STUDIES AND DOCUMENTATION IN THE HISTORY OF POPULAR ENTERTAINMENT

Edited by
Anthony Slide

WORDS AT WAR

World War II Era Radio Drama and the Postwar Broadcasting Industry Blacklist

Howard Blue

Studies and Documentation in the
History of Popular Entertainment

The Scarecrow Press, Inc.
Lanham, Maryland, and Oxford
2002

SCARECROW PRESS, INC.

Published in the United States of America
by Scarecrow Press, Inc.
A Member of the Rowman & Littlefield Publishing Group
4720 Boston Way
Lanham, Maryland 20706
www.scarecrowpress.com

PO Box 317
Oxford
OX2 9RU, UK

British Library Cataloguing in Publication Information Available

Library of Congress Cataloging-in-Publication Data

Blue, Howard, 1941–
Words at war : World War II era radio drama and the postwar broadcasting industry blacklist / Howard Blue.
p. cm. — (Studies and documentation in the history of popular entertainment ; no. 5)
Includes index.
ISBN 0-8108-4413-3 (alk. paper)
1. Radio broadcasting—United States—History. 2. Radio plays, American—History and criticism. 3. Blacklisting of entertainers—United States. I. Title. II. Series.

PN1991.3.U6 B59 2002
384.54'0973—dc21

2002006523

∞™ The paper used in this publication meets the minimum requirements of American National Standard for Information Sciences—Permanence of Paper for Printed Library Materials, ANSI/NISO Z39.48-1992. Manufactured in the United States of America.

For Debby and Julie
and the memory
of H. and G.

CONTENTS

ACKNOWLEDGMENTS

I wish to thank the many people whose cooperation with my research efforts made this book possible. My wife, Deborah Goldberg, now an expert on old-time radio, frequently critiqued sections of the manuscript, urged me on when my spirits flagged, restrained me when I sometimes charged ahead without looking to see if any "trucks were barreling down the street," and tolerated my obsessions.

Norman Corwin honored me by contributing generously of his time, answering my letters quickly, and providing expert advice regarding research matters and the methods of negotiating the labyrinth leading toward a publishing contract. Dave Siegel of Yorktown, New York, and Larry and John Gassman of Whittier, California, opened their extensive old-time radio archives and provided me with much-needed information on short notice. Without their help, my research task would have been substantially more difficult. Jerry Haendiges, Max Schmid, Jim Widner, and many others in the old-time radio community also provided me with useful tapes. Jay Hickerson, who prepares an annual old-time radio convention in Newark, New Jersey, was often the source of information crucial to locating old-time radio actors.

When I first began my project, Professor Everett Frost of New York University pointed the way to a number of important resource people.

Linda Sullivan Baity, Andrea End, Patricia Rosten Filan, Frances Lee Pearson, and Tess Wishengrad Siegel deserve special mention. Linda did a wonderful interview of Millard Lampell for me; Andrea volunteered a humorous account from Arnold Moss's (her late father's) unpublished manuscript; Patricia gave generous access to the papers of her father, Norman Rosten; Frances (who became a good friend) opened her home to me for several days while I examined her late husband's Canada Lee's papers; and Tess went out of her way to send me many useful materials from her father's papers. William L. Bird Jr. was helpful in providing me with information about Peter Lyon. I very much regret the passing of Ken Wiegel, a very knowledgeable source of information about wartime radio.

In the early stages of my research, this book was to be an anthology of U.S., Soviet, British, and German wartime drama. My partner then, the late Irene Schlegel, provided moral support and did some interesting work, which is not, however, reflected in this volume. Next, I offer heartfelt thanks to the many people who granted interviews. They include Arthur Anderson, George Ansbro, Jackson Beck, George Berger, Gilda Block, Frank Bresee, Harry Bartell, Walter Bernstein, George Braziller, Art Carney, Cliff Carpenter, Tommy Cook, Jeff Corey, John Eisenhower, Howard Fast, Bob Foreman, Madeline Lee Gilford, Larry Haines, Vincent Hartnett, Bruce Hunt, Kim Hunter, Lucille Lewis Johnson, Teri Keane, John Milton Kennedy, Polly Keusink, Emily Kingsley, Marjorie and Patricia Kirby, Mary Ann Kutner, Ramona Lampell, Ruth Last, Arthur Laurents, Roz Leader, Mildred Leipzig, Jane Lyon, Gil Mack, Leonard Maltin, Arthur Miller, Eleanor Oboler, Nancy Perl Real, Elliott Reid, Josie Roschiele, Ken Roberts, Al Schaffer, Ira Skutch, Pete Seeger, Robert Shayon, Peter Straus, and Robert Vaughn. Many of these people also answered written queries, as did Lois Culver and the late Bill Lipton. I also acknowledge my gratitude to the following people who granted interviews, who have since passed away: Erik Barnouw, Bert Cowlan, Clifton Fadiman, Raymond Edward Johnson, Millard Lampell, Ring Lardner Jr., Abe Polonsky, Allan Sloane, and Miriam Wolfe.

Carolyn Hoffman and her husband Bob Kann kindly put me up in their home in Madison, Wisconsin, during my research visit to their fair city, as did Tom and Jane Taussik in Havant, England, during my visits to the BBC archives in the early stages of my research. I am also grateful to Tom Taussik, John Gebhardt, Dan Lucas, Julie Blue, and Bill Streitwieser for their careful reading of sections of the manuscript and for their helpful comments. I especially appreciate Wendy Sleppin for her encouragement, for reading and editing the entire manuscript, and for helping me to put it into a suitable professional condition to send to a publisher. Rachel Goldberg did a masterful job in editing many chapters. John Gallagher, Robert Karen, and Gerald Nachman gave me advice of various sorts relating to publishing. Anthony Slide, my editor at Scarecrow Press, a highly accomplished and respected author, was very helpful.

Special thanks to Richard Fish of Bloomington, Indiana; Wayne Johnson of Conyers, Georgia; Ted Meland of Madison, Wisconsin; Sandy Tidwell in Provo, Utah; and Pat Wilson in Greenlawn, New York, who provided research assistance in libraries that I might otherwise have not been able to access. Julie Miller, former archivist of the Jewish Theological Seminary's Ratner Center, was extremely helpful; David Pfeiffer and his colleagues at the National Archives gave me invaluable assistance during my several visits there; Brad Bauer, former special collections librarian at the Thousand Oaks (California) Library, expertly guided me through the Norman Corwin Collection; Michael Henry of the Library of American Broadcasting at the University of Maryland gave me numerous leads and periodically sent me much needed material. Ginny Kilander of the American Heritage Center at the University of Wyoming sent me useful materials; Harold Miller at the State Historical Society of Wisconsin, Jean Ashton at Columbia University's Rare Book and Manuscript Library, Jessica Wiederhorn at Columbia's Oral History Research Office, and Sean Noel of Boston University's Special Collections Department were instrumental to the success of my research efforts. So were Chantel Dunham at the University of Georgia in Athens and Kelly Bullock and James D'Arc at Brigham Young University. Broadcast historian and journalist Elizabeth McLeod was a frequent and rapid source of information regarding details that often eluded me. I also acknowledge my indebtedness to Carolyn Kelly and Harriet Edwards, and their reference staffs at the Huntington and East Meadow (New York) Public Libraries, respectively, who fielded numerous inquiries and efficiently processed endless requests for materials via their interlibrary loan systems. Finally, I express gratitude to Jim Cox, Martin Grams Jr., Ted Kneebone, Jim Widner, and the many other old-time radio hobbyists, too numerous to mention, who answered my frequent questions posted on the "Old Time Radio Digest" (see http://lists.oldradio.net/).

I gratefully acknowledge permission from Betty Barnouw for quotations from Shannon Shafly's and Mark Langer's interview of Erik Barnouw; Stephen Burrows to quote a poem by Joseph Julian; Larry Beinhart for a quotation from the correspondence of Irving Beinhart; Norman Corwin for numerous quotations from his diaries, correspondence, and Jerrold Zinnamon's interview of him; Doris Davis to quote a passage from Dwight Weist's letter to Ann Case; Stephen Davis for quotations from two of Mark Blitzstein's radio plays; Anne Fadiman for quotations from the correspondence of Clifton Fadiman; Ian Freebairn-Smith for a quotation from an unpublished letter by Thomas Freebairn-Smith; Thomas Howell to paraphrase material in his doctoral dissertation on the Writer's War Board; Gerhard Horton to paraphrase various passages from his doctoral dissertation "Radio Goes to War: The Cultural Politics of Propaganda during World War II"; Marjorie Kirby to paraphrase excerpts from Edward Kirby's essay on American broadcasting during World War II; and Arthur Laurents to quote from his correspondence.

I also appreciate permission from Roz Leader to quote from Anton Leader's letter to Morton Wishengrad; Nanette Fabray Mac-Dougall for quotations from Ranald MacDougall's correspondence and from his radio play "Barbed Wire Sky"; Frances Lee Pearson for a quotation from Canada Lee's letter to Ed Sullivan; Richard McAdoo for excerpts from Archibald MacLeish's correspondence and radio play "The States Talking"; Arthur Miller for quotations from his correspondence and from Erik Barnouw's interview of him; The New York Public Library—American Jewish Committee Oral History Collection, Dorot Jewish Division, NYPL, for permission to quote from interviews of Milton Krents and Norman Rose; Sally Norton to paraphrase excerpts from her doctoral dissertation "A Historical Study of Will Geer"; Harold Ober Associates for quotations from Langston Hughes's correspondence and from Hughes's radio play "Brothers"; Leo Raikhman to paraphrase material from his essay about Ida Shlain; Nancy Perl Real for a quotation from Arnold Perl's radio play "The Empty Noose"; Shirley Robson to quote from the correspondence of William N. Robson, from his radio play "Open Letter on Race Hatred" and from John Hickman's interview of him; Betty Roper to quote from a letter by Milard King Roper; Norman Rose to quote from the New York Public Library's unpublished interview of him; Patricia Rosten Filan to quote from Norman Rosten's correspondence and from his radio play "Concerning the Red Army"; Barbara Savage to paraphrase material from her doctoral dissertation "Broadcasting Freedom: Radio, War and the Roots of Civil Rights Liberalism 1938-1948; the Schomburg Center for Research in Black Culture to quote from several episodes of *New World A-Coming*; Tess Siegel to quote from Morton Wishengrad's correspondence with Anton Leader and Norman Rosten; Eloise Sloane to quote from the author's interviews of Allan Sloane and from his letter to the author; Eleanor Straub to paraphrase two sections of her doctoral dissertation "Government Policy toward Civilian Women during World War II"; and Abigail Yager to quote a brief passage from her unpublished essay "The Life of Morton Wishengrad."

INTRODUCTION

Every tomato we pick today makes Gordon's job as a soldier a little easier. Because these tomatoes are going to war, Bill. They're
going to war as food for war workers, for our armed forces, for our
fighting Allies.

—Home Forces: "U.S. Crop Corps," *Uncle Sam*

On August 3, 1922, the *New York Times* published an article concerning the fatal poisoning of six people in the Shelbourne Restaurant
at 1127 Broadway in New York City. Each of the victims had eaten a
piece of pie that had been prepared by Charles Abramson, a pastry
cook who was the chief suspect in the incident. Also on August 3, the
Times carried an advertisement for "Girls' Black Sateen Bloomers, 2
for $1" at Bloomingdale's. A second ad, from another establishment,
promoted the sale of men's pure wool, one-piece bathing suits, at
$3.25 each. The *Times* did not make note, however, of a play entitled
"The Wolf" that was aired on station WGY in Schenectady, New York,
the same day as the article about the poisoned pies.[1]

"The Wolf," by Eugene Walter, was the first "on-air" drama. After its
broadcast, the station received two thousand letters from listeners within
a fifty-mile radius. The play featured a scene in which a character
screamed. One letter recounted that a policeman, hearing the scream

through an open window, was so convinced by its realism that he came bursting into the house to stop the "assault." The play's success was also apparent from the fact that, in the fall, the WGY plays became regular features. "The Wolf" and the other early radio plays were literal readings of famous stage plays. The classics were the most successful of these non-radio radio plays. They depended less on visual images than did modern plays of the 1920s. On Friday nights, WGY began to offer stage plays over the air: "The Garden of Allah," "Seven Keys to Baldpate," and periodically some classics such as the plays of Henrik Ibsen. Each show ran two and a half hours and used a live orchestra for musical bridges.[2]

The gradual development of radio drama, which broadcast of "The Wolf" initiated, was one of a number of factors that helped make possible the creation of a long-overlooked but substantial body of American war-related radio drama in the World War II era. Before and during that war, between 1936 and 1945, the commercial networks, Hollywood stars, private agencies, and the government cooperated to alert Americans to the threat of fascism, both within the United States and abroad. Much of this effort focused, of course, on stimulating support for American participation in World War II. That such stimulation was necessary is clear if one considers the results of two surveys. An opinion poll of June 1941, only five months before America entered the war, showed that 79 percent of the American people favored neutrality.[3] A second survey, a year later, revealed that a full 50 percent had no clear understanding of what the war was about.[4]

The broadcasting of radio drama was paramount among the ways in which various organizations attacked American apathy or even hostility toward fighting fascism. A group of writers created a unique body of shows, sketches, and whole series to create support for American participation in the war. They also stimulated morale, showing how all Americans could support the fight against fascism, even if some just grew tomatoes.

In February 1943, the magazine of the American Federation of Radio Artists (AFRA) carried an essay entitled "Toward A Better World" by Robert Landry of CBS. "When the history of this war comes to be written, considerable credit will be due to the so called radio documentary programs, those lectures in dramatic form on the nature of our enemies, on the magnitude of our problems, on the challenge of our future. The documentaries have raised vigorous rallying voices of realism, and at the same time, helped articulate the new global concepts of future decency."[5]

Landry might well have broadened his statement to include not just radio documentaries but other forms of radio drama as well. As he implied, as they worked directly on the war effort, many radio writers simultaneously advanced a progressive agenda to fight the enemy within: racism, poverty, and other social ills. But America was not prepared to accept that agenda. When the war ended, many of those writers would pay for their idealism by suffering blacklisting. So would many of the actors.

A number of factors led up to the development and use of these radio dramas of the World War II era. We can look at the various elements in the history of their development as the recipe for a dish with an elaborate set of ingredients.

Recipe for American World War II Era Radio Drama

Serves: 100,000,000

Ingredients

Radio	A dozen advertising agencies
The concept of radio drama	Several dozen major sponsors
FDR's pioneering propaganda	Several dozen progressive,
broadcasts for the New Deal	creative, and dedicated
	writers and directors
Orson Welles's production of	Several score of creative,
"The War of the Worlds"	dedicated actors
The concept of the sponsored	Two wartime government
program	propaganda agencies
The concept of the non-sponsored	Four or five private agencies
"sustaining program"	One war

Directions:
1. Mix in radio, drama, the ideas of the sustaining and sponsored programs, and the influence of FDR's broadcasts of the 1930s and Orson Welles's panic broadcast.
2. Add the war.
3. Blend in the writers and directors with the actors.

4. Beat while pouring in the advertising, private and government agencies, and the sponsors.
5. Lay this on a bed of semi-receptive, cautiously liberal radio networks.
6. Serve in generous portions to a skeptical national radio audience.

And there you have it, American World War II era radio drama.

The first "ingredient" of American war-related radio drama came into being in 1895 when Guglielmo Marconi sent radio communications through the air for the first time. Eleven years later, the human voice made its premier appearance on radio. Then, in 1920, the first regular commercial broadcasting took place with the establishment of stations KDKA in Pittsburgh and WWJ in Detroit. Within five years, radio began its role as a major source of family entertainment. By the mid 1930s, it had caught on. It was a relatively new but incredibly important cultural phenomenon. Actor Elliott Reid remembered how, when the phenomenally popular *Amos 'n' Andy* show was being broadcast, during the summer he could walk to a friend's house and never miss a word of the show because he could hear it from each house that he passed on his way to his destination.[6]

Sometimes the radio bore the brand name of Atwater Kent. Stromberg-Carlson was another popular brand name. Radio was so important that by the time of the Depression, when numerous families were forced through repossession or other reasons to give up their furniture or other belongings, repeatedly they clung to one most-treasured item, their radio. By the time of the attack on Pearl Harbor, 90 percent of the American people had at least one set in their home. The average American listened for about four hours daily.[7]

Among the millions of radio owners was the family of Samuel and Rose Corwin, who lived in a three-story tenement on Bremen Street in East Boston, Massachusetts. Samuel Corwin was the son of Russian Jews who emigrated to England where he was born and raised. As a young man, he, in turn, emigrated to the United States. Rose was an emigrant from Hungary. Norman, the third of the Corwin's four children, remembered a neighbor calling out to him, "Harold Merchant down the block just got this thing called a radio and you can hear things through the air." Corwin replied, "How can that be?" But it was true. Corwin went to the Merchants' house and, via a crystal set, heard his first radio transmission.[8]

The MacDougall family of Schenectady, New York, also listened to early radio. Their son Ranald, made one of the first sets in the city by winding cotton-covered wire around an oatmeal box.[9] And then there were the Millers of Harlem, Isidore and Augusta and their three children. The Millers bought their first radio, a superheterodyne set, in the early 1920s from a young neighbor who built it himself and powered it with an acid battery. Arthur, the middle child, remembered it with its tinny sound. Often it was out of commission, the victim of his older brother Kermit's penchant for "fixing" things.[10] Miller remembered how, at age eight, he heard his first broadcast, an orchestra performance from station KDKA in Pittsburgh, which he thought was close to Europe.[11]

Families who may have been the first in their neighborhood to have a radio found neighbors and even strangers often flocked to their house oblivious of their intrusion. Jackson Beck remembered this from his childhood in Far Rockaway, New York. As he told the author, "In 1923 I was about ten years old. After my father brought home our first radio, word got out and not only neighbors but even strangers from nearby towns started coming to our house. We used to go to bed fairly early and often people were coming to our door so late that they were waking us up. On Sundays they came in very large numbers. Finally we had to put up a sign 'Don't come in.'"[12] In adulthood, Miller, Norman Corwin, Ranald MacDougall, and Jackson Beck got to know radio from another perspective, the first three as writers for the medium and Beck as one of its most ubiquitous actors.

The first important demonstration of radio's potential for mobilizing public opinion was Franklin Delano Roosevelt's creation of a series of "fireside chats" to promote his New Deal programs. His goal was to help the nation get out of the Depression, which had hit it shortly before the election that brought him to power. He pulled out all the stops in arguing that America was fighting an enemy: unemployment, economic stagnation, and low national morale. In the process, he showed how powerful the new medium was, even mightier than the combined strength of all the nation's newspapers. However, there were some problems with the Roosevelt administration's use of radio as a tool of persuasion. In August 1933, one of the members of the Federal Radio Commission, predecessor of the Federal Communications Commission, sent a letter to all radio stations. He demanded that they reject any sponsor or advertiser who refused to cooperate with the codes of the National Recovery Administration, an agency established to help America deal with the economic problems brought on by the Depression.[13] The letter backfired, and some newspapers criticized Roosevelt for his administration's strong-arm tactics.

In 1936, lightning struck radio in the form of the *Columbia Workshop*, a newly created showcase for experimental radio drama. The *Columbia Workshop* was the brainchild of Brooklyn-born Irving Reis, who came into radio quite by chance.[14] Reis lost a month's pay buying bootleg gin and getting drunk for the first time. He tried to borrow $80 from a friend who worked for a radio station. The friend, who remembered that as a boy Reis had played around with amateur radio, invited Reis to apply for a job with the same station, a CBS affiliate. Reis first worked as a "log engineer," standing by for distress signals, on a shift from 4 P.M. to station closing at 2 A.M. At the time, the Federal Communications Commission required coastal stations to immediately stop broadcasting upon interception of an SOS. After his first year, when a studio engineer had to quit because of illness, Reis was promoted to fill the man's role.

Reis visited Europe where he learned that the British and the Germans had been experimenting with radio drama as early as 1926. On his return, he lobbied CBS to give him a chance to try to do an American version of what he had observed abroad. Reis finally got that chance in 1936 with the arrival to the network of its new programming chief William B. Lewis. The *Columbia Workshop* succeeded so well that some 7,000 plays a year flooded into the network from playwrights hoping to see their work given a chance.[15] Radio drama had come into its own. One sign of this was the publication of hundreds of radio plays in magazines and anthologies that appeared in libraries and bookstores around the United States.

Radio, of course, also came into its own as a business. Its goal, like all business ventures, was to make money. During its first several decades, to a great extent the networks sold time, not shows, to the advertising agencies. The agencies themselves produced many early shows for the sponsors and then used the networks' radio studios for the actual broadcasting. In 1934, about one-third of network time was sold for sponsored programming, and more than half of network revenue came from advertising agencies. Only after World War II did the networks themselves begin to develop commercial shows for sale through the agencies to the sponsors.

The development of unsponsored "sustaining programs" such as the *Columbia Workshop* came about as a result of the Communications Act of 1934, which required radio stations and networks to fulfill a public service obligation. "Sustaining shows" were an important alternative to the early practice of the agencies of producing shows. The networks themselves produced these shows, and they filled an important gap. Some of the most important war-related shows of the late 1930s and the war period were sustaining shows. Whereas sponsored shows generally avoided current political and other problems, the sustaining shows were more inclined to deal with them.

The producers of sustaining shows and of commercial shows functioned in spheres so totally different that they seemed at times to be even in different universes. Norman Corwin, the most acclaimed writer of sustained shows, told a story that illustrates this fact. In about 1943, Corwin attended a Peabody Award dinner. The Peabodys were, and are, the highest form of recognition for excellence in the radio broadcasting industry. At one point during the evening, a man seated at his left introduced himself and asked, "And are you in radio, Mr. Corwin." "Yes," Corwin replied. "I am with CBS." "That so? What line of work," the man continued. "Well, dramatic . . . sort of." Later Corwin learned that the man was president of the biggest advertising agency in the country. Yet they had never heard of each other.[16]

With the establishment of both sponsored and sustained radio programs, there were vehicles for broadcasting radio shows. And with evidence from the analysis of public reception of FDR's Depression-era fireside chats, there was also reason to believe that radio could affect people's morale. But could it move people to action? The answer to this question was provided by a trio of men: John Houseman, Howard Koch, and twenty-three-year-old Orson Welles.

Orson Welles's contribution to wartime radio drama was multifaceted. He not only acted in some of the most important radio dramas, he also wrote at least one. But his most significant work on radio was with coproducer John Houseman and writer Howard Koch on the Halloween 1938 panic broadcast, "The War of the Worlds." The show, based on the science fiction story by H. G. Wells about an invasion of earth by Martians, created a mass hysteria among the listening public. People in dozens of towns and cities around the country fled from the imaginary invaders described in the broadcast. The panic created traffic jams; flooded police, newspaper, and radio station switchboards; and sent scores of people to seek medical treatment for shock and hysteria. The factors that influenced it, the context in which it appeared, and the precedent that it set gave it an important role in the creation of war drama.

An important factor that governed people's reactions to Welles's broadcast was a state of anxiety resulting from a political crisis in Czechoslovakia that began several months earlier. The crisis, which culminated in the Munich Pact in late September, involved Adolf Hitler's demands that Great Britain and France accede to his wishes to annex a part of Czechoslovakia containing a large German ethnic minority. Its high point involved negotiations that saw British Prime Minister Neville Chamberlain fly twice to meet with Hitler. Particularly during these negotiations, radio bulletins repeatedly interrupted regular American programming, sometimes a dozen or more times a day, to bring out the latest news. Typical was one that featured reporter Max Jordan on the day that the pact was signed:

> In just a few moments the National Broadcasting Company hopes to bring you via retransmission from Europe, from Munich, the official communiqué just released of the results of the four-power conference between Prime Minister Chamberlain, Premier Daladier, Signor Mussolini and Herr Hitler. We, we [sic] plead for your indulgence for just a few moments while we make sure of all facilities in order to take you across the sea to bring you this important communiqué. We now take you across the sea.
>
> Hello, NBC, this is Max Jordan calling from Munich, Germany. It is now eight minutes to two o'clock AM local time. Exactly seventeen minutes ago Premier Chamberlain of England, Premier Daladier of France and his [sic] and their delegations walked out of the assembly room at the Führer's Palace here.[17]

To millions of Americans the world seemed to be on the brink of war. It was. And to many of those listeners, the crisis pointed to the possibility that the United States might be dragged into the war and, perhaps less plausibly at the time, even be invaded by an enemy force. Welles's broadcast started with an introduction that clearly identified the show as a work of fiction. But in imitating the interruptions of the broadcast with "news bulletins" regarding the "invasion," it copied the realistic style to which listeners had become accustomed.[18] The broadcast had its greatest impact on many people who tuned in late, missing the introduction. A study commissioned by Princeton University concluded that of the 6 million who heard the show, 1.7 million accepted its reports as authentic news and 1.2 million were genuinely frightened. Many, first hearing the program in mid broadcast, came upon it as it shifted realistically from one "on the spot field reporter" to another, and they were totally conned. In imitating the style of the previous weeks' bulletins, the broadcast achieved credibility that exceeded anyone's expectation. The recollection of one listener, decades later, illustrates how some people came to accept the broadcast as a factual one: "My wife and I were driving though the redwood forest in northern California when the broadcast came over our car radio. . . . All we could think of was to try to get back to L.A. to see our children once more. And be with them when it happened. We went right by gas stations but I forgot we were low in gas. In the middle of the forest our gas ran out. There was nothing to do. We just sat there holding hands expecting to see those Martian monsters appear over the tops of the trees."[19]

Without the anxiety that the previous weeks' bulletins about the Munich Crisis raised, Welles's program would undoubtedly have had less impact. Even generations later, young people continue to be fascinated with the power over its listeners that radio demonstrated in October 1938. The lesson was noted by later radio writers and producers. In an undated memo to an official of the Office of War Information, written most likely in 1942, radio writer George Faulkner acknowledged the influence of "The War of the Worlds" broadcast. "When will we really believe that radio is a tremendous power?" asked Faulkner. Referring to the Welles broadcast, he wrote of the "terrific mass suggestibility of the American radio audience, made clear by that tragi-comic episode."[20] In short, Faulkner and his colleagues had seen proof positive that the public could be sold a bill of goods or, to put it less cynically, could be swayed to take action that it had never intended to take.

President Roosevelt's creation of several propaganda agencies was also essential to the development of radio drama during World War II. The agencies had a difficult birth as a result of the nation's experience with a World War I propaganda organization, the Committee on Public Information (CPI). During World War I, President Woodrow Wilson established the agency, the nation's first great experiment with propaganda, and appointed George Creel, a short, stocky, muckraking journalist from Missouri, as its head. Unfortunately, in trying to garner support for the war effort, Creel used a high-handed style that offended Congress and hordes of plain citizens.

In addition to using a wide variety of propaganda techniques, Creel introduced "voluntary guidelines" for the news media. In essence, it was censorship. The CPI also helped to pass the Espionage Act of 1917.[21] Because of the wording of a section of the new law, it was used to imprison Americans who spoke out or wrote against the war. As a result of Creel's tactics, a lingering resentment developed. When the war ended, Congress took its vengeance out on him, canceling his committee's appropriations so quickly that he was left without enough money to close down his office and organize its records.[22]

The Creel legacy was an unwelcome one to any president who wanted to establish his own propaganda agency. Roosevelt knew that many Americans feared not only foreign propaganda but, as a result of their memory of Creel's CPI, the domestic variety, too, for which reason they were particularly wary of having a government propaganda agency. For this reason, although events and the times called for creation of some sort of major propaganda bureau from 1939 through 1941, the administration overtly rejected the idea. Yet at the same time, it prepared to establish a coordinated propaganda agency.

In 1939, FDR established the Office of Government Reports (OGR) under the direction of Louis Mellett. The OGR and several other agencies were given severely limited powers and scope. Three administration officials, Vice President Henry A. Wallace, Secretary of War Henry Stimson, and Secretary of the Navy Frank Knox made an early call for a government propaganda agency, but Mellett and FDR rejected the idea. The President still believed that establishing such an agency before America entered the war would invite attacks on it by his political enemies. Nevertheless, in addition to the OGR, in June 1940, the administration established the Office of Emergency Management, another agency that handled propaganda assignments; and by late 1941, the infrastructure for government-supervised propaganda campaigns was ready.[23]

Roosevelt finally created his first real propaganda agency, the Office of Facts and Figures (OFF), in October, only two months before America entered the war. But even this agency had severely clipped wings. OFF's successor agency, the Office of War Information (OWI), had slightly more powers.

The war part of the recipe was easy to come by, too easy, thanks to one Adolf Hitler, a compliant German nation, and Hitler's like-minded colleagues in Italy and Japan. Radio could not get away from the dramatic events taking place in Europe and elsewhere. "Tonight, after rehearsals," Norman Corwin wrote in his diary on March 18, 1939, concerning a show he was preparing, "[I] wrote in a special section to deal by unmistakable implication, with the latest development in Hitler's case of rabies—the nauseating grab of Czechoslovakia."[24]

Eventually, of course, America was pulled into the war. From the start it was evident that people wanted reassurance. During the depths of the Depression, President Roosevelt had provided it through broadcast of his fireside chats.[25] Now, people wanted it at least as much as they had during the 1930s. They also often sought some level of personal contact with the people who spoke to them on radio. The numerous letters from listeners to the networks, hosts of radio shows, and the Office of War Information illustrate this last point. "I'm a native of Illinois and left penniless at age 59, am doing War Department Work, filing important papers and records. . . . Just established a record of one year in service, with no annual or sick leave and never late to work," wrote a listener to Cecil B. DeMille, "producer" of *Lux Radio Theatre*. "Please give us something bright and cheerful [in] these troubled times," wrote a second listener, also to DeMille. And in a third letter, a young listener inquired after hearing broadcast of "The Navy Comes Through," "I would like to know if you put on this play at my suggestion." A month earlier, after seeing the film on which the broadcast was based, he had written to DeMille, proposing that *Lux Radio Theatre* air an adaptation.[26]

Where did the radio actors and the writers of radio drama who emerged in the late 1930s and 1940s come from? Some writers, Norman Corwin and Allan Sloane, for example, got their start as print journalists. Others were "lent" or "given" to wartime radio by another primary calling. Archibald MacLeish, Stephen Vincent Benét, Langston Hughes, and Edna St. Vincent Millay were poets. Bill Robson first worked as a film script writer, and Millard Lampell was a folk singer.

Fredric March, Melvyn Douglas, and John Garfield were film stars. Joseph Julian, Art Carney, and Jackson Beck came directly to radio as young men. Carney, for example, got his start in radio almost as soon as he got into show business. His first job, when he was fresh out of high school, was as a mimic and announcer with Horace Heidt's Musical Knights, a big band touring troupe. He specialized in mimicking President Roosevelt and New York State's colorful governor, Al Smith. In addition to playing some of the country's largest clubs, the band appeared on a variety of radio programs, including, in 1938, "Pot O'Gold," a money giveaway program.[27]

Regardless of their experience prior to radio, virtually all of the most prominent radio writers and many of the actors shared a common set of concerns with each other and with a broad array of people in the arts, education, the labor movement, and various other fields.[28] The Depression, Hitler's rise to power, the fascist attack on democracy during the Spanish Civil War (1936–1939), and racial oppression in the United States, especially the lynching of Negroes, heavily influenced American leftists who came of age in the 1930s. They developed a pro-union, antifascist, internationalist-minded, and racially tolerant orientation that sought to create social and political change. The struggle in Spain especially appeared to American writers as a black-and-white model of the struggle between good and evil.

By 1940, the factors described earlier coalesced to form the mass of war-related radio drama. The first such show, "Fall of the City," appeared on the *Columbia Workshop* in April 1937. A variety of similarly focused plays followed it. Two things occurred in radio drama as the nation inched closer and closer to war. First, radio moved away from its position of neutrality. Initially, the name "Hitler" hung over events but rarely appeared in radio drama scripts. But after the attack on Pearl Harbor, show after show blasted away at him. Second, even before the Japanese attack, radio gradually began to give less and less time to lighter fare. Many of the comedy and other types of more frivolous shows that remained were cut from one hour to half-hour time slots. In 1940, more than 10,000 hours of drama were broadcast over the air. This represented more than 30 percent of the available air time.[29] After the attack on Pearl Harbor, the percentage of hours devoted to war-related drama increased even further.

NOTES

1. "Poisoned Pies," "Sure Poisoned Pie Was Meant to Kill," 1:3; Girls' Bloomers, 4:1; Men's Bathing Suits, 7:8. *New York Times*, August 3, 1922.

2. Connie Billips and Arthur Pierce, *Lux Presents Hollywood: A Show-By-Show History of the Lux Radio Theatre and the Lux Video Theatre, 1934–1957* (Jefferson, N.C.: McFarland, 1995), 1.

3. Michelle Hilmes, *Radio Voices: American Broadcasting, 1922–1952* (Minneapolis: University of Minnesota. Press, 1997), 235.

4. Gerhard Horten, "Radio Goes to War: The Cultural Politics of Propaganda during World War II," (Ph.D. diss., University of California at Berkeley, 1994), 177.

5. Robert Landry, "Robert Landry Ventures a Prophecy," in *Stand By*, Vol. 4, No. 4, February 1943, 6.

6. Elliott Reid to author, October 24, 1998.

7. Horten, "Radio Goes to War," 163.

8. Ken Burns, producer, *Empire of the Air: the Men Who Made Radio*, Turner Home Entertainment, produced in association with WETA TV, 1996. Videotapes.

9. Erik Barnouw, *Radio Drama in Action* (New York: Farrar & Rinehart, 1945), 252.

10. Arthur Miller, *Timebends* (New York: Grove Press, 1987), 15.

11. Arthur Miller, letter to the author, February 17, 2000.

12. Jackson Beck, telephone interview by the author, July 30, 1998.

13. Mitchell Dawson, "Censorship On the Air," *The American Mercury*, Vol. 31 (March 1934), 267, as cited in Horten, "Radio Goes to War," 44.

14. The account of Reis's career and role in creation of the *Columbia Workshop* is based on an untitled autobiographical document in the Reis Collection, ACAD.

15. John Dunning, *On the Air: The Encyclopedia of Old Time Radio* (New York: Oxford University Press, 1998), 170.

16. Norman Corwin, "Remarks," in Hollywood Writers Mobilization, *Writer's Congress; the Proceedings of the Conference Held in October 1943 under the Sponsorship of the Hollywood Writers' Mobilization and the University of California* (Berkeley: University of California Press, 1944), 153.

17. Jordan began this bulletin from Munich at 8:52 P.M., September 29, 1938, interrupting an NBC broadcast of swing music. This was a giant scoop for NBC.

18. "Ladies and gentlemen, we interrupt our program of dance music to bring you a special bulletin from the Intercontinental Radio News." From "The War of the Worlds," CBS, broadcast October 30, 1938.

19. Howard Koch, *The Panic Broadcast* (New York: Avon, 1970), 89.

20. Memo from George Faulkner to W. B. Lewis, n.d., Lewis Collection, BU.

21. Thomas Fleming, "World War I Propagandist George Creel." *Military History*, Vol. 12, no. 5, December 1995 (viewed on unpaginated website www.thehistorynet.com/militaryhistory/ar.../12955_text htm on May 8, 1999).

22. Fleming, "World War I Propagandist George Creel."

23 Horten, "Radio Goes to War," 62–63.

24. Norman Corwin, *Diary*, March 18, 1939, Corwin Collection, TOL.

25. According to Erik Barnouw, Roosevelt's first "fireside chat" engendered one-half million letters from listeners, forcing the White House to hire additional assistance to open and read them. Erik Barnouw, *The Golden Web: A History of Broadcasting in the United States, vol. 2, 1933–1953* (New York: Oxford University Press, 1968), 7.

26. All three of these quotes are from letters in the Cecil B. DeMille Archives, MSS 1400, L. Tom Terry Special Collections, BYU: "native of Illinois," Wilma Erickson, n.d., Box 1121, folder 16; "give us something bright," M. Crawley, Dec. 29, 1943, Box 1122, folder 1; "The Navy Comes Through," Irwin Doutt, Jr., May 4, 1943, Box 1122, folder 3.

27. Michael Starr, *Art Carney: A Biography* (New York: Fromm International Publishing, 1997), 21–22.

28. For an interesting but somewhat controversial account of what Michael Denning sees as a cultural front, see Denning's *The Cultural Front* (New York: Verso, 1996), 14–18. Denning, a professor of American Studies at Yale University, discusses how the shared interests of these people resulted in

their participation in the Popular Front, a loosely structured "broad and tenuous left wing alliance" that emerged during the upheavals of the Depression. The movement united Socialists, labor unionists, Communists, community activists, and émigré antifascists in support of the development of "laborite social democracy." Denning argues that the Popular Front created a "movement culture" that was responsible for a vast array of left-wing creativity in radio, film and theater, and folk, jazz, cabaret, and classical music. However, as one reviewer, Adam Shatz, noted in *Nation* magazine (March 10, 1997, 264, no. 9, 25), Denning engages in extensive hyperbole, discussing a culture front that never existed. According to Shatz, Denning has illusions about the Popular Front's power and mistakenly attributes to it works that had nothing to do with its goals. As an illustration of this point, Shatz cites Denning's discussion of Orson Welles's "The War of the Worlds" broadcast. Whereas Denning views the show as "one of those anti-fascist 'air raid' stories, Shatz implies that it was just a highly successful science fiction piece.

29. Norman Weiser, *The Writer's Radio Theater* (New York: Harper & Row, 1941), ix.

THE WRITERS

The writer of the 1930s and 1940s belonged to a generation in rebellion. He was an accuser . . . and the enemy was poverty, war,
fascism, corruption in high places or low.

—Norman Rosten, *New York Post Magazine*

Norman Rosten's comment about his generation of writers was
echoed by a number of his contemporaries. William Robson, a CBS
scriptwriter and producer, expressed typical progressive attitudes in a
letter to a friend. "I feel that the responsible radio writer . . . , " he
wrote, "will constantly seek to inject, where it is gracefully possible,
ideas of tolerance and equality."[1] Allan Sloane, whom Robson first
brought into radio writing, expressed similar views. Sloane sought to
"change the world" with the microphone. On the question of racism in
radio, for example, he believed that the responsible radio writer should
seek to help radio move away from its biased hiring practices and become an equal opportunity employer by taking the initiative and creating roles for black actors. The question remains, however, as to why
these radio people and their progressive and liberal colleagues in journalism and other fields were so motivated to push for social change.
What common experiences pushed them into seeking the same things?

NORMAN CORWIN

Six foot, bushy haired, and long lived, Norman Corwin was without doubt the most prominent of the radio writers of the 1940s. With genes inherited from his father who lived past 110, Corwin, at age 91 at the time of this writing, continues to be an active writer and teacher. Author, producer, and director of radio plays at CBS, Corwin had an instinctive grasp of the medium of radio from an early age. A gentle man who throughout his life rarely uttered a harsh word about another person, Corwin earned the respect of generations of colleagues and radio listeners. In a letter to the author, Allan Sloane described his first meeting with Corwin in 1943.[2]

Sloane was working late one evening when "a tall, moustachioed gent with bushy hair and a harried look" ran into him in a corridor on the eighteenth floor of CBS, where the producers and directors had their offices. With no introduction or fanfare, the man asked, "Would you by any chance know how to make a Molotov cocktail?" "Sure," Sloane replied, and told him how. "Thanks," the man said and started back to his office. Then he stopped, headed back to Sloane's office, cleared his throat, and stuck out his hand. "My name's Corwin," he said. "I know," Sloane replied and he introduced himself. "Oh yes," Corwin replied. "You're the one who's writing all those good words for Robson. Let's do something together some day." Sloane wrote of Corwin, "In my deepest heart, I worshipped his work. His talents added up to genius. . . . I could comfortably walk into anybody's office, but not Norman's. The busy, rattle of his typewriter warned me away from daring to disturb him."

The record of the development of Norman Corwin's civic consciousness is one of the clearest among the radio dramatists. One of the earliest influences on him was the infamous Sacco-Vanzetti case that developed in 1927 when Corwin was beginning his career, working initially as a newspaper journalist. Two immigrant Italian anarchists, convicted of murder more on the basis of their beliefs than on evidence, were about to be executed. On the night of the scheduled executions, anticipating a flood of telephone calls because the newspaper office was receiving cabled reports, Corwin's editor assigned him to field the inquiries. Thus, at age seventeen, Corwin found himself a spokesman to the public concerning one of twentieth century America's most blatant injustices. "Yes, Sacco has been executed," he found himself telling the first caller. "Yes. Four minutes ago. Vanzetti is now on his way to the chair."[3]

In a 1933 letter to his brothers occasioned by the death of their maternal grandmother, Corwin gave his opinion of the influence of his maternal grandparents on the family. "I think," he wrote, "we owe to them our heritage of a fairly liberal streak handed down to Ma . . . of a sympathy with the insensitive hum drum fellow who minds his business and patches your stovepipes."[4]

In the same year, Corwin made a memorable vacation trip to Europe. In Heidelberg, Germany, he came face to face with Nazism in the person of the seventeen-year-old son of the owners of the pension where he was staying. The boy followed Corwin all over as he toured the city, proudly telling him how Nazism was restoring respectability to Germany and how the party would purge "the pollution of race." Only on the last day of his stay, just after they had walked up to Heidelberg Castle, did Corwin tell the boy that he himself was a Jew. They walked back down the castle's ramparts and back to the pension in silence. [5]

Later, while Corwin was traveling on a train in France, he got into a conversation with a young Frenchwoman who told him of her hatred of the Germans as a result of the previous war. At this point in his life, Corwin was a pacifist and he replied "We are beyond thinking of war as an instrument of political expediency. If we are really earnest about peace, there need never be another war."[6]

Several years later, in 1935, Corwin saw the spillover of fascist influence in his home state. While still a print journalist in Springfield, Massachusetts, his paper assigned him to do a story about an organization calling itself the "Italian Red Cross," which had sought permission to use the town's municipal auditorium for a "humanitarian" fund raiser. In Ethiopia, Italian pilots were dropping bombs on unarmed people and mechanized Italian troops were firing on people armed with little more than spears. Yet the proceeds were to be used "to help Italian soldiers injured during their attack on Ethiopia." When four antifascists and a black clergyman protested against allowing the group to use the town facility, a hearing was held to decide the issue.[7]

The Italians received permission to hold their fund raiser and Corwin attended, covering the story. Decades later, he remembered his shock at seeing their use of the Fascist salute and hearing their denouncement of the local antifascists as Communists.

In 1935, Corwin's social consciousness was further raised through his exposure to antiunion bias. He had moved over to radio, working at a Cincinnati station. Station policy forbade reference to strikes during news broadcasts. But in a contribution to an employee suggestion box, Corwin innocently commented that ignoring strikes that newspapers reported might diminish listener confidence in the station. For this he was fired. Corwin left Cincinnati and returned east.[8]

In New York, Corwin's brother Emil helped him find a job in 20th Century-Fox's publicity department, writing interviews and commentaries to be used on radio. After a while, however, Corwin started hearing the call of radio again. He wrote a letter to WQXR, a classical music station, suggesting a program dealing with poetry. Apparently at least partly because the station had a highbrow listenership, he wound up getting an audition and then a job that ran for twenty weeks. This, in turn, led to his being invited to direct CBS's prestigious *Columbia Workshop*. It was a giant step from $50 per week at a local station to $125 per week for a national network. Corwin's career grew quickly at CBS. Late in 1938 he was given his own show, *Norman Corwin's Words Without Music*, a program of dramatized poetry. It was instantly acclaimed. Having made the big time, he was now poised to become a household name.

In February 1939, Corwin wrote and directed his first antifascist radio play, "They Fly Through the Air With the Greatest of Ease." The project was the first of many that he undertook to lend his support to the fight against fascism. A workaholic, he periodically found his health suffering from his frantic pace. At one point, while working on a series, he retired to a thatched-roof cottage in New Jersey and led an almost monastic life, seeing no films or plays and spending little time with his girlfriend. A courier traveled across the George Washington Bridge to collect pages from him and bring them into the city, and a cook came by to prepare his meals.

Besides carrying on his work, Corwin also spoke out in public forums and in print about how radio needed to fight fascism. During a meeting of the Institute for Education by Radio at Ohio State University, he lashed out at the domestic obstacles to unity in the war effort. "Why have there not been at this convention names named?" he asked. "Let us talk about the Fascists within, who are the equivalent of six battleships or a couple of Panzer divisions in effect upon morale. Whom do I mean? I will name names—Lindbergh, Coughlin, Patterson, McCormick, Hearst, the *News*, the *Tribune*, the *Star*, the *Christian Front*."[9]

Corwin was also bothered by fear and hatred of America's new ally, the Soviet Union. In an anthology of his plays he wrote, "I never subscribed to the belief, as did so many sympathizers in this country, that the Soviet Union could do no wrong. But it seemed to me, from where I was sitting, that the USSR was doing things less wrong than what was being charged by the kind of witch-hunters who pronounced Shirley Temple a Red."[10]

Corwin's remark about the Soviet Union's capacity to do wrong understates the horror of a system that murdered millions of Ukrainians in a forced famine. His skewed perception of the Soviet Union reflects a problem that characterized many Americans of his generation on the political left. There were several important factors responsible for it. One was inadequate information. The Hearst newspapers and some others in Great Britain and the United States reported accurately on the forced famine. However, other western newspapers, notably the *New York Times*, the American newspaper of record, were silent about this massive instance of genocide. Other sources have discussed in detail the reasons for this major failure, for example, the role of *Times* correspondent Walter Duranty whose relationship with a Russian mistress was used to manipulate him into submitting stories in which he lied about conditions in Ukraine.[11] "The populace from babies to old folks, looks healthy and well nourished . . . ," Duranty wrote in September 1933 of the Ukrainians he had seen.[12] Liberals chose to accept such accounts partly because they distrusted the Hearst newspapers' inclination to soft pedal the abuses of Nazism and their bias against organized labor and all things Soviet.

A 1943 letter that Corwin wrote to the New York *Herald Tribune* states fairly succinctly his political outlook and that of many other progressives of the era. Corwin counted among his concerns the plight of displaced persons; the persecution of minorities, particularly the lynching of Negroes; infringements of civil liberties; smears; miscarriages of justice; domestic purges; censorship; libelous attacks; and committee investigations of his liberalism.[13] As a result of Corwin's dedication and hard work he earned himself the distinction of being radio's foremost dramatist and a major influence on a whole generation of writers, among whom were Rod Serling, Charles Kuralt, Norman Lear, and Ray Bradbury.

ARCH OBOLER

Along with Corwin, NBC's Arch Oboler was the other most prominent writer, producer, and director of radio drama. Oboler grew up in Chicago, where his boyhood ambition was to be a naturalist, an interest reflected in the presence in his bedroom of turtles, frogs, salamanders, and scorpions.[14] He was a short, dark, energetic man who wore casual clothing to work: polo shirts, baggy pants, and a trademark porkpie hat. He was also rather self-centered and somewhat controversial, often known to give interviewers a difficult time. Some descriptions of him emphasize the genius that he displayed in his field, whereas others stress the flashy and gimmicky quality of his writing. Because of his habit of self-promotion, the not-very-full record of his life contains claims that remain somewhat suspect. According to one account, Oboler sold his first story at age ten, after a visit to a zoo gave him the idea for it.

Oboler wrote several dozen radio plays before selling his first one, "Futuristics," to NBC, which used it to celebrate the opening of Radio City Music Hall. At the time, he was a student at the University of Chicago. In the next few years, he wrote for several shows, among them the *Chase and Sanborn Hour,* in the process gaining important experience in developing his radio drama technique.

According to Oboler, in 1936, he approached NBC with a complete folio of plays in an attempt to start an experimental theater. The proposal may have been influenced by word that CBS was about to launch the *Columbia Workshop.* "Radio is not mature enough for such productions," an NBC executive told Oboler. Instead, that spring the network offered him a position as writer for *Lights Out*, a popular horror series created by Wyliss Cooper, who was moving on to Hollywood. The series was known for its superb combination of first-rate writing and dramatic sound effects. Oboler accepted the offer, and the series became so identified with him that Cooper's role has often been forgotten.

In addition to his use of realistic sound effects, Arch Oboler had a particularly declamatory style and a remarkable stream-of-consciousness technique. He was also filled with a seemingly boundless energy. Unlike the usual production man who directed shows from within a glass-lined control room, Oboler, a short man, would often jump onto the central table in the middle of the studio, with earphones on his head, and direct the performance almost right on top of his actors.

Lewis Titterton, an administrator in the NBC hierarchy, recognized Oboler's talent early on. In the spring of 1939, after NBC had received some 225 letters in response to Oboler's plays, Titterton wrote to a higher up, "they are truly inspirational. If sentiment like these could reach people all over the world, if copies for American schools and peace organizations could be obtained, they would aid in preparing a saner and better future for humanity."[15]

Several months later, Oboler received one more letter worthy of note concerning a play, unfortunately not identified by name, that had a strong moral message. "Please do not think me a religious fanatic," wrote a listener in Connecticut, "if I tell you I have always believed the second coming of Christ would be a man or woman who could tell the world in terms even children could feel and find the living God. . . . You are doing just this."[16]

The message fell on fertile ears. Oboler already possessed a certain arrogance. Back during his short stay in college of less than a year, he became embroiled in an argument with the professor of his course in writing short stories. The professor criticized him for being ignorant of the elements of pulp writing. In reply, Oboler blurted out, "I've published more than a dozen stories. You've done only a couple. You don't know what you're talking about." Subsequently, according to one account, Oboler was charged with insubordination and left the university. The incident gives insight into the personality of the scrappiest and most competitive of all of the radio writers.

In later years Oboler published an article boasting of the superiority of Chicago radio drama over that of New York and Hollywood. "New York radio was rarely able to break loose of the pattern of plays written for the theatre," and Hollywood radio drama "was too screenplay conscious." He claimed it was Chicago radio alone (with the implication that "Chicago" meant Arch Oboler) that was "free of old influences" and that provided the right "sounds of words . . . effects, and orchestral accompaniment" that enabled the listener to create his own mental pictures.[17]

Among actors and others who worked with Oboler there is sharp division about him. Some, like actor Tommy Cook, who was only twelve when he started to work for Oboler, remember him with great affection. But others saw him as a contentious, highly opinionated, egotistical person. "Call me "Mr. O.," not "Arch," he once told a friend of several years.[18] Actress Irene Tedrow, who worked with both Corwin and Oboler, once described Corwin as "a very dear, gentle man, such a loving person." She said of Oboler, however, "Arch is a neurotic. He yells and sometimes he's very difficult."[19]

The fact cannot be denied that repeatedly throughout his career Oboler came into conflict with others, sometimes with big-name Hollywood stars. Once, several months before the entry of the United States into the war, MGM "lent" him Walter Pidgeon for one of Oboler's patriotic radio plays. In rehearsals, Pidgeon was terrible. Pidgeon was not the only big-name film actor to find it too difficult to rely strictly on his voice for a performance. "As many people [will] hear you in this next hour of broadcast as have heard you in all the motion pictures, and all the theater productions you have been in during your life time . . . ," Oboler told Pidgeon. "Therefore, I would appreciate it very much if you went home."[20]

Ronald Colman was another Oboler antagonist. During an ill-fated twenty-one-week radio collaboration the two came to detest each other. The experience was characterized by the slamming of doors and by Oboler and Colman addressing each other by "Mr." For one thing, Colman and others were annoyed with Oboler's screaming and ranting. The actor also became fed up with Oboler's habit of producing a script at the last moment as though he had just dashed it off between more urgent business. In addition, Colman, a fastidious

dresser, was disgusted by Oboler's wardrobe of "dirty dungarees, no
socks, sandals, and a hat with a grease-stained band." Oboler's explanation for his dress style was that he was a man ahead of his time.[21] In
1949, Oboler also came into conflict with James and Pamela Mason
soon after the beginning of a dramatic series that Oboler was hired to
write. Oboler and the Masons soon parted.

Writer Barbara Merlin, who worked as Oboler's assistant during the
war, called him "an inveterate liar." She alleged that he would lie to
any agency and say that he had been up all night for three nights writing a show that he also got in under the wire. According to Merlin,
there was one unusual occasion when Oboler submitted a script a few
days early. But, she alleged, he had stolen the entire script from another show.[22] Oboler was also involved in an angry tug-of-war with a
writer who was romantically involved with the famed German refugee
writer Bertolt Brecht. The writer claimed that she gave Oboler a radio play about the fight for freedom in Norway and that he then
broadcast it under his name.

The matter of Oboler producing a script at the last minute was apparently a common thing with him. Broadcast historian Erik Barnouw
recalled attending a party at Oboler's Frank Lloyd Wright house,
which sat cantilevered over a cliff. During the party Oboler disappeared. On inquiring about his host, Oboler's wife told Barnouw,
"He's writing a script." Shortly afterward, Oboler reemerged, the
script complete. He was a fast writer and an eclectic man.

Oboler's quirks and contentiousness aside, he deserves credit for attempting as early as 1938 to wake up America to the dangers of fascism through a variety of anti-Nazi plays. In 1941, six months before
the United States came into the war, at a conference, Oboler spoke of
his frustration over what he perceived as the networks' lack of courage
in accepting plays on controversial themes. He talked about what he
saw as the great need for plays encouraging young men to become flying cadets and of network reluctance to cooperate in the endeavor. In
fact, there was at least one such show in the pre-Pearl Harbor months,
From Oxford Pacifism to Fighter Pilot, a series that promoted sympathy for the pilots of the Royal Air Force who were defending Britain
from the German Luftwaffe. More importantly, by this time, too,
there was a broad array of programs designed to create support

among the listening public for intervention. Oboler's plea at this point may have reflected a lag in his perception of how programming had changed. In any case, between 1939, when he produced his first war-related play, and 1945, when the war ended, Oboler produced more than seventy "Beat the Axis" plays.

ARCHIBALD MACLEISH

He "had the long bony face of an aristocrat, the good looks of a rich man, and the smile of an administrator." Thus did writer Donald Hall describe his former professor at Harvard, the noted poet Archibald MacLeish.[23] MacLeish had been a strong pacifist as late as 1935. But after a trip to Japan, the overthrow of democracy in Spain, and Hitler's successful takeover of both Austria and Czechoslovakia, MacLeish changed his views and began to speak in favor of action against fascism. He advocated American aid to the Loyalists in Spain and support for Britain. Finally, before the idea gained widespread acceptance, he pushed for intervention against the Nazis.

One of the most dramatic parts of MacLeish's crusade against fascism appeared in 1937. With Ernest Hemingway and several other prominent writers, he produced *The Spanish Earth,* a documentary film about the Spanish Civil War, one of the great progressive theatrical events of that year. Also in 1937, in March, the *Columbia Workshop* produced MacLeish's antifascist "The Fall of the City," the first radio play in verse. Two months later, MacLeish chaired a meeting of the League of American Writers in New York at which he commented to those who believed that fighting fascism might bring on a war that the war for freedom had already begun. Similarly, during Phi Beta Kappa ceremonies at Columbia University, he read "Speech to the Scholars," a pro-intervention poem. The poem was a polemic that the war against fascism differed from others in history because the agencies of propaganda were now being used in sophisticated ways to seduce people into believing the lies of totalitarian states.

Later in 1937, MacLeish took his campaign to the White House. Accompanied by another playwright, and acting on behalf of an informal group, the two appealed to President Roosevelt to aid the Loyalist government in Spain. Roosevelt gave an evasive answer, but he thought highly enough of MacLeish two years later to appoint him Librarian of Congress. In 1941, two months before the attack on Pearl Harbor, MacLeish took on further responsibility with the government, this time as head of a new federal propaganda agency.

WILLIAM ROBSON

When radio director and writer William Robson died at the age of 88 in 1995, a good part of an era died with him. Arthur Laurents immortalized Robson as "Big Bill Verso," a man with flair, in his novel, *The Way We Were*: "the heavy door from the outside corridor opened and Bill Verso stalked in: a big man with a big black mustache and a big head of always tousled hair. Verso cultivated looking and moving like a director: he wore a Hemingway trench coat and strode straight to the control room without a good morning or an apology. Nor was anyone surprised at the sleepy, elegant redhead who trailed behind him in a sleek raincoat."[24]

Bill Robson grew up in Pittsburgh and was educated at Yale. For a short time after college, he wrote film scripts. Then, in 1933, he moved over to a Los Angeles radio station, writing *Conquerors of the Sky*, a series about World War I flyers. Robson also began to write for *Calling All Cars*, a crime show that aired on the West Coast in the early 1930s. Within a short time he was moved from writing to directing the show. This began a long association with CBS as a producer and director. Robson was responsible for, among other things, some of the best war-related programs heard on the air.

Robson's career more or less defined radio's Golden Age. It spanned the era's beginning, with production of Archibald MacLeish's "The Fall of the City," on which he worked, and its end, with the conclusion of the war and the emergence of television. Robson worked with, influenced, and was influenced by many major writers and producers of the era. In addition to MacLeish and Laurents, these included Norman Corwin, Arch Oboler, Ranald MacDougall, Allan Sloane, and Irving Reis. Along the way Robson won several Peabody prizes, some for plays that he himself wrote.

Robson's career also shows how radio of the era functioned as a national conscience, or at least as a prod to it. "As broadcasters, we have certain responsibilities," he said in 1943 on a panel at a meeting of the Institute for Radio Education in Columbus, Ohio. Robson frequently acted on that belief, using radio to try to clarify crucial social issues. In 1938, working with documentarian Pare Lorentz, he produced a program about the unemployed for the *Columbia Workshop*. Implicitly endorsing the New Deal, as it was, the program was controversial. Robson and Lorentz knew this and decided that with the hate campaign against FDR gaining strength, they had best not circulate the script around CBS. They even delayed showing it to Bill Lewis, the vice president of programming, until before noon on the Saturday of the broadcast. As it turned out, Lewis had tickets for a doubleheader at Yankee Stadium and he had to make a choice of either going to the ball game or reading the script. Luckily for Robson and Lorenz, he selected the game, because, as he told them after it aired, had he read the script before its broadcast, he would have canceled it.[25]

Throughout Robson's life he was concerned about the plight of minorities, particularly black Americans. Speaking further during his presentation in Columbus, he said "We have a little back-yard cleaning right here: we cannot fight to protect the Jew in the ghetto of Warsaw and allow the Negro to do only spade work in the armed forces or to patrol the border at Fort Huachuca or to be a messman aboard a Navy fighting ship. If we are going into this war to make the world safe for all peoples . . . we had better be sure that we mean it at home."[26]

ALLAN SLOANE

As a boy, Allan Sloane sometimes stood on the top of the hill in East Side Park in his home town of Paterson, New Jersey, and watched the beckoning gleam of sunlight on the roofs of the skyscrapers in Manhattan.[27] Sloane was one of two writers (Millard Lampell was the other) to come to New York and to radio from Paterson. The two met when Sloane was twenty-two and Lampell was seventeen. Despite the difference in their ages, and because of Lampell's precocity and their common interest in literature, for a while they were close friends, with

Sloane serving as Lampell's mentor. Lampell found Sloane's home full of books: Hemingway, Fitzgerald, Balzac, Melville, and Maupassant.

Like most of the other writers of wartime radio drama, Sloane was greatly affected by the Depression and the worldwide political turmoil of the 1930s. In the fall of 1931 he enrolled at the College of the City of New York (CCNY). They were exciting years, and the experience helped to politicize him. At the time, the college was a hotbed of radical politics, one of the most important progressive centers in the city. The milieu helped shape Sloane's thinking, as it did a number of influential writers and intellectuals who attended this "Poor Man's Harvard."

In the fall of 1934, while Sloane was at City College, its president, Frederick Robinson, hosted a visit from sixteen Italian university students, part of a larger group that the Fascist government of Benito Mussolini sent to tour American universities. The visit turned out to be a fiasco. First a group of antifascist undergraduates, including Sloane, demonstrated the morning before the Italian students' arrival. Sloane witnessed Robinson berating the demonstrators and even whacking several of them with his umbrella. Later, after a conflict-torn ceremony of welcome, Sloane participated in another demonstration in the college's stadium where he and a friend carried a device they had made, a long pole with two heads on it. Two people stood on either side of the contraption. When the device was pulled from one side, up popped an arm with an umbrella. When it was pulled from the other, up came a caricature of Mussolini. The protest was short lived because Robinson called the police, who came and broke it up with nightsticks. Sloane was among those struck during the fracas.

After graduation from CCNY, Sloane studied journalism in a graduate program at Columbia University. Subsequently, he worked as a newspaper reporter for several years. Early in 1941, believing that he was about to be drafted, he joined the Army. Barely more than two weeks after the attack on Pearl Harbor, Sloane received a medical discharge and returned to journalism. Within a few weeks, he moved in with his friend Lampell, who had an apartment in Brooklyn. Lampell was singing with a folk song group, the Almanac Singers, and Sloane met and even sang several times with them.

Sloane spent 1942 and part of the following year hopping from job to job: with the Associated Press, *Newsweek*, the newspaper *PM*, and

Parade magazine. The stint with *Parade* proved to be his last experience with journalism. One day in 1943, the managing editor called him into his office and fired him, the result apparently of a clash of egos.

Sloane checked the grapevine to see who was hiring, fearful that he might have to go back to smalltime papers. Then one evening in early July, while flipping stations on his radio, he came upon a broadcast of the *Man Behind the Gun*, a Robson series. Inspired by what he heard, Sloane decided to try his hand at writing a radio script for the show. He chose as his subject a fictional invasion of Sicily by the Allied Forces. Unannounced, Sloane then visited Robson's office at CBS. Robson was unavailable, so he left the script with a secretary. Two nights later, the telephone rang at Sloane's home in Connecticut. "Sloane, is that you," a voice asked. "Yes, who is this?" Sloane replied. "Bill Robson." "Who?" "Bill Robson at CBS. You left the script for me." "What do you think of it?" Sloane inquired. "What do I think of it? Haven't you been listening to the radio? Don't you read the newspaper?" Sloane had missed the news story that was headlined in the *New York Times* two days earlier. The allies had invaded Sicily.[28]

Subsequently, Sloane received his first paycheck for the show. It was for $250. "Easy money," he said to himself. He was flabbergasted. But when he mentioned the amount of the check to another staff member, she yelled at him. Robson had been paying his other writers $375. "He's robbing you because you're the new kid on the block!" the woman told him, after which she nearly attacked Robson and shamed him into giving Sloane equal pay.

For a short time in the 1940s, Sloane belonged to the American Communist Party. Lampell had already joined, and one day in early 1943 he brought Sloane with him to a party meeting. Sloane remained a member until the summer of 1944 when he quit after some disagreements with party leadership.[29]

STEPHEN VINCENT BENÉT

Among the most patriotic of the radio writers was the poet Stephen Vincent Benét. In 1929, Benét, a balding, bespectacled Yale graduate, was awarded a Pulitzer Prize for a book-length poem, *John Brown's Body*. In his earlier years, Benét was rather indifferent to politics, but during the 1930s he grew increasingly interested in national and international events. By the late 1930s he had widespread friendships among European refugees. He had also developed a personal link with events in Spain when his nephew joined the International Brigade to fight the fascists there. In October 1941, Benét also joined the Council for Democracy and served as a member of its executive committee. He was an excellent, fascinating, and yet tragic choice to enlist in the production of radio propaganda. In addition to his primary reputation as a poet, Benét had already developed experience as a writer for radio. He had a sense of its fluidity and was attracted to its direct appeal to the human mind.

By the time of the attack on Pearl Harbor, Benét was driven to assist the war effort, attending meetings, giving radio readings of his poetry, and writing a pledge of allegiance to be taken by civil defense workers. Norman Corwin called him a "one man task force." Benét also wrote an article for Russian Relief that sent food parcels and bandages to the Soviet Union and wrote original materials for radio. His best-known contribution to the war effort was a radio drama in verse, "They Burned the Books."

Benét was aware that writing propaganda might damage his reputation in the postwar years. This had happened to many American writers who had taken it up during World War I. In fact, he was prescient. Decades after Benét's death, writer Paul Fussell criticized him for having been persuaded that the war effort required the laying aside of all normal standards of art and intellect.[30] There was also the problem that the bulk of Benét's war writing, radio scripts, was perishable. None had the permanence of a book. Most were free verse dramas intended to be broadcast only once, although many were re-broadcast. But Benét focused on the positive aspects of radio, which he curiously labeled "as old as the human heart." And he wrote of the war: "This one is for our skins and the chips are down."

Besides sacrificing his reputation, Benét refused any personal profit from war writing. In 1941, *Life* sent him a check for $500 for a poem entitled "Listen to the People." Despite financial problems, he endorsed it and sent it to the USO.

NORMAN ROSTEN

Norman Rosten was born in New York City on New Year's Day in 1914. For a while his family had a farm in upstate New York and he had plans to be a farmer. He attended the Agricultural College of Cornell University with that goal in mind. According to one story, when the family farm burned down, they and he returned to the seaside Brooklyn community of Coney Island, about which he wrote extensively.

In 1935, Rosten graduated from Brooklyn College intent on becoming a teacher. Unable to find a job, however, he decided to become a writer. He received part of his training on a graduate fellowship at the University of Michigan, where his talent was also recognized with a Hopwood Award in poetry and drama. Two years later, having completed his studies, he received a Yale Series of Younger Poets Award, an event that apparently helped him make the acquaintance of famed poet Stephen Vincent Benét, a graduate of Yale who became his mentor. For a short time Rosten worked for the New York Federal Theatre. Then, in 1941, through a recommendation from Benét, he began writing patriotic radio plays for NBC's *Cavalcade of America*. Rosten credited the broadcast of MacLeish's "Fall of the City" for making him realize what "a wonderful carrier for poetry" radio was. From there, Rosten became one of the most prolific writers of radio plays of the 1940s. After Rosten's first successes in selling radio dramas, he decided that the medium did not offer him sufficient freedom of expression. But the needs of the war attracted him back. He threw himself into producing morale boosting plays for the Treasury Department and the Office of War Information.

The social and political turmoil of the 1930s had a profound effect on Rosten, as it had on most of his friends and colleagues, and Rosten was inspired to fight for a more just society. As early as his graduate school years he published a variety of articles, plays, and poems reflecting his thoughts and feelings about the Spanish Civil War and other issues of the day. Many of them show a clear influence of the philosophy that also shaped the Communist Party, and they appeared in publications such as *Mainstream* and *Soviet Russia Today*, which had links with it.

Two of Rosten's early works, a dramatic poem on the tragic history of the Chicago Haymarket Riot and a script for a pageant depicting the lives of Lenin and two other working-class leaders, sponsored by the Young Communist League, both written in 1937, show his socialist orientation.

Like Benét and so many others, Rosten was quite caught up in war fever. In an undated letter to Benét, written on a hot summer day, he claimed "One thing that makes the heat worth taking is knowing that Hitler is finally getting his shoulders pinned to the mat. Methinks the road that started in Spain will end in Moscow, in reverse!"[31] In a second letter to Benét (also undated), Rosten revealed further the war's grip on him. "I've had a kind of talk with myself in a cloakroom over the week end and I've decided not to rush into teaching. . . . I'm going to try to get into aircraft work. It's more important and I suspect I'll be a better writer because of it."[32]

It appears that, in fact, Rosten never did go into aircraft work. He occasionally had some commercial success with his writings, but he never held a real job. Rosten always lived a simple life; too simple, his wife is reported to have complained at times, referring to their finances. Essentially a poet and a romanticist who fled from hard analysis of issues, his income was often minimal—poets rarely make much of a living—but he shared what he had. In 1942, his first volume of poetry won him a Guggenheim Award that carried a prize of $1,000. Rosten sent half of it to his sister.

During the war years the Rosten apartment was often the venue of a literary salon attended by many others in the arts who were also living on the fringe. Some called Rosten and his group "The Broken Wing Society," an appellation used more as a sympathetic than as a pejorative one.

Boyishly handsome with a shock of brown hair, Rosten was an extremely well-liked man. Novelist Norman Mailer, himself a much more controversial and angry writer, said of Rosten, "[he was] the most easy decent man, totally relaxed and affable. Norman's manner was one of the models of behavior for me. . . . He was a guy who'd treat the postman with the same dignity as a world famous author."[33]

LANGSTON HUGHES

Missouri-born Langston Hughes, yet another poet who wrote for wartime radio, had many fewer opportunities with the medium than his white peers had.[34] Racial discrimination hampered his career in many ways. His earliest experience with it was in Topeka, Kansas, in the late summer of 1908 when he was six and his mother tried to enroll him in a white neighborhood school. She was told instead to enroll him in a black school, some distance away. After arguing fruitlessly with the principal, she appealed to the school board and won. From the first day, Hughes's teacher tried to break his will, seating him, for example, in a corner in the back of the room, out of the alphabetical order in which she had the rest of the class organized. One day she took a stick of licorice away from a white boy saying loudly, "You don't want to eat these. . . . They'll make you black like Langston."[35]

Hughes rose from obscurity partly with the help of the poet Vachel Lindsay. The two met as Lindsay was dining in a Washington, D.C., hotel where Hughes was working as a bellboy. One day Hughes quietly put three of his poems next to Lindsay's plate. After Lindsay read them, he told a newspaper reporter that he had "discovered" a new poet. The resulting article gave Hughes his first publicity outside the black community.

Langston Hughes was at the center of a group of writers and actors trying to create an independent black theater in Harlem. He was also involved in the political and social issues that concerned Harlem's leadership. Hughes had one of the widest world views of the various radio writers of war-era drama. He was also one of the writers most critical of American social life.

In 1931, Hughes began a dramatic move to the far left. He visited Spain at the time of its Civil War, and he traveled extensively throughout the Soviet Union. In both countries he was mesmerized by an apparent absence of racism. In Spain, he was impressed that American blacks were fighting alongside whites on the Loyalist side, sometimes even in positions of command over whites. He saw the Soviet Union as "the world's new center," characterizing it by the phrase "no colonies, no voteless citizens, and no Jim Crow cars."[36]

Hughes also joined the John Reed Club of New York, part of a se-ries of Communist Party–supported groups of left-wing writers and artists that helped organize a radical urban subculture. Like the party, the club was committed to fighting racism. Here he worked alongside Whittaker Chambers as a director of the left-wing Suitcase Theater. The club's publication, *New Masses*, became the leading outlet for his poems, some of which were bitterly anticapitalist.[37]

Hughes was outspoken in his opposition to many forms of racism and persecution, attending public forums that addressed the issues of Nazi persecution of Jews and racism against American blacks. Through various writings he attacked all forms of oppression. In the fall of 1942, he published "Klan or Gestapo? Why Take Either?" an ar-ticle in the *Chicago Defender,* America's largest circulation black weekly. "It is the duty of Negro writers," Hughes proclaimed, "to re-veal the international aspects of our problems at home, to show how these problems are merely a part of the great problem of world free-dom everywhere."[38]

Because of his leftist views, Hughes was an early target of right-wing groups. In 1938, Dr. Theodore Graebner of Concordia Seminary in St. Louis, Missouri, testifying before the House Un-American Ac-tivities Committee (HUAC), attacked radicals in the nation's universi-ties and referred to Hughes as a "Communist poet." Two years later, members of the Four-Square Gospel Church and the Angelus Bible College organized by evangelist Aimée Semple McPherson organized a protest against a speech by Hughes that was scheduled in Pasadena, California.[39] The incident inspired the FBI to begin gathering infor-mation about him.[40]

Hughes's role in radio began in 1940 when CBS asked him to write some scripts for *Pursuit of Happiness,* a series directed by Norman Corwin. Jobs for blacks in radio were quite scarce, and Hughes was delighted to accept. CBS accepted one script on Booker T. Washing-ton, although it rejected two others.

Shortly after the attack on Pearl Harbor, the Writers War Board, a private organization, invited Hughes to join its advisory committee. Formed to help the war effort, it included among its members such prominent writers as Pearl Buck and William Shirer. Although Hughes accepted the invitation, he did so with a keen awareness of his status as the group's token black, and he dealt with the Writers War Board with a profound sense of independence. On the one hand, he viewed Nazi racism as close kin to the racism of the lynch mobs of the American South and to racism in general throughout America. But he also saw through the hypocrisy of blacks fighting to defend a democracy whose fruits they could not fully share.

Hughes had no doubt that the defeat of Nazi Germany was as much in the interest of American blacks as it was for whites. At the time, the climate of American race relations seemed to be improving: the Office of Facts and Figures, the Roosevelt administration's first wartime propaganda agency, was attempting to implement a policy for a more dignified presentation of blacks than had generally been network practice.[41] As the war moved forward, Hughes continued to be harassed for his progressive views. At the end of the summer of 1944, he was to go on a poetry-reading tour of high schools in New Jersey and Philadelphia. It was sponsored by the Common Council for African Unity, which included among its goals the need to instill pride in black students and promote the perception of blacks as human beings among white students. But in early October, a staff member of HUAC denounced Hughes as "a leading member of the Communist Party for some twenty years." Later in the month, a newspaper columnist in the *New York Sun* joined in the attack. Within a day or so, the principals of several of the schools Hughes was to visit quickly canceled the planned appearances.

MILLARD LAMPELL

Millard Lampell was born into a liberal Jewish family; his father was a garment worker who had emigrated to New York from Austria-Hungary, as had Lampell's mother. Lampell was handsome, short, athletic, aggressive, ebullient, and, in his youth, fond of stylish clothes.[42] In his early years, he worked as a silk dyer, fruit picker, coal miner, and folk singer.

Lampell sold his first piece of writing while studying at the University of West Virginia. It was an article based on the experience he and his roommate had with fascist groups on campus to whom they presented themselves as being interested in forming a fascist student organization. After Lampell completed the requirements for his degree, he left West Virginia for New York City without waiting for graduation. There he got a job spying on the American Destiny Party, a fascist organization with some 350 followers, and its "führer," Joe McWilliams. McWilliams, who traveled New York in a covered wagon, called himself "the anti-Jew candidate for Congress," drawing crowds in one instance as large as 2,000 people.[43]

In 1941, Lampell traveled and wrote and sang folk music and peace songs with the Almanac Singers, a group that featured Woody Guthrie and Pete Seeger. The Almanacs were strongly antifascist, pro-union, and antisegregationist with a touch of anti-Rockefeller thrown in. Lampell, a born operator, with a devil-may-care attitude, faked a hill-billy accent and claimed Kentucky origins.[44] Also, unlike the others in the group, Lampell saw the Almanacs as an adventure to get involved in temporarily. Guthrie's biographer, Joe Klein, described the folk singing group as being "so fertile and so clever, and their conversation so rapid, that they were now the first major group of entertainers turning out war propaganda in New York . . . and CBS radio, for one, was interested in using them as morale builders." Klein added, "There was even some talk of the Almanacs being hired by the networks to write songs describing each new major event in the war."[45]

One Sunday, just as the Almanacs finished a concert, a thin-faced man in a suit approached Lampell.[46] The man, Hi Brown, one of radio's most important producers, asked Lampell if he had ever considered writing for radio. Apparently word of Lampell's talent as writer of some of the Almanacs' songs as well as articles for the *New Republic*, had gotten around. Dangling the prospects of Lampell's making some good money, Brown tried to sell him on the idea of writing for him. He even needled the younger man about the sloppy college-dormitory–like conditions in which Lampell was then living with his friends.

At first Lampell was put off by Brown's manner. But Brown was not one to take "no" for an answer. He explained that the Office of War Information had asked him to put together a series about ordinary people and their lives during the war and offered Lampell $50 just for trying to write a script. "I'll send you some old ones," he said. "Use them as models. And if I can use what you write, you'll get a total of $200." Lampell gave in.

As a boy, Lampell gained experience telling stories to his friends sitting on the steps in front of his house. Now, almost effortlessly he typed up a script about a grain farmer burdened with insects, weather problems, and threats of bank foreclosure. When the farmer's grandson joins the Marines, the farmer gets a new determination to help the war effort by overcoming his problems and making the farm succeed. On finishing his script, Lampell took it to Brown's apartment on Manhattan's West Side. Instead of an office, Brown worked out of his home. Brown looked over the script, smiled, and immediately offered Lampell a job.

In 1942 and 1943, Lampell wrote for several radio programs: *It's the Navy*; *Men, Machines and Victory*; and *Green Valley, U.S.A.* It was also in early 1942 that he met Norman Rosten just as Lampell was starting to write for radio. He had never met a poet before, and he was very impressed. The two began a close friendship, frequently taking long walks together through Brooklyn, especially on the esplanade overlooking the docks in the Navy Yard.

In June 1943, Lampell was drafted. After training, he was assigned to the Air Force radio section in New Haven, Connecticut, where he wrote, produced, and directed Air Force radio programs on all the networks. In the summer of 1944, Lampell was released from the Air Force to visit veterans hospitals around the United States and gather material for radio scripts about returning soldiers. On completing the project based on this research, he subsequently lectured on radio writing at several New York area colleges. In 1946, Lampell went to Hollywood as a contract writer at Warner Bros.

ARTHUR MILLER

Perhaps the most artistically gifted of the radio playwrights of the war era was Arthur Miller, who is best known for *Death of a Salesman* and other stage plays. At least partly by choice, Miller has had one of the lowest profiles as an author of radio plays. Although he wrote perhaps twenty-five of them between 1939 and 1946, most war-related, few histories of broadcasting acknowledge his radio role.

Miller grew up in an initially well-to-do family in Harlem in the 1920s.[47] The Depression hit his family hard, forcing his grandfather to give up his home and move in with Miller's family, where the two had to share a bedroom. Miller also saw his father, a garment industry manufacturer, go broke. The family lost a life of privilege, which included the services of a chauffeur, a seven-passenger National, and ownership of a summer bungalow. Miller saw how the experience caused his father to grow into himself and lose his powers. These observations combined to make him question the capitalist system.

Miller attended the University of Michigan, where he met his classmates and friends Norman Rosten and Rosten's soon-to-be wife, Hedda Rowinski. The college had some of the atmosphere of City College in New York whose night program Miller had briefly attended. Michigan was one of the few midwestern universities at the time where Marxism could be openly discussed in its classrooms. Here, during the rise of fascism in Europe, Miller began his career as a playwright, winning the University of Michigan Hopwood Award for two of his plays. He also developed a progressive political outlook characterized initially by faith in socialism and by a lifelong devotion to human rights concerns. Like others he began to see Soviet socialism as a preferred alternative, ignoring the Soviet Union's glaring defects. Referring in his autobiography to Russia in the early stages of World War II, he noted: "Russia in 1940 had no colonies, had annexed no neighbors (the division of Poland with Germany and the occupation of the Baltic republics were explained away as defensive acts), and could therefore claim a clean anti-imperialist record; and it had no unemployment, unlike every major European country."[48]

Elaborating further on how he and other leftists were blinded to the faults in the Soviet system, he added wistfully, "It was really quite simple: we had to hope and we found hope where we could, in illusions, too, providing they showed promise. Reality was intolerable with its permanent armies of the unemployed, the stagnating . . . spirit of America, the fearful racism everywhere, the waste of everything precious, especially the potential of the young. . . . All that could save us was harsh reason and socialism, production not for profit but for use.[49]

After graduation , Miller moved back east, hoping to begin a writing career. Within a few months, a representative of 20th Century-Fox offered him $250 a week to come to Hollywood to write film scripts. Miller, an idealist, rejected the offer, opting instead for a job at $22.77 per week with the Federal Theatre. During his school breaks he had periodically attended performances of the left-wing Group Theatre in New York, whose social consciousness reverberated in him. He viewed his friends who accepted the film studios' generous offers and were shipped to Hollywood in "cattle cars" as prostituting their artistic freedom.

Miller's job with the Federal Theatre lasted only six months, after which the government terminated the agency. At around the same time, his radio writing career began with a play for CBS's *Columbia Workshop*. Although the series featured the work of a number of already established writers, such as Archibald MacLeish and Stephen Vincent Benét, most of its scripts came from new writers such as Miller. Miller wrote scripts for other series, too, including the *Cavalcade of America,* to which he was referred by Norman Rosten.

When the United States became involved in the war in 1941, Miller was rejected for military service because of a knee injury.[50] The experience left him feeling alienated and frustrated with what he described in his autobiography as "the inevitable unease of the survivor." For any man in good or reasonably good health, being a civilian during the war meant having to answer to external and sometimes internal questioning about why he was not in uniform doing his part for the country. Miller also failed in his efforts to get a job with the Office of War Information. The situation left him feeling "part of nothing, no class, no influential group; it was like high school perpetually, with everybody else rushing to one or another club and me still trying to figure out what was happening."[51]

Seeking some feeling of community, Miller got a job in the Brooklyn Navy Yard, where he helped recondition ships for service. Recalling the era further, he wrote "Rejected for military service, I had to justify my existence by throwing myself into writing patriotic war plays for radio. We were all one big happy family fighting the common enemy, but the more expert I became the more desiccated I felt writing the stuff which was more like a form of yelling than writing. . . . Still it was an easy dollar." [52]

As a child growing up in the 1920s in a largely Jewish environment, Miller rarely encountered overt anti-Semitism. Yet subtle forces in his family milieu had instilled in him a need to be on guard regarding his Jewish identity. Once, as he was applying for his first public library card, the librarian asked his father's first name. It was "Isidore," a very Jewish name. Suddenly, young Arthur froze up and then without replying, bolted out of the library and into the street.

Now, in his twenties, working in the Navy Yard, Miller experienced direct anti-Semitism. The 1930s and 1940s were rampant with it. Periodically, it was expressed on the radio and in newspaper real estate and want ads. Miller was on lunch break one day with a Czech welder with whom he had begun to strike up a friendship. Suddenly something set the man off, and he let loose a display of vicious anti-Semitic comments. He did not know that Miller was Jewish, and his remarks were not directed at him. But Miller was so stunned that it put a quick end to the friendship. Altogether these and other similar incidents made a sufficient impression on him that he wrote a novel about anti-Semitism and devoted a number of pages to these incidents in his memoir. He also became an activist in PEN, the international writers organization that fights for the right to free expression.

Miller spent only three months per year writing for radio. He worked very quickly, completing a half-hour play in less than a day. The rest of the year he wrote stage plays. Others, too, of course, had misgivings about writing war propaganda. However, his regrets apparently exceeded most other writers, who may have disliked doing wartime propaganda work but otherwise enjoyed writing for radio. In 1947, by which time Miller ceased writing for radio, he wrote, "really fine radio drama or first rate comedy is an impossibility."[53]

ARTHUR LAURENTS

Arthur Laurents is the son of a humanitarian orthodox Jewish father and an atheistic and socialistic-minded mother. He attended Cornell University, graduating in 1940. Soon after college, at the urging of a friend, Laurents enrolled in a radio course with William Robson at New York University.[54] To Laurents's disappointment, Robson showed up only five weeks after the course began. But when he did, he was so impressed with Laurents's work that he took a play that Laurents wrote for the course and sold it to CBS, for the *Columbia Workshop.* Although the show usually paid $100 for scripts, Laurents received only $30 for his, coincidentally the cost of his tuition for the course. But through his contact with Robson, the fledgling writer began his career, writing for numerous half-hour commercial shows.

In the summer of 1941, Laurents was drafted into the Army. Although he was supposed to be there only five days, he spent his first six weeks in the service at Camp Upton, Long Island, now the site of the Brookhaven National Laboratories. He was then sent for basic training to Ft. Monmouth in New Jersey. On Sunday, December 7, while on leave in New York, Laurents was showering in the apartment of a friend when she called in to him, "They bombed Pearl Harbor. All military leaves are canceled and all soldiers have been ordered to report back to their bases." Laurents finished his shower quickly, dressed, and left.

From Monmouth, through an error in Laurents's classification number, and much to his misery, the Army sent him to Ft. Benning, Georgia, long before anyone else from the base was sent out. He was a writer who was now being classified as a photographer. One weekend at Ft. Benning, Laurents found himself the only soldier in his unit who had not been granted leave. When he complained, the officer on duty responded with unexplained hostility. He soon found out its cause. The whole unit, with the exception of Laurents, was going overseas. Laurents was being sent to New York! At Monmouth, he had made two friends, who had now arranged for him to be transferred to a unit making training films in Astoria, New York, across the East River from Manhattan. One of them was Bob Hopkins, the son of FDR's chief advisor Harry Hopkins. The other was a man named Harry, who had admired Laurents because of the latter's experience in radio, under a false impression that Laurents fostered that he knew many radio stars. Harry worked in a classification center and he did the actual paperwork.

Toward the end of 1943, Laurents was transferred from Astoria to a radio writing unit in Manhattan. The following year, while attending a meeting of the Radio Writers Guild, he spoke out in favor of a bill that was intended to rectify a voting problem that had been responsible for only a small percentage of soldiers being able to vote in national and other elections. Southern Democrat and many Republican politicians had vehemently opposed the bill, because polls showed that young people, soldiers, and others tended to support the New Deal. The bill would provide a simplified ballot system to allow soldiers to vote in federal elections starting in 1944.[55]

Laurents had attended the Radio Writers Guild meeting in uniform, and playwright Russell Crouse had noted his outspokenness. As Laurents learned from a friend, Crouse later repeated Laurents's comments to the Army chief of radio during a visit to Washington, referring to Laurents as a communist. A prominent member of the Writers War Board, Crouse was a political conservative. As a consequence, Laurents was summoned to Washington and questioned about his views. Subsequently, he was required to have all his scripts cleared in Washington. It seems likely, too, as he speculated, that the incident also served to block him from any promotions.

Laurents is a homosexual and, as such, encountered numerous instances of bigotry. As a boy of seven, with his sexual identity far from self-evident, he suffered the pain of rumors that circulated about him. By his early twenties, having had both heterosexual and homosexual experiences, he was plagued with confusion. While in the Army, his problem was intensified by the Army's zero tolerance for homosexuality. Living in fear, he told none of his fellow soldiers. Seeking psychological help with his problems, he had the misfortune to find himself with a psychoanalyst who claimed that he could "cure" Laurents of his homosexuality. Only some years later did he find a therapist with a humanistic outlook.

As with Arthur Miller, instances of anti-Semitism contributed to sensitize Laurents to racial and other forms of bigotry. "Sheeny," a man in a passing car yelled out at him one day when he was ten, while he was standing and waiting for a trolley. Another time, when he was in high school, his French teacher, angry because he had been inattentive, burst out "You . . . always spoil my class. You Jews poison the class." Later, at Cornell, he encountered a professor of a play-writing course who did not hesitate to start a sentence with the words "You Jews. . . ." One other incident occurred in the Army at Monmouth. A sergeant, explaining procedures for barracks inspection, commented on how badly "the kikes cleaned up." Suddenly, Laurents's friend Bob, a gentile, decked the sergeant, knocking him onto the barracks floor. As Laurents explained in his autobiography, the consequence of all of these factors was that he came to conclude that America was plagued with problems of bias concerning—in order starting with those most victimized: homosexuals, blacks, and Jews.

MORTON WISHENGRAD

Morton Wishengrad was born in New York's lower east side in 1913 to Orthodox Russian–Jewish immigrant parents. He was a tall, thin, modest, and reserved man. Wishengrad shared many of the concerns of the progressive-minded writers of his generation. He considered himself a liberal, although in his case, a determinedly anti-Communist one.

Wishengrad died young, at the age of 49, and never had a chance to write his memoirs. Years later a nine-year-old granddaughter who never knew him wrote an eight-page biographical sketch of him, describing how he met his wife at a meeting "of young people who were interested in helping poor people fight the great depression."[56] Like his fellow radio writers and so many of his generation, Wishengrad was a strong labor advocate. One of his first jobs was with the International Ladies Garment Workers Union, for which he worked as an editor, researcher, teacher, and educational director. Subsequently, he was named the American Federation of Labor's director of a joint Labor Short Wave Bureau that broadcast via the Office of War Information to organized labor in free and German occupied territory. Late in 1942, the Congress of Industrial Organizations (CIO) Textiles Workers Union asked him to write a script for NBC's *Labor for Victory* series. This led to his writing for NBC's University of the Air, the *Cavalcade of America,* and a Red Cross series.

Wishengrad stands out uniquely among a number of Jewish radio writers as perhaps the only one to clearly bring his Jewish consciousness to the medium. Initially, an encounter with a teacher in a Jewish religious school who taught "more by the rod than by the book" prompted him to reject both Judaism and anything to do with Jewish themes. Years later, after he started to work in radio, while doing research about Christopher Columbus he read about Spain's expulsion of the Jews. This led to his reading about the Spanish Inquisition, which called to his mind a parallel with Nazism. Instead of writing about Columbus, he wound up writing about the Jews. The program so impressed the American Jewish Committee that it asked him to write a script about Yom Kippur. Feeling, however, that he did not know enough about the inner significance of the holiday, Wishengrad volunteered instead to do one about the battle of the Warsaw ghetto.

CONCLUSION

Wishengrad, Corwin, and another dozen or so radio dramatists dominated the field of radio drama during the World War II era. During one week alone in 1944, NBC broadcast a total of five one-half-hour radio dramas by Wishengrad, resulting in a network news release calling the week "Morton Wishengrad Week." Most of these writers were quite young when they got their start. They also shared an early expressed opposition to fascism even before Pearl Harbor was attacked, and they lent their talents to the war effort, sometimes at great cost to themselves.

Why were radio dramatists so determined to seek social change? What in their background attracted them to it? Part of the answer is that they were all exposed to the horrors of the Depression. Arthur Miller saw his grandfather lose his home and his father go broke. Miller, Arthur Laurents, Langston Hughes, Allan Sloane, Millard Lampell, and Norman Corwin also had early encounters with American-grown anti-Semitism, Jim Crow bigotry, or rabid anti-Communism. Laurents and Hughes both first personally experienced bigotry while they were still in elementary school. As adults, both also encountered right-wing bigots who threw at them the epithet "communist." These things sensitized them to persecution and other forms of social injustice and influenced their writings. In Hughes's case they inspired him to visit both Spain and the Soviet Union in search of tolerant societies.

Another influence on these writers was their exposure to the social movements, such as the CIO labor movement, set in motion in the 1930s. Norman Corwin saw how the radio station for which he worked intentionally refused to report on labor union strikes. Morton Wishengrad worked for a union. All of them supported unionism, and except perhaps for Hughes, who received only a few radio commissions, they all appear to have belonged to the Radio Writers Guild.

In addition to exposure to the economic havoc wreaked by the depression, to racial bigotry, and to labor strife, Norman Corwin and Millard Lampell had direct contact with undistilled fascism. Corwin's occurred both in Massachusetts and during a visit to Germany; Lampell's took place while he was still in college. The consequence of all these factors was the creation of a whole body of wartime radio drama with a progressive coloration by writers who saw the war as an effort to defeat not just the Axis powers but also a variety of other illnesses in the world.

NOTES

1. William N. Robson to Erik Barnouw, April 13, 1945, Box 38, the Barnouw Collection, COL-RB.

2. Allan Sloane to author, n.d.

3. Norman Corwin to Robert Young, February 7, 1993, in Norman Corwin, *Norman Corwin's Letters*, ed. A. J. Langguth (New York: Barricade Books, 1994), 439.

4. Norman Corwin to Emil and Alfred Corwin, June 23, 1933, in Corwin, *Norman Corwin's Letters*, 17.

5. Except where otherwise indicated, the rest of this profile of Corwin is based on material from the author's interviews of Corwin and on R. LeRoy Bannerman, *On a Note of Triumph: Norman Corwin and the Golden Age of Radio* (New York: Lyle Stuart, 1986).

6. Norman Corwin, *Untitled and Other Radio Dramas* (New York: Henry Holt, 1945), 486.

7. Corwin, *Untitled and Other Radio Dramas*, 65–66.

8. Erik Barnouw, *The Golden Web: A History of Broadcasting in the United States, vol. 2, 1933–1953* (New York: Oxford University Press, 1968), 119.

9. Josephine H. MacLatchy, ed., *Education on the Air: Thirteenth Year-book of the Institute for Education by Radio* (Columbus: Ohio State University, 1942), 90–91.

10. Corwin, *Untitled and Other Radio Dramas*, 401.

11. State Education Department, Bureau of Curriculum Development Handout, A-13.7 in *Case Studies: Persecution/Genocide, The Human Rights Series, Volume III* (The University of the State of New York), 87.

12. Walter Duranty, "Big Ukraine Crop Taxes Harvesters," *New York Times,* September 18, 1933, 8.

13. Norman Corwin to editor, *New York Herald Tribune*, March 6, 1943, "Definition of a Liberal," *New York Herald Tribune*, March 13, 1943, reprinted in Corwin, *Norman Corwin's Letters,* 111–112.

14. Maxine Block, ed., *Current Biography* (New York: H. W. Wilson, 1940), 622.

15. Lewis Titterton to John Royal, April 20, 1939, USS MSS 17AF, Box 71C, folder 41, NBC Collection (WISC). Titterton wrote this concerning Oboler's April 15, 1939, broadcast of three brief plays.

16. Mrs. W. Snedeker to Arch Oboler, July 30, 1939, USS MSS, 17AF, Box 71C, folder 41, NBC Collection, WISC.

17. Arch Oboler, "Windy Kilocycles," *Theatre Arts,* 35 (1951): 46.

18. Martin Halperin, telephone conversation with author, November 15, 1998.

19. John Dunning, *On the Air: The Encyclopedia of Old Time Radio* (New York: Oxford University Press, 1998), 38.

20. Ira Skutch, ed., *Five Directors: The Golden Years of Radio.* (Lanham, Md., Scarecrow Press, 1998), 149.

21. Juliet Benita Colman, *Ronald Colman, A Very Private Person: A Biography* (New York: Morrow, 1975), 207.

22. Milton Merlin and Barbara Merlin, interviewed by Dan Haefele, Studio City, Ca., n.d., private collection.

23. Scott Donaldson and R. H. Winnick, *Archibald MacLeish: An American Life* (Boston: Houghton Mifflin, 1992), 406. In addition to the quote, this entire profile of MacLeish is based on Donaldson and Winnick's work.

24. Arthur Laurents, *The Way We Were* (New York, Harper & Row, 1972), 6.

25. Pare Lorentz, *FDR's Moviemaker: Memoirs and Scripts* (Reno: University of Nevada Press, 1992), 78–79.

26. Josephine H. MacLatchy, ed., *Education on the Air: Fourteenth Year-book of the Institute for Education by Radio* (Columbus: Ohio State University, 1943), 58.

27. This profile is based on interviews of Sloane and on an undated letter to the author.

28. "Allied Troops Start Invasion of Sicily," *New York Times*, July 9, 1943, 1.

29. U.S. House Committee on Un-American Activities, *Communist Methods of Infiltration (Entertainment—Part 1). Hearing before a subcommittee of the Committee on Un-American Activities* (83rd Cong., 2nd sess., January 13, 1954), 3856–3858.

30. Paul Fussell, *Wartime: Understanding and Behavior in the Second World War* (New York: Oxford University Press, 1989), 175.

31. Norman Rosten to S.V. Benét, n.d., Benét Collection, YALE.

32. Rosten to Benét, n.d., Benét Collection, YALE.

33. Peter Manso, *Mailer* (New York: Penguin, 1986), 98.

34. Except where otherwise indicated, the following account of Hughes's life is based on Arnold Rampersad, *The Life of Langston Hughes: Volume I: 1902–1941, I, Too, Sing America* (New York: Oxford University Press, 1988), 12–13, 117, 215–217, 350, 390, and *Volume II: 1941–1967, I Dream A World* (New York: Oxford University Press, 1988), 89–90.

35. The quotation concerning his first experience with racial discrimination is from Rampersad, *I, Too, Sing America*, 13.

36. Eric J. Sundquist, "Who Was Langston Hughes?" *Commentary* 102 (December 1997), 55–59.

37. Rampersad, *I, Too, Sing America*, 215–216.

38. Faith Berry, *Langston Hughes, Before and Beyond Harlem* (Westport, Conn.: L. Hill, 1983), 309.

39. Graebner's testimony is discussed in Rampersad, *I Dream A World*, 90. The McPherson protest is discussed in Rampersad, *I, Too, Sing America*, 390.

40. Rampersad, *I Dream A World*, 92.

41. Rampersad, *I Dream A World*, 45.

42. David King Dunaway, *How Can I Keep from Singing* (New York: McGraw-Hill, 1981), 8.

43. Mike Landon (pseud. for Millard Lampell), "Is There a Fuehrer in the House," *New Republic*, August 12, 1940, 212–213.

44. Joe Klein, *Woody Guthrie: A Life* (New York: Knopf, 1980), 193.

45. Klein, *Woody Guthrie*, 193

46. This account of Lampell's meeting with Hi Brown and his entry into radio is based on an unpublished memoir by Lampell.

47. Except where otherwise indicated, much of the rest of this profile of Miller is based on material from the author's interviews of him and on Arthur Miller's memoir, *Timebends* (New York: Grove Press, 1987).

48. Miller, *Timebends*, 85.

49. Miller, *Timebends*, 71.

50. Arthur Miller. The Reminiscences of Arthur Miller, June 1959, p. 928, CUOHROC.

51. Miller, *Timebends*, 223

52. Miller, *Timebends*, 203.

53. Arthur Miller, Introduction to radio adaptation of *"Three Men on a Horse,"* in H. William Fitelson, ed., *Theatre Guild on the Air* (New York: Rinehart, 1947), 205.

54. Except where otherwise indicated, much of the rest of this profile of Laurents is based on material from the author's interview of him and on Laurents's memoir, *Original Story By: A Memoir of Broadway and Hollywood* (New York: Alfred A. Knopf, 2000).

55. The following account is based on "Why Soldier Votes Are Feared," *The New Republic*, December 13, 1943, 837.

56. Abigail Yager, *The Life of Morton Wishengrad*, unpublished, courtesy of Abigail Yager, n.d.

THE ACTORS

Oh we are radio soldiers
Prepared for all emergencies
Though we sell soap and Sloan's Linimum
For the usual AFRA[1] minimum
We serve our country on land and on the seas.
We use a special kind of poison gas
Our Casualities are oh so light!
Whether it's snowing or whether its raining
With only a few hours basic training
We're ready for the toughest kind of fight!

—Joseph Julian, "Radio Soldiers," in *Stand By*

In addition to radio dramatists, the story of the radio plays of the World War II era also touches on the lives of many actors and actresses. Some, such as Joseph Julian and Jackson Beck, worked predominantly in radio. Others, some of Hollywood's brightest stars, more or less "moonlit" on radio. Bette Davis, Raymond Massey, James Cagney, Olivia De Havilland, Lloyd Nolan, John Garfield, Ingrid Bergman, Walter Huston, Lionel Barrymore, Groucho Marx, and Edward G. Robinson all appeared in wartime radio plays. If they worked for a commercial show, *Lux Radio Theatre*, for example, they were very well paid. But many of them were happy to work on Oboler's and Corwin's non-sponsored shows that were less directed toward entertaining and more focused on boosting morale. For these there was often little, and sometimes even no, pay.

Generally, Hollywood actors seemed to have a low regard for radio as a medium. Their involvement was partly because radio work could be fun. "Radio," said Agnes Moorehead, "is a cinch compared to the screen."[2] For one thing, you didn't have to memorize your lines. In addition, if the broadcast was war related, you were doing the patriotic thing. For John Garfield, who had a serious heart condition, doing patriotic radio dramas functioned as a substitute for serving in the military. If you couldn't or didn't serve your country by putting on a uniform, at least you could do so by urging others to do so. Some may have shared Ingrid Bergman's and Mercedes McCambridge's attitude, for both of whom radio work was a quick means of picking up a few dollars. Bergman sometimes did it to pay for her hotel room and transportation when she came to New York for a few days to get away from Hollywood.[3] McCambridge put it like this: "When I'd get really hard up, I'd go to some radio man I knew and beg him to write in a part for me, just for a few days."[4]

Many actors shared the progressive views of the radio dramatists. Family, work experience, and, for those so educated, perhaps influences felt at college helped shape their views and their social consciousness. Will Geer recalled how his years at the University of Chicago played an important role in this for him.[5] A talk by the noted attorney Clarence Darrow particularly impressed him. Darrow came to Chicago in 1924 to defend two young men, Nathan Leopold and Richard Loeb, then on trial for a sensational and notorious thrill killing. Geer recalled that in talking with students at the college, Darrow sought their opinion on some heavy philosophical issues. For Geer, the experience of hearing a prominent attorney soliciting his opinion started him thinking in ways that he had not done so earlier. For Joseph Julian, Arthur Miller, and Orson Welles, their early work experience with the Federal Theater Project played a key role.

Among Hollywood actors who performed in wartime radio dramas, Melvyn Douglas, Fredric March, March's wife, Florence Eldridge, and Burgess Meredith were particularly known for their outspoken antifascist attitudes. In 1936, Douglas and his wife Helen Gahagan were returning by ship from Europe.[6] While seated at the captain's table at dinner, they were shocked to hear a group of Midwestern businessmen speak admiringly of Hitler and how he had brought order to Germany. The businessmen also told of their contempt for "that cripple in the White House." The experience helped energize the couple to activism, including association with an anti-Nazi organization in Hollywood. On their return from Europe, they threw themselves into work for progressive causes.[7]

Meredith, March, and Eldridge also took leadership roles in Popular Front anti-Nazi organizations. Months before the attack on Pearl Harbor, Burgess Meredith and Helen Hayes cochaired the National Stage, Screen, Radio, and Arts Division of the Fight for Freedom Committee, an organization that urged the United States to join the Allies to fight Hitler.[8] March and Eldridge initially threw parties for refugee film persons from Nazi Germany when they arrived in Hollywood.[9] But later they took more serious action when along with Melvyn Douglas, Paul Muni, and John Garfield, they participated in founding the Motion Picture Artists Committee (MPAC) to aid Republican Spain in the fight against fascism. The same group also helped establish the Hollywood affiliate of the nationwide Joint Anti-Fascist Refugee Committee. After the International Brigade withdrew from Spain, veterans of the Spanish Civil War had formed the committee to give aid to Spanish refugees interned in camps in France.[10] In addition, the Marches supported the Hollywood Anti-Nazi League, organized in mid 1936. The League supported the Spanish Loyalists in their struggle against the Fascists, lobbied for American economic pressure against Germany to force the Nazis to stop their aggression, and sponsored a radio serial written by Donald Ogden Stewart. In addition, it pushed for passage of an abortive anti-lynching bill that was before Congress.[11]

One American actor with direct knowledge of the fear that Nazism inspired was Cliff Carpenter. In 1938, shortly after the Germans took over Austria as a result of the infamous "Anschluss," Carpenter visited Vienna. Signs saying "Jews Forbidden" and hideous anti-Semitic drawings on shop windows and kiosks greeted him. On his arrival, Carpenter had difficulty finding lodging. The city was filled with visiting Germans who came to celebrate Austria's union with their country. In search of a place to stay, Carpenter called up a young woman, a Viennese university student to whom a college friend had referred him. A frightened voice answered the phone, asked him to call back the next day, and hung up. Carpenter called her back in the morning, and she invited him to visit.

Attending a party in the woman's home, Carpenter asked during a lull in the conversation, "So, how do you feel about the Anschluss?"[12] Suddenly all talking ceased and everybody looked at him. "Well, we're all Jewish, here," his hostess said in reply. Later, on learning that Carpenter planned to visit Paris after leaving Vienna, the parents of a young woman asked him to take some bonds with him. "Later we'll come and get them," they told him. Carpenter agreed and took them. "You're crazy," an American friend told him. "You'll get arrested." But before he could leave the city, the Austrian asked for them back. "If they find them on you, they'll trace them back to us," the man explained nervously.

JOSEPH JULIAN

Joseph Julian was one of the busiest actors in radio drama. Julian was brought up in Baltimore, where he was orphaned at twelve.[13] He spent part of his childhood in an orphanage and a home for working boys, during which time he sold newspapers and worked in a shoe factory.

Julian got his first acting experience, a brief one, as an extra with a stock company, earning $1 a night. In the early 1930s he moved to New York where he worked part time as a shoe salesman. Otherwise, he hung around Times Square, the heart of the theater district, eavesdropping on "theater types" and eventually making a contact who helped him get his first radio job, as an extra on CBS's *March of Time*, a dramatized news show. The cast, which was like a stock company, included Art Carney, Orson Welles, and Bud Collyer, all among the crème de la crème of radio actors. Repeating to himself "Heard by millions, heard by millions," Julian enjoyed his first taste of national exposure, although he himself had just one line.

Next Julian got a job with the Works Progress Administration (WPA), the New Deal program that sponsored the Federal Theater Project. For a while he worked at WLW in Cincinnati, the most powerful station in the country, both as an actor and, when a new program manager decided to do some "housecleaning," as an assistant sound effects man.

At age 26, Julian returned to New York and resumed his acting career, appearing in, among other radio shows, a unique soap opera, *Against the Storm,* which dealt with war-related themes right from its start, more than two years before the attack on Pearl Harbor. In 1942, he landed his first lead in another war-related production, "To The Young," part of a Norman Corwin propaganda series sponsored by the Office of War Information. Working for Corwin began what Julian called "the most rewarding relationship of his career." Like so many others, he was delighted with Corwin's writing. "I know of no peer on his level of achievement," he wrote about Corwin in his memoir. Subsequent to Julian's work on "To the Young," his career grew, both on radio, where he was heard on more than forty shows, and on the stage.

Julian was a favorite actor of Corwin. His big hands, large head, solid jaw, and sturdy build even gave him the appearance of the "common man," whom Corwin frequently depicted in his plays. Although this did not matter because Julian was working on radio, more importantly, his voice and speech rhythms gave him the sound of a stereotypical worker. In 1942, CBS sent Corwin to London to write and direct *An American in England*, a series, for the Office of War Information. Corwin easily cast the British roles for the series but, dissatisfied with the few American actors available in England, he sent for Julian to play the role of the series's protagonist, an American narrator. Julian jumped at the opportunity and travel was arranged for him via a B-25 bomber ferry departing from Montreal.[14]

On Julian's return from London in the fall, he resumed his regular work routine. He also submitted two poems to *Stand By*, the newsletter of the American Federation of Radio Artists.[15] One of them, "Out Damned Spot," criticized fascist thinking in the United States.

During his free time, Julian also occasionally attended gatherings connected with the war. He accepted an invitation from a group called the Artists' Front to Win the War to read a poem about artists who died fighting fascism. The meeting, at Carnegie Hall, was held to promote the idea of opening a second front in the war in Europe, which at the time President Roosevelt and most American military leaders were supporting. But Julian's participation at the meeting came back to haunt him after the war as "evidence" that he was a "subversive."

WILL GEER

In the 1970s a whole generation watched Will Geer play the role of Grandpa Walton, a rural character with a homespun philosophy on the popular television series *The Waltons.* Many might be surprised that the actor behind "Grandpa" was in reality a political and social radical. Geer, the man with the blue swivel eyes and the deft comic sense, was a well-traveled, rock-solid, antifascist and antiwar activist, as radical an actor as walked on any American stage in the twentieth century.

In the 1930s he became involved with a number of small Popular Front workers' theaters, or "agit prop" groups as they were called, that sprang up around the country.[16] At a time of great economic turmoil, the political left used them as one of its strategies to try to achieve social change. On two occasions, Geer's political activism put him in physical danger. On Memorial Day, 1933, he was present at a meeting in a park in San Diego, California, where several actors performed at a National Youth Day Demonstration. Accounts of the day vary, but it appears that the city council refused to grant a group a parade permit because they would not guarantee not to fly a red flag. The sponsors went ahead with the parade anyway. When police tried to break it up, swinging clubs and trying to tear down the group's banners, things became violent. During the altercation a woman was fatally injured. Geer and seven others were arrested; three were charged with felonies, and Geer and the remaining four were charged with misdemeanors. A month later, after the jury trying the misdemeanor cases reached impasse, the case against Geer was dismissed.

Two years after the San Diego incident, Geer directed two plays by social playwright Clifford Odets at the Hollywood Playhouse. On May

20, the day before the plays were to open, a threatening note appeared at the theater. "Manager, you know what we do to the enemies of New Germany. If you open." It was also accompanied by two crudely hand drawn skull-and-crossbones and a swastika. Nine days later, four men with German accents forced Geer into a car and kicked and beat him. They particularly objected, so they said, to a scene in the play that Geer just directed in which a character tore Hitler's picture off the wall. They then dumped Geer half-conscious in the hills above Vine Street. He painfully and slowly made his way to Hollywood Receiving Hospital where he was treated for severe bruises of the head, chest, and back.

Not long after he recuperated, Geer visited the Soviet Union. A year earlier, as the result of his meeting a delegation of Russian film-makers who were touring the United States, he had been invited to visit Russia to act in *Circus,* a Russian film dealing with racial tolerance. Geer played the role of the leader of a mob of rednecks. In Russia, Geer became very impressed by government support for the theater. He took to Soviet drama's emphasis of the theme of building a new social order and saw the arts as a catalyst for social change.

On Geer's return home in September and throughout the rest of the decade, he participated in hundreds of benefit performances. Early in 1938, he became associated with the Theater Arts Committee (TAC), formed to aid the Spanish loyalists. Also standing for defense of civil liberties, TAC produced a number of progressive plays. In the summer of 1938 Geer took part in a summer tour through Maryland and several other states. This tour and several other activities in the late 1930s put him into contact with many others in broadcasting who shared at least some of his concerns. Among them were critic Clifton Fadiman, radio and later film director Joseph Losey, composer Marc Blitzstein, former politician turned social activist Wendell Willkie, and Communist Party General Secretary Earl Browder. In this same period, Geer also got to meet and, in many cases, work with actors Orson Welles, Ralph Bellamy, House Jameson, Raymond Johnson, Florence Eldridge, Cliff Carpenter, and John Garfield and with folk singers Burl Ives and Woody Guthrie. With Guthrie, it was the beginning of a life-long friendship. With the exception of Browder, all of them were connected with significant war-related dramatic radio productions.

Frequently, Geer appeared in socially themed productions such as *The Cradle Will Rock* and *Of Mice and Men*. In show after show, he garnered complimentary reviews—all the while delivering pro-worker, antifascist messages to capacity New York audiences. Later, as theater opportunities dried up in the 1940s, the tall stentorian-voiced foghorn of a man moved into the relatively apolitical but lucrative medium of radio drama. Soon his dry Indiana accent (once described by Guthrie as resembling "a stick in the fire") was heard in living rooms around the country.[17] Geer's first radio work was on the *Columbia Workshop* in 1936. By early 1942, he also appeared in at least five other major radio shows. Later, he acted in others, including the *Cavalcade of America* series, which featured a number of war-related shows. Geer believed that radio acting was a form of prostitution. Unlike his stage work, through which he delivered his message of progressivism, most of Geer's radio work was apolitical, but it put bread on the table.

In June 1941, German troops invaded the Soviet Union, defying the non-aggression pact that the two nations signed two years earlier. Until then, Geer, Guthrie, the Theatre Arts Committee, and a number of other leftist organizations and individuals opposed American entry into the war. At the time they regarded it as designed to benefit the capitalists at the expense of the working man who supported many of the soldiers. Writer David Dunaway described how Pete Seeger, Guthrie, and their friends reacted on hearing news of the invasion. They were holding a rent party in New York City on the day of the invasion. "The Nazis have invaded Russia," Allan Sloane shouted as he burst into the room.[18] Suddenly the singing stopped and there was silence. In a few minutes, the silence turned to arguing as the group tried to sort out what to do. The attack prompted the vast majority of American Communists and fellow travelers, minus Geer, to do a sudden about-face and support the war effort.

Will Geer marched to his own drummer. He was clearly dissatisfied with the movement of the United States toward involvement with the war, and his position remained the same after the attack on Pearl Harbor. No one could say that it was a matter of cowardice. By the time the United States entered the war, he had two children and was ineligible for the draft both because of his family status and his age. It was not easy for a pacifist to know where to draw the line. In response to calls to support the war effort, he restricted his cooperation primarily to occasionally doing some war relief benefits and working with the victory garden program. For example, in July 1942, at a meeting in Helen Hayes's home, he helped plan a benefit for Russian War Relief. In regard to victory gardens, Geer not only grew huge quantities of vegetables, he also taught others how to plant them and he prepared such an impressive planting guide that county farm agents copied and sold it.

ORSON WELLES

Film, television and radio actor, film director, magician, gourmand, and glutton, Orson Welles was born in Wisconsin in 1915. Welles was an unforgettable man to behold. John Houseman, who worked closely with him in Welles's most productive years, described his friend as possessing a pale-pudding face with violent black eyes and a button nose with a wen to one side of it. According to Houseman, Welles walked with a shuffling, flat-footed gait. Furthermore, continued Houseman, a deep runnel met his well-shaped mouth with very small teeth.[19] Welles was "an original."

Welles began his show business career at the age of ten and produced Shakespeare in high school, where he also coauthored a book with his principal. In 1931, at the age of sixteen, he traveled to Ireland. In Dublin, he boldly presented himself uninvited to the directors of the newly formed Gate Theater seeking an audition for a role. Impressed by Welles's imposing physical appearance and his rolling basso voice, the directors granted his request. Welles was accepted and given a role in a stage version of *Jew Süss*, by Lion Feuchtwanger. An Irish reviewer for the *New York Times* commented that the packed house was struck by the naturalness and ease of the novice actor's performance on his first appearance.[20]

In 1933, as the result of a meeting with the playwright Thornton Wilder, Welles received letters of introduction to various people in New York, including literature and drama critic Alexander Woollcott. Woollcott, in turn, recommended Welles to the producer-director husband of famed stage actress Katherine Cornell. This resulted in Welles obtaining a role in *Romeo and Juliet* in Cornell's traveling repertory company.[21]

Orson Welles was perhaps the most important Popular Front artist, working for and lending his name and talents to numerous organizations and projects, including the California Labor School, the Hollywood Independent Citizens Committee of the Arts, Sciences and Professions, the League of American Writers, and the Progressive Citizens of America. Throughout much of his professional career, Welles's film, radio, and theatrical work as well as his journalistic output reflected his strong critique of fascism. Welles opposed racism and the abuses of the free enterprise system. He was critical of the rich, whom he perceived as being generally evil and corrupt, although he was not an opponent of the system itself.

Besides his role in the controversial "The War of the Worlds" broadcast, between 1935 and 1941 Welles also participated in four productions expressing clear left-wing critiques of American society. In 1935, John Houseman invited Welles, who was only nineteen, to participate in his production of Archibald MacLeish's verse play *Panic*. Welles played the lead role of a fifty-five-year-old tycoon. The play, with its social message about the 1929 stock market crash and the Great Depression, was in sync with Welles's own political views. In the following year, Houseman took Welles on as a director in a most unusual endeavor. Houseman had been hired as one of two joint heads of a Negro Theater Project sponsored by the WPA. The project fit in well with Welles's personal interest in promoting race relations. For one thing, he was a critic of the "mammy" and other stereotypical roles to which blacks had hitherto been restricted.

In 1936, the Negro Theater took on the ambitious idea of staging *Macbeth*. The play featured a memorable ghost scene by the black actor Canada Lee in the role of Banquo. A third and very controversial play with a progressive theme about the evils of capitalism was Marc Blitzstein's *Cradle Will Rock*. The play offered an interpretation of the severe economic problems in which the United States was caught up in the middle of the Depression. Unfortunately, four days before its first scheduled preview, it became the victim of federal budget cuts that were quite possibly influenced by a desire to censor the play. On the day of its first official performance, federal officials suddenly ordered a contingent of WPA guards to seize the building and block the play's production. In addition, Actors Equity ordered the play's cast not to appear on stage unless the WPA sponsored the production. But Houseman and Welles were not to be stopped. Someone found an empty theater. They hired it, and a large crowd of cast members, musicians, and audience made their way to the new theater where Will Geer and the other actors who had not been scared off performed their lines from their seats in the audience.

Finally, in 1941, Welles directed a stage version of *Native Son*, Richard Wright's protest novel. The play starred Canada Lee as a young black man caught up in overwhelming rage brought on by racism in American society. It proved to be a smashing success for both Welles and Lee.

Had Orson Welles not done any of his film or stage work, or even the broadcast of "The War of the Worlds," he might still be remembered just for the rest of his radio work. Arthur Miller paid tribute to Welles's radio acting and to the latter's "baritone-basso" voice. Welles was a genius with the microphone, Miller recalled. "He seemed to climb into it, his word carving voice winding into one's brain. No actor had such intimacy and sheer presence in a loudspeaker . . . he . . . had [a] . . . loose and wicked belly laugh and the noble air of a lord."[22]

Welles's first major radio role was as the narrator of Archibald MacLeish's "Fall of the City," a parable about the rise of a dictator. The role established Welles as one of radio's great artists. The following year he won the role of Lamont Cranston, The Shadow, possibly radio's most famous fictional crime fighter. By 1939 he was so busy on radio that on a number of occasions he chartered an ambulance that rushed him with red light flashing and sirens screaming to meet a tight deadline.

In addition to his radio, film, and stage work, Welles also did some journalism. In 1944, he wrote for *Free World*, a leftist magazine. For the July issue, he wrote "Race Hatred Must Be Outlawed," an editorial that argued that the war was being fought against the causes of race hatred.[23] Early in the following year, Welles began to write a column two or three times a week for the *New York Post* discussing politics and the end of the war. Influenced by journalists George Seldes and I. F. Stone, he wrote in a February 1945 column about Nazi-influenced German-language newspapers in the United States that praised Mussolini and Franco.[24] In others, he criticized efforts to obstruct the Nuremberg trials and railed against rumors that many Nazis might be restored to political power after the war.

CANADA LEE

Canada Lee was a legendary man with an amazing career: jockey, band leader, successful prize fighter (until he lost an eye in a fight), and then finally actor.[25] He received rave reviews for his starring roles in the stage adaptation of *Native Son* in 1941 and in *Cry, the Beloved Country*, the antiapartheid film, eleven years later.

Lee had a wonderful and sometimes outrageous sense of humor. Once, he was present at the performance of a play that featured a friend, Lloyd Gough, whom he had not seen for several years. While Gough was on stage, Lee went backstage. He stood in a place where he was visible to him but not to the audience. Gough saw Lee still and attentive and continued with his scene, turning his back to Lee for a moment. When he turned around again, Lee was still standing there quietly, with a solemn look on his face. But suddenly, Lee's trousers dropped down to his ankles, his legs bare. Gough managed to hide his reaction.[26]

As a black American who rose from obscurity to phenomenal success, Lee could have turned his back on the have-nots whom he might have left behind. Instead, he became an outspoken advocate for social justice. "I would not fight in an army in which there exists racial segregation," he told students at a December 1942 rally at City College.[27] The statement was reported to the FBI, and a few weeks later the bureau opened a file on him. The character of the case was labeled "Custodial detention—C Sedition."[28] A report in the file characterized Lee as being active in agitating for a revolt by Negro soldiers. The identity of the informant who made this allegation is hidden; the FBI agent who reviewed the file before sending it to the author blacked it out. Another document reported that Lee was "the head of an unofficial organization consisting of Negroes for the purpose of gaining equality for the Negro in the Army and that Lee has openly and publicly stated the time is not far distant when the United States Army will give the Negro what he is entitled to or face mutiny on the part of all Negro troops."[29]

The City College statement and the allegation that Lee was trying to spark a revolt antagonized the FBI at the highest level, and J. Edgar Hoover himself took personal interest in the case. In a May 1943 memo to the Justice Department's Criminal Division, the FBI director asked whether there might be sufficient basis to prosecute Lee for violations of a sedition statute. Five months later, one suspects much to Hoover's disappointment, Assistant Attorney General Tom C. Clark advised him that the division was "not requesting any specific investigation at that time."[30] Nowhere in the file is there any mention that, despite Lee's statements early in the war, he did, in fact, come around to believing that blacks needed to support the war effort. Having lost an eye, he was unable to enlist, but he spent many an hour at USOs. In addition, in recognition for his consistent efforts in helping to sell war bonds, the Army even gave him an award.

Lee fought injustice wherever he saw it. He opposed racial segregation in its many forms: in the Armed Forces, in baseball, and wherever else it existed. Beyond fighting for equality specifically for African-Americans, he also fought more broadly for social justice for all Americans, attacking anti-Semitism and supporting New Deal programs. He found it very difficult to turn down an invitation to make a speech for a cause he supported. In 1944, he actively campaigned for Roosevelt's reelection. Four years later, in recognition of Lee's interfaith work, a branch of B'nai B'rith awarded him its "meritorious interfaith medal."

Lee's fight against racism often crossed over into his professional life. In 1944 he played the role of a black mess man in the Alfred Hitchcock film *Lifeboat*. The original script called for his character to be a stereotypical, subordinate black, but Lee refused to go along with this conception, insisting, for example, that his character address the white characters as Mr. or Miss only if all the other characters did so, too.[31] Lee performed in a variety of radio plays. But at a time when two white men were playing the roles of blacks in the hit radio series

Amos 'n' Andy, although Lee's speech was perfectly compatible with white roles, he was hired only to play blacks.

Like his roles in other media, much of Lee's radio work promoted social equality. His earliest war-related dramatic role on radio, and possibly one of his first radio roles in general, was in 1941 in "Freedom's a Hard-Bought Thing," a play in a pre–Pearl Harbor series entitled *The Free Company*. At the time, German and Japanese propaganda was trying to exploit all possible opportunities to increase the amount of anti-interventionist sentiment among Americans, including appealing to blacks by emphasizing racial injustice in the United States. The series was produced to counter Nazi propaganda. Later that year, Lee took part in *America's Negro Soldiers*, a War Department series that also sought to answer German propaganda. It tried to appeal to blacks by showing that they had a tradition of loyalty and devotion to the country. Lee also attempted to form a company to produce a thirteen-week test series of half-hour radio dramas based on Negro life. His intention was to avoid the demeaning stereotypes of the *Amos 'n' Andy* characters. There would be no persecution complexes or fast-stepping night-lifers. Lee got as far as presenting the idea to the broadcasting chains, but the idea proved abortive. He also played a role in a series entitled *Green Valley*.

FREDRIC MARCH

Fredric March's true claim to fame as an actor is without doubt for his film work. But like a number of other film actors in the 1930s and the 1940s, he also had an important career in radio. Like most of them, March's film reputation so overpowers his work on radio that his biographers generally overlook it. The relative impermanence of radio broadcasts compared with film also contributed to this state of affairs.

Born in Racine, Wisconsin, in 1897, March's original name was Fred Bickel. He joined the Army in 1918, attended officer's training school, and was commissioned a second lieutenant in artillery. But he was retained in the United States as an instructor of equestrianism.[32] After the war, March was initially a banker. One day in the fall of 1920, however, while at work, March suddenly doubled over in pain. His colleagues, not realizing the severity of his situation, helped him to get home. Once there, his landlady realized that he needed immediate medical attention. While March waited for an ambulance, to divert his attention from his pain, she told him a series of anecdotes concerning her days in the theatre. When March later awoke in the hospital after an appendectomy, recalling her stories, he resolved to become an actor.[33]

In 1928 with the advent of the talkies, the tall, broad-shouldered March got his first big break in films. With his handsome looks and trained voice that was capable of booming with a sonorous timbre, he was a natural for the screen. Within a couple of years he was a star.

In the late 1930s, the Marches were activists against fascism. Their participation in a number of artistic enterprises gave voice to their antifascism. In 1939, they appeared in a play in New York, *The American Way*, which attacked the German-American Bund.[34] In 1942, March starred in "Your Navy," a play in Norman Corwin's government propaganda series *This Is War*. Two years later, March made a tour of the European theater, where he entertained troops. On his return, he appeared in "Untitled," another Corwin play. Years later, Corwin remembered March fondly as a principled, idealistic, and considerate man who showed up for a broadcast one day wearing a face mask to minimize the chance that others would catch his cold.[35] Besides his work for Corwin, March also served as master of ceremonies for seventeen broadcasts of the *Treasury Star Parade* series.

There were other ways, too, in which March supported the war effort. In August 1943, along with William O'Dwyer, the soon-to-be mayor of New York City, and a number of others, he was a sponsor at the Hotel Biltmore of a "United Nations in America" dinner. In addition, four months after the war ended, March and Helen Hayes performed a skit at a rally sponsored by the American Society for Russian Relief at Madison Square Garden.[36] For March's efforts in support of the war effort, in 1945, he received the Eisenhower Medal as the actor who had done the most for democracy. Yet in spite of March's prewar clearance on charges of being a communist and in spite of his medal, his name came under scrutiny again after the war.

BUD COLLYER

New York–born Collyer was one of the most successful actors to be associated with wartime radio drama. "Collyer" was actually the name of his mother's family, which included many generations of actors. He rejected his given name Clayton Heermance Jr.

Following in his father's footsteps, Collyer became a lawyer. However, he quickly discovered he could make more in a month or so on the air than he could in a year in the legal field. Collyer was one of the busiest of radio's actors, routinely doing approximately 34 shows a week, among them *Superman,* for which he played the title role for more than a decade, and the *Cavalcade of America,* on which he worked as the announcer. Part of the reason he was able to maintain his hectic pace was that he had an amazing ability whenever he had a few minutes without dialogue to go into a state of deep sleep in the studio, sometimes on top of a piano, and wake up refreshed and totally alert.

If Orson Welles and Fredric March represented the liberal and somewhat populous end of the political spectrum among wartime actors, Collyer represented a very conservative part of it. As described by Collyer's one-time friend, actor Jackson Beck, Collyer was "a brilliant guy with a dark side politically."[37] Quite popular among his colleagues, Collyer had a jovial disposition, genial manners, and perky enthusiasm. But in addition to these qualities, he exhibited some of the behavior commonly associated with what decades later is described as the religious right. It was not that he once considered becoming a minister or that he taught Sunday school for more than twenty years while living in Greenwich, Connecticut. His sense of religious duty went beyond these manifestations of his spiritual interest. Religion was almost the exclusive object of Collyer's thoughts and conversation. He referred to God as "the realest member of our family." He even claimed that God had helped his daughter pass her exams and had advised his family and him on business contracts. Of people who did not believe in God, he said, "I feel sorry, not for them—but for the elements that cast them in that mold. And if it fell my way, I would do anything I could to change their minds and convince them."[38]

Although Bud Collyer's name figures into this volume because he hosted the *Cavalcade of America,* a more important reason for including it in these pages is the adversarial role he played vis-à-vis many of his progressive colleagues in the postwar years. In his self-appointed role of protector of America from the threat of communism, Collyer was a significant player both within the American Federation of Radio Artists and in a private capacity in trying to force a number of his colleagues out of their profession.

BURGESS MEREDITH

Burgess Meredith grew up in Cleveland where his father was a doctor. He attended and flunked out of Amherst College. During the subsequent five-year period, he worked as a reporter, salesman, editor, clerk, Wall Street runner, and merchant seaman. In 1929, with his resonant, ironic voice, offbeat manner, and bushy eyebrows, Meredith made his first mark on public consciousness by appearing in several Broadway plays by Maxwell Anderson. Among them was *Winterset,* a drama based on the Sacco and Vanzetti case.

Although Meredith's autobiography gives a skimpy view of his progressive views, periodically he took an activist stand against the repressive forces that grew increasingly menacing in the late 1940s and the 1950s.[39] An ardent trade unionist and a noncommunist liberal, he served as president of the Actors Equity Association in the late 1930s. In the process he worked with a number of leftists who drew the wrath of a competing union that accused Equity of being a "Soviet menace." In an article published in 1939, Meredith defended his work with these "Reds" and wrote, "These fellow travelers work with a glorious vitality; they are always there when the others don't show up. They are up to a certain point reliable and idealistic writers."[40]

In the World War II era, Meredith frequently appeared on radio. By 1941, he was well known for his interventionist views. In August of that year, obviously feeling that Meredith was a kindred spirit, a listener to a variety show for which he served as host wrote to him. She suggested that he publicize her idea that the government market what she called "V" stamps, which she proposed would have the words "An

Allied Victory," printed on them. They would be sold like Christmas seals and the proceeds could be used for defense, for such purposes as building air raid shelters and manufacturing gas masks.[41]

By the time Meredith received the woman's letter, he had already become involved with the Fight for Freedom Committee. Apparently in connection with that role, both before and after the attack on Pearl Harbor, he met several times with William B. Lewis, head of the Radio Bureau of the Office of Facts and Figures. In one instance, a meeting included writer John Steinbeck. Meredith also became involved with the committee's staging of "Fun to Be Free," a musical revue designed to raise the public's consciousness about the war. Starting in New York in Madison Square Garden in October and continuing after the attack on Pearl Harbor in St. Louis, Cleveland, and Washington, D.C., the revue satirized the Axis powers. During the week after Pearl Harbor, at the end of the St. Louis performance with Melvyn Douglas, Humphrey Bogart, and other celebrities in the city's 12,000-seat municipal auditorium, Meredith got into an all-night discussion with Douglas.[42] The topic was what the show business community could do additionally to support the war effort. By the next morning, the two had worked out a plan for an agency to coordinate the work of show business people to help in the dissemination of war-related information. They flew to Washington, D.C., to see Archibald MacLeish. Meredith's role in the matter ended with this one meeting, but Douglas went on to take a position with the Office of Civil Defense.

Meredith's most significant appearances were in the war-related shows of Norman Corwin, Orson Welles, and Archibald MacLeish. In February 1942, Meredith and his friend actor James Stewart, who was then sharing his house with Meredith, came home to learn that they had both been drafted. In his autobiography, Meredith recalled that they sat around listening to a recorded version of MacLeish's "Fall of the City" in which Meredith had played an important role.[43] Meredith served in the Army Air Force from February 1942 until late October 1944.

In March 1948, Meredith participated in a meeting of the Stop Censorship Committee in the Grand Ballroom of the Hotel Astor. During the meeting he recited the names of famous people who have been censored down through history: "Socrates. Michaelangelo.

Galileo. DaVinci. Dante. Beethoven. Moliere. Balzac. Zoller. Goya. Rousseau. Paine. Cervantes. Ibsen. Whitman. Thoreau. Emerson. Darwin. All these men were censored. But, can you name their inquisitors? Their censors? Can you name the 'Un-something' committee on which they served? The creative giants of the past brought us to ever higher stages of human achievement. To cherish the men of art, science and creative thought is the duty of all men towards man's understanding of man."[44]

CONCLUSION

The progressive politics of most of the actors discussed in this chapter upset the Red baiters of their time. Because most had high profiles, they were even easier targets than were the writers. Prominent among the militant opponents of the New Deal, of labor, and of the struggle for civil rights in the 1940s was U.S. Representative Martin Dies, a big, beefy, cigar-smoking Texan with a broad smile and a sharp tongue. The six-foot, three-inch Dies was chairman of the House Committee on Un-American Activities. In 1940, the committee was investigating allegations of communist infiltration of Hollywood. Fredric March, his wife Florence Eldridge, Franchot Tone, and James Cagney were four of the actors on whom the committee focused its attention.

The source of allegations that March and the others were Communists was John L. Leech, a former secretary of the Communist Party of Los Angeles. Leech claimed that the Marches had bought "Communist stamps" on the corner of Hollywood and Vine. His testimony to a Los Angeles County grand jury was leaked to newspapers, and quickly the allegations received nationwide distribution. When the Marches learned of this accusation, they called Dies, volunteered to appear before his committee, and, on August 17, confronted and discredited Leech.[45] Chairman Dies even issued a statement to the press that there was no evidence that they were Communists. But, unapologetically, he also urged the Marches that in the future they should consult the American Legion or the local Chamber of Commerce before participating in any other organizations.

In addition to the Marches, actors Orson Welles, Burgess Meredith, and Will Geer were also early subjects of right-wing scrutiny. The earliest attention to any of the four was accorded to Welles in March 1941 when the special agent in charge at the FBI's New York office sent a letter to J. Edgar Hoover. The agent advised the FBI director that the New York office would soon be sending reports about Welles to the Dies Committee.[46] A month later, Hoover sent a memorandum to the Attorney General's office noting that the Dies Committee had collected information about several organizations, allegedly communist in character, with which Welles was associated.[47] Two of them were the Negro Cultural Committee and the Foster Parents Plan for War Children.

Meredith's social activism prompted the FBI to begin keeping tabs on him as early as June 1942. The earliest entry in his FBI file alleges that he had a "past history reflecting Leftist activities . . ." including his having signed a 1938 petition that urged severing of economic relations with Germany.[48] Periodically, the American Legion fed the agency information about Meredith; in June 1943, the agency prepared what they called a "summary memorandum" on him.[49] Prominent in his file is discussion of his role in radio, particularly concerning the series *The Free Company,* mentioned already in connection with Canada Lee.

Geer attracted greater FBI scrutiny than did Meredith. Because of his connection with various groups on the left, the FBI perceived him as an enemy of the state. Ironically, they made their first report on him just at the time that his activism was abating, in July 1941. FBI agents submitted his name for "Custodial Detention" purposes in the event of "national emergency."[50] The investigation was deferred a year later, then taken up early in 1943, but closed when the only significant facts uncovered were Geer's association with Ella Reeve Bloor, his wife's grandmother, who was a cofounder of the American Communist Party, and news coverage about him by a Delaware newspaper that was considered to be communist.[51]

Reflecting on the substance of FBI reports, it is clear that the government had a paranoid view of the so-called threat that these actors posed to American society. The FBI deemed Lee's and Welles's opposition to racial segregation and Meredith's "premature anti-

Nazism" as evidence of such a threat. The bureau had a similar view of the fact that Geer was married to a woman whose grandmother was a communist. It bears repeating that in his and Lee's cases, the FBI was considering custodial detention. It should not be a surprise, then, that radio dramas reflecting progressive themes periodically became the subject of official scrutiny.

NOTES

1. American Federation of Radio Actors.

2. Cincinnati, Ohio, *Billboard,* July 18, 1942, Box 143, in Agnes Moorehead Collection, WISC.

3. Ingrid Bergman and Alan Burgess, *Ingrid Bergman: My Story* (New York: Delacorte Press, 1980), 3.

4. Gladwin Hill, "Tough as a Kitten," *Colliers,* September 9, 1950, 11, 68.

5. Evan Finch, "Will Geer: Frankfort's Supporting Actor," *Traces* 10, no. 4 (Fall 1998): 7.

6. Erik Barnouw, *The Golden Web: A History of Broadcasting in the United States, vol. 2, 1933–1953* (New York: Oxford University Press, 1968), 106.

7. Larry Ceplair and Steven Englund, *The Inquisition in Hollywood: Politics in the Film Community, 1930–1960* (Garden City, N.Y.: Anchor Press/Doubleday, 1980), 97.

8. Helen Gahagan Douglas, *A Full Life* (Garden City, N.Y.: Doubleday, 1982), 172.

9. Ceplair and Englund, *The Inquisition in Hollywood*, 96.

10. Ceplair and Englund, *The Inquisition in Hollywood*, 114.

11. John Cogley, *Report on Blacklisting: II. Radio-Television* (New York: Fund for the Republic, 1956), 36.

12. This account of Carpenter's visit to Vienna is based on the author's interview at Carpenter's home in Pawling, N.Y., December 2, 1999.

13. Except where otherwise indicated, this section is based on material from Joseph Julian, *This Was Radio: A Personal Memoir* (New York: Viking Press, 1975).

14. Julian, *This Was Radio*, 80–81.

15. Joseph Julian, "Out Damned Spot," *Stand By*, June 1942, 6; and Julian, "Radio Soldiers" (see n. 1).

16. Except where otherwise indicated, this section is based on material from Sally Norton, "A Historical Study of Actor Will Geer, His Life and Work

in the Context of Twentieth-Century American Social, Political and Theatrical History" (Ph.D. diss., University of Southern California), 1980.

17. Finch, "Will Geer: Frankfort's Supporting Actor," 9.

18. David King Dunaway, *How Can I Keep from Singing: Pete Seeger* (New York: McGraw-Hill, 1981), 84.

19. John Houseman, *Run-Through: A Memoir* (New York: Simon & Schuster, 1972), 150.

20. J. J. Hayes in the *New York Times*, as quoted by Charles Higham in *Orson Welles: The Rise and Fall of an American Genius* (New York: St. Martin's Press, 1985), 59.

21. Frank Brady, *Citizen Welles: A Biography of Orson Welles* (New York, Charles Scribner's Sons, 1989), 48–50.

22. Arthur Miller, *Timebends* (New York: Grove Press, 1987), 205.

23. Charles Higham, *The Films of Orson Welles* (Berkeley: University of California Press, 1971), 214.

24. Higham, *The Films of Orson Welles*, 76.

25. Except where otherwise indicated, this section is based on material from a series of interviews of Frances Lee Pearson conducted by the author at Ms. Pearson's home in Doraville, Ga., on March 18–20, 1999.

26. Lloyd Gough to Frances Lee Pearson, November 21, 1981, CL.

27. FBI Agent E. Conroy to J. Edgar Hoover, April 29, 1943, Canada Lee FBI file.

28. Conroy to Hoover, April 29, 1943.

29. Report of unidentified special agent (name blacked out by the FBI) concerning Canada Lee, April 29, 1943, Canada Lee FBI file.

30. Assistant Attorney General Tom Clark, memo to FBI Director, October 21, 1943, Canada Lee FBI file.

31. Frances Pearson, interviewed by the author, Doraville, Ga., March 20, 1999.

32. Deborah Peterson, *Fredric March* (Westport, Conn.: Greenwood Press, 1996), 15.

33. Peterson, *Fredric March*, 22.

34. Edward Barrett Jr., *The Tenney Committee: Legislative Investigation of Subversive Activities in California* (Ithaca, N.Y.: Cornell University Press, 1951), 378.

35. Norman Corwin, interview by author, Los Angeles, July 3, 1997.

36. Barrett, *The Tenney Committee*, 386.

37. Donald Myers, "The Voice of Experience," *Newsday,* January 18, 1990.

38. Edith Efron, "Bud Collyer Discusses Bud Collyer," *TV Guide*, 10, no. 21 (May 26, 1962): 23–25.

39. Burgess Meredith, *So Far, So Good: A Memoir* (New York: Little, Brown, 1994), 92–97, 106, 120.

40. Burgess Meredith, "Confessions of a Fellow Traveler," *Common Sense*. VIII, no. 10 (1939): 3–6.

41. Ann Stevenson to Burgess Meredith, August 10, 1941, Box 15, folder 9, Fight for Freedom Collection, Seeley G. Mudd Manuscript Library, Princeton University.

42. This account of Meredith's brief collaboration with Douglas is recounted in Melvyn Douglas and Tom Arthur, *The Autobiography of Melvyn Douglas* (Lanham, Md.: University Press of America, 1986), 116–119.

43. Meredith, *So Far, So Good,* 105–106.

44. The tape containing Meredith's comments is found in a folder on the committee in the Edward Choate Collection. Choate was an officer in the Committee, WISC.

45. Barrett, *The Tenney Committee*, 224.

46. B. E. Sackett to J. Edgar Hoover, March 24, 1941, Orson Welles FBI file.

47. J. Edgar Hoover to the Assistant to the Attorney General, April 24, 1941, Orson Welles FBI file.

48. Untitled memorandum, June 6, 1942, Burgess Meredith FBI file.

49. Memorandum from D. M. Ladd to E. A. Tamma, June 8, 1943, Burgess Meredith FBI file.

50. Norton, "A Historical Study," 378.

51. Norton, "A Historical Study," 378.

4

ON THE EVE OF WORLD WAR II: EXPRESSING ANTIFASCISM THROUGH ALLEGORY

An order . . . came down from that little god who sits on top of the [NBC] corporation's topmost salary bracket, that until further notice, the war was to be ignored by the radio dramatists.

—Arch Oboler, *This Freedom*

Storm clouds gathered over Europe in the 1920s and the 1930s. The ascension to power of first Mussolini in Italy and then Hitler in Germany foretold to many that bad days were coming. A 1936 *New York Times* front-page headline, "Hitler Sends German Troops into Rhineland,"[1] told a part of the story. In violation of the Versailles Treaty, the Nazis took the first of a series of steps to expand German power. Two years later, in November 1938, another *Times* headline summed up an even more frightening story: "Nazis Smash, Loot and Burn Jewish Shops and Temples."[2] The headline referred to the Nazis' Kristallnacht attack on Jews throughout Austria and Germany. The road to Auschwitz was "under construction." And war was coming closer and closer.

These events, of course, were reported on American radio as well as in the newspapers. But radio, particularly, limited itself to reporting the facts. The country was reluctant to confront the implications of the growth of the cancer that was fascism in Spain, Germany, and Italy. Until the attack on Pearl Harbor, with the exception of establishing its lend-lease program, the United States maintained a strict policy of neutrality. And so, more or less, did the American media. In the United States, war-related radio drama slowly got its start in the 1930s.

It was clear from a 1940 statement by Janet McRorie, head of NBC's Continuity Department, that neutrality was network policy for more than just radio drama at NBC. "When commercial copy comes up for consideration," wrote McRorie, "we ask the sponsors not to tie the program up with the war; also to avoid individual protestations of loyalty. The aim is to maintain the same tenor of broadcasting as before the war, because the bulletins and commentaries from overseas are tragic enough."[3]

Other networks maintained similar policies. Danish-born Sandra Michael wrote for a high-brow soap opera, *Against the Storm*, which appeared on the Mutual Network. Late in December 1939, she found that one of the "higher-ups" in the network rejected a script that she had written for the show's New Year's Day 1940 broadcast. In the script a German professor, a refugee living in New York, talked about the Nazis' brutal persecution of people whom he knew. "We would rather not take such a definite stand against Nazism," wrote the network official. "If these references are eliminated, the script is okay."[4]

In June 1941, CBS broadcast Norman Corwin's radio play "Appointment." He had been hearing frequent expressions of the desire from what he called "otherwise mild and benign folk" to kill Hitler. This inspired him to write a play containing the message that it was concerted action by groups of people, not individual acts of terrorism, that was needed to defeat fascism. Corwin's original plan was to convey this message in the story of the foiling of a man's plot to kill a dictator. But the network forced him to change the plot to an allegorical one involving an escaped political prisoner's plan to kill a prison commandant.[5]

The networks' paternalism or cold feet notwithstanding, there was a more substantive reason for the avoidance of war talk on radio. They were afraid they might offend some of their audience, who were, after all, customers of network sponsors. One of the clearest examples of this occurred in 1935 and involved radio host Alexander Woollcott. Woollcott openly attacked Nazism and Fascism on his weekly radio program "The Town Crier." Cream of Wheat, his sponsor, voiced vigorous objection that the attacks might offend various racial groups.[6]

Which groups might be offended by Woollcott's attacks? Nazi sympathizers and Italian Fascists visiting or residing in the United States were likely ones. In the late 1930s, the attraction of Nazism was sufficiently strong for the German-American Bund to attract 22,000 people to a pro-Hitler rally at Madison Square Garden. The presence of Italian fascism was evident from more than Norman Corwin's encounter with the attempt by the "Italian Red Cross" to raise funds for the "poor Italian soldiers" injured during their attack on Ethiopia. Arthur Miller recalled "the occasional beatings of British sailors by Italian-American workers who would ambush them . . . in the middle of the night because Britain had 'betrayed' Italy by declaring war on her."[7] So Cream of Wheat may have been right to worry. Their Bundist and Fascist listeners may have turned against their product.

Alexander Woollcott persisted with his attacks on Nazism and Fascism. Finally, the company threw down the gauntlet: "Either drop all matters of a controversial nature or leave the show." Woollcott quit, walking away from a contract that was paying him $80,000 a year.[8]

Broadcaster H. V. Kaltenborn's experience in 1939 mirrored that of Woollcott. A year earlier the Czechoslovakia crisis resulted in the Munich Pact and the German invasion of the Sudetenland section of Czechoslovakia. CBS cleared the boards of other programming and gave Kaltenborn carte blanche to cover the crisis.[9] He repaid the debt by providing radio accounts that held listeners in rapt attention to his every word. In the process his salary leaped from $100 a week in early September to $600 a week in December, at which point Kaltenborn was to do a fifteen-minute Sunday night commentary sponsored by General Mills, the makers of Gold Medal Flour.

One provision of Kaltenborn's contract was that he inform an executive of General Mills of the subject of each week's talk in advance. Kaltenborn ignored this provision, but the company allowed him to continue nevertheless. However, when he used his program to strongly denounce Nazi propaganda, some listeners began to complain. Initially, the company stood by him. But then three things happened. First, an association of bakers made up largely of members of German ethnic background announced a boycott of Gold Medal Flour. General Mills relayed their concern about this to Kaltenborn, but they continued to stand by him. Second, many listeners wrote in, complaining about Kaltenborn's attacks on Spain's Francisco Franco, which they interpreted as being anti-Catholic. And, finally, a priest, the associate editor of a Catholic family weekly in Indiana, wrote a three-and-a-half page single-spaced typed letter to General Mills. He condemned the anti-Franco forces, citing atrocities they had allegedly committed. He also threatened to publicize the notion that General Mills was associated with supporting the Loyalist causes in Spain. By March, General Mills had dropped Kaltenborn.

The development of American war-related radio drama was also delayed because of several factors connected to the American experience with World War I. One, mentioned earlier, was President Woodrow Wilson's establishment of the Committee on Public Information (CPI), a propaganda agency.[10] George Creel, head of the CPI, deserves credit for the imaginative quality of its most unusual propagandistic scheme, his creation of the "Four Minute Man." A message was posted on the stage curtain in movie theaters across the country before or after the main feature announcing the imminent appearance of a local member of a cadre of prowar volunteers. At the appointed time, each volunteer made a four-minute speech on a topic such as "Why We Are Fighting" and "What Our Enemy Really Is." However admirable the innovative nature of the scheme, it did not offset the resentment toward the CPI's overall program. The use of "voluntary guidelines" for the news media, which offended journalists and many others, was only one of a number of programs that created ill will toward the CPI. Twenty years after the end of World War I, the CPI was still strong in public memory.

A second factor relevant to World War I that inhibited American radio's discussion of events in Europe in the 1930s was the issue of war profits. Several years after the end of World War I, a committee headed by North Dakota Senator Gerald Nye looked into the earnings of the Du Pont corporation, a manufacturer of gunpowder and chemicals. The inquiry showed that Du Pont had produced 40 percent of the propellant powders used by the Allies, garnering a $238 million profit. The report horrified the nation. In response, Du Pont hired an advertising agency, Batten, Barton, Durstine and Osborn, to help improve its image. The agency took on the responsibility of creating a radio series sponsored by Du Pont to emphasize humanitarian themes. Thus, in the fall of 1935 began the *Cavalcade of America* series on American history. There was one important caveat. The new show would generally avoid war themes, particularly battle scenes, whenever possible.[11]

As a result of all these factors, for the most part in the 1930s, when radio dramas dealt with the rise of fascism in Europe and the consequent outbreak of hostilities, it did so indirectly. There were three writers who were most prominent in this regard: Archibald MacLeish, Norman Corwin, and Arch Oboler. A fourth, actor and writer Orson Welles, also deserves mention.

ARCHIBALD MACLEISH ON THE EVE OF WAR

Archibald MacLeish wrote the first radio play to deal with the rise of European fascism, "The Fall of the City," which was also radio's first play written in verse. Poetry had found a new vehicle. "The Fall of the City" is a morality play about a people who are warned that they must fight for their freedom, but, ignoring the warning, they fall prostrate before an approaching conqueror. As one scholar noted, "Each character is drawn broadly and simply to present one viewpoint. Names are not even given to these characters. The Orator is the pacifist who bolsters his speech with false ideals, . . . the General is the realist who sees that it is necessary to fight for freedom."[12]

MacLeish was influenced in writing the play by an Aztec myth that maintained that in 1519, just before the Spaniards conquered the city of Tenochtitlán, a woman rose from the grave to warn the city of a conquering army. To enable the play to come across as a parable with the force of universality, however, it purposely avoids using time or place reference.

In many ways, "The Fall of the City" is a model of how a dramatist can properly use the unique medium of radio. MacLeish realized that although a stage audience will not get up and walk out on a play that starts slowly, a radio audience can easily turn a knob and switch to another station. Consequently, his radio plays use attention-getting beginnings. "The Fall of the City" starts:

> Ladies and gentlemen:
> This broadcast comes to you from the city.[13]

MacLeish understood, too, that because the words of the radio dramatist must substitute for the sense of sight, radio drama must repeat important ideas. Other than words, the radio dramatist has at his disposal only sound effects and music to substitute for the scenery, costumes, lighting effects, and the other accoutrements of the stage playwright. Thus, in "The Fall of the City" MacLeish has different voices repeatedly utter a single statement, "Masterless men will take a master."

One weakness is that MacLeish failed to exploit an important advantage of radio. The limitations of stage mechanics prevent the rapid shift from scene to scene. But on radio it is not necessary or even desirable to keep a single set. MacLeish has a messenger race into the scene to inform the audience of action elsewhere instead of shifting scenes to the site of the action itself.

> There has come the conqueror!
> I am to tell you.

The half-hour drama was broadcast in April 1937 by the *Columbia Workshop*, which Irving Reis established the previous year.

MacLeish's was an inexpensive production: He, himself, received a pittance. Its young stars, Orson Welles and Burgess Meredith, also worked for low wages.[14] But it was electrifying. MacLeish sought through the production to show that people can be persuaded to accept what they see as their fate.

The play dealt with a somber theme, but its production involved some humorous incidents related to the "fly by the seat of your pants" nature of early radio. Frequently, there were some loose ends left showing. "The Fall of the City" included a crowd scene featuring 150 college students who were needed to produce the "oohs" and "ahs" of the masses adulating the approaching conqueror. Partly for this reason it was produced in a large National Guard Armory in New York City. The armory had to be specially hooked up to lines for the broadcast with microphones lying all over. In addition, the producer had to build an isolation booth for Welles.[15] On the Saturday before the broadcast, the first day of rehearsals, a group of obviously well-heeled "Park Avenue type" gentlemen, carrying tennis rackets, came into the armory insisting that they had it reserved for their game. They were quickly escorted from the armory. On the following day, a dress rehearsal was planned for an hour before the 7:00 P.M. broadcast. Suddenly six minutes before the rehearsal was to begin, the huge, noisy metal door at the end of the armory was opened from the outside. One after another, National Guard trucks came barreling into the armory, returning from bivouac, almost sending Reis into shock.[16]

A later, repeat version of "The Fall of the City," broadcast in the fall of 1939, managed to avoid even more serious intrusions. Performed in the open, in the Los Angeles Coliseum, it took place within three blocks of a hospital, an area normally characterized by ambulances coming and going, their sirens screaming. It was also directly under the north-south air flight line to San Diego. In addition, there were potential problems with streetcar bells. Fortunately, a CBS "fixer" from a local station with the right connections took care of matters. Nobody knew for sure how he did it, but no planes flew overhead and no ambulance sirens or streetcar bells were heard during the broadcast.[17]

Critics and the public hailed "The Fall of the City's" artistic quality. "After a few moments," one listener wrote, "I closed my eyes and was actually in the Square. There was no microphone; gone was my receiving set—both obliterated." A man from New Orleans wrote to "whoever wrote that thing! At 7:00–7:30!" The letter writer described how he had a regular routine on Sundays that consisted in part of going out in the afternoon, playing golf or tennis until he was tired. He specified the hours when he played. Then he came home, filled his bathtub, brought his radio into the bathroom, and then got into the tub. "On this day," the man continued, meaning the day of the broadcast of "The Fall of the City," "I played my game, and got tired, came home and filled the tub, turned on the radio, got into the tub, and the goddamn thing began spouting poetry at me! And if I could've got it, I'd have choked it, but I couldn't! And you want to know something? It's great!"[18] Despite the general acclaim for "The Fall of the City," there was a curious absence of focus on the political message and relevance of the play among the critics, who discussed it solely as an artistic achievement without any reference to events unfolding in Europe and Asia.

Almost immediately after the broadcast of "The Fall of the City," CBS began to receive verse plays from other poets. Stephen Vincent Benét and a variety of other luminaries began to submit their work to radio stations. A young Arthur Miller upon hearing the production decided that "radio was made for poetry." Years later, referring to the broadcast's effect on radio, he asserted that "MacLeish lifted it to a gorgeous level."[19] Miller's friend, poet Norman Rosten, came to the same conclusion. "The Fall of the City" may also have influenced the theme for Rosten's own antifascist radio play in verse, "Prometheus in Granada." The latter, written in 1939, concerned the execution several years earlier of Spanish poet Federico Garcia Lorca. Lorca had been dragged during the night to a clearing in a forest near the city of Granada. There, illuminated by the headlights of an automobile, he was killed by the Fascist forces of General Francisco Franco.

In June 1938, MacLeish wrote "Air Raid," his second radio drama in verse. The play, set in a town somewhere in Europe, tells of defenseless women who are lulled into thinking that war is a man's activity and has no direct influence on them. They refuse to believe that they will be attacked. But, indeed, bombs targeting both women and children do fall, killing them.

"Air Raid" was clearly influenced by the Spanish Civil War, the conflict that the political left generally viewed as the beginning of the fight against fascism. MacLeish even acknowledged the influence on him of *Guernica,* Picasso's famous painting of the Fascists' aerial bombing of the city by the same name. "I no longer remember where or how I first came face to face with *Guernica,* he wrote "I only know that when I saw it first I heard it."[20]

Just as in "The Fall of the City," "Air Raid," too, has what Norman Corwin calls a "socko" beginning:

When you hear the gong sound
The time will be
Ten Seconds past 2 A.M. precisely[21]

And again in "Air Raid," MacLeish demonstrated his understanding
of the need to repeat important ideas. The sergeant in "Air Raid" em-
phasizes the fact that the fascist enemy will not spare women: "The
wars have changed with the world and not for the better!" A little later
he says: "It may have been thought: This enemy kills women." A few
lines after that he makes the same statement:

It may have been thought: This enemy kills women.
Meaning to kill them![22]

He then goes on to make the same point two more times. Unlike in
"The Fall of the City," in "Air Raid," he allows scenes to shift "rapidly
from the women to the lovers to the children to the announcer with
scarcely a second's interruption."[23]

The broadcast of "Air Raid" took place in October 1938. As with
"The Fall of the City," CBS presented it as part of the *Columbia
Workshop*. William Robson, who directed the crowd scenes in "The
Fall of the City," was also involved in the production of "Air Raid," although this time working on the audio part of the show. It was something for which he demonstrated a keen sensitivity. Recalling the production years later, Robson commented, "We had . . . German fighter
bombers coming in from a great distance over a small town in north-
eastern Spain. . . . I wanted the effects of planes [coming] before you
see them, before you really hear them. There's this kind of strange
sound that develops into the sound of an airplane. So I said to the
sound-effects man, 'I want the effects of these planes coming in to
start under sixteen cycles per second.' The guy looked at me and said,
'You're crazy! That's the threshold of hearing.' I said, 'Yeah, I want it
to start at twelve.' He said, 'But nobody will hear it.' But by God, it
started from nowhere."[24]

Although it escaped the notice of all but a few listeners, "Air Raid"
featured a technical mistake resulting more from the novel quality of
aerial warfare than from the oversight of MacLeish. The script describes the bombers strafing the women on the ground below with

machine gun fire. That, as even casual students of modern warfare know, is beyond the capability of bombers.

"The Fall of the City" and "Air Raid" earned MacLeish a reputation as a prophet. In April 1938, just short of a year after the first broadcast of "The Fall of the City," German troops marched into Austria initiating the Anschluss with Germany, the unification under Hitler of the two nations. Viennese citizens lined the streets cheering their conquerors. The "city" had fallen for real. Shortly after the second broadcast of "The Fall of the City," a Yale classmate called MacLeish and said, "I heard your 'The Fall of the City.' . . . Did you know that the Nazis were going to enter Austria and just at that time? . . . What happens in your play is exactly what happened in Austria and I want to find out from you whether you have prophetic gifts or whether you are a phony who stumbled on secret information and made use of it."[25]

Many years after its broadcast, MacLeish described the circumstances in which he wrote "The Fall of the City." In a letter to Erik Barnouw, he wrote that "Anschluss was imminent and Nazism wrenched my bowels and all I could think about was the metaphor of the play and the terrible probability that it would turn true even in the U.S. There was an uncanny almost unnatural relationship between the poem and the events which followed. A friend cabled me from Vienna asking if Goebbels wasn't plagiarizing me."[26]

In the case of "Air Raid," the historical parallel was with the German invasion of the Sudetenland section of Czechoslovakia. In late September, two months after MacLeish wrote the play, Hitler obtained the reluctant agreement of the British and the French to stand by while his forces entered the Sudetenland. The following day, German troops crossed the border. As in "Air Raid," Czechs huddled in fear of aerial bombardment, but, unlike the play, none took place. Nevertheless, the aggression featured in "Air Raid" struck some listeners as uncanny, considering that MacLeish wrote it before the seizure of the Sudetenland.

In late October, *Time* reflected on MacLeish's work and its association with recent events: "In spite of the fact that the situation is a straight projection of . . . [September's] . . . Czechoslovakian crisis, when a man listened for war at his loud speaker like a frightened bell boy at a murderer's key hole, prescient poet MacLeish began it in the spring, rewrote it in August."[27]

The *New York Times* wrote about the same phenomenon several days after the broadcast: "The 'Air Raid' Mr. MacLeish wrote last June and he had the novel experience of hearing parts of it enacted in real life, almost as he had envisaged it. He tuned in on the September broadcasts from Czechoslovakia in which announcers described the blackout, the fear of bombers and the preparation for the air attacks."[28]

Writer James Boyd added his commentary concerning MacLeish's unique role, "You are the first serious writer radio has had," Boyd wrote in a 1940 letter to MacLeish, "and the first to show how serious a medium the radio can be."[29] But despite all the recognition that "The Fall of the City" and "Air Raid" gave him, MacLeish had a major misgiving. In an interview conducted not long after the broadcast of "The Fall of the City," he deplored the fact that his six months of preparation and a huge financial investment yielded just a single half-hour performance.[30]

NORMAN CORWIN ON THE EVE OF WAR

Like MacLeish, Norman Corwin was quite clearly influenced by events in Spain. Corwin's first foray against fascism was inspired after he read a remark by Vittorio Mussolini, the pilot son of the Italian dictator. The elder Mussolini had sent a military force to Ethiopia to secure an African colony for Italy. Vittorio wrote how while flying missions there he obtained great pleasure watching the explosion of bombs that he dropped on men and horses. He compared the spectacle to the unfolding of a rose.

Subsequent to reading this comment, Corwin wrote "They Fly Through the Air with the Greatest of Ease," which dramatized a ruthless bomber crew's lack of concern for human life while they dropped bombs on homes and civilians. In the course of the play, the pilot comments to the radio operator how gunning down fleeing civilians is similar to mowing wheat, to which the radio operator responds "Nice symmetrical pattern, isn't it?"[31]

Like MacLeish in "The Fall of the City," in "They Fly Through the Air" Corwin, seeking to give his parable the force of universality, avoided specific time and place references. In fact, he even gave the fliers typical American speech, although they were obviously European fascists.[32]

Unlike MacLeish, Corwin traveled in "They Fly Through the Air," shifting from scene to scene. The announcer starts with the men in the bomber, then leaves them to describe the peaceful life in the town, even going behind closed doors to reveal petty family quarrels and crying babies; back he then goes to the men in the bombers as they strafe the refugees. As Milton Kaplan pointed out in his unique and incisive volume *Radio and Poetry*, the play is also characterized by masterful use of sound effects, depending "on throbbing airplane motors, gun shots, the dull explosion of bombs far off, the tinkling of a piano, and the wail of a baby to provide poignant contrast in his bitter commentary on fascist warfare."[33]

"They Fly Through the Air with the Greatest of Ease" was broadcast on CBS in February 1939 as a part of Corwin's *Words Without Music* series and narrated by the commanding voice of Corwin's friend Martin Gabel. Immediately after the broadcast, Bill Robson rushed into the control room grabbed Corwin's hand and, almost crippling it in the process, exclaimed, "Norman, you're a major American poet."[34] The broadcast was a turning point in Corwin's career, giving him instant national recognition. The New York *Daily News* called it "the best radio play ever written in America."[35] CBS received 1,000 letters. Four people from as many separate states each wrote in that they had been listening while driving their cars and eventually had to pull over to the side of the road to hear it to the end. "This is the first 'fan' letter I have ever written . . . ," the chairman of a high school English department in Pennsylvania wrote to Corwin. "They Float [*sic*] Through the Air" was the most convincing argument against the madness of war that I could conceive. I went to school today and wrote on the front board in large letters: YOU MUST LISTEN TO NBC'S *WORDS WITHOUT MUSIC* ON SUNDAY."[36] Some time later the film rights to the script were sold to Warner Bros. One of the roles was to be played by a young actor named Ronald Reagan.[37]

Broadcast of "They Fly Through the Air" was a bold step for CBS at a time when increasing isolationism was making just mention of "war" controversial. The fact that CBS did not try to censor the play was evidence of the network's liberal leanings. But seven months later, just a few days after England and France declared war on Germany, the network canceled a planned repeat broadcast. The planned film was also canceled.

ARCH OBOLER ON THE EVE OF WAR

Arch Oboler may have been the only Jew who ever received a written commendation from Father Gerald Coughlin, the vicious and well-known anti-Semitic and super patriot Catholic priest of the 1930s air-waves. "Gentlemen," wrote Coughlin to NBC in an undated letter, "kindly convey my appreciation to Mister Arch Oboler for his presentation of 'The Mirage.' It was worth a dozen sermons."[38] But Oboler had not yet fully hit his stride with the kind of antifascist plays that would be a significant part of his hallmark and that Coughlin would have been loath to praise.

Like his radio colleagues Rosten and MacLeish, Oboler wrote some of his first anti-Nazi plays in allegorical form. For Oboler, producing socially conscious and antifascist radio drama was a passion. His NBC series *Lights Out* was essentially a horror series. But he inserted themes dealing with world problems into a significant percentage of its shows.[39] One example of this genre was "Genghis Khan," a January 1938 (somewhat embarrassing) story concerning a black man in Harlem who runs amok with a "spirit" at his side. The real subject was Hitler and his "voices."[40] In the summer of the following year, Oboler also produced "Ivory Tower," an overtly anti-Nazi play whose characters bear German names. Oboler's only concession to NBC's policy of caution was that he held back from saying that the locale was Germany. In his typical competitive fashion Oboler pointed out that "Ivory Tower" far predated Corwin's more successful "They Fly Through the Air" (which in fact it did not).[41] In "And Adam Begot," heard two months later, Oboler wrote a parable of appeasement in which he attacked the British and French betrayal of Czechoslovakia at the Munich Conference a year earlier. In "And Adam Begot," three twentieth-century people experience an automobile crash and somehow wind up back in time. They encounter a Neanderthal man who is

clearly going to kill them. Geoffrey, a diplomat, initially takes the attitude, "I'll meet him half way. He'll listen to me." But after the crea-
ture nearly kills him, he realizes that there is a time for talk and a time
for action. "But you can't reason with *unreason*, can you?" he says to
his friends. "When you're facing brute force, words and ethics and
logic and good faith don't mean anything, do they?" And with that,
Geoffrey grabs a gun, shoots, and kills the monster.[42]

Oboler's experience in trying to broadcast plays dealing with the
approaching war gives perhaps the clearest illustration of the problem
of prewar censorship. In the introduction to the published form of
"Genghis Khan," he complained of what he called "the guardians of
the kilocycle purity" whose mission was to see to it that NBC radio
dramatists toed the line in ignoring the war. "In other words," wrote
Oboler, "with one swoop of an inter-office memo, the network abol-
ished reality."[43]

Oboler's experience with the play "This Precious Freedom" further
illustrates the prewar network censorship problem. The play, the second installment in *Everyman's Theater*, a sponsored series, was broadcast late in 1939, two years before U.S. entry into the war. It told of a
man returning from a one-month vacation in the Canadian wilds.
While he was away, a dictatorship arose. What happened in Europe
was now being repeated in the United States. Much to Oboler's frustration, after NBC saw an advance copy of the manuscript they decided that the play was "dangerous" and might arouse the public.
Network officials, concerned, too, that it could be interpreted as criticizing the government's preparedness efforts, nearly canceled the
play's broadcast.[44]

Because Oboler sometimes seemed to stretch the truth, it is sometimes difficult to be certain of the accuracy of his stories. According to
one account by Oboler, he sent the script of "This Precious Freedom"
to Washington, D.C., where the Army Intelligence Division approved
of it, after making a few changes. Allegedly, the Army changed the in-
troductory line from "This is a situation . . . that we hope will never
happen here" to "This is a situation . . . that can NEVER happen
here."[45] Another account, also by Oboler, states that he and Raymond
Massey, the play's star, made a cross-country flight to New York where
they successfully persuaded network officials to permit its broadcast.[46]

Later, the Institute for Education by Radio named "This Precious Freedom" the outstanding commercial broadcast of the year.

THE FREE COMPANY

Early in 1941, Archibald MacLeish participated in the production of an unusual noncommercial CBS radio series, *The Free Company*. The series was initiated at the instigation of then U.S. Solicitor-General Francis Biddle. President Roosevelt had assigned Biddle, himself a playwright and poet, to develop propaganda programs.[47] The goal was to alert Americans to the threat from the Nazis and to combat foreign propaganda.

One German attempt to influence Americans involved a purported "station" calling itself "The Station of All True Americans." Heard in the United States at 8:30 each evening, it began and ended its broadcasting day with American patriotic songs. It specialized in attacks on FDR and other broadcasts designed to foment racial tensions. The broadcast pretended to come from within the United States. Its main speaker, "Joe Scanlon," had a Midwest accent. Actually it originated from Germany.

The *Free Company*'s coordinator was author James Boyd, whom Biddle hired on a dollar-a-year basis to work on the project. Boyd got started in November of the previous year after contacting MacLeish, John Steinbeck, and various other prominent writers. "So far most efforts in this country have been directed to attacks on [Axis] propaganda," Boyd explained in his initial contact with these writers. "But the best defense would be the positive restatement in moving terms of our own beliefs."[48]

Once the baton was passed from Washington, Boyd, MacLeish, Orson Welles, Pulitzer Prize–winning playwright Marc Connelly, and a number of other prominent writers began to put the series together. Ernest Hemingway, who was originally supposed to participate in the project, had to pull out at the last minute because of a trip to China. In his autobiography, Burgess Meredith, the series's narrator, described how Biddle regularly phoned him during the weeks that it was on the air. "He said he felt like a midwife," wrote Meredith, "responsible for the birth of the series."[49] Another unique feature was its use of the pro bono services of a group of actors sympathetic with its objectives. After getting permission from the Screen Actors Guild and the American Federation of Radio Artists (AFRA), besides Meredith, the *Free Company* utilized the services of such actors as Melvyn Douglas, Franchot Tone, Paul Stewart, Paul Muni, and John Garfield.

Three broadcasts in the *Free Company* series, MacLeish's, Welles's and Connelly's, turned out to be controversial. MacLeish's contribution, "The States Talking," a play in allegorical form, elicited a couple of comments in the newsletter of the American Federation of Radio Artists. It consisted of a variety of voices from various regions of the country presented to disprove the Nazi claim that "The States would never amount to anything because of their mixed blood" and that "The pure bred nations of the old world . . . would run the world. . . ."[50] In "The States Talking," MacLeish let the states speak out to refute the Nazis' racist views. The problem with his offering was that in the process of asserting the positive qualities of a multinational society, it went overboard in sneering at societies with homogeneous populations. The play first establishes that the Nazis are critical of the racial makeup of America:

There's talk says Illinois . . .
Talk about what says Dakota? . . .
I gather they don't like us says Maine . . .
What's wrong says Utah.
Something we did?

The essence of the criticism is that "It's the women we married. . . . They don't like it. . . . We married around. . . ." And now MacLeish answers the Nazis back:

I gather they're pure bred, says Maine. They're superior people.
So's snakes says Texas. So's potatoes.
Potatoes are pure bred.
The superior people . . . I remember Them! Standing behind in the doors . . . afraid of travel . . . afraid of changes . . . afraid of strangers. . . . Stayed home and stuck to their kind . . . married their kind. . . . Married their cousins who looked like their mothers.

There is even more derision when these words are heard or read in context. "Who would they marry? says Florida. Who could they find? The girls we left behind us says Missouri. *Sound* (The laughter becomes a tremendous shout)."[51] The point is clear.

One of the reactions to "The States Talking" came from an actor who wrote anonymously to the AFRA newsletter, describing the play as an "orgy of dramatized hate." MacLeish's allusion to the inward-looking character of the Nazis, their xenophobia, fear of travel, and change when presented as a national characteristic, was bound to offend some. And so even did his derision of the Nazi Aryan super-race concept via the epithet of a people who "married their cousins who looked like their mothers." After all, even more than fifty years later, the idea of America as melting pot has been proved to be a myth. "To preach inferiority of people, as MacLeish did in his opus today," the actor wrote, "is not my idea of explaining the Bill of Rights, which the *Free Company* boasts as its purpose." However, the writer's apparent isolationist views might be surmised from his additional comment, "There are bastards responsible for the war all right, but I don't think America's hands are clean on that score either."[52] The writer chose not to elaborate on this last allegation, which referred after all to the war that officially began when, after a string of earlier territorial conquests, Hitler's troops attacked Poland.

Connelly's and Welles's plays produced much stronger reaction than MacLeish's. Soon after their broadcast, the American Legion, the California Sons of the American Revolution, and the Hearst papers went on the attack. Connelly's play "The Mole on Mr. Lincoln's Cheek" was an appeal for freedom to teach and a plug for "honest textbooks." He was inspired to deal with this theme by the case of an actual attack on a social studies textbook series.

In 1938, Harold Rugg, a professor at Teachers College, Columbia University, published *Man and His Changing World*, a progressive series.[53] It was received well by teachers and became one of the most widely used textbook series at the time. In a relatively short time, nearly half of the social studies students in the United States were reading it in their courses. *Man and His Changing World* advocated racial understanding, citizenship, democracy, and social justice. It also championed national economic planning, although not government

ownership of industry as right-wing critics alleged in their rush to try
to tar Rugg with the label "Marxist."

Rugg's series was also fairly candid, citing innocuous truths that
showed some of the warts in American history. It referred, for example, to some smuggling that John Hancock, one of the signers of
the Declaration of Independence, had done. The critical approach
of Rugg's and other textbooks raised the hackles of business leaders,
among them H. W. Prentis, president of the National Association of
Manufacturers (NAM). In a 1940 speech, Prentis charged that certain textbooks were responsible for introducing "creeping collec-
tivism" to the younger generation and thereby undermining their
faith in private enterprise. Next, the NAM commissioned Ralph
Robey, a professor of banking at Columbia University, to review the
social studies textbooks used in the public schools. When Robey
completed his task, he, too, concluded that they were too critical of
the capitalist system. His findings were disseminated widely, and the
business community, the American Legion, and other groups then
campaigned nationwide against Rugg's books. As a result, many
school boards stopped using them and their sales dropped by 90
percent. In a few communities, they were not only banned but also
publicly burnt!

The Connelly play inspired by the textbook case starred Melvyn
Douglas and the actress who was perhaps best known for her film
role as the Wicked Witch of the West in *The Wizard of Oz*, Margaret Hamilton. It concerns a young teacher, Miss Thatcher, whom
the head of the local Veteran's League and a member of the school
board are seeking to fire for "unpatriotic statements" about American heroes, such as Hancock. They also want to ban the textbook
that she has her students use. Both her principal and her school su-
perintendent defend her at a raucous school board meeting. So,
surprisingly, does a second board member, Mr. Roberts, at the last
minute.

Roberts initially appears to be a witch hunter, but at the last minute
he changes his tune. Speaking in her defense, he refers to the mole on
Lincoln's cheek, letting it symbolize how Americans want the truth,
even about imperfections in their heroes: "if any painter or sculptor
dared to show us Lincoln without that mole, there ain't anybody over

eight years old in America wouldn't say, 'Put that mole back.'"[54] Berating the chief reactionary further, he tells him "if parts of our history ain't pretty to look at, let's face the facts and then make improvements as we get the chance to." Roberts then goes on to contrast the American educational system to Germany's. The critical reference to Germany was a rare phenomenon in a decade when CBS and radio in general were wary of offending anyone. "If you want to see what happens to a country that has nothing but little tin gods in it," Roberts continues, "look at Germany. School children there are being taught by your system. All their leaders are perfect and all their histories are being rewritten to prove it. Well, do you want *our* kids to be told about America that way? We know that everything considered, it's one of the best countries ever organized. And we want to keep it that way. And that means not being afraid to learn what made it tick in the beginning and what keeps it going today."

The other play attacked by the Hearst papers and their allies, "His Honor, the Mayor," written and directed by Orson Welles, actually received the brunt of the criticism. As *Time* pointed out, the timing of the attacks suspiciously coincided with the release dates of *Citizen Kane,* Welles's thinly veiled and quite critical film portrayal of publisher William Randolph Hearst. But, like Connelly, Welles, too, stepped on the toes of the American Legion.

Welles's play depicted how Bill Knaggs, a small town mayor, supported the right of assembly by allowing a gang of antilabor, anti-Semitic, right-wing "White Crusaders," among them some witch-hunting members of a "Veterans League," to conduct a meeting but then outwitted them by holding an even larger meeting of his own.

In the process of defending the right of right wingers to hold a public meeting, Welles was also subtly arguing that those on the political left should be able to do the same.[55] The play also contained an autobiographical touch reflecting on Welles's own prodigious appetite and weight problem. Knaggs says: "Take my word for it, when responsibilities get to be almost unendurable, a man on a diet takes to his sugar and starches as an addict retreats to his opium pipes, or a drunkard to his bottle."

According to Burgess Meredith, just before it was to be broadcast, a CBS executive took him aside. The brass feared that Meredith or

Welles might be tempted to interrupt the program and give their personal opinions about Hearst. "I must warn you, Mr. Meredith," the executive told him, "There's to be no ad libbing on the program and no references to Hearst whatsoever. The network is not to be involved in Mr. Welles's dispute with Hearst. And I want this passed on to Mr. Welles."[56]

Even without additional provocation, the Hearst newspaper chain ripped into Welles's broadcast on their front pages. Many of the articles sounded more like editorials than objective reporting. They cited searing criticism from American Legion and Veterans of Foreign Wars posts in Los Angeles and New York. *The Free Company* said these self-appointed guardians of American security were "unpatriotic, communistic and full of subversive propaganda." A spokesman for a Legion post in Brooklyn suggested that the very name of the series sounded suspiciously communistic. The chairman of the Legion's National Americanism Commission characterized the broadcast as "cleverly designed to poison the minds of young Americans." But by the time the smoke cleared, none of the critics cited any particulars to support their conclusions.

In response to the attacks, *The Free Company* made only a mild reply. Burgess Meredith read a long-winded explanation of the series's purposes and philosophy and pointed out that many of its members had served in the Army. According to Marc Connelly, because those associated with the series had been asked not to disclose Biddle's role as instigator of the series, they held back from trying to counteract the charges out of fear that any response might provoke further investigation. The series soon ended. Initially to many, it seemed un-American to have a corps of propagandists. This may have been a residue of the resentment created by the Creel Commission. Perhaps, in addition to the pressures, the series failed partly because of this attitude.

One other consequence of the series deserves mention. It prompted some Hearst sympathizers to begin sending communications to the FBI alleging that Welles was a subversive and spurred an FBI investigation of him that lasted for years. Its purpose was to determine any possible communist affiliations. One document in the FBI file criticized the *Free Company* for "deriding our National Defense system."[57] It gave no specifics. A reading of the plays in the series finds no basis for the allegation. However, if one bears in mind that within months of the last of the *Free Company* broadcasts, the Japanese bombed U.S. navy ships at Pearl Harbor virtually with impunity, had the *Free Company* actually made such an allegation it would have performed an important public service.

The same FBI document also attempted to lend credence to the idea that the series was following the Communist Party line, which initially opposed American participation in the war but then did an about-face after the June 1941 German attack on the Soviet Union. To this end, the report claimed that "Following Russia's entry into the war the broadcasts were discontinued." In fact, the series was discontinued more than a month before the German attack.

The FBI also examined various organizations with which Welles was affiliated, including even the innocuous-sounding Foster Parents Plan for War Children. They spied on bookstores that Welles frequented to learn what kind of political works he was reading. The FBI looked not only at Welles's associates but also, in connection with their focus on Welles, at the associates of his associates.

In March 1941, Hoover himself sent a memo to the assistant attorney general that referred to the "Communist character" of the organizations to which Welles belonged. In the end the most damning thing that the bureau could say about Welles (according to a special agent's report to J. Edgar Hoover) was that he "consistently followed the Communist line." What that meant was apparently never spelled out, however. But, for the FBI, opposition to racism, anti-Semitism, and Spanish fascism were among the signs that the subject of an investigation was a possible communist. In addition, "being a premature antifascist" also meant to the FBI that an individual deserved their attention. Clearly, the investigation never succeeded in establishing that Welles was a member of the Communist Party.

The termination of *The Free Company* series occurred approximately six months before the attack on Pearl Harbor. Subsequently, the networks and the government took off their gloves. American radio underwent a radical transformation, speaking out overtly against fascism and naming names.

NOTES

1. "Hitler Sends German Troops into Rhineland," *New York Times*, March 18, 1936, 1.

2. "Nazis Smash, Loot and Burn Jewish Shops and Temples . . ." *New York Times*, November 11, 1938, 1.

3. "Impact of War On the Air," *New York Times*, August 18, 1940, IX, 104.

4. Sandra Michael to Erik Barnouw, n.d., Box 38, the Barnouw Collection, COL-RB. Michael actually cited this incident as an exception to what she believed was Mutual of Omaha's general policy at the time of permitting the show to speak out against fascism. Whether Mutual of Omaha was more tolerant of such candor at the time than NBC and CBS is a subject of study that might be undertaken elsewhere. It is worthy of mention that in the same letter, without noting the network, Michael cited a similar incident concerning a script for a show other than *Against the Storm*, about an occurrence during the Spanish Civil War.

5. Norman Corwin, *Thirteen by Corwin: Radio Dramas by Norman Corwin* (New York: Henry Holt, 1942), 313.

6. Samuel Adams, *Alexander Woollcott: His Life and His World* (New York: Reynal and Hitchcock, 1945), 245–246.

7. Arthur Miller, *Timebends* (New York: Grove Press, 1987), 201.

8. Edwin P. Hoyt, *Alexander Woollcott* (Radnor, Pa.: Chilton, 1973), 274–275.

9. The following account concerning Kaltenborn is based on David G. Clark, "H. V. Kaltenborn and His Sponsors," *Journal of Broadcasting* (Fall 1968): 310–319.

10. The following account of the "Creel Committee" is based on Thomas Fleming, "World War I Propagandist, George Creel," *Military History*, vol. 12, no. 5 (December 1995).

11. Erik Barnouw, *The Golden Web: A History of Broadcasting in the United States, vol. 2, 1933–1953* (New York: Oxford University Press, 1968), 87–88.

12. Milton Kaplan, *Radio and Poetry* (New York: Columbia University Press, 1949), 90.

13. The text of the play can be found in Archibald MacLeish, *Six Plays* (Boston: Houghton Mifflin, 1980), from which this and the following two quotes were taken from pages 69, 74, and 75, respectively.

14. Scott Donaldson and R. H. Winnick, *Archibald MacLeish: An American Life* (Boston: Houghton Mifflin, 1992), 268.

15. Frank Brady, *Citizen Welles: A Biography of Orson Welles* (New York, Charles Scribner's Sons, 1989), 107.

16. "The Reminiscences of William Robson," Part I, vol. 2, June 15, 1966, 8–9, CUOHROC.

17. "The Reminiscences of William Robson," Part I, vol. 2, 10, CUOHROC.

18. Bernard A. Drabeck and Helen E. Ellis, eds., *Reflections: Archibald MacLeish* (Amherst: University of Massachusetts Press, 1986), 108.

19. Donaldson and Winnick, *Archibald MacLeish*, 269.

20. MacLeish, *Six Plays*, 98.

21. MacLeish, *Six Plays*, 99.

22. Kaplan, *Radio and Poetry*, 79.

23. Kaplan, *Radio and Poetry*, 71.

24. Leonard Maltin, *The Great American Broadcast: A Celebration of Radio's Golden Age* (New York: Dutton, 1997), 69.

25. Drabeck and Ellis, *Reflections,* 108.

26. Erik Barnouw to Archibald MacLeish, January 2, 1968, Box 1, Barnouw Collection, COL-RB [see MacLeish's reply in margin].

27. "Air Raid," *Time,* October 31, 1938, 32:30.

28. Orrin E. Dunlap Jr., "Exploring in Drama," *New York Times*, October 30, 1938, IX, 12:1.

29. James Boyd to Archibald MacLeish, November 27, 1940, Box 3, James Boyd file, LOC.

30. Signi Falk, *Archibald MacLeish* (New York, Twayne, 1965), 96.

31. Norman Corwin, "They Fly Through the Air with the Greatest of Ease," in Norman Corwin, *Thirteen by Corwin*, 69.

32. Kaplan, *Radio and Poetry*, 92.

33. Kaplan, *Radio and Poetry*, 94.

34. Corwin diary, February 19, 1939, Corwin Collection, TOL.

35. Ben Gross in the New York *Daily News* as cited in Corwin, *Thirteen by Corwin,* 79.

36. Paul Overdorf to Norman Corwin, February 21, 1939, Box 9, Corwin Collection, BU.

37. Untitled clipping, *Miami Daily News*, August 10, 1939, Box 9, #VIII Corwin Collection, BU.

38. Fa. Charles Coughlin to NBC, April 1, 1939, Box 71C, folder 41, NBC Collection, WISC.

39. Erik Barnouw, *Radio Drama in Action* (New York: Farrar & Rinehart, 1945), 386.

40. Arch Oboler, *This Freedom: Thirteen New Radio Plays* (New York: Random House, 1942), 77–100.

41. Oboler to Barnouw, May 23, 1945, Box 38. Barnouw Collection, COL-RB.

42. Oboler, *This Freedom,* 49–68.

43. Oboler, *This Freedom,* 78.

44. Oboler, *This Freedom,* 218; and Arch Oboler, *Oboler Omnibus* (New York: Dual, Sloan, & Pearce, 1945), 157–158.

45. This quote is from "'This Precious Freedom' Gets on the Air," an article in the library of Old Time Radio collector David Siegel. The clipping does not indicate its source.

46. Oboler, *Oboler Omnibus,* 157.

47. Burgess Meredith, *So Far, So Good: A Memoir* (New York: Little, Brown, 1994), 118.

48. James Boyd to Archibald MacLeish, November 27, 1940, Box 3, James Boyd file, Archibald MacLeish Collection, LOC.

49. Meredith, *So Far, So Good*, 119.

50. Donaldson and Winnick, *Archibald MacLeish*, 339.

51. James Boyd, ed., *The Free Company Presents* (New York: Dodd Mead, 1941), 223–234.

52. Anonymous letter to the editor, "An AFRA Actor Protests Free Co.," *Stand By*, II, no. 7 (May 1941): 7.

53. The following account is based on Frances FitzGerald, *America Revised: History Schoolbooks in the Twentieth Century* (Boston: Little, Brown, 1979), 36–37; S. Alexander Rippa, *Education in a Free Society: An American History* (New York: Longman, 1997), 255–256; Joel Spring, *Conflict of Interests: The Politics of American Education* (New York: Longman, 1993), 186–187.

54. Marc Connelly, "The Mole on Mr. Lincoln's Cheek," in Boyd, *The Free Company Presents*, 25–53.

55. Simon Callow, *Orson Welles: The Road to Xanadu* (London: Jonathan Cape, 1995), 555.

56. Meredith, *So Far, So Good,* 119.

57. Memorandum from SAC, Los Angeles FBI office, to FBI Director, November 3, 1944, 4, Orson Welles FBI file.

5

CORWIN AND THE OFFICE OF FACTS AND FIGURES

Praise God from whom all blessings flow. Tonight's broadcast wrote the enlistment papers for 100,000 free American volunteers tomorrow morning.

—Irving Cobb in a letter to Norman Corwin

Your name is Johnny. You are a farmer in Acworth, Georgia. It is October 1941. War has been raging in Europe for two years. German submarines have just sunk thirteen American merchant ships in the North Atlantic.[1] Your father served in World War I, in the artillery. It appears that the government is trying to get the country into a second war in Europe. You oppose this. You heard that some of the American propagandists who worked for the government during the Great War of 1914–1918 confessed and even bragged about inventing atrocity stories to help bolster support for American intervention in that war. You don't want your family to have to make the same sacrifices that it made twenty years ago. You don't believe the government's interpretation of what is going on in the world—and, for good reason.

The question of how to convince Johnny and other Americans of the threat that the Axis powers presented was a thorny one. President Roosevelt knew that the United States had to get into the war. It concerned America's vital interests, threatening, among other things, to destroy Britain, our closest ally, and wipe out all vestiges of democracy on the European continent. However, in addition to popular wariness of any government propaganda agency, there was the problem of strong American isolationist sentiment. Among prominent congressional isolationists were Republican Representative Hamilton Fish of New York and Senator Gerald Nye from North Dakota and Democratic Senators Burton Wheeler of Montana and David Walsh of Massachusetts. Fish, who detested Roosevelt personally and politically, chaired the National Committee to Keep America Out of Foreign Wars. Nye was a fervent isolationist who defended former aviation hero-turned-isolationist Charles Lindbergh when Lindbergh verbally attacked Jews and the Roosevelt administration.

As a result of the efforts of Nye and his colleagues, the 1940 Republican Party platform, while calling for "preparedness," opposed American involvement in foreign wars. Moreover, thanks to Wheeler and Walsh, the 1940 Democratic Party platform contained a plank that pledged to keep the United States out of overseas conflicts "except in case of attack." Had it not been for Roosevelt's insistence, the last clause would even have been left out.

The two government departments most involved in the pre–Pearl Harbor period dissemination of war- or defense-related radio drama were War and Treasury. The War Department began working with the radio industry on programs about military training camps in late 1940. In April of the following year, it established a radio division in its Bureau of Public Relations. Subsequently, the new division cooperated with NBC, which produced *Wings of Destiny*, a series of dramatized stories about the U.S. Army Air Corps. It also worked with CBS on *Spirit of '41*, a series that dramatized episodes about the Army, Navy, and Marines.[2]

The Treasury Department got into the act in early 1941, collaborating with the networks to promote the sale of defense bonds. Its most successful show, the overtly propagandistic *Treasury Star Parade*, was first broadcast in the summer of 1942 and ran through 1943. It was taped in New York City at the facilities of the World Broadcasting System, a syndication company in the old NBC studios on Fifth Avenue. William Bacher, who started out as a dentist in New Jersey, directed the series. A short, intense man with reddish brown hair and the reputation of a genius, Bacher conducted his rehearsals with a firm hand.[3]

The *Treasury Star Parade* featured plays and statements that were filled not only with patriotism but also with the indignation and even hatred that many Americans felt in the year after the Pearl Harbor attack. Like a number of other shows, it featured performances by film stars who donated their services. It was offered via transcriptions to all radio stations; and by the summer of 1942 there were 830 of a possible 920 subscriptions. Besides *Treasury Star Parade*, in the summer of 1942, Texaco donated a full hour on CBS for the *Treasury Hour*, a variety show. The new series featured seven-minute dramatic spots by Arch Oboler. As a result of Treasury's sponsorship of these two shows and two other network programs, it exceeded its initial goal months before the deadline and fulfilled its 1942 first-quarter quota before January 1, 1942. The War and Treasury Departments' early efforts notwithstanding, important people within or near the top leadership circle continued through early 1941 to push for creation of some sort of centralized agency that might educate the public about the realities of the war. Chief among them was Eleanor Roosevelt.

As a result of the various expressions of isolationist sentiment and distrust of government, President Roosevelt was wary of creating a real propaganda agency, preferring instead a multiplicity of agencies with limited powers. He also wanted control of wartime news and information in the hands of his own press secretary.[4] However, in the fall, as the United States edged closer to war, he finally gave in. But avoiding any of the traditional names, he insisted on naming the new propaganda agency the "Office of Facts and Figures" (OFF), "the place in Washington where you could, if you were a newspaper reporter, go and get your government-wide facts and figures. . . . "[5] OFF, established in the Office of Emergency Management, was to "advise with" government departments and agencies concerning the dissemination of war information.

To head the new agency, the president appointed Archibald MacLeish, who was already the Librarian of Congress. The president felt that he could do both jobs. MacLeish's appointment seemed to be a wise one. He had a record as a strong interventionist. Also, in spite of his background as a poet, he had practical talent as an administrator. One of the first things that MacLeish did was to establish the theory and theme of OFF's effort as "the United People's Strategy of Truth."[6] However, OFF and MacLeish as its head were doomed from the start.

For one thing, initially Roosevelt gave OFF no funds for operating costs and MacLeish had to scratch and fight until he finally got some. In addition, in the beginning, OFF had no decent headquarters; its first offices were in an apartment house in the most remote part of the city. Also, particularly before Pearl Harbor, an anti-interventionist press went on the attack. Most of the venom was directed at MacLeish personally from such sources as Colonel Robert McCormick's *Chicago Tribune.* But journalists also targeted and ridiculed OFF itself, calling it "The Office of Fuss and Feathers."[7]

MacLeish had problems with the FBI and with allegations concerning his political views. He had a background of frequent association with communists, who were in the forefront of the interventionist movement. Moreover, his staff, like himself, were antifascist liberals. When the FBI investigated a number of MacLeish's appointments, he complained to Francis Biddle, who by now was attorney general. However, Biddle merely passed on the complaints to FBI Director J. Edgar Hoover. This, in turn, led to the FBI compiling a dossier on MacLeish that eventually reached 600 pages.[8]

In April 1942, the Norristown *Times Herald*, a small-town Pennsylvania newspaper owned by Ralph Strassburger, a pre-war isolationist, made an editorial attack that was typical of the far right.[9] The editorial concerned a column by journalists Drew Pearson and Robert Allen that had appeared in newspapers around the country just a few days earlier. Pearson and Allen "indicated publicly to the enemy," as Strassburger put it, the location of the meetings of the Joint Chiefs of Staff. They did it, Strassburger added, "apparently without the censorship of Archibald MacLeish and other communists now employed in the Censorship Office at Washington." "Sue them for libel," Biddle suggested when MacLeish asked his view of the situation.[10] But after some thought, MacLeish decided to ignore the provocation.

Although OFF was short-lived, lasting only eight months, it had a profound impact on radio drama. For one thing, a ready-made coterie of writers flocked to the agency, eager to provide their services. Many of them regarded the war as a clear-cut struggle between good and evil. A letter from Orin Tovrov, an occasional writer of propaganda radio dramas and a long-time writer for *Ma Perkins,* one of radio's most popular soap operas, illustrates this.[11] Seeking a writing position with OFF, he described how of their own volition, he and his colleagues sought to insert material to help the war effort into various scripts. "Each day I cull my mind to a facet of the war effort, and then have "Ma" or somebody mention it or do something about it."

Much of OFF's impact had to do with MacLeish's selection of William B. Lewis as head of OFF's radio division. Lewis was CBS's large, dark-haired, and gruff-voiced vice president of programming who originally hired Norman Corwin. Lewis's first foray into the federal government took place in the summer of 1941 when he took a position as radio coordinator under former New York City Mayor Fiorello LaGuardia at the Office of Civilian Defense (OCD), established during the previous spring.[12]

"WE HOLD THESE TRUTHS"

Even at OFF, the bearish-looking Lewis continued to function as Corwin's guardian angel. In the fall of 1941, shortly after Lewis's move to OFF, Lewis hosted a group of friends, including Corwin, at a birthday party for Lewis's wife. During the evening, he briefly mentioned to Corwin that he would soon be calling him about "something big." Lewis phoned Corwin several days later. That "something big," as Lewis explained, was to be a one-hour-long, four-network dramatic program to commemorate the 150th anniversary of the Bill of Rights. Lewis wanted Corwin to do it.[13] At first, Corwin declined the offer. He had just concluded a grueling eight-month series, *26 by Corwin,* and he was exhausted. But Lewis prevailed.

On November 17, Corwin arrived at a hotel in Washington where he shared a room with Lewis and had a late-night discussion concerning the pending program. Corwin learned for the first time that President Roosevelt himself was involved in the project and might even make a short speech at the broadcast's conclusion.

With a deadline of twenty-six days, Corwin began his research in the Library of Congress. He even got permission to work there after closing hours. On December 4, with the script only three-fourths complete, it was time for Corwin to depart. It was clear that he would have to write the rest of the program on the train en route to the West Coast.

Early in the planning, Corwin envisioned actor James Stewart as narrator. Stewart, who was now a corporal in the Army Air Corps, was stationed at a base in California. At each stop along the way, Corwin sent telegrams to try to line up his cast.[14]

On Sunday, December 7, while en route, Corwin decided to take a break from the writing and he rang for the porter to get a radio. His play, "Between Americans," starring Orson Welles was scheduled for a rebroadcast. But the porter shook his head. All the radios were in use. "Why suh," said the porter, "th' Japs have bombed Pearl Harbor." One of Corwin's first thoughts on hearing the news was that it meant cancellation of the Bill of Rights program. He dashed off a telegram seeking confirmation. In reply he received word that MacLeish had met with the president. The program was now being viewed as even more important than when it was originally conceived. The emphasis was to shift to presenting the Bill of Rights as a symbol of what America was defending.

"We Hold These Truths" featured a star-studded cast, including Edward Arnold, Lionel Barrymore, Walter Huston, Edward G. Robinson, Orson Welles, James Stewart, and Rudy Vallee. It also included a central role played by Orson Welles that demanded a powerful style of delivery.

Welles's schedule did not allow him to arrive in time for the start of the rehearsal for "We Hold These Truths," so the cast worked around his role. When he arrived, he was even later than he planned. On being handed the script, with no warm-up, he strode up to the microphone to read his part. "Cold reading," radio folks call it. It was the first time he was seeing the script. His role was a long one, with rising emotion, magnificent skill, and passion. His peers were all years older and more experienced than he. They listened in silence that continued for a moment after he concluded his reading. Then they burst into applause.[15] One rarely saw this at rehearsals. There was another memorable scene, at the end of the actual broadcast. When his long dramatic part finished, Stewart pulled off his earphones and excused himself from the studio. He made his way to a more private spot and broke into tears.[16] Later, he told Corwin, "If I were not already a star, this show would have made me one."[17]

Welles was not the only prima donna involved with the broadcast. There was also Bernard Herrman, who wrote the show's score. One of the nation's finest dramatic composers, Herrman was a temperamental as well as a talented man. He was overly sensitive to perceived threats of betrayal, and he had difficulty expressing affection. But Corwin and Herrman managed a friendship, and they went on to collaborate on other important works after "We Hold These Truths." Corwin called Herrman "a rara avis who behaves like a genius and at the same time is one."[18] He credited Herrman's score with expanding on and improving the script's basic dramatic ideas by adding color and dimension to it.

When the show ended, Corwin stood outside the control room as his cast departed, like a minister at the church door bidding his congregation farewell at the end of a service.[19] Afterwards, dejected, mopping his brow, he waited for the phone to ring. It did not. He was certain that despite all his hard work and the show's million-dollar cast, it had been a colossal flop. Some 300 people had called the station after some of his previous broadcasts. However, apparently no one wanted to congratulate him on this one. It had been broadcast on eighty-eight stations. Why was there not a single call? Suddenly, just as Corwin was getting ready to leave the control room, the phone rang. Corwin lunged for it.

"May I speak to Corwin?" the caller inquired.
"This is he," he replied.
"This is Joy," the woman told him.
"Joy?"
"Yes—don't you remember—we met at Lucy's last Christmas."
"Oh, sure. How are you."
"Fine. I just heard your program."
"Oh, yes. How did you like it.
"It was okay. Look, I'm giving a party next Tuesday night. Would you like to come?"[20]

Only the next day did Corwin learn the truth. Because the program had three points of origin, New York, Washington, D.C., and Hollywood, listeners had been uncertain where to call. But now, the congratulatory messages arrived. One half of the country's population, 63 million people, had heard the broadcast. And coming as it did it eight days after the attack on Pearl Harbor, it gained a historic significance. Corwin had created the prototype of a new role for radio. Although "We Hold These Truths" was planned before Pearl Harbor, the Japanese attack and America's entry into the war resulted in it acting as radio's de facto preface to the conflict. This was the first of several times when Corwin found himself at the center of a national crisis.

It was now two months since the creation of OFF. Quickly the United States came into the war not only against Japan but also against its allies, Italy and Germany. Regular programming adjusted to the new situation rather slowly. It took a while to develop a frank approach to the realities of war. Months before Pearl Harbor, broadcast executives decided that if the United States became involved in the war, in addition to providing normal programming, radio would focus on three other objectives. It would provide prompt news, air government appeals, and promote "provocations of patriotic activity." But beyond formulating these objectives on America's entry into the war, it was evident that there was no operable plan for using radio to act meaningfully to reinforce America's resolve.

In the months after Pearl Harbor, radio underwent tremendous change. So did those associated with it. This partly involved sacrifices by many actors and others in the industry similar to those made by the rest of the country. Within six months the staffs at NBC and CBS experienced a tremendous turnover. Burgess Meredith was one of many actors to be drafted. "I had two wonderful movies lined up, which I was sorry to lose," he wrote to Corwin in March of the New Year, "but what the hell, they will probably be shooting pictures in four dimensions in the next life."[21] Corwin was offered a commission as a major a year earlier, to take charge of the Army Air Force's radio program activities. He turned it down, however, preferring to stay with CBS, where as a civilian he had a wider latitude and greater independence producing sustaining programs.[22]

Because of the war, various government branches and the Armed Forces began to cooperate with radio networks and a variety of other non-government groups. Unions, the entertainment industry, and newly formed committees such as the Writers War Board and the Council for Democracy worked to create a huge mass of propaganda writing, much of it in the form of radio plays, to help create public support for the war effort. The majority of radio writers became involved in this war writing, and their works blanketed the networks in the United States and around the world. Even the Du Pont–sponsored *Cavalcade of America* series abandoned its prewar avoidance of military themes.

THIS IS WAR

To bring radio into the fray, OFF, in the persons of MacLeish and Lewis, and a variety of other government leaders met with a number of radio executives. They agreed that "a major effort of emotional programming should saturate the country."[23] The effort would take the shape of a militant thirteen-part domestic propaganda series called *This is War*. The series was intended to make "an honest and convincing presentation of the issues of the war" to America. It was also agreed that once again Norman Corwin would be asked to direct an OFF project. MacLeish saw the series as a part of his "United People's Strategy of Truth."

Corwin learned of the plans for the new series on New Year's Day of 1942 when his bosses at CBS summoned him east from California for "an important assignment." In New York they quickly briefed him and then sent him to Washington. There he participated in a day-long conference to formulate policy and plans for the series. In addition, an OFF official brought him to the FBI for a briefing. Even after Corwin's departure for New York, OFF continued to feed materials to Corwin and his writers, soliciting materials from the Federal Communications Commission (FCC) and other federal agencies. From the FCC, OFF requested records of Nazi propaganda on such themes as Jew baiting and anti-British sentiment.

Corwin had reservations about the series from the start. "I hope it will represent the finest things radio can contribute to the war effort," he wired Bill Lewis, "but from details of proposed material and treatment so far advanced, I fear . . . [we are] . . . more likely to bore listeners than to inspire them."[24] Corwin also expressed a concern that if the series were to succeed, as was the case with the Bill of Rights program, it needed some top Hollywood talent. He was given what he wanted. Robert Montgomery narrated the first play in the series. Jimmy Cagney, James Stewart, and Raymond Massey appeared in later ones.

This Is War departed radically from radio's long-standing position of impartiality. The series began on Valentine's Day in February 1942 with "America at War," one of six of the thirteen installments that Corwin wrote himself. The inclusion of Montgomery as narrator was a clever decision. The six-footer, who walked like a West Point cadet, was the first Hollywood actor to go overseas to take part in the war. As was reported widely in the press the previous year, Montgomery served seventeen days at the front in France, driving an ambulance with the American Field Service volunteer ambulance corps.[25] In the summer of 1940, after the fall of France, Montgomery returned home. And, like Stewart, Montgomery, now a lieutenant, volunteered for military service (in the Navy) even before Pearl Harbor.

During the play, the radio audience heard the sounds of gunfire, of typing, and of machinery in war plants. Then Montgomery spoke. "These are all battle noises," he proclaimed. "They're all related to the roaring cannon. . . . Songs will rise up from our singing people, some well worth the nation's ear. Songs to work to, and to fight to and songs to set our quotas to."[26] The Almanac Singers, a folk group featuring Woody Guthrie and Pete Seeger, began singing "Round and Round Hitler's Grave," a bouncy square dance tune that Millard Lampell converted into a war song. The play praised President Roosevelt's policies. "We were busy educating our people," Corwin wrote in the very first script, "giving them a decent slant on things, trying to see that the hungry got fed and the jobless got work, trying to remember the forgotten man, trying to deal out a better deal around the table."[27]

The second show, "The White House and the War," by William Robson, was a review and a paean to presidential leadership during wartime. First, it briefly surveyed three earlier presidents' roles during wartime. Then it discussed Roosevelt, lauding first his leadership during World War I when he was assistant secretary of the Navy: "Those who know this President by more familiar names than Franklin Delano Roosevelt, these men who know the Commander-in-Chief of the Army and Navy and what he was before he came to live in the house, they know that he is better trained for war than any President before him."[28] Such praise is typical of war propaganda whose crucial element is its potential to persuade a people that they have a God-given right to victory. One means of doing this is to publicize the virtues of both the people and their leader.[29]

Among the writers of the other six programs in *This Is War* were twenty-seven-year-old Ranald MacDougall, who wrote two of them, and Stephen Vincent Benét and playwright Maxwell Anderson, who wrote one each. MacDougall, from Syracuse, New York, had started writing quite early. By age seventeen he had sold several pieces of his writing to Fawcett Publications, which a year later offered him an assistant editorship until they learned his age. Then he was told that it "wasn't fitting that one so young should be editing the work of his elders." Four years later he got his first job with radio as a mimeograph operator at NBC. Within a few years he was working as a writer.[30] After a salary dispute at NBC, MacDougall left the company and shortly thereafter got his assignments for *This Is War*. Despite MacDougall's youth, Corwin recognized his talent, particularly his keen ear for dialogue.

An average weekly audience of some 20 million people heard *This Is War* on four networks.[31] The series was America's first comprehensive attempt to use radio as a wartime tool to promote civilian morale. The timing could not have been better. Even those associated with the broadcast were glum about the war's progress. "Home in a cold rain," Bill Lewis wrote in his diary one day in early April during the middle of the series, "as discouraged about the war and the world as I ever have been."[32] Lewis's mood was well founded. "75 Japanese Planes Raid Ceylon" a newspaper headline reported the previous day. The same issue also told how a U.S. freighter that outran four German submarines was sunk by a fifth. Morning headlines for the same day that Lewis recorded his glum outlook spoke of the first Japanese air raids on the mainland of India and of a Japanese bombing raid in Burma that left the city of Mandalay in ruins.

While the nation needed its morale boosted, *This Is War* drew wildly mixed reviews. In the process it earned itself the reputation of "the most criticized program in radio history." Many credited it with jolting America's neutral stance and helping to arouse Americans to make appeasement a dead issue. *Variety,* the show business weekly, enthusiastically greeted the initial program, calling it "a hypodermic of emotional vitamins" and "a tough-talking, spade-calling, spine-walloping propaganda of pugnacity."[33] One much-told account of its reception concerns a group of travelers aboard a club car on a train crossing the Rockies. During the thirty-minute broadcast, the passengers were so gripped by the intensity of the program that absolute silence reigned during the time of transmission. The dean of a college in Kentucky sent a note of appreciation for a show in the series that challenged discrimination against blacks by defense industries and unions. The script argued that such discrimination was acting as a brake in the effort to achieve all-out production. "I am sure that thousands of Negroes and liberal-minded citizens applauded," wrote the dean. Another listener wrote in, as the series was concluding, "it was heartbreaking to have *This Is War* discontinued. . . . My eleven and seven year old offspring were as tense as I, listening to that broadcast. At its end, the seven year old, from her bed, was heard to mutter, "We just must *win* this war."[34]

For the most part, the most vociferous comments were critical. From the left, there were attacks on OFF for canceling the planned broadcast of a play by screenwriter Donald Ogden Stewart. Stewart, a leftist, was the president of the Hollywood Anti-Nazi League, and his political views made him a frequent target of the right.[35] His play "This Is Morale" had been scheduled for broadcast on March 21, but OFF was displeased with it and dropped it. Enter George Seldes.

Seldes was one of a small number of great independent American journalists of the twentieth century.[36] In 1922, he traveled to the Soviet Union where he met Lenin and Trotsky. He spent a year reporting from there until he was expelled for not bowing to Soviet censorship of the news. In the same decade, Seldes also visited Fascist Italy to chronicle the rise of Mussolini. From here, too, he was expelled when he refused to write what the Fascisti wanted him to write. On his return to America, Seldes established *In Fact*, the first publication in America solely devoted to press criticism. He published it from 1940 to 1950, and it had a peak circulation of 176,000 before being Red-baited out of existence.

When OFF dropped "This Is Morale," Seldes published a large excerpt from the script in *In Fact* along with an account about how OFF had canceled its broadcast. This spurred the complaints. A letter to MacLeish from a New York reader of the "Seldes" version was typical of those concerning cancellation of the Stewart broadcast. The writer accused MacLeish of appeasing "our fifth column." He noted that a week after MacLeish canceled the show, Colonel McCormick, the isolationist publisher of the *Chicago Tribune,* who was also MacLeish's nemesis, rose at the Associated Convention and called MacLeish a communist. "If you refuse to permit propaganda against the fifth . . . column," the letter writer wrote, "you strengthen it to the point where it will . . . defeat our whole foreign policy."[37]

A reading of *In Fact*'s version of the play suggests that OFF canceled Stewart's play for good reason. "This Is Morale" was a polemic for a number of actions to bring about social change.[38] It had little to do with the proposed purposes of the series, to boost support for the war effort. Instead it reflected Stewart's image of himself. In a 1975 autobiography he described how he underwent a profound social change in 1935, after which he considered himself a "romantic communist." "Gradually in my mind began to form the image of a "worker," wrote Stewart, "whom I wanted to have the same sense of freedom and brotherhood that I had had at college. . . . And over in the corner of my imagination, behind the worker there crouched an image of a little man who needed my help—the oppressed, the unemployed, the hungry, the Jew under Hitler, the Negro."[39]

Stewart's reaction to his play's cancellation also seemed to indicate that he was a man out of touch. When he heard about the cancellation, he called MacLeish in Washington. "Don, there's a war on!"[40] MacLeish yelled at Stewart before hanging up on him. Stewart did not have a clue about why it had been rejected.

It is likely that instead of boosting morale, Stewart's play would have caused widespread controversy. A large number of the radio plays of the war era pushed progressive themes. Many of them were subjected to hyperbolic criticisms that they were pushing "communism." Generally, most of these criticisms were based on a poor understanding of the nature of communism. But a small part of Stewart's play appeared to advocate that farmers adopt the kind of collective sharing of farm equipment that was distinctly characteristic of Soviet collective farms.

OFF officials responded to criticisms of the play's cancellation by explaining that it contained several statements that were "Not in accord with the government's policy and that it advocated action that the government could not approve."[41] According to OFF, Stewart's script advocated that individual citizens and community groups mobilize independently of any nationwide effort, and "it tended to deprecate the activities of the Federal Government."[42] William B. Lewis gave additional explanation, alleging that even after Stewart was asked to make some alterations in the script, he failed to do so.[43]

As another letter indicated, even without the broadcasting of Stewart's play, a number of themes in the plays that did air appealed to the left. In late April, Gus Hall, then county secretary of the Communist Party in Cuyahoga County, Ohio, and later the party's national head, wrote to OFF requesting a transcript of "The United Nations," the fifth script in the series.[44] The script, about America's wartime allies, dealt in part with the Red Army. Hall wanted to use it in a rally in support of beginning a western offensive. Had the Red-baiters known about his letter, surely they would have raised their cry even more shrilly. As seen time and time again, for such people, Communist Party approval of a writer's work was sufficient to prove that the writer was a communist.

Among the milder criticisms, *PM Daily*, a liberal New York newspaper, complained that the first show, "lacked the logic electricity; the jolting overwhelming urgency required to knock America out of its complacency."[45] It needed to be bold enough to attack politicians such as Senators Byrd and Tydings, two anti–New Deal Democrats. Other critics said the series was unduly aggressive. They perceived it as paralleling the propaganda efforts of the Nazis. The Radio and Publicity Committee of the Buffalo (New York) Council of Churches accused it of increasing hatred and using patriotism for the sake of profit. To this argument, MacLeish responded that the show was advocating hatred of evil not hatred toward persons. And Corwin argued that "We cannot be too squeamish about our reference to the enemy." He contended that he had to reveal the horrors of Nazism to aid the understanding of the principles for which Americans were fighting. The issue of whether Americans should hate the Germans continued to crop up periodically and was fiercely debated in the following months.

Even George Faulkner, author of the show that Gus Hall admired, acknowledged the problems in the series. In a letter in late April, Faulkner wrote that the series reflected a confused state of mind in Washington. Taking a shot at Corwin, he wrote "I think . . . [he] . . . is too fond of sound effects and production subtleties in general. These things rejoice the ear of a quick listener, but the slower brethren just get lost and too often the words themselves are obscured in a cloud of music and sound. . . . My mother who is a pretty average audience, says: 'Why do they have so much clatter.'"[46]

Critics on the far right attacked the first show for its liberal message or because of the politics of those involved with it. The New York *World Telegram* reported "The program's backers were much upset today to learn that the Almanac Singers have long been the favorite balladeers of the Communists and their official publications, the *Daily Worker* and *New Masses.*"[47]

The *World Telegram* also took a shot at Corwin, claiming "Mr. Corwin is not entirely unaware of Communist activities. For January a year ago he was listed as one of 'a brilliant array of talent' who agreed to write the script for a coast-to-coast broadcast in behalf of the American Rescue Ship Mission which was then under fire as a Communist front."[48]

The *World Telegram* article and a similar one in the *New York Post* spelled a quick end to the commercial career of the Almanacs. Their banning from the networks as a result of the journalistic Red-baiting was a harbinger of things to come. In fact, Seeger, Lampell, and at least one other group member were members of the Communist Party. However, what that meant or should have meant in a democracy has remained to this day a highly debatable question. For all three, it was the party's opposition to racism and support of various progressive causes that attracted them to it. The group was somewhat alienated by the party's dogmatism. They even composed a few songs parodying the party's heavy use of Marxist jargon.[49] Also, like the vast majority of those who joined the American Communist Party in that era, there is virtually no evidence that they or their friends had even a remote interest in overthrowing the U.S. government.

One angry listener, a member of the Daughters of the American Revolution, wrote that the first program "was to any thinking person so blatant—so patently Jewish hate [*sic*]—that it acted as a boomerang. . . . I realize that we have a huge percentage of foreign born *peasants* but you only antagonize 8th generation Americans as most Americans are."[50] Perhaps the most vitriolic letter was from a member of the Arizona State legislature who wrote, "Why is it that we have to have everything pertaining to this war effort given to us by some pig-headed Jew or strained for us through a sieve of nauseating Jewish psychology. If this nation will divorce itself from the international Jewish mountebanks, racketeering labor leaders, and Hollywood guttersnipes, there will then be no reason for propaganda broadcasts. Good Americans with names that can be pronounced will do the rest."[51]

There were other arguments against the series. Some looked at the four networks' use of time as forced listening. Others, hostile to the Roosevelt administration, took potshots at what they saw as "the President's own show." For according to one story, the initiative for the series originated in the White House.[52] There was some revulsion at an "official" government series, particularly because it praised FDR and his policies. Roosevelt's enemies in Congress and elsewhere did not accept that war propaganda automatically confers legitimacy on the leader. But for the moment, their hands were tied. They could only complain. But they bided their time and eventually took it out on the administration's propaganda apparatus.[53]

Corwin was not very happy with *This Is War*. On the one hand, he felt that it helped kill *Social Justice*, one of the most treasonable fascist publications in the United States of its day.[54] But the series was beset with problems. Some were endemic to efforts to coordinate the efforts of a disparate group of people and meet difficult deadlines. Writer George Faulkner was one of those problems. During preparation for broadcast of his play "The United Nations," he intervened in the production process, telling Corwin how to handle such things as sound effects and generally interfering with Corwin's attempts to do his job as director. Finally, Hay McClinton, the series producer, had to ask Faulkner to stay away from the studio.[55]

In the process of producing the seventh play in the series, Corwin ran into trouble between the first and second broadcast when his narrator, actor John Carradine, was found drunk. Some forced coffee drinking resolved the problem only moments before air time for the second broadcast to the West Coast. Corwin was also disappointed or annoyed with at least one of the stars who performed in the series. "Cagney was a slow study and never reached the drive I expected of him," he wrote in his diary.[56] The series was a rush job, put on two months earlier than Corwin wished. The combined problems resulted in so much stress, manifested in increasingly low blood pressure, that a doctor whom Corwin consulted was dubious about the wisdom of his continuing to work on the series.[57]

Subsequent to its broadcast, Corwin regretted that there had not been more time to study its topics more thoroughly. In addition, he had been disturbed by problems that resulted from the conflicting jurisdictions of various governmental agencies: "it was the experience of *This Is War* that multiple points of view always canceled out; that, for example what one half of the OFF liked, the other half didn't; that what a Navy liaison man found objectionable . . . was the very thing that made the War Production Board very happy to have said on the air."[58]

Talking to an interviewer decades after the broadcast, Corwin said of *This Is War*, "I don't remember [it] with much charity . . . it was as close as I ever came to writing propaganda, and I think that's what bothered me."[59] In fact because of the times in which he was writing, as that same interviewer wrote, most of Corwin's scripts of the war period fell into the category of propaganda. This also applies to much of the writing of a number of other radio dramatists of the era. Arthur Laurents and Millard Lampell both bridled at the use of the word in reference to some of their works of the war period. But if "propaganda" has an unpleasant sound to it, the term nevertheless realistically characterizes much of their work as well.

OFF: BROAD STRATEGY AND A SHORT TENURE

In addition to commissioning the networks to do Corwin's "We Hold These Truths" and *This Is War*, OFF's Domestic Radio Bureau established several approaches to expand production of programs for radio.

One was the Domestic Radio Bureau's direct production of programs. Two others were the April 1942 organization of commercial radio for the transmission of propaganda via a Network Allocation Plan and, eight months later, creation of the Special Assignment Plan. These and related plans affected tens of thousands of broadcasts, and war and propaganda campaigns became a daily part of American life.

OFF produced several dramatic series, among them *Keep 'Em Rolling* and *You Can't Do Business with Hitler*. Technically, *Keep 'Em Rolling*, begun in November 1941, was a variety series. It had its pick of top stage and screen stars. Clifton Fadiman served as its host. In addition to typical variety show acts, each show featured a short play." *You Can't Do Business with Hitler*, a fifteen-minute show featuring heavy-hitting classical propaganda, was launched in December 1941. Twenty-eighty-year-old Frank Telford, an advertising executive who also wrote some of the scripts, directed the series. Most of the episodes contain a fictionalized interpretation of some Nazi policy or law. The series was aired via electrical transcriptions by more than six hundred stations.

The Network Allocation Plan was OFF's most important long-range scheme. It carried out a fusion of American warfare with regular radio programming. Its focus was on helping develop programming for action messages: save fuel; collect scrap; enlist; or buy bonds. OFF played the role of consultant for stations and networks that produced their own radio dramas and other related propaganda. The scheme facilitated a rational decision-making process to help plan what topics should be emphasized on radio broadcasts. The question was: "What information needs deserved priority on network programs?" To assist in answering it, the same month that OFF established the Network Allocation Plan, it also established an Intelligence Bureau. The bureau's task was to provide OFF's Domestic Branch with factual information to further its effective relations with the press, magazine and book publishers, and radio.[60] To gather this information, it conducted weekly polls and man-on-the-street interviews and cooperated with existing polling organizations.

Once OFF (and later its successor agency, the Office of War Information) made its decisions, it attempted to distribute war messages among the networks. Its main task in regard to programming was to recommend particular themes at given times. An OFF memo issued in March 1942, on the eve of the implementation of the Network Allocation Plan, highlighted the plan's basic principle. "[It] . . . must be to give the greatest amount of repetition to the smallest number of ideas possible," Seymour Morris of OFF's Allocation Division suggested to a colleague. "If we scatter our effort across some 20 or 30 ideas, we will probably only confuse people and achieve no clear-cut results. On the other hand, by making a "drive" on a limited number of subjects we can undoubtedly drive these points home."[61]

The most eye-catching part of the memo was its last sentence, "it's . . . interesting to reread the chapter on propaganda in *Mein Kampf* in this connection." For the sake of FDR's and Archibald MacLeish's blood pressure, it was a good thing that this reference to Hitler's book never became public knowledge during the war. As it was, a month earlier OFF received a letter concerning *This Is War* from an Arizona critic who said of the February 22 broadcast, "It was not patriotic; it was anti-democratic. . . . It was a . . . clear case of Heil Roosevelt."[62] The FDR administration did not need its own people fueling the fires of its critics.

Usually the Network Allocation Plan obtained voluntary cooperation. The Radio Bureau had no authority to enforce it. When it occasionally encountered resistance, the bureau worked through advertising agencies to obtain the cooperation of radio sponsors. It cited the contributions of the sponsor's competition or used friendships and connections to exert subtle pressure.[63] One agency that proved stubborn for a while was owned by Milton Biow. In this case, Seymour Morris sought the help of a friend at Procter and Gamble, a radio sponsor. Morris wrote to his friend about the Biow agency "which is doing the poorest job for us on the Allocation Plan assignments. . . . The situation was unfortunate enough when it was simply a case of doing a poor job for us on every message they delivered. . . . They now want to be excused altogether from any cooperation on this program . . . you as an individual could be extremely helpful to us if—when a convenient occasion arises—you could drop into Mr. Biow's ear a few of the opinions which your Company has about the Network Allocation Plan and the job it has done to date."[64] A week later, a friend at Procter and Gamble assured Morris that he would take care of the problem.

In contrast with the Network Allocation Plan and its focus on action, the Special Assignment Plan spotlighted things that the citizen needed to know and understand about the war effort to play a constructive role in it. These included such topics as the issues involved in the war, the need for all-out production of the working forces, and the nature of the jobs and training of the fighting forces. The plan started out servicing fifty-six programs weekly, which translated to approximately eight a day or two per network per day.

Keep 'Em Rolling aired its last show in May 1942 while *You Can't Do Business with Hitler* lasted until March 1943. By the end of the spring of 1942, however, OFF itself was on its way to oblivion. From the start it had been a makeshift arrangement with weak authority. If it did not achieve dazzling success in its collaborations with Corwin, it accomplished even less with its print publications. Its first such effort was *Report to the Nation,* a dull and flabby pamphlet that was intended to present an account of the nation's war effort. *Report to the Nation* was poorly received, as were several other similar efforts. Generally, OFF proved inept at handling its principal assignment, coordinating war information. The various federal agencies that were releasing war information to the public did what OFF told them only if it suited them, and OFF was powerless to do anything about it. In addition to the weakness of its authority and its failure to establish good press relations, it also suffered from internal administrative difficulties. It was overstaffed, and it lacked forceful direction. Bill Lewis said as much in his diary in a mid-April notation: "Present status of OFF: Operations Bureau only one getting anywhere. Intelligence behind; Liaison not well administered; Production a mess. Reorganization of government information services stalled. MacLeish, a bad executive, trying hard."[65]

In June, the Office of War Information, a new agency that the Roosevelt administration created, absorbed OFF and much of its staff. The Office of War Information continued the production of dramatized propaganda programs.

NOTES

1. Scott Donaldson and R. H. Winnick, *Archibald MacLeish: An American Life* (Boston: Houghton Mifflin, 1992), 339.

2. Gerhard Horten, "Radio Goes to War: The Cultural Politics of Propaganda during World War II" (Ph.D. diss., University of California at Berkeley, 1994), 65–66.

3. Mary Jane Higby, *Tune in Tomorrow* (New York: Cowles, 1968), 61.

4. Donaldson and Winnick, *Archibald MacLeish*, 350.

5. Bernard A. Drabeck and Helen E. Ellis, eds., *Reflections: Archibald MacLeish* (Amherst: University of Massachusetts Press, 1986), 147.

6. R. LeRoy Bannerman, *On a Note of Triumph: Norman Corwin and the Golden Age of Radio.* (New York: Lyle Stuart, 1986), 99.

7. Donaldson and Winnick, *Archibald MacLeish*, 355.

8. Donaldson and Winnick, *Archibald MacLeish*, 354–355.

9. Norristown *Times Herald,* April 14, 1942. This article can be found in the Archibald MacLeish Collection, container 3, LOC.

10. Francis Biddle to Archibald MacLeish, MacLeish Collection, April 16, 1942, LOC.

11. Orin Tovrov to Douglas Meservey (OFF), June 5, 1942, NA 208–103–647, Records of Allocation Division.

12. Box #428, folder, W. B. Lewis, Biographical Collection, Lewis Collection, BU.

13. Except where otherwise indicated, discussions of Corwin's 1942 radio plays are based on Bannerman's well-documented biography of Corwin or on the author's interviews with Corwin.

14. Bannerman, *On a Note of Triumph*, 78.

15. Norman Corwin, in Museum of Broadcasting, *Orson Welles on the Air: The Radio Years* (New York: Museum of Broadcasting, 1988), 42.

16. Gary Fishgall, *Pieces of Time* (New York: Scribner, 1997), 159.

17. Norman Corwin, interview by author, Los Angeles, November 20, 1998.

18. Stephen Smith, *A Heart at Fire's Center* (Berkeley: University of California Press, 1991), 90.

19. Norman Corwin, *More By Corwin: 16 Radio Dramas* (New York: Henry Holt, 1944), 93.

20. Corwin, *More By Corwin*, 93–94.

21. Burgess Meredith to Norman Corwin, March 19, 1942, COR 00635, Corwin Collection, TOL.

22. Norman Corwin telegram to Nat Wolfe, January 13, 1941, COR 00999, Corwin Collection, TOL.

23. Bannerman, *On a Note of Triumph*, 76.

24. Norman Corwin telegram to William B. Lewis, n.d., COR 00999, Corwin Collection, TOL.

25. Untitled newspaper article in Robert Montgomery folder of newspaper clippings, ACAD.

26. Norman Corwin, "This Is War," in Corwin et al., *This Is War: A Collection of Plays About America on the March by Norman Corwin and Others* (New York: Dodd, Mead, 1942), 20.

27. Corwin, "This Is War," in Corwin et al., *This Is War*, 8–21.

28. William N. Robson, John Driscoll, and Norman Corwin, "The White House and the War," in Corwin et al., *This Is War*, 33–34.

29. Horten, "Radio Goes to War," 111.

30. Ranald MacDougall to Erik Barnouw, May 2, 1945, Box 38, Barnouw Collection, COL-RB.

31. *Variety*, March 18, 1942, 32.

32. W. B. Lewis diary, April 8, 1942, Lewis Collection, BU.

33. "This Is War—II," *Variety*, February 25, 1942, 26.

34. Virginia Meredith to Henry Pringle (of OFF), June 1942, NA-4–24, folder 370 "Radio and Television." June 1942 A.

35. *Current Biography: Who's News and Why—1941* (New York: H. W. Wilson), 826.

36. For an interesting autobiographical account of Seldes's long and fascinating life, see George Seldes, *Witness to a Century* (New York: Ballantine Books, 1987).

37. Irving Beinhart to Archibald MacLeish, n.d., NA 208–5–22, folder 370 "Radio and Television," April 1942.

38. An abbreviated version of the play was published in *In Fact*, April 27, 1942, a newsletter published by George Seldes.

39. Donald Ogden Stewart, *By a Stroke of Luck* (New York: Paddington Press/Two Continents, 1975), 217.

40. Stewart, *By a Stroke of Luck*, 260–261.

41. John C. Baker (of OFF) to Richard Rasmusson, April 30, 1942, NA 208–5–22, folder 370 "Radio and Television."

42. William B. Lewis to Irving Flamm, April 28, 1942, NA 208–5–22, folder 370 "Radio and Television."

43. Lewis to Flamm, April 28, 1942.

44. Gus Hall to OFF, April 21, 1942, NA 208–5–22, 370 "Radio and Television."

45. "Pugnacity Is Needed for 'This Is War,'" *PM Daily* II, no. 173 (February 16, 1942): 23.

46. George Faulkner to W. B. Lewis, April 22, 1942, NA 208–5–23, folder 370 "Radio and Television," April 1942.

47. "Singers on New Morale Show also Warbled for Communists," *New York World Telegram*, February 17, 1942, 3.

48. "Singers on New Morale Show, " *New York World Telegram*.

49. Pete Seeger, telephone conversation with author, July 21, 1998.

50. Zella Hazen to "Propaganda Department," February 15, 1942, NA-5–21, folder 370 "Radio and Television," 1941–February 1942.

51. J. Lee Loveless, member of the Arizona House of Representatives, to Archibald MacLeish, February 23, 1942, NA 208–5–21, folder 370 "Radio and Television," 1941–February 1942.

52. Richard Lingeman, *Don't You Know There's a War On?* (New York: Putnam, 1970), 225.

53. Horten, "Radio Goes to War," 111–112.

54. Corwin, *More By Corwin*, 295.

55. George Faulkner to William B. Lewis, March 15, 1942, Box 22, Correspondence file "F," Lewis Collection, BU.

56. Corwin diary, April 25, 1942, Corwin Collection, TOL.

57. Corwin diary, March 30, 1942, Corwin Collection, TOL.

58. Norman Corwin, *Untitled and Other Radio Dramas* (New York: Henry Holt, 1945), 161.

59. Norman Corwin, interview by Jerrold Zinnamon, July 6, 1982, Jerrold Zinnamon, in "Norman Corwin: A Study of Selected Radio Plays by the Noted Author and Dramatist." (Ph.D. diss., University of Florida, 1984).

60. Horten, "Radio Goes to War," 181.

61. Seymour Morris to Douglas Meservey, March 17, 1942, NA 208–5–22, folder 370 "Radio and Television," March 1942.

62. John Fryer to Bamberger Broadcasting, February 22, 1942, NA 208–5–21, folder 370 "Radio and Television."

63. Horten, "Radio Goes to War," 182.

64. Horten, "Radio Goes to War," 182.

65. W. B. Lewis diary, April 11, 1942, Lewis Collection, BU.

THE OFFICE OF WAR
INFORMATION AND OTHER
GOVERNMENT AGENCIES

Elmer, as you know is the chief of that weird, hydraheaded monstrosity of government mismanagement known as the Office of War Information. . . .

—Malcolm Bingay, *The Detroit Free Press*

You own a hardware store in Houston, Texas. Your heroes are Senators Gerald Nye, Burton Wheeler, and Millard Tydings. America is at war. You firmly believe that we should not have gotten into it and that we should get out as quickly as possible. The fact that America and its allies are not doing well in the war only reinforces your belief. There has been a string of Allied defeats: Guam, Wake Island, Borneo, Singapore, Hong Kong, and, worst of all, the fall of the Philippines. As far as you are concerned, America should cut its losses. You are willing to see the government consider a peace offer from the Germans even if it means a de facto victory for them. A newspaper editorial of February 1942 expressed your current view. "The point is that if the arsenal of democracy is stripped of too many of its own defenses it will be laid open to invasion and conquest."[1] "Amen," you said when you read it. A few months later, the same newspaper published a letter that you sent in response to President Roosevelt's request for suggestions as to what to call the war. You wrote in "Several suggestion for F.D.R. about naming the war: the

Pyrrhic Victory, The Raw Deal, the Slaughter Pen, the Revenge of the Patriots." [2]

You are also quite unhappy with many of the people in the Roosevelt administration. Vice President Henry Wallace is a bit too "pink" for your taste. So is MacLeish who heads that thing they call "OFF" in the papers.

As a result of all of the negative reaction to Archibald MacLeish and the Office of Facts and Figures (OFF), President Roosevelt decided by the spring of 1942 to replace OFF with a new agency to channel the flow of public information. The decision was long overdue. Sometime earlier, Roosevelt had told an aide that he wanted the broadcaster "with the funny voice, Elmer—Elmer something" to head the new agency.[3] In May, FDR invited fifty-two-year-old CBS news broadcaster Elmer Davis to the White House. Rex Stout of the Writers War Board had recommended Davis through Robert Sherwood. Actually, Davis thought others might be more suitable for such a position. Ironically, at some point earlier, he had written to presidential adviser Harry Hopkins to suggest Stout, Edward R. Murrow, or William L. Shirer as possible choices to assume the new position.

Davis was an ungainly, white-haired man with jet black eyebrows and a head that seemed a bit too large for his body. He had a somewhat droll appearance and gave an impression of great seriousness. But he was also a baseball lover with an explosive sense of humor. Some time before the meeting, Davis himself blasted the mess into which OFF had gotten. "The whole government publicity situation," he complained on one broadcast, "has everybody in the news business almost in despair, with half a dozen different agencies following different lines."[4] Now with Roosevelt having decided on Davis to assume the role of chief of the new agency, Davis found himself having to eat his words. As he later recalled the meeting, he was not offered the position, he was ordered to take it.

The following month, Executive Order No. 9182 was put into effect creating the new agency. The Office of War Information (OWI) consolidated the functions of the Office of Facts and Figures, the division of information in the Office for Emergency Management, the Office of Government Reports, and the foreign information service of the Office of Co-Ordinator of Information. Davis was installed in office space that had been occupied by MacLeish's OFF in the Old Building of the Library of Congress.

Initially Davis was overwhelmed by his new administrative position. On his first day on the job, a secretary noticed him flipping through a stack of organizational charts. He had a look on his face that revealed obvious feelings of confusion and perhaps even intimidation. When she offered her assistance, Davis confided "I never could understand charts . . . do you suppose there's a typewriter around?" With the typewriter in front of him, Davis began to feel more comfortable and he got to work. His self-doubts did not disappear immediately, however. "What in hell am I doing here?" he asked an old friend. "I'm not an administrator, I'm a writer."

As if Davis's own doubts were not enough, he also had to contend with resentment and a lack of confidence in him from people in other government agencies. Two of his biggest problems were Chief of Naval Operations Ernest L. King and Secretary of War Henry Stimson. When a journalist once asked Stimson whether the OWI had power to oversee military communiqués, Stimson replied stiffly, "Is Mr. Davis an educated military officer?"

Some of the roots of Davis's and the OWI's problems go back to the first tastes of radio propaganda that OFF gave the country. Some of it praised President Roosevelt and his policies. Such praise was common for wartime propaganda, whose nature is to extol the virtues of the nation and its leadership. This is exactly what *This Is War* did in at least two of its programs.

Propaganda such as this disturbed FDR's enemies. And there is no doubt that in the process of trying to explain governmental acts, some of the staff of the OWI's domestic branch went out of their way to praise the FDR administration. By itself, that praise might have been sufficient to alienate Republicans and conservative Democrats from the idea of a federal propaganda agency bombarding the American people. Add to that memories of the resentment toward the Creel Commission. It was no wonder that the OWI became a whipping boy for Congress, particularly the House of Representatives. It was an easy target.

Like the staff of OFF, Davis and his people became targets of accusations of communist influence. Many OWI employees were, in fact, quite liberal; the agency had the highest percentage of New Dealers of any wartime agency. Among them were Peter Lyon, Joseph Liss, Bernard Schoenfeld, and, of course, Archibald MacLeish. Orin Tovrov, another radio dramatist, actor Joe Julian, Arthur Miller, and Norman Rosten, all of them liberals, too, had sought work with OFF or the OWI, although unsuccessfully.

Early in 1943, New York State Congressman John Taber, one of OWI's main gadflies, made a two-pronged attack.[5] First he criticized an OWI film short in which Vice President Henry Wallace spoke of the "People's Revolution" and declared that the "common people" of the world "are on the march toward even greater freedom." The film, said Taber, was filled with communist ideas. He also criticized an OWI radio play, "Old Joe Mazerak," about a legendary Paul Bunyan of the steel mills. The newspaper article that reported his criticism provided no specifics on this latter charge. One can only speculate that it was the glorification of a working class model, a practice also common in Soviet propaganda, that upset the congressman.

In April 1943, Davis received letters from two groups attacking the OWI for its alleged communist influence. One came from the chairman of an organization called the Social Democratic Federation. The writer alleged that there were "fellow travelers," individuals whose ideas and or organizational affiliations were too "sympathetic" toward communism, in the OWI's New York Office." "Your letter . . . echoes a complaint which has been made by others," Davis volunteered. "We do not keep any known fellow travelers on our rolls, though we have some who used to travel, but have since reformed." "I can assure you," he continued, "that no one who is now a fellow traveler is wanted in our office. However, we do not feel that it is impossible to repent of past errors when proof of a real change of heart is available."[6]

The other letter originated from the vice chairman of the Constitutional Educational League of New York, an extreme right-wing organization headed by Joseph Kamp, distributor of the "Benjamin Franklin prophecy," an anti-Semitic forgery.[7] The letter leveled the same type of criticism as the one from the Social Democratic Federation. Although the group had no sizable constituency, after the writer sent a letter to members of Congress alleging that OWI was "employing many Communists," he succeeded in getting word of its accusation published in an article in the *New York Times*.

As Davis reported to President Roosevelt shortly before the dissolution of the OWI, over a three-year period, he fired thirty-five OWI employees because of alleged past communist associations.[8] According to his report, their loyalty to the United States was too dependent on the vicissitudes of Russian foreign policy. He explained further, "During the period of the Nazi Soviet Pact they were anti war. But after Hitler attacked Russia, they became zealous for the war against fascism." The criticism was typical of that leveled against members of the American left during the era.

As FBI files later showed, allegiance to the Soviet Union, as distinct from admiration, was virtually nonexistent among writers and others who worked for radio during the war. Yet some of them were fired from their jobs. Despite attempts to portray them as possible traitors, the real issue was that their thinking was not following the government's lead. For more than two years after the August 1939 signing of the Nazi-Soviet Pact, the United States maintained a policy of neutrality regarding the conflict in Europe, a policy that it gradually abandoned in the months before the attack on Pearl Harbor. Some Americans on the left, however, such as Langston Hughes, dared to advocate antifascism "ahead of schedule." Moreover, others went beyond Hughes, who just lent moral support, and jumped the gun by joining the Lincoln Brigade, the military unit made up of Americans who assisted Spanish Loyalists in the fight against Fascism. Such actions made people suspect and often resulted in the FBI hounding them on their return home.

One other allegation, that the OWI was harboring communists, is worth noting. As part of the effort to drum up support abroad for the Allied cause, the American Federation of Labor and the Congress of Industrial Organizations sponsored the Labor Short Wave Bureau, for which Morton Wishengrad worked. The unions provided broadcast material to the bureau about American labor and the OWI staffed it. However, the unions became concerned that the OWI broadcasts were emphasizing the role of communist labor leaders in America. They also alleged that Peter Lyon, one of the most prolific writers of war-related radio dramas and head of the labor desk, had past communist associations. As a result, he was transferred to another OWI post. The incident was later cited by the Red-baiters as part of a litany of allegations. However, the removal of Lyon and other liberals was a bit late and the leftist label stuck to the organization.

In addition to the allegations that the OWI was riddled with communists, it was faulted for being too pro-Roosevelt. What critics meant by this, at least in part, was that it was too progressive. An article by *Newsweek* writer Ralph Robey said of one OWI publication, "On almost every subject which is controversial the discussion is one-sided, incomplete, and prejudiced.[9] And the prejudice is always on the side of the Administration and the bureaucrats." Robey also charged the OWI with consistently favoring the administration in any of its disagreements with Congress. But critics also attacked it because some of its propaganda focused on the injustice of the situation of blacks vis-à-vis the war.

On whom could they take revenge? They could attack Elmer Davis and the domestic branch of "his" OWI, Roosevelt's personal advertising agency, as they had come to see it. Their opportunity came during the appropriations hearings that began in early 1943.

OWI AS CONSULTANT

Like its predecessor, the OWI both acted as a consultant and produced its own shows. The need for a centralized government information agency was clear. In one instance, a network writer wrote into a script a set of her own air raid rules, causing consternation from coast to coast. On a number of occasions, the OWI advised the networks to make major modifications of shows that they were planning. CBS's original idea for its show *The Man Behind the Gun*, for example, was to reflect solely the activities of men in the American Armed Forces. However, on the eve of production, at the agency's urging, the network agreed to have the series also deal with soldiers in Allied armies.

The OWI's collaboration with producers Hi Brown and Norman Corwin also illustrates its role as consultant. Smooth-talking Brown, one of radio's most prolific radio producers, grew up in Brooklyn and got an early start in radio when he obtained the radio rights to the Dick Tracy comic strip.[10] Still active in radio drama into the new millennium, Brown long ago earned the reputation of a doer, producing twenty to thirty half-hour shows that he sent around the country, all without the benefit of having an office.

In 1937, Brown went on the air with *Main Street, USA*, a weekly half-hour dramatic series on CBS. The show, produced in collaboration with the Federation of Jewish Philanthropies, reflected the influence of Kristallnacht and other events in Europe. Between June 1938 and the beginning of the war, Brown produced some twenty-five half-hour episodes of *Main Street* that attacked Nazism and domestic anti-Semitism. One particularly bold dramatization told of a fictional New Hampshire town that rejected a several million dollar bequest that had been made with the proviso that no Jews would benefit from it. Unfortunately, outside of Jewish listeners, *Main Street, USA* received little attention. Soon after the United States became involved in the war, *Main Street* became *Green Valley, USA* (i.e., "Anyplace USA"). Brown frequently wound up spending a part of his work week in Washington conferring with government officials about appropriate war-related themes to include in his shows.

"They want a story about China," or "This week it's giving blood," Brown would tell a writer for *Green Valley, USA* on his return to New York. The writer would then turn out a five-part story. Sometimes writers tired of the directives. Once, Brown called up Allan Sloane. "We need a show dealing with the blood drive, Allan." "No, Hi." Sloane replied. "I just did one for you on blood." "All right, Allan, do this one using a different blood type," Brown cajoled his writer.[11]

Green Valley, USA was an interesting example of radio in wartime.[12] It dealt with subjects of national importance, yet it was not a documentary. It ran five fifteen-minute individual stories each week and featured the same grocer, the same postman, and the same schoolteacher throughout its three-and-a-half years of existence, like a soap opera. Yet with its honest characterizations and situations, it did not fit the mold of the traditional soap opera.

With occasional scenes such as a knock on the door and a soldier saluting and saying, "We have news about your son," *Green Valley, USA* was a show and a community to which listeners could relate. Its opening, spoken by actor Santos Ortega, went "Hello, neighbor. Welcome back to Green Valley. I've got a story for you, about some people you probably know . . . people just like you, . . . important people, whose story is the life story of America." Each segment then went on to deal with a war-related theme. Sometimes it was the black market, racial discrimination, the enemy, or Lend-Lease to Russia. At other times it was Victory Gardens or the need to buy war bonds or to keep one's mouth shut.

Hi Brown brought to *Green Valley, USA* both his talents as a producer and director and a small troupe of accomplished actors who required minimal direction. Some of them, Mason Adams, Larry Haines, Ethel Everett, and, especially, Joe Julian had worked extensively for Norman Corwin. At least two members, Richard Widmark and Mercedes McCambridge, later became successful film actors.

There was an interesting contrast to Norman Corwin. The latter usually rehearsed his actors thoroughly, whereas Brown just handed out the pages of a script and started his watch. Amazingly he did all this plus two daytime soaps back to back, *Joyce Jordan* and *Girl Intern*, and two night-time regular half-hour series, *Nero Wolfe* and *Inner Sanctum*.

Millard Lampell was the first writer for *Green Valley, USA*. After Lampell put in a good word with Brown about Allan Sloane, Sloane became one of a stable of writers who "wrote to order." In various ways, Brown became Sloane's teacher. Sloane would dream up a story, run it by Brown for the latter's approval, and then write a week's worth of shows in one day. "It wasn't as hard as it sounds," Sloane recalled, "because each week's stories really added up to one half-hour's worth of drama. And I learned how to write for Hi's 'stock company.'"

Once, when Sloane presented Brown with a script that was too jam-packed, Brown taught him a lesson in radio production efficiency. "Allan," Brown said, "The script is wonderful. But you give me all these sound effects. For example, I'm looking at the scene in the barber shop. You give me a whole script for the background, the customers, the scissors, the razor strop, the kitchen sink. Allan, you're wasting paper and time. The average radio set in America has six tubes—and what the audience hears with all the sound levels you're giving them—they think something is wrong with the set."[13]

What Brown did not say was that such a script required actors to "double," meaning to play additional smaller roles. If they just said "rhubarb, rhubarb" to simulate background sounds of a group of people, it did not cost Brown anything. But if an actor said just one line as a new character, he was entitled to extra pay. At the end of the war, Brown turned *Green Valley, USA* into a half-hour series, featuring stories of soldiers being reunited with their families and the rekindling of a whole new world in a peaceful new economy.

Norman Corwin's role as collaborator with the OWI involved his work on three series: *An American in England, An American in Russia,* and *Passport for Adams.* In broad outline, this work was similar to what he did for OFF on *This Is War.* He did all three series as a CBS employee, but, unlike *This Is War,* the other three were broadcast in a normal manner, on just the one network. *Passport for Adams* came about in 1943 when the OWI asked CBS to develop a goodwill series on the subject of America's allies. It premiered in August and focused on a small town editor, Doug Adams, played by Robert Young, who had been chosen to visit the nations allied with the United States. Accompanying Adams was "Quiz," a blunt, confident, prejudiced, and somewhat ignorant photographer, played by Dane Clark. "Chief," said "Quiz," early in the series, "you don't seem to realize you're sending me out around the world with a guy [who] edits the *Dingville Bugle.* . . . You're going to hurt my reputation if you couple me up with an Eagle Scout."[14] With his narrow-mindedness, Quiz served as a foil to help the more liberal and democratic-minded Adams enlighten the listener.

Billboard praised *Passport for Adams,* calling it "a program jam-packed with mass appeal. Should do more for the home front and the eventual winning of the peace than all the verbiage spouted by stuffed shirts in the past year."[15] But John Hutchens, a *New York Times* reviewer, reacted quite differently. Ranald MacDougall wrote four shows in the "Passport" series. Six months earlier, Hutchens praised MacDougall for his work on another show, writing, "His dialogue is terse, colorful, realistic and shot through with hard-boiled and honest humor."[16] But now, he faulted MacDougall for "a prosy travelogue that never captures the living impact of even a routine short wave broadcast from a far place."[17] Hutchens also complained that the show sounded as though the writer took a fast look at the encyclopedia to get background stuff and that it lacked "images that move in the mind." Apparently, CBS shared Hutchens's view. As a result, Mac-Dougall left and Corwin himself wrote the remaining ones.

After eight weeks, the series was cut short, allegedly so that Corwin could meet what he called "prior commitments." Young took the cancellation the hardest. He had given the series priority over some other projects because he believed in its mission, to help the country understand our allies better.

Besides consulting on these large audience shows, the Domestic Radio Bureau fielded questions from radio stations around the country. In the spring of 1943, the chairman of a Florida Defense Council sent the OWI a locally produced play about a simulated air raid.[18] Joseph Liss of the Radio Bureau wrote back, discouraging the council from continuing with the project.[19] He warned the Florida group that their project risked running into the kind of public reaction that Orson Welles had created with his "The War of the Worlds" broadcast. No matter how many times the broadcasters reiterated that the program was fictional, Liss advised, the effect on listeners would be the same.

The OWI's involvement in directly producing war-related radio dramas mainly involved three series, *This Is Our Enemy*, *Uncle Sam,* and *Hasten the Day*. Frank Telford, who first directed *You Can't Do Business with Hitler* for the Office of Emergency Management, produced *This Is Our Enemy* in the late spring and summer of 1942. The new writer now was Bernard C. Schoenfeld, who worked for the Department of the Interior before the war. The series' thirty-minute plays were allegedly based on eyewitness accounts "by prominent figures in public life." Its purpose was to provide Americans "with an accurate and realistic interpretation of the Nazi ideology as expressed in the institutions and methodology of Axis 'New Order,' both in the German homeland and in the occupied countries of Europe."[20]

As the quote implies, the show clearly continued to emphasize Germany as the chief enemy. Of its sixty-eight installments, fifty-nine concerned Germany, seven dealt with Japan, and only two focused on Italy. Why the emphasis on Germany? Part of the reason was that months after the United States entered the war, most Americans still had a distorted view of Germany. Even in late spring of 1942 some 65 percent of the American people thought that the Germans wanted to get rid of their Nazi leaders. The nation that labeled Corwin and others who opposed fascism in the late 1930s as "premature fascists" was still somewhat deluded.

The technical quality of *This Is Our Enemy* was better than that of *You Can't Do Business with Hitler*, but it, too, pulled no punches. The show featured the talents of Frank Lovejoy as well as the deep mellifluous voice of Arnold Moss, who was heard in a number of Corwin productions among numerous other radio assignments.

By their more propagandistic nature, the OWI's broadcasts were open to even more criticism for increasing hatred toward the enemy than were Oboler's and Corwin's initial wartime plays. Lacking any subtlety, their most prominent feature was a heavy-handed use of the exclamation point. Nevertheless, perhaps because the public had become accustomed to a candid portrayal of the Axis powers, Schoenfeld's plays received far less attention than Oboler's and Corwin's. After their initial broadcast, the scripts from *This Is Our Enemy* were lent out via a catalog to schools around the country for classroom use.

UNCLE SAM

The *Uncle Sam* series, consisting of fifteen-minute transcribed, dramatic programs, began in the late winter of 1942–1943. Among its writers were Don Quinn, who had earlier worked on the popular commercial radio series *Fibber McGee and Molly*, and Norman Rosten. Radio stations were permitted to sell the series to local sponsors, and by the spring of the following year more than 250 stations had done so.

Many *Uncle Sam* episodes dealt with domestic themes, attacking racial discrimination, private hoarding during wartime, absenteeism from work, or the purchasing of black market goods. Others dealt with the importance of food as a weapon of war and the need for women to work in war industries. Programs about the fighting forces hailed the work of the Air Transport Command, the Seabees, physicians, and women's military units such as the WAVES. A third group focused on Nazi atrocities in Russia or the fighting assistance that the people in Nazi-occupied countries were giving.

NOT FOR GLORY AND HASTEN THE DAY

The Office of Civilian Defense produced two series entitled *Not for Glory* and *Hasten the Day* that dealt with problems of the Home Front. *Not for Glory*, which ran for thirteen weeks in 1943, told how average Americans were meeting wartime problems in their own communities. It employed some unusual techniques to attain a high degree of authenticity. Although it was fictionalized, it used real names and places on the air and recordings were made of some voices of the people being portrayed so that the actors could imitate them with some precision. At the end of each broadcast, a representative of the group whose achievements were dramatized was presented with a citation.

Hasten the Day, a series of weekly recorded fifteen-minute programs, began in August 1943. After a year, the OWI took it over from the Office of Civilian Defense. The series told a complete story about a member of the "Tucker" family, consisting of a war plant worker, his wife, two older sons who were in the service, a teenage daughter, a teenage son, and a five-year old. Woven into each story was information about a particular government campaign such as a war bond drive, the need to hold down prices, victory gardens, home canning, rent control, local manpower shortages, car pooling, juvenile delinquency, better breakfasts, back to school, the "crop corps," or security of war information.

SCRIPT CLEARANCE

To sanitize scripts for public consumption, the OWI's Domestic Radio Bureau established a script clearance section. Its purview included shows produced by government agencies and even some commercial ones. Woe to the script writer who became too florid in his description of how yellow the "Japs" were (it might offend the Chinese) or who too strongly emphasized the dangers to soldiers. Script clearance replaced the phrase "our men who are going to fight and die for us" that appeared in the original version of a show in *Chaplain Jim*, an NBC (Blue Network) series, with "our men who are going to fight and maybe die for us."[21] Similarly, the too-passive words of a seventy-year-old man, "They (the war Shipping Administration) want me back to sea," in a *Treasury Star Parade* show, were replaced with the more active "I want to go back to sea." And finally, an editor deleted a whole line from "Queens Die Proudly," another *Treasury Star Parade* episode. A character says "Your bombs are laid, and in that split second you quit working for the government and begin to work for your wives and families." The explanation for the deletion was, "There should be no differentiation between the people and the government any time. The government is the people. This war is not the government's war. It's ours."

These examples notwithstanding, it was not the job of script clearance or the OWI in general solely to whitewash images that government-produced radio projected. When an overzealous scriptwriter included the phrase, "In our country the weak have never been oppressed," script clearance deleted the line and, slapping his hand, wrote in the margin, "This remark is not true." Within limits, Archibald MacLeish's claim that the U.S. government had a "Strategy of Truth" was a valid one.

For all of OWI's good intentions and despite, or perhaps because of, the crusading spirit of its staff, its radio work was short lived. The same partisan politics that thwarted development of a centralized government propaganda agency before the attack on Pearl Harbor was responsible. The opportunity for FDR's and the OWI's enemies to strike came when the issue of the prospective funding of government propaganda for fiscal year 1944 came before Congress. In the summer of 1943, with congressmen such as John Taber in the lead, the House of Representatives voted to abolish the appropriations for the OWI's domestic branch. When Elmer Davis threatened to resign if the Senate did not restore the funds, the Senate Appropriations Committee agreed to give him $3 million for fiscal year 1944. But he was prohibited from using it for films, radio scripts, or publications. The house gave Davis a last kick by removing $250,000. The budget of the domestic branch was now just a third of what it had been. As a result of the cutbacks, the OWI closed twelve regional branches and its motion picture bureau and gave up publications.[22]

From mid 1943, the Domestic Branch's main function was to coordinate work of government agencies with that of the advertising industry. Most of the domestic propaganda and other war-related broadcasting was left up to the commercial media. In its crippled condition, the OWI continued to do what it could until the end of the war. "Not much work to do here," Joe Liss wrote sadly to a friend in August 1943.[23] Two years later, in mid September 1945, Elmer Davis wrote his last memo to his staff, "Tomorrow OWI will pass out of existence, as a war agency should when the war is over . . . we have been criticized; but again and again we have had the gratifying experience of finding some hostile critics completely changing."[24]

NOTES

1. New York *Daily News*, February 25, 1942, as cited in Gerhard Horten, "Radio Goes to War: The Cultural Politics of Propaganda during World War II." (Ph.D. diss., University of California at Berkeley, 1994), 79.

2. New York *Daily News*, April 9 and 11, 1942, as cited in Horten, "Radio Goes to War," 79.

3. Most of the following discussion concerning Elmer Davis, including these four quotes, is based on Ray Boomhower, "Elmer Davis: Defender of American Liberties," *Traces* (Fall 1997), vol. 9 (unpaginated): "the broadcaster "with the funny voice. Elmer—Elmer something"; "I could never understand . . . typewriter around?" "What in hell . . . a writer"; "Is Mr. Davis . . . military officer?"

4. Roger Burlingame, *Don't Let Them Scare You: The Life and Times of Elmer Davis* (Philadelphia: Lippincott, 1961), 186

5. Alex Singleton, "OWI Films Partly Drivel, Says Taber," *Washington Post*, March 14, 1943, 12:1.

6. Elmer Davis to William Karlin, Social Democratic Federation, August 17, 1942, NA 208-6E-13, Records of the Historian.

7. Kenneth Stewart, "The OWI and Its Critics," *New Republic* 109, no. 24 (Dec. 13, 1943): 844.

8. "Report to the President," 13 VI 42–15 ix 45, NA 208-6E-13, Records of the Historian, Subject file, 194–46.

9. Ralph Robey, "Battle Stations for All: Prejudiced Propaganda," *Newsweek*, May 3, 1943, 21:61.

10. The following discussion of Brown's career and *Green Valley, USA* is mostly based on the author's March 14, 1997, interview with him.

11. Allan Sloane, interview by author, New Canaan, Conn., April 15, 1999.

12. This part of the discussion is largely based on an undated letter from Allan Sloane to the author.

13. Allan Sloane to author, April 18, 1998.

14. See Norman Corwin's commentary on *Passport for Adams*, in Norman Corwin, *Untitled and Other Radio Dramas* (New York: Henry Holt, 1945), 366.

15. Lou Frankel in *Billboard* as quoted in Corwin, *Untitled*, 533.

16. John K. Hutchens, "Man Behind the Gun," *New York Times*, March 21, 1943, II, 9:1.

17. John K. Hutchens, "Airwaves Journal," *New York Times*, September 12, 1943, II, 7:1.

18. M. Allen Barth, Chairman, Defense Council of Dade County, Fla., to Elmer Davis, April 16, 1943, NA 208-140-749.

19. Joseph Liss to M. Allen Barth, April, 22, 1943, NA 208-140-749.

20. From the introduction to Bernard C. Schoenfeld, *This Is Our Enemy*, John Hay Library, Brown University.

21. The following examples of the work of the script clearance section can be found in a series of memos from Joseph Liss to Philip Cohen and William Spire (or to Cohen and Douglas Meservey) entitled "Report on the Activities of the Script Clearance Section . . ." in NA 208-96-631, folder "Script Clearance." For example, reference to the "yellow Japs" appeared in "Queens Die Proudly," *Treasury Star Parade*, n.d., Joseph Liss (and Helen Turner) to Philip Cohen and William Spire, "Report on the Activities . . . from May 18, 1943 to June 1, 1943," Memo dated June 1, 1943. Modified versions of phrases that Script Clearance altered appear next to the original versions, often with an explanation. In the example just cited, the censor explained that the phrase "our little yellow men" was cut "because the Chinese are also yellow-skinned. . . . This phrase smacks too much of typical racial prejudice."

22. John Morton Blum, *V Was for Victory* (New York: Harcourt Brace Jovanovich, 1976), 41.

23. Joe Liss to Brewster Morgan, August 3, 1943, Box 55, Liss Collection, BU.

24. Elmer Davis to all staff, September 14, 1945, NA 208-6E-13, Records of the Historian Subject file 1941–1946.

PRIVATE AGENCIES

A new propaganda organization has been set up in Washington recently, consisting of some 3,500 writers, headed by Rex Stout, well-known detective and pulp magazine writer. . . . Now we have the explanation why so many of the war stories released in Washington have so strong a flavor of Chicago gangsterism.

—German Ministry of Propaganda shortwave broadcast

Your name is Stanley. You live in Cincinnati, Ohio. It's 1939. For years you have been hearing people talk about Father Gerald Coughlin, the radio priest, whose ranting against President Roosevelt and against Jews is heard throughout the United States. At first, in about 1930, Father Coughlin's program of "social justice" got you thinking. It was a radical challenge to unbridled capitalism and you thought perhaps Coughlin was on to something. But gradually he became more and more of an extremist. You still have reservations about some of FDR's programs and you do not consider yourself a progressive. However, you voted for Roosevelt twice because you believed that he provides the leadership that the country needs in these hard times of the 1930s.

Father Coughlin's hatred of Roosevelt and his virulent anti-Semitism astound you. In November of last year, a week after the newspapers were filled with stories about the "Crystal Night" attacks on Jews in Germany and Austria, you heard him comment on the attacks. Instead of clearly condemning them, he called on Jews to join him in criticizing persecution of both Jews and Christians. Later, in another broadcast, as he has often done, he harped on what he called the prominent role that Jews had played in the birth of Soviet Communism.

In an argument with a friend who always defends Coughlin, you pointed out that even if Coughlin's interpretation of the role of many Jews in the Soviet government is accurate, American Jews deserved no more condemnation because of that than American Catholics deserved because many German Catholics helped create the German Nazi Party. You also heard Coughlin try to minimize the scope of the Crystal Night occurrence when he claimed that despite it, not one Jew was put to death officially for his race or religion. In addition, he condemned American Jews for wanting the United States to go to war allegedly under "the leadership of Jews" because of an "internal problem in Germany." Last week you asked your priest why the church didn't excommunicate Father Coughlin. "The church's umbrella is wide enough to cover people of many views," he replied. The answer did not satisfy you and you wondered where his own views lay.

In the months leading up to the attack on Pearl Harbor, a number of private organizations began to take steps to counter the broadcasts of bigots such as Father Coughlin and the Reverend Gerald L. K. Smith and help clarify what the Nazis really stood for. Among these organizations was a relatively new one, the American Council Against Nazi Propaganda, and some older ones, such as the American Jewish Committee and the National Council of Christians and Jews. In addition, both before U.S. entry into the war and immediately afterward, several other private groups, including the Hollywood Writers Mobilization (HWM), a Popular Front organization, the Council for Books in Wartime, and the Writers War Board, also came into existence. They, too, sought to help unify the nation and, now, overtly to support the war effort using radio.

THE AMERICAN JEWISH COMMITTEE

The American Jewish Committee (AJC) was founded in 1906. It first became involved with war-related broadcasting in 1937 when it contacted NBC and asked the network to nominate a Jewish employee to take a job with the AJC to start a radio unit. The AJC was interested in counteracting Nazi and domestic propaganda efforts to divide and conquer the American people. NBC had very few Jewish employees, and quickly the name of Milton Krents was proposed.[1] Krents, a native of Massachusetts, had moved to New York several years earlier to attend New York University. In 1935, he finished its law school and then, because of the scarcity of jobs due to the Depression, took a part-time job in the mail room at NBC. Some time later, he moved over to the accounting department, where he was working when he was nominated for the job with the AJC.

Krents turned out to be more than a good choice. He was able to comfortably wear many hats, knowing which one to put on when. He was also imaginative, confident, and a bit daring. At some point after he came to the AJC, a friend at station WMCA proposed an idea regarding the hated German-American Bund that was whipping up anti-Semitic sentiment through a series of public rallies. The Bund was scheduled to hold a large rally at Madison Square Garden. Would Krents be interested, asked his friend, in helping to plant a wire recorder underneath the rostrum at the Garden to record the rally's proceedings? Krents jumped at the chance and found funding for the project, and his friend successfully obtained a word-for-word account of the fascist supporters' speeches. After the war, Krents made them available to the prosecution at the trial of Fritz Kuhn, the head of the Bund, and his Bund associates.

At the AJC, Krents gradually went about the task assigned him. One strategy he employed was to cultivate contacts among advertising agencies and other organizations. His task was made easier because, in addition to his primary role at the AJC, he served as radio consultant for another organization, the Council for Democracy, which shared many of the AJC's concerns about the Nazi threat.

In early September 1941, Krents visited Washington, D.C., to become acquainted with radio officials connected with government agencies.[2] The trip illustrates the war-era connections between the various private agencies and the Roosevelt administration. The Council for Democracy wanted to cooperate with the government on research and program ideas. Krents met with officials of the Justice Department and the Treasury Department, as well as with Bernard Schoenfeld, radio director of the Office of Production Management and Emergency Management. During one of his meetings, Krents learned that the Department of the Army was seeking assistance in strengthening morale, particularly the morale of the families of draftees, whom it described as "largely responsible for the discontent and weak morale in the army which had been aroused through letters from home."

Working from the AJC, eventually Krents was able to integrate into existing programs ideas about intergroup relations to try to counter the poison of Nazi "divide and conquer" broadcasts. The *Uncle Don* show for children, for example, on Mutual's station WOR tried to teach children how to recognize antidemocratic propaganda. Krents also facilitated production of some dramatic shows about Jewish war heroes. Among them were two aired in the spring of 1943: a network broadcast about a machine gunner Wineberg and a program about the experiences of Sidney Cohen, an American who had joined the Royal Air Force.

THE COUNCIL FOR DEMOCRACY

In August 1940, a group of activists including Charles P. Taft, a moderate Republican from Ohio, and Freda Kirchwey, a politically leftwing journalist, organized a private agency, the Council for Democracy.[3] The council described itself as "devoted solely to the cause of democracy and broad enough to unite all loyal Americans." It's purpose was to counter both anti-Semitic propaganda from overseas and a broader range of domestic appeals to prejudice. It also developed a clear interventionist stance regarding the war in Europe. The council criticized racism in the military and elsewhere and took prolabor positions such as opposing legislation banning strikes.

At the beginning, the council was under the heavy influence of *Time* and *Life* magazine publisher Henry Luce. Its first president was Charles Douglas ("C. D.") Jackson, a multitalented, imaginative, and internationalist-minded Princeton graduate who had been brought up in Switzerland. By 1937, Jackson had worked his way up to general manager of *Life*. Among his talents was a knack for public relations, a quality that served the agency well.

Like several of the private agencies, the council had an elite membership and was well connected with the Roosevelt administration, with an impressive array of talent at its disposal. A council publication quoted prominent journalist and broadcaster William Shirer, who predicted that Hitler would attack the United States. In August 1941, the council sponsored a National Emergency Rally at Madison Square Garden. Fifteen thousand people came to hear Admiral Richard Byrd, poet Carl Sandberg, and others speak out in favor of national unity. Byrd called for "a spontaneous reawakening of all the people . . . exactly as if we were fighting a shooting war for our national self preservation against the dictator world."[4]

One of the council's hardest working and most gifted members was Pulitzer prize–winning poet Stephen Vincent Benét, who wrote most of the radio dramas that the council sponsored. Benét disliked many of the principles on which the Luce publications operated. Generally, they gave scant attention to the genocidal policies of the Nazi in regard to the Jews. And, in turn, so did the propaganda films and the propaganda radio plays and rallies that the council sponsored. However, Benét worked quite well with the *Time* employee whom Luce assigned to work with the council. It was the council that commissioned most of Benét's scripts of 1941 and 1942.

One of the council's most important successes involved the 1942 production of a six-part series of dramatized letters entitled *Dear Adolf*. The series began when Milton Krents approached NBC and proposed that the network do a prodemocracy program. He realized that he had to come up with something that the network would not normally be able to do itself. Thus, he proposed the idea of a dramatized series of letters to Hitler that would answer German propaganda. Krents also proposed Stephen Vincent Benét as author of the series. Krents had become friendly with Benét through contacts that he and his wife had with a literary agency in New York for which he also served as a radio consultant. Krents visited Benét at the poet's brownstone on 68th Street, and Benét readily agreed to the project.

The preparation for the series further illustrates the cooperation that took place among groups involved in producing wartime propaganda.

In early May 1942, Marshall Shulman of the council contacted the Office of Facts and Figures (OFF) requesting "valuable raw materials" in the numerous letters OFF received in response to broadcast of *This Is War*. The council wanted to get the authentic feel for the broadcasts. Shulman explained that he was aware that "many recent representations of the common types on the air have sounded phony."[5] He sought reports with sentiments of the farmers, businessmen, and four other groups that would be represented in the Benét series. Specifically, he wanted human interest incidents, reports concerning feelings about the war, and, in the case of farmers, accounts of the types of personal problems that they faced as a result of the war. In response, OFF obtained materials from the Department of Agriculture for Benét's use and had the Library of Congress send a set of recordings to give Benét "authentic voices of the people as we have recorded them."

Dear Adolf featured performances by Raymond Massey, Helen Hayes, Melvyn Douglas, James Cagney, and William Holden. Although the series was started at Krents's instigation, partly because of fear of anti-Semitic backlash, the AJC stayed in the background and the council was identified at the start of each of the broadcasts as the sponsor. The AJC also wanted to have the idea conveyed that the struggle was between the Nazis and the American people as a whole and not just between the Nazis and the Jews.

The various letters in the series, from a businessman, a housewife, a soldier, a worker, and an immigrant, were "enlivened by a sharp literacy and technical proficiency." "We'll choke you with wheat and corn, Adolf," says the Farmer, "we'll drown you in New York State milk." "Benét was making literary history," wrote Charles Fenton, one of the poet's biographers.[6] Apparently some listeners agreed. A young sailor heard one of the segments on a car radio while hitching from Milwaukee back to boot camp. "The program sounded at first like something from the *Farmer's Almanac*, he wrote afterwards to the Council. "Mr. Massey (the actor) was just to the point where he was listing the farm assets of the country as he went on interjecting a few satirical *Dear Adolf*s. I . . . immediately became conscious of the fact that I was listening to a masterpiece of satire delivered by a consummate artist. . . . I am city born and city bred. . . . I never had too much respect either for the farmer in general or for his particular value in our present war effort. However, as I listened to this letter, as the hundreds of Wisconsin Dairy Farms rolled by I felt a new confidence born of a new ally. In the future I shall think of the Army, the Navy, the Marine Corps and the Farmer."[7]

After six broadcasts, the series terminated in early August. *Time* praised *Dear Adolf* at its conclusion, calling it "The most engaging of U.S. fight-talk programs," and said of the decision to discontinue it, "Unlike many another morale program, it is quitting before the tread shows through the tires."[8] But network officials were so pleased with the series that they tried to talk Benét into continuing it with several more segments. An employee of the council even told Benét that NBC promised him a good job if he persuaded Benét to continue the series.[9] By 1942, however, the poet was a very sick man. In his better days he was a tall, loose-limbed man. But now he was gnarled, bent with arthritis, and dependent on pills to get a decent night's sleep. A friend wrote of him at this time, "He was the unhealthiest looking man I ever saw." Despite his weariness, Benét sought no easing of his propaganda load. The tragedy of his intensive propaganda work was that it may have hastened an early death. He died at the age of 44 only months after completion of *Dear Adolf*.

THE WRITERS WAR BOARD

The Writers War Board (WWB) was the most notable group that worked with the networks and the government to support production of war-related propaganda.[10] It began when Julian "Pete" Street, the head of the Treasury Department's writing staff, asked playwright Howard Lindsay to find some professional writers in New York to assist in the effort to sell war bonds. Lindsay's friend Russell Crouse pushed the process further by suggesting the idea of creating a committee of writers and recommended writer Rex Stout to head it.

Stout, a mystery writer, was the creator of Nero Wolfe, one of America's best-known fictional detectives. When approached, he agreed to take on the task if three conditions were met: that the committee be independent, that he have a free hand to personally select its members, and that the committee be able to finance its work in its own way. Lindsay agreed, and shortly after the New Year, the WWB had its first meeting, in the East 39th Street office of the Authors League in New York.

Like Alexander Woollcott, the goat-bearded and cigar-smoking Stout was a liberal and an early outspoken critic of Nazi Germany. One of his targets was "America Firster" and Hitler apologist Charles Lindbergh. Before the United States entered the war, Stout once predicted during a radio talk that if the Nazis succeeded in conquering the world, Lindbergh would be the collaborationist president of the United States.[11] Stout's outspokenness made him a controversial figure whom at least two critics publicly attacked. The first one, Congressman Hamilton Fish, called him "more dangerous than Earl Browder."[12] Browder was the head of the American Communist Party. The second person was Merwin Hart, a Nazi propagandist from Utica, New York. During the beginning of the McCarthy-blacklist era, citing Stout's founding of the journal *New Masses* as evidence, Hart told a congressional committee that Stout was a communist. Ironically, Stout had terminated his affiliation with the publication in protest at its adoption of the communist line.[13]

Although planned originally as a part-time endeavor, by the spring the WWB evolved into a quasi-official agency under the Office of War Information (OWI). With the help of an annual $34,000 government subsidy, it functioned as a clearing house to mobilize writers in support of the war effort. The group was closely tied to Washington. Mrs. Stout had met President Roosevelt in 1940 at a Hyde Park luncheon.[14] At various times, Stout and Clifton Fadiman, his chief aide, were in direct contact with the White House and with President and Mrs. Roosevelt themselves. Like Stout, Fadiman, the book review editor of the *New Yorker*, was a highly disciplined man with sharp perceptions. For many more than Stephen Vincent Benét, propaganda was now the order of the day.

Like its chairman, the WWB took a clearly liberal position on most of the issues that it addressed. As Thomas Howell, a scholar, pointed out, most of its villains were Republicans such as Senator Robert Taft and the conservative Congressman from New York, Hamilton Fish. However, the WWB was composed of members of both parties.[15]

Despite the WWB's subsidy and closeness to the government, it remained a fairly small group of about twenty members, and Stout continued as its chair. The group's core members met on a regular basis, usually on Wednesdays. Meetings began at mid afternoon and often lasted until late in the evening. Their purpose was to coordinate production of newspaper and magazine articles and stories, stage shows, and radio broadcasts with varying degrees of propaganda messages. Frequently, Stout would pose a problem and those present would then discuss how to solve it.[16]

The WWB's Radio Committee was one of its key divisions. It included among its members Arch Oboler; Erik Barnouw, NBC's Dutch-born director of scripts; and Carlton Morse, one of radio's most prolific producers, writers, and directors. Beginning in July 1942, the committee selected a "Script of the Month" and distributed it to radio stations and schools around the country. The first so designated was Stephen Vincent Benét's "They Burned the Books." Because of the WWB's cooperation with the OWI, the themes of the approximately seventy-two scripts that it distributed during the war often reflected the priorities that the government had decided to emphasize. The titles of some of them were "The Nature of the Enemy," "Foreigners Settled America," "Hate Incorporated," and "War Criminals and Punishment."

The WWB devoted special attention to problems of morale and recruiting, helping the Army, the Army Air Force, and the newly organized women's divisions of the military. Like Corwin and Oboler, it sought to convince Americans of the cancerous nature of the enemy and promote racial tolerance and harmony. Apparently, the new organization quickly got under the skin of the Hitler regime, because not long after the WWB's formation, the quotation at the beginning of this chapter appeared in a German Ministry of Propaganda broadcast. The reference to Washington (the organization remained based in New York) appears to be a convenient error.

One other focus of the WWB's work was to persuade Americans of the need for international cooperation and even world federation in the postwar era. "Most of us are . . . convinced that some form of international association is necessary after the war if we are not to commit world suicide in 1960," Fadiman wrote in a January 1943 letter to Stephen Vincent Benét.[17] Fadiman expressed the sentiment of some of the WWB's members: "Our first task, I think, is to make ordinary people see that it is possible."

To make the point that international cooperation was possible, and to try to convince Benét of the need for a radio play to persuade the public to support the idea, Fadiman cited the Soviet Union, "which has successfully blended 169 . . . races into what hardly can be called a democracy but is certainly a going concern." Fadiman suggested that Benét dramatize how the original thirteen colonies sacrificed part of their sovereignty to create a republic. "Today is the world's 1783," he argued, referring to the beginning of the republic. Fadiman clarified that he did not mean to imply that the nations needed to come together at once to form a world republic. But he argued that the type of world association that he had in mind did require that each nation give up at least "some of its sovereignty in the interest of the greater whole." The record does not show Benét's response to these suggestions. Although it appears clear that he never produced anything along the lines of what Fadiman was suggesting, in May 1945 the WWB did distribute copies of "They Shall Be Heard," a dramatic commentary about the founding of the United Nations in San Francisco, written by Benét's protégé Norman Rosten.

Most of the WWB's focus was on Nazi Germany rather than on Japan. WWB members believed, probably with some justification, that too many Americans felt that Germans were a people of good will who had been temporarily misled by their Nazi leadership. The group also was convinced that partly as a result of the attack on Pearl Harbor, American public opinion had been sufficiently mobilized against Japan and that many more Americans held hostile attitudes toward the Japanese than against the Germans. Public opinion polls tended to validate this perception.

Toward the end of the war, the WWB fell into disfavor in Washington. A federal official's report a month before the end of the war claimed that the WWB was making inefficient use of its government subsidy. The report also described the WWB's dozen employees as "engaged in doing very little, in a rather spacious office."[18] The observer criticized the WWB for hiring a private firm to do duplication and stamp and mail thousands of pieces of mail. Edward Klauber, assistant director of OWI, was instrumental in cutting off WWB's subsidy, calling it a political liability. Klauber viewed the organization as being too involved in what he characterized as "pri-

vate" projects, such as campaigns against the use of racial stereotypes in the media.

THE HOLLYWOOD WRITERS MOBILIZATION

The Hollywood Writers Mobilization (HWM), the WWB's west coast
equivalent, was also established immediately after the attack on Pearl
Harbor. Like the WWB, the HWM served as a clearinghouse, enlisting some 3,500 writers. Whether because of an inevitable rivalry or because the criticism was warranted, several critics, one of them a WWB
member, viewed the HWM in a negative light. In an undated memo,
he reported to WWB Chairman Stout about the west coast organization, apparently after visiting Hollywood. "Hollywood Mobilization
talks a great deal but does not accomplish much," he alleged. "There
are some first class people who want to help, . . . but better action is
secured when OWI goes to them direct rather than through the committee. . . . They have no regular organization of their own. . . . They
seem to have an inferiority complex. . . . They live in the shadow of the
Hollywood Victory Committee . . . [and] the Writers War Board, which
seems to be physically closer to Washington. . . . Hollywood radio writers seem to know more about the War WWB than about the Hollywood Mobilization. They say the WWB is composed of leaders in their
lines, HMC [sic] is not."[19]

One project backed by the HWM was a series entitled *Free World
Theatre* that NBC's wunderkind Arch Oboler produced in the first
half of 1943. Oboler had produced at least seventy "beat the Axis" radio plays in the previous year alone. His first post–Pearl Harbor series, *Plays for Americans,* premiered the same month as Corwin's *This
Is War.* Its first offering was a short piece starring James Stewart and
Mercedes McCambridge.[20] Reviewing the first five plays, the *New
York Times* gave it a generally favorable judgment: "The significance
of Mr. Oboler's current series," wrote the *Times* critic, "is that they
were written for this time and that behind them is the urgency of his
indignation. . . . Had he waited or worked more slowly they might
have acquired a certain polish; almost certainly they would have lost a
(great) deal of immediate force."[21]

Free World Theatre arose from Oboler's discussions with the OWI, the WWB, and the HWM. Its purpose was to illustrate the war and peace aims of the United Nations, as the western Allies called themselves. As Oboler began to work on *Free World Theatre*, he grappled with the same problem that Corwin encountered: trying to produce quality scripts while under pressure.

In the preface to a published version of the *Free World Theatre* plays, Oboler hinted at the trouble that seemed to beset the series right from the start. He had decided to base each play on a quote from a prominent world figure. To this end he spent a month writing individual letters to leaders all over the world asking each for an idea, a quote, suitable for radio dramatization. Aldous Huxley sent a four-page reply in an almost illegible handwriting. German novelist Thomas Mann sent a vitriolic summary of the growth and meaning of Nazi doctrine. But George Bernard Shaw and several others were unimpressed. Shaw replied bluntly "I don't think the project will prove workable."[22] In his typical scrappy manner, Oboler saw fit to mention this in his preface. "It is amusing to remember," Oboler commented, "at this moment of recapitulation, the skepticism of numerous radio-wise individuals who warned that this sort of collaborative venture could never succeed in a medium such as radio, where work must be produced for a split-second deadline."[23]

In addition to the discouragement contained in Shaw's warning, Oboler encountered problems from the WWB, with which he met at the end of October. Initially, the group gave some support. But later it concluded that he was trying to bite off more than he could chew. "There simply is not an adequate supply of sufficient first grade talent to furnish so large an amount of exceptional work in so short a time," they advised the OWI in Washington.[24] Rex Stout of the WWB wired a similar message to Oboler.[25] In reply, Oboler told Stout during a subsequent telephone conversation, "Look at the record. Thirteen of the *Plays for Americans* out of a series of 23 plays I recently did are now on the book stands . . . remember further that these ideas were all original with me." Oboler complained that a series "which I can do very easily . . . is now being theorized to death." In his vintage style, Oboler also boasted, "I know enough name authors personally (out here we have Thomas Mann, Aldous Huxley and a dozen more name authors, and I'm sure that a cable to Mr. Churchill from me would get some answer) but I do want to do this series through the WWB as you suggested."[26]

In the end, the OWI overrode Stout's objections and the series went ahead. Its first program was a collection of quick sketches of two wounded soldiers on a Pacific Island and of families in Norway and Holland, all heartened by a speech that they heard on shortwave radio from America. "Oboler . . . threw away his own small candle," wrote *Newsweek*, "and started illuminating the victory road with a battery of bigger and brighter lights."[27] However, by April, Cornwell Jackson of the OWI's West Coast office perceived the series quite differently. "I think the OWI credit line should be withdrawn from *Free World Theatre*," he wrote to Washington. "There is rarely any relationship between the as-broadcast scripts and the statements that allegedly inspire them." He went on to describe the show as becoming "dangerously close to political propaganda," and added insult to injury saying "perhaps most important of all they aren't very entertaining."[28] Two days later, OWI headquarters replied. "We accept your judgment. . . . Ask that credit be withdrawn."[29]

In the fall of 1943, the HWM convinced Robert Sproul, president of the University of California, Los Angeles, to cosponsor a congress of writers on the university campus. The congress was to discuss the role of writers in the war. Once word of the planned conference got out, California State Senator Tenney tried to persuade Sproul to cancel the congress, arguing that it was communist inspired.[30] When Sproul ignored Tenney's request, Tenney held two days of hearings on the congress and on the HWM. In fact, although there were communists within the HWM, it was hardly a communist-run organization. Some HWM members sponsored a large demonstration against American Nazi Gerald L. K. Smith, the sort of activity that appealed to the radical left. Otherwise, to a great extent the left was largely submerged within the HWM.

In 1944 the HWM sponsored a series of seminars that dealt with the problems of the returning soldier. The seminars focused realistically on the broad problems of adjustment that both soldiers and civilians would need to make as a result of the demobilization that would soon occur. One result of the seminars was production of a series of radio plays entitled *Reunion, USA*.

THE COUNCIL FOR BOOKS IN WARTIME

Like the WWB and the Council for Democracy, the Council for Books in Wartime was located in New York City. It, too, was effective in spreading a great deal of war propaganda. A group of publishers, notably from Farrar and Rinehart, created the organization. It was based first in a room of the Book Publishers Bureau and then in an office on Madison Avenue.

Like both of the other organizations, the 'Books Council' was adept at public relations. One of its first steps was to contact NBC's Erik Barnouw to propose a quiz show. Barnouw responded with a counterproposal for what he saw as a better idea, a series of dramatized adaptations of war-related books. Thus, beginning in the spring of 1943, NBC presented *Words at War,* a program based on the Barnouw format and with Barnouw as editor. For most of its run, the series was sustained, except during a brief period when it was sponsored by Johnson's Wax.

Words at War was one of the best quality shows of the war. Among its directors were Anton Leader and Joseph Losey. Boston-born Leader was an ascetic-looking, slim man with pale green eyes. "He looked like an artist," said an actor who recalled him years after Leader's death in 1988. Leader was a founder of the Radio and Television Directors Union and served for a while as its president. In contrast to a director such as William Robson, Leader had a quiet manner in the control room. Like Corwin and other radio principals of his generation, he loved the public service end of radio. He often succeeded in inserting social content messages into the show in the fashion of latter-day television programs such as *The Twilight Zone*, *M°A°S°H,* and *Star Trek*.

Words at War frequently addressed major issues, particularly on the home front. Sometimes, however, Barnouw and his staff had to fight to be able to broadcast such "social action" programs. For example, once the brass vetoed a program attacking anti-Semitism that Barnouw proposed. Barnouw was told, "This will open us to the charge that we are 'Jew dominated.' And this would be embarrassing to Mr. Sarnoff."[31] David Sarnoff, NBC's president, was a Jew. To get around such problems, the staff became adept at presenting programs that avoided the obvious but subtly got a message across.

In April 1945, the show presented an unusual broadcast, "They Left the Back Door Open," that touched on the topic of the Spanish Civil War.[32] The war in Spain, a controversial one for Americans, had been more or less taboo as a subject for radio drama. Americans on the left tended to see it as a clear-cut struggle between the fascists, aided by Hitler and Mussolini, and an antifascist coalition. However, many Americans, particularly the vast majority of conservative American Catholics, sympathized with the ultimately victorious fascist Franco forces. They perceived Franco as an ally of the church at the same time that they viewed the Loyalists who had international communist support as its enemies. "They Left the Back Door Open" concerns Bill Donaldson, a Canadian who moves to Britain during the time of the war in Spain. Bill joins the British Army and then, when Britain refuses to help the Spanish loyalists, deserts just before his unit is to be sent to India and travels to Spain to join the Loyalist side.

One of the show's most recognized broadcasts was "Assignment USA," based on a book that reported on a nationwide tour by its author Selden Menefee. The broadcast praised the war effort and showed an understanding of sectional problems. But it startled listeners, boldly castigating specific American cities and regions for their racism, anti-Semitism, and economic discrimination. Boston, for example, had earlier experienced riots. "We'll have to set about getting Boston into the United States," listeners heard.[33] Of Mobile, Alabama, a city full of war wealth and resulting problems of vice, the broadcast proclaimed "Mobile ain't fit to live in." "Assignment USA" also cited racial prejudice in the South, isolationist movements in the Midwest, anti-Semitic activity in New England, and labor management clashes throughout the country. The script related these problems to their effect on the war effort. The broadcast was one of the first war dramatizations to deal with the dangerous conflicts and undercurrents affecting national life in peace and war. *Variety* praised "Assignment USA" and recommended its rebroadcast. But Boston station WBZ and a station in Alabama banned the repeat program. Among other books that provided the basis for dramatizations were *One World* by Wendell Willkie, *Here Is Your War* by Ernie Pyle, and *A Bell for Adano* by John Hersey.

Words at War featured two prominent commentators: literary critic Carl Van Doren and Clifton Fadiman. Fadiman was with the show for a number of months until July 1944 when he resigned out of protest at the proposed broadcast of "Traveler from Tokyo." The script and the book on which it was based promoted the theory that Japan had fallen into the hands of a small group of gangsters. Fadiman believed that this theory was too soft on the Japanese. Just as he believed in the collective guilt of the German masses, he blamed the Japanese for consciously accepting evil. In a letter to Richard MacDonagh, manager of the series's script division, Fadiman wrote, "The patriotism of yourself and the Council is, of course, unquestioned. Yet without meaning to do so, I firmly believe you are impeding victory and certainly miseducating the American citizen by your proposed presentation of [the] book."[34]

Words at War was honored in March 1945 with a citation from *Variety* "for dramatizing some of the finest words that have come out of the war dealing with the vital issues that confront the country today." Unfortunately, the series came to a controversial end in the spring of 1945.

THE RED CROSS

The American Red Cross was founded in 1881 to help with disaster relief, services to the Armed Forces and veterans, and public health and safety programs. Among private organizations, it was one of the most prolific producers of wartime radio drama. Virtually all of its radio productions, dramatic and otherwise, sought to promote Red Cross programs and needs. During the war these included coordinating blood drives, recruiting nurses, promoting first aid education, and providing assistance to the Armed Forces.

Because of the "motherhood" and "apple pie" status of the Red Cross and its work, doors opened easily for the organization and it obtained the support and volunteer efforts of many prominent people. Among the film stars who performed in Red Cross–sponsored radio dramas were Fredric March, Helen Hayes, Ralph Bellamy, Paul Muni, and Richard Widmark. Peter Lyon and Milton Geiger were among the writers.

Thus We Live was one of the four or five major wartime Red Cross series. An April 1942 broadcast was typical of the way the series promoted the organization. It tells of a soldier who develops a morale problem after receipt of a letter from his wife Rose and how the Red Cross helps him to resolve it. The broadcast was atypical, however, in one respect. The usual wartime radio drama featured a protagonist with a WASP name, perhaps "Bob Dawkins" or "Pete Harris" or an occasional Irish-American name. This show, however, features "Johnny Torelli," "a husky broad shouldered American of Italian ancestry."

The listener knows Johnny has a problem when he tells a fellow soldier "Look fella, the way I act is my own business! I'm not askin' any favors from you and I don't want any advice either!"[35] The root of Johnny's problem is that Rose is having difficulty with her "stepmother and the stepmother's lazy good-for-nothing daughters." The stepmother and her daughters are taking most of the money that Johnny sends home each month, money Rose needs "to buy oranges and things like that for the baby." In this case the Red Cross comes to the rescue by sending a Home Service Worker who helps Rose get a new place to live—and a job. And more. The Red Cross arranges for a home furlough for Johnny.

CONCLUSION

The Writers War Board and the other five agencies described in this chapter all helped disseminate programs to promote morale among the American people during World War II. In fact, four of these agencies owed their very existence to the war effort and were disbanded soon after the war. Despite the government connections and even subsidies that some of these agencies possessed, their wartime roles largely reflect American faith in individualism. Nazi Germany, in contrast, as befit a totalitarian system, allowed only one avenue for mobilizing mass opinion, the German Ministry of Propaganda, headed by Joseph Goebbels. Even in democratic Britain, the government held a monopoly on the means of propagandizing its people, the BBC. Besides the shows that the WWB and its sister agencies produced, another type of show, commercially sponsored ones, joined the flood of war-related radio dramas.

NOTES

1. The following account is based on Milton Krents's interview by Jill Levine, New York City, 1979, NYPL-AJC.

2. Milton Krents, report on Washington trip, September 1941, Box 235 file "1940–1941," files of the American Jewish Committee at the YIVO Institute for Jewish Research.

3. Robert Herzstein, *Henry R. Luce: A Political Portrait of the Man Who Created the American Century* (New York: Charles Scribner's Sons, 1994), 217.

4. *Action: A Fortnightly Newsletter for Defence* (New York: Council for Democracy), no. 4 (September 1, 1941), 4.

5. Marshall Shulman to Philip Cohen, May 7, 1942, NA 208-5-21.

6. Charles A. Fenton, *Stephen Vincent Benét, the Life and Times of an American Man of Letters, 1898–1943* (New Haven, Conn.: Yale University Press, 1958), 369.

7. Milard King Roper to Council for Democracy, n.d., Benét Collection, YALE.

8. "Dear Adolf," *Time*, August 3, 1942, 50.

9. "Dear Adolf," *Time*, 50.

10. Except where otherwise indicated this section is based on John McAleer, *Rex Stout: A Biography* (Boston: Little Brown, 1977).

11. Thomas Howell, "The Writers War Board: Writers and World War II" (Ph.D. diss., Louisiana State University, 1971), 18.

12. McAleer, *Rex Stout*, 333.

13. No doubt Hart intended his testimony as retribution. Seven years earlier, Stout had a hand in publicly labeling him "an American Quisling" for which Hart unsuccessfully sued him for libel. See McAleer, *Rex Stout*, 325–326 and 381.

14. McAleer, *Rex Stout*, 281.

15. Howell, "The Writers War Board," 508.

16. McAleer, *Rex Stout*, 311.

17. Clifton Fadiman to Stephen Vincent Benét, January 12, 1943, UNCAT Za Benét Collection, YALE.

18. Harold Craske, Regional Attorney, O.D., N.Y., to Thomas Bracken, General Counsel, O.D., April 18, 1945, RG 208-6A-5, Records of the OWI, Records of the Historian, Relating to the Domestic Branch, 1942–1945.

19. Bob Colwell to Rex Stout, n.d., Box 126, WWB Collection, Hollywood Writers Mobilization folder, LOC.

20. Arch Oboler, "Letter at Midnight," in *Plays for Americans* (New York: Farrar & Rinehart, 1942), 3–19.

21. John Hutchens, "Angry Writer," *New York Times,* March 8, 1942 ,VIII 10:1.

22. Arch Oboler, *Free World Theatre: Nineteen New Radio Plays* (New York: Random House, 1944), xiv.

23. Oboler, *Free World Theatre,* xiii–xiv.

24. William B. Lewis to Arch Oboler, November 2, 1942, NA 208-92–594.

25. Oboler mentions this in a letter; see Arch Oboler to William B. Lewis, November 3, 1942, NA 208-92-594.

26. Oboler to Lewis, November 3, 1942.

27. "Oboler's Free World," *Newsweek,* March 1, 1943, 74.

28. Cornwell Jackson to Donald Stauffer, OWI Washington office, April, 10, 1943, NA 208-95-625.

29. Philip Cohen to Cornwell Jackson, OWI Washington office, April, 12, 1943, NA 208-95-625.

30. Nancy Lynn Schwartz, *The Hollywood Writers' War* (New York: Knopf, 1982), 199–200.

31. The Reminiscences of Erik Barnouw, 1975, p. 37, CUOHROC.

32. L. S. B. Shapiro, "They Left the Back Door Open," adapted by Edward Jurist, episode 93, April 17, 1945, Box 499, folder 4, *Words at War,* NBC Collection, WISC.

33 Selden Menefee, "Assignment USA," adapted by Richard McDonagh, episode 37, February 22, 1944, Box 501, folder 1, *Words at War,* NBC Collection, WISC.

34. Clifton Fadiman to Richard McDonagh, July 19, 1944, Box 22, folder 4, The Council of Books in Wartime, Public Policy Papers, Princeton University Library. Published with permission of Princeton University Library.

35. Script #2, *Thus We Live,* April 1942, American Red Cross Central File, 1935–1946, Group 3, NA 200, Box 40, 020.32 (#1-10).

8

SPONSORED RADIO DRAMAS

Opening in the war's most critical year, *Words at War* hit the air
with a punch that no postwar "now it can be told" rehash could
ever match . . . the success of *Words* was the immediacy of its subject matter. . . . This atmosphere—of a country fighting for its
life—gave the stories maximum impact, with no holds barred save
those of government-imposed security.

—John Dunning, *On the Air*

Your name is Barbara.[1] *You live in an apartment in New York City, in the
Borough of Queens. Your family has been living with the war for a year
and a half. As it has intensified, so, too, have the air raid drills. They usually take place as soon as it gets dark enough, which means there can be
no lights anywhere. Last night, as your family often has done, they gathered around the radio in the kitchen to listen to the* Lux Radio Theatre.
*It's one of the weekly highlights of your lives. While you were listening,
an air raid drill began. You, your brother, and your mother, of course,
quickly turned out the lights, drew the curtains and blinds, and then returned to the radio. A few minutes later, much to everybody's surprise,
the warden yelled out, "Lights out on the 4th floor apartment." You all
realized that it was the radio. It was powered by lighted tubes. You were
loath to turn it off but had no choice. You certainly did not want to see*

the city of New York go up in flames from the bombers homing in to the radio's light. But your mother suddenly solved the problem by covering the kitchen table with blankets that went to the floor. You all crawled into the makeshift dark room and finished listening to the program without uttering a sound.

Unlike *Lux Radio Theatre,* most of the radio dramas that promoted the war effort were part of unsponsored "sustained" series. As *The Free Company* or *This Is War* series demonstrate with their attacks on racism, such shows often reflected the progressive values of their writers. CBS particularly, through Norman Corwin, Bill Robson, and a number of others, provided a remarkable voice against repression and in favor of tolerance.

Commercially sponsored shows not surprisingly often reflected more conservative values than did sustained ones. Some of the same progressive writers who worked on sustained shows, Allan Sloane, Norman Rosten, Peter Lyon, Morton Wishengrad, and Arch Oboler, for example, also wrote for commercially sponsored ones. However, under the watchful eyes of the companies' or the sponsors' supervisors these writers toed a more conservative story line.

Foremost among the commercially sponsored dramatic shows that included at least some important level of war-related material were the *The March of Time* and the *Cavalcade of America,* both produced by Batten, Barten, Durstine and Osborn (BBD&O), the advertising agency, and *Lux Radio Theatre. The March of Time,* begun in 1928, was a dramatized newsreel, in a class by itself. The other two series also began before the war, but as shows of pure entertainment. After Pearl Harbor was attacked, however, these series devoted significant amounts of air time to the war. Two other commercial shows, *The Doctor Fights* and *Ceiling Unlimited,* only began during the war and were devoted totally to supporting the war effort.

THE MARCH OF TIME

The March of Time used dramatic techniques, although none of its broadcasts could truly be called dramas. Originating with a series of ten-minute broadcasts at Cincinnati station WLW, it was radio's first newsreel.[2] The program was the brainchild of Fred Smith, the station's manager, who wanted to provide radio with an alternative source to the wire services, which at the time were offering their facilities only to the print media. As a result, radio could only rewrite stories from the day's newspapers and then broadcast bulletins as though they were fresh news.

Smith came up with the idea of dramatizing the news to give it an immediacy that would bring listeners right into the events they were hearing. In pursuit of his plan, he contacted *Time*'s circulation manager, Roy Larson, and proposed a collaboration. The station obtained the ability to present timely news reports, and *Time* got publicity and a chance to get new advertising accounts. The success of the show spawned a number of imitators as well as a film version that *Time* produced for movie theaters.

Despite its initial success, in late 1931 *The March of Time* was reported to be losing money for *Time,* which announced that it would soon be discontinuing the series. When word of the planned cancellation reached the public, 22,000 listeners wrote letters of protest. "If *The March of Time* goes off the air," wrote one man, "my radio set goes out the window with a bang that will be heard from Madison, Wisconsin, to the east end of New York's Forty-Second Street." The company backed down, and for a while CBS absorbed the production costs, presenting it as a sustaining show, while *Time* continued to get the credit from the announcement that preceded each show: "Presented by the editors of *Time*." Eventually several commercial sponsors, including Remington Rand and Wrigley Chewing Gum took it on. Wrigley terminated its sponsorship in the late 1930s after a number of German groups complained about *Time*'s increasing anti-Nazism.

For much of its run, *The March of Time* featured a core company of ten New York actors, including Orson Welles, all of whom imitated the most regular newsmakers. Art Carney regularly played the role of Franklin Delano Roosevelt, finely imitating his patrician accent. Ted de Corsia mastered the voices of Benito Mussolini and Pierre Laval; Agnes Moorehead and Jeanette Nolan imitated Eleanor Roosevelt; Dwight Weist did renditions of Adolf Hitler, Joseph Goebbels, William Randolph Hearst, and Father Charles Coughlin, among others. In addition, the *March of Time* maintained a list of another 700 actors who had special talents, such as voices of Swedes, gnomes, babies, and others.

A number of stories testify to the proficiency of cast members' imitations. Once, actor Gil Mack's wife was at home listening to *The March of Time*. Her husband was playing the role of FDR delivering the memorable inaugural address in which he uttered "The only thing we have to fear is fear itself." Just then, a man who regularly stopped by to sell fresh eggs knocked on the door. "Shhh," Mrs. Mack told him as she let him into the house. "I'm listening to my husband." The man left quickly after giving her a strange look, never to return.[3]

Dwight Weist once described his experience in mimicking Adolf Hitler over a period of at least six years. Initially it involved depicting Hitler's increasing confidence as he rose to power. Later, Weist found himself imitating the Führer's increasingly nervous speech characteristics as the Allies step by step thwarted his plans of conquest. Elaborating, Weist wrote "inflection is the first element of a voice that impresses a listener, next tonal quality, and lastly pitch. . . . An impersonator is faced often times with certain compromises in order to convey the correct impression to the listener. For example, most of us recognize Hitler by the high-pitched hysterical quality he uses during the climaxes . . . of his speeches. His normal voice is rather low (baritone), and it is only when he shouts that his voice becomes high, as does anyone's. In playing a conversational scene, however, that impersonator must always bear in mind that the normal quality is not the quality that the listener is accustomed to hear. The impersonator must cheat a little and raise the pitch and add a few hysterics, even if the scene does not require it."[4]

The March of Time demanded more from its actors than just proficiency. Frequently, it broadcast breaking news stories with no time for rehearsal. This meant that actors had to do sight readings, working with scripts that they were seeing for the first time. They learned to read ahead two lines while voicing ones they had already read.

With the training and experience that *The March of Time* gave its cast, it became a major spawning ground for some of radio's best actors and a couple of its best directors. In pioneering the practice of restaging history for a mass audience, it also provided a model for many subsequent shows. Calling the program the finest thing done on radio, radio director Bill Robson acknowledged its impact on him and credited it with influencing the whole era of radio's Golden Age.

Periodically, critics from both the left and the right attacked the show. Communists occasionally blasted it as a fascist program, and William Randolph Hearst, who banned mention of it in his newspapers, labeled it as communist propaganda. Germany also banned the program, and, at one point, President Roosevelt demanded that the show pull its impersonators of him off the air.

In 1938, Hitler was the most imitated person on the show, Stalin and a Japanese political figure tied for second place, and FDR was third. The following excerpt from a September broadcast of that year gives a little flavor of the show. It concerns British Prime Minister Neville Chamberlain, whose name came to be synonymous with "appeasement." Chamberlain is about to fly to meet with Hitler to try to resolve the Munich Crisis.

> RADIO: One moment, sir . . . Could you just say a few words, Mr. Chamberlain . . . to our listeners?
>
> CHAMBERLAIN: Very well. I am going to see the German Chancellor because the situation seems to me . . . to be one in which discussions between him and me may have useful consequences. My policy has always been to try to ensure peace . . . and the Führer's ready acceptance of my suggestion encourages me to hope that my visit to him will not be without much result.
>
> RADIO: Thank you, sir . . . thank you . . .
>
> CHAMBERLAIN: Well, Halifax, I'll keep in touch with you through Neville Henderson . . .
>
> HALIFAX: The very best of luck, Neville . . .
>
> CHAMBERLAIN: I hope so. I sincerely hope so. Good-by . . . good-by . . .
>
> SOUND: PLANE DOOR SHUTS . . . MOTOR GUNNING.[5]

The year after this broadcast *The March of Time* was discontinued, only to be revived in 1941. This pattern occurred twice more during the war years. In 1942, it changed from a full half-hour of dramatizations to a combination of only one or two such broadcasts with a series of "on the spot" reports. The dramatic spots tended to deal with news that while important had not likely been presented already. For example, instead of presenting the life of Mussolini after his fall from power in July 1943, a subject with which many other programs were dealing, *The March of Time* dramatized the less familiar story of the background to the fall of Corsica. It also dramatized news events such as the Dutch aerial and naval counteroffensive, MacArthur's heroic stand on Corregidor and Bataan, and the march of 100,000 Chinese troops to relieve Burma. The show ran through the war years and then was finally discontinued for good in 1945.

CAVALCADE OF AMERICA

In 1935, BBD&O began to produce the *Cavalcade of America* on NBC for the Du Pont Company.[6] Du Pont's goal was to improve its image by its association with a show that dramatized positive features of American history. Initially, the series featured broadcasts such as the two-part "The Spirit of Competition," which presented one segment about the Oklahoma land rush and a second about a Mississippi steamer race. Later came biographical sketches of people such as Samuel Morse, Daniel Boone, John Paul Jones, and Charles Goodyear, inventor of vulcanized rubber. Even the series's war-related broadcasts stuck to established ways of saying things and avoided focusing on ideas or on clarifying problems and issues.

The series was noted for several prejudices. For years, it generally steered clear of historical events beyond the 1890s, avoided black-related themes, and refused to employ black actors or handle scripts that criticized the rich. "It has been called to my attention," wrote Anne Tanneyhill of the National Urban League to Truman Gibson, the black civilian aide to the Secretary of War, "that it is almost impossible to 'crack' *Cavalcade* with scripts [about black Americans] and when one does the advertising agency so restricts the scriptwriter that the original meaning and intention are often lost."[7] *Cavalcade's* policy was also to avoid any "heavies." The joke at BBD&O, according to Bob Foreman, retired head of creative programming at the agency, was that the one exception was King George III, who could be bad mouthed in shows that dealt with the American Revolution. But saying anything negative about Hitler, Franco, or Mussolini was taboo.[8]

During the 1930s, the Du Pont Company helped finance the Liberty League, a far-right pressure group composed of financiers, industrialists, conservative Democrats, and corporate lawyers. Nevertheless, by the end of the decade, the company's expansion into textiles and plastics, reports of various breakthroughs in its laboratories, and the *Cavalcade*'s adroit projection of the company's image resulted in an improved public perception of it.

With America's entry into the war in 1941, the producers finally altered their view of history. Now history came more and more to include what had happened a few months ago on the African front or in Burma. In dealing with major themes such as freedom of religion, for example, instead of the often-told story of Roger Williams, the *Cavalcade* presented Arthur Miller's "Listen to the Sound of Wings," a show about the German Protestant Pastor Martin Niemoller.[9] This broadcast described how Niemoller stood firm on his religious beliefs, defied Hitler, and then suffered eight years of imprisonment.

By early 1943, the *Cavalcade* was regularly presenting shows to help support the war effort. But the shift notwithstanding, BBD&O's and Du Pont's dealings were characterized by a pronounced political conservatism as well as some anti-Semitism. Arthur Miller remembered that once while he was visiting the studio, Homer Fickett, the show's director, noticed that Miller was carrying a copy of *New Masses*, a leftist publication.[10] Fickett made him hide it deep in his coat pocket before some "closely shaved executives" found him out. Among those "closely shaved executives" was Bruce Barton, one of the agency's founders, a political conservative and isolationist who served in the House of Representatives for several years. He was a staunch opponent of Roosevelt and the New Deal, and he gave his public relations expertise to many Republican candidates over the years.

The anti-Semitism was subtle but clear, as it often was in the corporate world of the 1930s and 1940s. Miller also recalled Fickett saying, "They told me they'd rather you and Rosten not be around here." A few years later, when Eric Barnouw served a stint as the series editor, the name of Morton Wishengrad came up for consideration as a possible regular staff member. "Oh, no, that wouldn't be fair to him," commented one executive. "Why," asked Barnouw. "Because he's a

Jew. His career would be hampered because he wouldn't be able to work on the Du Pont account," was the reply.[11]

The Du Pont Company also zealously watched for anything in *Cavalcade* scripts that might tarnish the company's image. In two instances, this involved petty censorship. The July 1943 broadcast of Stephen Vincent Benét's "Listen to the People" contains a soliloquy by a "totalitarian voice." "We can give you your own Hess, your own Himmler, your own Goering," he says at one point. The play's original text continues with the words "all home grown and wrapped in cellophane."[12] But cellophane was a Du Pont product protected by a trademark. Apparently nervous at having listeners envision a Nazi leader wrapped in a Du Pont product, the producers substituted the word "tissue" for "cellophane" when the play was broadcast.[13]

Arthur Miller encountered an even pettier instance of censorship. In 1944, BBD&O asked him to write a script about the Army's Canine Corps. Miller wrote a humorous script. Early in his story when Joe, the story's canine protagonist, is still privately owned, his owner refers to times when Joe bit salesmen who dared to ring his doorbell. "We'd like you to delete the reference to his biting," Miller was told. "Why," he asked incredulously. "Well, you know," he was told, "many Du Pont products are sold door-to-door by salesmen and we don't want them to be disturbed by reference to a dog biting a salesman."[14] Miller offered to change the doorbell ringer's identity, and his suggestion was kicked upstairs to the agency honchos. After some discussion, the salesman became a government employee, a postman.

A team of eleven writers, among them some of the best in radio, worked for the *Cavalcade*. Besides Benét and Miller, there were Morton Wishengrad, Peter Lyon, Norman Rosten, and Erik Barnouw. The series also featured a fairly regular acting troupe, which included Wally Maher and Will Geer. If the episodes of the *Cavalcade of America* reflected the political philosophy of Bruce Barton, the same could not be said about all of its actors, at least not about Geer. However, the closest that Geer's personal beliefs ever came into play in the *Cavalcade* studio was the day he brought in a huge bag of vegetables from his victory garden, which he distributed to everyone in the studio.[15]

LUX RADIO THEATRE

Lux Radio Theatre was the most important dramatic show in radio despite its derivative status. It started in New York in 1934 presenting adaptations of stage plays.[16] Two years later it moved to Hollywood, where it switched to broadcasting adaptations of films. The show opened at the 965-seat Music Box Theater on Hollywood Boulevard. Along with the *Cavalcade of America, Lux Radio Theatre* made the most use of some of Hollywood's biggest name stars. Fred MacMurray and Loretta Young were the ones who appeared most frequently. Among others who made repeat broadcasts were Claudette Colbert (24), Barbara Stanwyck (23), and Cary Grant (22).

At the height of *Lux Radio Theatre*'s popularity an audience of 40 million people heard its broadcasts. Film director Cecil B. DeMille was key to *Lux*'s success during a seven-year period that included almost all of the war. DeMille, who had already directed epics such as *The Ten Commandments* (1923) and *The Crusades* (1935), was hired in 1936, soon after the show arrived in Hollywood. Given the value of his name, the show's promotion tried to make out that he was "the boss" and he was given the title of "producer" and host. A salary of $2,000 for a three-hour work week accompanied the title. At a time when many working men were earning perhaps only $17 or $18 a week, this amounted to approximately $11 for each minute that he worked.

Although DeMille may also have consulted on proposed plays for the series, for the most part he was really only its master of ceremonies. However, he did his best to keep up the illusion implied by his title, pacing up and down before the studio audience, after he read his own lines, and periodically checking his pocket watch or the studio clock.[17] He also made notations on his copy of the script and checked off scenes as they were completed. The charade included his arriving directly from a movie set in "director-type puttees spattered with mud." Another time, when he was recovering from surgery, he arrived at the theater in an ambulance and the press photographed him speaking his lines from a stretcher.[18] A whole year after John Milton Kennedy had been working as the show's announcer, one day when someone mentioned Kennedy's name to DeMille, the latter asked with a puzzled look on his face, "Who the hell is John Milton Kennedy?"[19] The "producer" really did not know his own show. He was not even required to be present at the rehearsals on Fridays and Saturdays.

The bombing of Pearl Harbor caught *Lux Radio Theatre* off guard. A frivolous comedy entitled "The Doctor Takes a Wife" was scheduled for broadcast the day after the attack. Writer George Welles recalled that the program opened with the playing of the national anthem rather than with the usual *Lux* musical theme. Furthermore, acknowledging the unusual circumstances of the moment, DeMille solemnly remarked that "Throughout America tonight this inspired music lifts every heart to new patriotism, as all of us join you in pledging full allegiance to our country. We've asked the Columbia Broadcasting System to interrupt our program tonight with any important news developments."[20] In fact, during the second act of the play, CBS newscaster John Daly reporting from New York interrupted the show with a five-minute update on the war, during which he delivered a late bulletin that fifty unidentified airplanes were observed heading for San Francisco.

During the war, *Lux Radio Theatre* continued to offer many of the same type of plays that it had offered earlier. However, partly because more and more war stories had crept into Hollywood's film repertoire, adaptations of war-related films became a regular feature of the series. Among such shows in 1942 were "This Above All," a love story set in wartime England, and "Arise My Love," about a female foreign correspondent and a "soldier of fortune" flyer whose lives became embroiled in the war. Such shows were in the minority in the first year of the war. But their number increased significantly in 1943.

Unlike many other war-related broadcasts, *Lux Radio Theatre* used war themes as a byproduct of its main focus, providing entertainment. DeMille stated the show's approach to the war in a broadcast of October 1942: "In times of stress in the world," he explained, "there's more satisfaction than ever in the production of plays for the *Lux Radio Theatre*. That's because trouble knits families and nations closer together, and we know for one hour each week a great family sprawls across the whole continent and turns its ears to this stage. . . . Our job is to make you laugh, to stir you with drama and for one little hour to help you forget. . . . this is one of the most important services that a national theatre can render to our country in these times. . . ."[21]

The beginning of American involvement in the war placed special demands on drama series that dealt with the conflict. One was the need for musical themes appropriate for stories concerning the war. *Lux* musical director Louis Silvers who had a background as a staff arranger-conductor-composer at Columbia and Warner Bros., filled this need. Like DeMille, Silvers came to *Lux* soon after it arrived in Hollywood. Silvers stayed with *Lux* for fifteen seasons.

Music's primary purpose in radio drama is to tie scenes together. Silvers was very adept at writing bridges that reflected first the mood of the scene that has just taken place and then altering its character, preparing the audience for the scene that is about to come. Now, during the war, Silvers created special musical cues that he called "Attack," "Menace," and "Foreboding." "Foreboding" was used to depict Nazi activities. At the time it was common to interpolate the music of Richard Wagner into music representing the German Army. "Foreboding" quoted briefly from Wagner's "The Ride of the Valkyries (from *Die Walküre*) and his "Siegfried's Funeral March" (from Wagner's opera *Gotterdammerung*.) Numerous film scores quoted these two pieces, but Silvers wove them into a new synthesis with unusual effectiveness.

As it did on other shows, the war also impacted *Lux Radio Theatre* by taking away some of its actors. On two occasions in 1942, DeMille announced during curtain calls that the stars of the respective shows, William Holden in "I Wanted Wings" and Tyrone Power in "This Above All," were enlisting in the armed forces. The announcement regarding Power hit at least one listener rather hard:

> While all of us have got to help stop this vicious slaughter, still I'm sure you will understand what I mean when I say that we fans put our favorites on pedestals and it is quite overwhelming to realize that they are human beings after all, and can be killed by an enemy . . . just like anybody else. Up until now it's been glamorous, romantic, ethereal Hollywood which has been going all out in an effort to keep up the morale of our boys in the service, and now Hollywood itself is being torn apart.
>
> One actually recovers from the shock of the loss of a screen star but the emptiness stays with one for such a long time.[22]

Jeff Corey, another *Lux* actor who left for the service, the Navy in his case, wanted to do one last broadcast before he went away. The day that he was sworn in, the Navy wanted to do some publicity photos. "For God's sakes," Corey blurted out, "I've got to do a show for *Lux Radio Theatre*. There's a dress rehearsal at 5:00 and a performance at 6." "You're in the Navy, now," an officer told him. Corey had no choice but to stay until the publicity shots were completed. Miraculously, although he missed the dress rehearsal, he reached the studio five minutes before air time. Someone had stood in for him during the dress rehearsal. Corey did the performance. Afterward, DeMille came to him, took Corey's right hand into his own and said, "Son, I envy you." And Corey had the feeling that "What C. B. was saying was 'I wish I could direct World War II.'"[23]

Partly because *Lux* was a commercial show with big-name actors and a big-name host, it drew a different type of fan mail than sustaining shows with their less well-known actors. For one thing, when "Cecil the Great" encouraged letters concerning the sponsor's product, fans responded as though he, himself, might have a personal interest in their cosmetic concerns. "I thought if I wrote to you, you could tell me what to use for freckles and pimples," one fifteen-year-old girl wrote.[24] Some letters even came from soldiers at the front—often via a family member stateside. The father of a soldier stationed in the Middle East sent a letter describing a dinner at which his son was a guest of a sheik. The main course was a large barbecued lamb served on an enormous tray. In apparent accord with local custom, the Americans joined their hosts in literally tearing "the poor beast to shreds" with their fingers. The writer went on to quote his son about the dinner's aftermath: "when we had our fill," he related, "[we] were directed to a native servant to wash our hands and Mom, what do you think we were given to wash our hands with—LUX, yes LUX. Right away I thought of you and Pop on a Monday evening, the *Lux* Hour, quiet please."[25]

Besides discussing the product, listeners also replied to DeMille's request for suggestions with comments typical of film star fans, often requesting that their favorite actors be featured on a *Lux* show. In this regard, Alan Ladd was very popular. Ticket requests and complimentary and critical comments were also common topics of the letters.

DeMille's secretary handled the correspondence, dividing it into four or five main categories and replying usually with a form letter. She consulted DeMille himself regarding letters from prominent persons or those that stood out in other ways.

Lux Radio Theatre provoked some uniquely critical reactions. Take the case of "The Fighting 69th," one of its most popular broadcasts. Aired in April 1942, it starred Pat O'Brien and concerned a renowned American regiment during World War I. All but one of the twenty or so letters it inspired were complimentary. The critical one came from a Protestant listener, who was offended by the broadcast's use of the term "non-Catholic." "Members of the Roman Catholic minority happen to be a minority in this country," she wrote, "and the use of the term 'non-Catholics' seems to imply that all persons outside of this particular faith are inferior. . . . People belonging to other faiths when speaking of Catholics always refer to them as Catholics and I doubt if you have ever heard the term 'non-Protestant' used in this connection. As a Protestant, I object to being classed as a 'non-Catholic'—I am a Protestant and want to be called just that. . . . Furthermore, it seems that whenever any religious theme is portrayed in the movies, it is always the Catholic faith which is shown in an inspiring light. Members of other religious faiths are usually blackguards and renegades . . . . this letter is not written with the intention to slur any religious group but simply a plea for fair dealing to all."[26]

As DeMille's reply to the listener demonstrates, he missed the key problem in her letter. There were no Jews, Muslims, or Hindus in her world. Glossing over her myopic assumption that "non-Catholic" refers only to Protestants, he wrote, "Frankly, we did not think of the objection you mention, but I know you will understand that we are . . . constantly on the alert for anything that will detract from the enjoyment of a play."[27]

The writer of a second letter, concerning another show, aroused DeMille's ire and he was less patient with her. She complained that "In your Monday night Program . . . you showed Damn poor taste broadcasting a play about a soldier being all shot up and returning home to his girl. It certainly makes [people] like myself think of discouraging things, this sort of stuff does not help morale a Damn bit."[28] "Mr. DeMille . . . strongly advises you to take a tonic for your nerves,"

DeMille's secretary replied on his behalf, departing from their usually diplomatic tone.

Broadcast of another show, "Air Force," based on the John Garfield film by the same name, also attracted some critical reaction. The film version became embroiled in a small controversy concerning false allegations contained in it. After the attack on Pearl Harbor, rumors circulated alleging sabotage by Japanese-Americans. One held that Japanese trucks in Hawaii were used to put several American planes out of commission. Another alleged that Japanese planted dynamite in Hawaii before the attack. Both Honolulu's police chief and the Office of Military Intelligence found the rumors to be unfounded.[29] However, *Air Force*, the film, was found to have content based on at least one of the rumors, and the producer had to delete some scenes before it could be shown in Hawaii.

Now, following the announcement that *Lux* planned to broadcast a radio version of the film, a Mrs. Thayer, chairwoman of the Committee on American Principles and Fair Play, a California organization, wrote to DeMille.[30] She expressed concern that the radio version might retain the inaccurate content of the original version of the film and urged DeMille not to foster racial hatred or "weaken the war effort by increasing suspicion of Japanese-Americans."

DeMille's secretary often replied to listeners' letters, even if the writer was just praising Lux soap and likely hoping for an autographed letter from DeMille. However, there is no record of Mrs. Thayer's response to the show as it was broadcast. But the content of another listener's letter suggests that her broad concerns about racism were well founded. "We especially enjoyed tonight's program," a corporal based in Virginia wrote to DeMille about "Air Force." "It makes us mad to hear the story of Pearl Harbor again. . . . The day will come when those Nips, who think they are the superior race will be sorry they jumped the gun on us. It will be the biggest display of fireworks they're [*sic*] ever seen."[31]

Reactions to two other 1943 *Lux* shows about the American Armed Forces also validated Thayer's concerns. Two listeners wrote in concerning "Salute to the Marines" and "So Proudly We Hail," both broadcast in early November. "Salute to the Marines" concerns a Marine sergeant major and his pacifist wife. "So Proudly We Hail," featuring Veronica Lake, Paulette Goddard, and Claudette Colbert, told the story of a group of American Army nurses who were evacuated from the island of Corregidor just as the Japanese forces took it over.[32] The story featured comments such as, "Oh, then the rest of those girls are in the hands of those filthy . . . " and "I'm going to kill Japs—every bloodstained one that I can get my hands on."

A man from Washington State referring to "Salute to the Marines," asked, "Must we always be "propagandized to [the] extent of having all pacifists be Nazis? Propaganda has its place but it will be most effective if it reflects good taste and good judgment. We resent being bombarded with racial hatreds, fictitious threats and fears. Give us realism. We can take it and Lord knows, we need it. Only give us play selections that stick to the truth."[33]

The second listener, a young woman writing from Idaho, focused on the distorted portrayals of the Japanese in both shows. She also speculated whether the shows' stars were themselves internalizing the bigotry that characterized the roles that they were playing. "You see I am a fourteen-year-old Japanese girl (nisei)," she explained, "and although now, I live in a Japanese detention camp I am an American. And . . . 'So Proudly We Hail' and 'Salute to the Marines' made me feel as if I was one of the 'Japs' they want to kill. . . . And it also seems that I am right because people in California are threatening to kill any 'Japs' that intend to live there afterwards. But I hope that all of this is not true."[34]

Another Japanese-American girl, Jane, wrote to DeMille from her home in Hawaii. She briefly thanked him for the presentation of a third play, "The Pied Piper." Jane voiced no direct complaints, but her letter too reflected how she felt like an outcast. "I'm very interested in being an actress," she wrote, "but what have I got to show, Nothing. Absolutely nothing. Not pretty no nothing. . . . I wish with all my heart . . . I will go to California. You see I happened [sic] to be a Japanese girl of 12. 13 this month. But I wished I wasn't one. Maybe you hate the Japanese. In a way Yes because they started the world war. . . . I can't be an actress because I'm a Japanese. Anyway whoever in a world has ever heard of a Japanese actress in Hollywood."[35] The Lux files of letters from listeners usually contain copies of the replies that DeMille's office sent to those who wrote in. He did not appear to have replied to the last two letters.

By mid 1943, some *Lux* listeners were fed up with war-related radio dramas. Earlier, listeners to other war-related shows had expressed sentiment along these lines. A "night chemist" in Salt Lake
City wrote to Elmer Davis in February complaining about the *Uncle
Sam* series. "I wonder if you have ever considered your office as a recruiting service for the Gestapo," he grumbled. "When I am finished
with long hours of work and the mechanism of living, I settle into a
chair and turn on my radio at about 10:30 A.M. . . . out comes *Uncle
Sam,* . . . after listening to 15 minutes of drivel I am forced to conclude that either the mass of the american [*sic*] people are morons,
or else the OWI has a mistaken impression of the nation and its audience. . . . Being tired to start with, that program brings me to a state
of nervous irritation which precludes any interest on my part in the
outcome of the war."[36]

More than network-sustaining shows or commercial ones, *Lux Radio Theatre* was particularly vulnerable to such complaints. After all,
for years before Pearl Harbor was bombed, the show had offered a
diet of pure entertainment. Typical of criticisms of some of *Lux*'s
wartime offerings was a letter received in June 1943. "I'm getting so
dam [*sic*] sick of war, war and more war stories and movies," the writer
whined. "Ronald Colman is my favorite star but I'm not listening even
to hear him—that's how sick I am of war movies. For God sake give
us more comedy. There's so much tragedy all around. So surely for re-
laxation one should not have to listen to more tragedy—dramatized at
that. I work in a war plant inspecting shells."[37]

Another listener claimed to speak for the many mothers in the listening audience whose sons were in the service and who "are trying to find
entertainment to take their thoughts off their loneliness. Why force
them to listen to war stories or shut off their radios. . . . A woman with a
son in the service, when she settles down for an hour of entertainment
in the evening wants . . . something else besides the war. . . . She . . . is
making one of the biggest sacrifices of the war."[38]

DeMille left *Lux* in January 1945, as the consequence of a dispute
with the American Federation of Radio Actors (AFRA). AFRA was
opposing Proposition 12, a proposed "right to work" law that would
permit people to work in radio without requiring them to join a union.
To fight the bill, AFRA assessed each of its members $1. Claiming it

was an issue of freedom, DeMille refused to go along with it or to let anyone pay it on his behalf. The dispute dragged on through 1944.[39]

THE DOCTOR FIGHTS

The Doctor Fights, which CBS created as a summer replacement, dealt with the role of physicians in the war effort. The Biow Agency produced the series for its sponsor, the Schenley liquor company. However, because the word "liquor" could not even be mentioned on the air, the public heard "sponsored by Schenley Laboratories."[40] Schenley actually did own laboratories. However, the company had much less need to advertise the laboratories to the public than it did liquor.

Arthur Miller and his friends Joseph Liss and Norman Rosten contributed plays to *The Doctor Fights*. A typical one concerned a Dr. Grinker who used sodium pentathol on downed pilots suffering from trauma to help them remember and deal with their stress disorder. Another show was Miller's "Lips for the Trumpet," which aired in July 1945 and starred Gene Lockhart. Still another one featured Gregory Peck in the role of a medical officer aboard a destroyer who was faced with the dilemma of whether to use his small stock of penicillin for a group of German prisoners of war or keep it in reserve for possible need by American men.

Al Schaffer, a sound effects man who worked on *The Doctor Fights*, recalled that like Bill Robson, Dee Engelbach, who directed *The Doctor Fights*, was in love with sound. During the war years the Federal Communications Commission put strict limits on the maximum sound level that radio could broadcast. Schaffer recalled, "We were forbidden from going over the "0 point."[41] If we did, the station could be fined." Engelbach, however, was constantly pressing his engineers for louder and louder sound levels. Finally, one of them got Engelbach off his back by concocting a dummy sound meter with a cardboard dial that appeared to indicate that the sound had reached the maximum level possible.

Despite Miller's work for various radio series, he had little respect for the medium as a vehicle for artistic expression. In 1947, by which time he had left, he wrote, "really fine radio drama or first rate comedy is an impossibility."[42] Miller was frustrated by radio's need to get on with the story, which robs a play of the kind of nuance that can be achieved in a stage play. On the stage, however, it is possible and often desirable to include material in a scene that does not necessarily serve to advance the story.

CEILING UNLIMITED

In September 1942, Orson Welles became involved in multiple capacities in creating *Ceiling Unlimited*, a weekly series sponsored by the Lockheed Vega aircraft corporation to glorify the aviation industry. Initially it appeared that Arthur Miller was going to be the series principal writer. The two men had several things in common. Both were then twenty-seven, and both had been employed for a while by the Federal Theatre Project.

Welles had recently met Miller for the first time in NBC's huge studio 8-A when Miller dropped by to give director Homer Fickett a script that he had just finished for *Cavalcade of America*. By accident, the writer walked in just as the bulky actor was having a temper tantrum during rehearsal for a show, yelling at Frank Monaghan, the Yale professor, whose job it was to check *Cavalcade* scripts for accuracy. Welles was upset that Monaghan had not deleted some corrections that he had made. Miller quietly approached Fickett just as Welles's fury had started to subside and whispered that he thought Welles would be excellent as the Mexican protagonist in the play that Miller had just completed. Fickett seized on the suggestion, partly as a way out of the tense situation. He scanned the script, brought Miller over to Welles, handed it to him and introduced the two. Welles glanced at the script's novel opening, in verse, read further, and suddenly moved over to a microphone into which he then continued to read aloud. Soon the whole cast became involved in the reading. When it was over, Welles walked over to Miller and gave the taller man a bear hug.[43]

Now, involved in a series of his own, Welles asked Miller to create its format. Miller's reply was "I've been thinking about it today, however, and I feel sure about one thing. You don't want any. Your voice is a format. The only two things that must be heard at the beginning of the show every week are your voice and Lockheed Vega . . . but around those two things the variety should be infinite. . . . They alone and by themselves do everything any format can possibly attempt to do. Your voice if I may say so, portends much."[44]

In fact, as Miller told the author, he never did take such a role. From the beginning, Welles himself was producer-director-writer and narrator. To familiarize himself with the airplanes that would be the subject of the series, particularly the B-17 Flying Fortresses, Welles visited the sponsor's airplane manufacturing factories in California. Sporting an employee badge and a hard hat, he spoke to assembly line workers and shared box lunches with company executives. He quickly found himself becoming seduced by the romance of flying. To increase his poetic sense of it he read *The Little Prince* and several other stories by Antoine de Saint-Exupéry.

Just as the Du Pont Company had been concerned about its public image, as the following excerpt from a Lockheed executive's letter shows, Lockheed, too, was a bit worried about how the public perceived it.

> Lockheed does not want to appear in the role of either a prophet or a maker of munitions, and not especially, as an advocate of more and greater munitions (armed planes) after the war. Quite frankly, we are faced with a good deal of confusion as to what should be a solid and continuous line of thought that will enable us to go safely ahead and build up a backlog of scripts. The only rocks of Gibraltar are: one, the slogan "Look to Lockheed for leadership"; and two, dependability. . . . We want to show that airplanes deliver goods on schedule, that failure of parts or motors is the exception rather than the rule, that routine is the order of the day.[45]

Departing from the usual type of wartime shows about heroes, instead of concentrating on the pilots or other crew members, the first broadcasts of *Ceiling Unlimited* focused on individual airplanes as the stars. "This is the story of 'Cactus Sal' or 'Snoozy,' listeners heard Welles say as he introduced a show. He then narrated a dramatization about American planes fighting off attacks from enemy aircraft as they destroyed railroad yards and aircraft plants in Berlin, Rotterdam, or Rouen.

One of the more remarkable shows in the series is "Going to Run All Night," starring Wally Maher as a marathon runner who covered thirty-five miles through enemy lines to get help for his friends. The show was a brilliant collaboration between Maher and a sound effects man. Maher delivered his lines in a constant out of breath, stream-of-consciousness manner while the other man jogged in place in a box of gravel. Three microphones were needed: one for Maher and two for the sound effects man; a tall one picked up the latter's labored breathing, and a shorter one broadcast his footsteps.[46]

As it happened, Welles worked with the series for only a short time. In early February 1943, just before air time, he had an argument with a man from the advertising agency that was handling the show for the sponsor. Welles stormed out of the studio, never to return. After his departure, the series continued, now featuring stories of war heroism with big name Hollywood stars such as Edward G. Robinson, Ronald Colman, Cary Grant, Alan Ladd, Basil Rathbone, and Charles Boyer.

By the fall of 1944, *Ceiling Unlimited*, *Words at War*, *The Doctor Fights*, and Norman Corwin's and Arch Oboler's relatively short-term war-related series had run their course. In contrast, the *Cavalcade of America* and *Lux Radio Theatre,* both of which began in the prewar years, continued into the early 1950s, gradually, of course, decreasing their use of war themes.

NOTES

1. I am grateful to Barbara Thomas for this account concerning her family, which she related to me during a telephone conversation on January 8, 1999. This story is also related in Connie Billips and Arthur Pierce, *Lux Presents Hollywood: A Show-by-Show History of the Lux Radio Theatre and the Lux Video Theatre, 1934–1957* (Jefferson, N.C.: McFarland, 1995), 29.

2. Except where otherwise indicated, this account of *The March of Time* is based on Raymond Fielding, *The March of Time, 1935–1951* (New York: Oxford University Press, 1978), 19, and on Ann Case, "A Historical Study of the 'March of Time' Program Including an Analysis of Listener Reaction." (Master's thesis, Ohio State University, 1943), 61.

3. Gil Mack, interview by author, Lynbrook, N.Y., October 27, 1999.

4. Dwight Weist to Ann Case, October 1, 1943, as quoted in Ann Case, "A Historical Study," 63.

5. The complete text of this script about the Munich crisis was available on the Internet (in December 2000) at www.otr.com/marchtime.htm.

6. This discussion of the themes of *Cavalcade of America* shows is based on John Dunning, *On the Air: The Encyclopedia of Old Time Radio* (New York: Oxford University Press, 1998), 141.

7. Anne Tanneyhill, National Urban League, to Truman Gibson, December 7, 1943, NA 107-188-240 folder, "Radio Operators and Technicians."

8. Bob Foreman, telephone conversation with the author, August 6, 1999.

9. "Listen to the Sound of Wings," *Cavalcade of America*, vol. I, Radio Spirits.

10. Arthur Miller, *Timebends* (New York: Grove Press, 1987), 203.

11. Erik Barnouw, *Media Marathon* (Durham, N.C.: Duke University Press, 1996), 77.

12. Stephen Vincent Benét, *We Stand United and Other Radio Scripts* (New York: Farrar & Rinehart, 1945), 137–154.

13. William L. Bird Jr. *Better Living* (Evanston, Ill.: Northwestern University Press, 1999), 114.

14. The Reminiscences of Arthur Miller, June 1959, CUOHROC.

15. Sally Norton, "A Historical Study of Actor Will Geer, His Life and Work in the Context of Twentieth-Century American Social, Political and Theatrical History." (Ph.D. diss., University of Southern California, 1980), 371.

16. Except where otherwise indicated, this discussion of the *Lux Radio Theatre* is based on Billips and Pierce, *Lux Presents Hollywood*.

17. Ring Lardner Jr., "The Sign of the Boss," Box 29, folder 7, DeMille Collection, BYU.

18. Dunning, *On the Air*, 47.

19. John Milton Kennedy, telephone conversation with author, November 8, 1999.

20. *Lux Radio Theatre*, December 8, 1941.

21. As quoted in Jay Berkowitz, "An Historical Survey and Analysis of the Lux Radio Theatre 1934–1955." (Master's thesis, Temple University, 1967), 49. DeMille's comment was made during the October 26, 1942, *Lux Radio Theatre* broadcast of "Wake Island."

22 Louise Hynes to C. B. DeMille, September 30, 1942, Box 1116, folder 9, DeMille Archives, BYU.

23. Jeff Corey, telephone conversation with author, December 8, 1998.

24. Irene Stankiewicz to C. B. DeMille, n.d., Box 1122, folder 8, DeMille Archives, BYU.

25. Charles Fogle Jr., to C. B. DeMille, May 31, 1944, Box 1128, folder 6, DeMille Archives, BYU.

26. Sophie Meyer to C. B. DeMille, April 7, 1942, Box 1116, folder 8, DeMille Archives, BYU.

27. C. B. DeMille to Sophie Meyer, April 16, 1942, Box 1116, folder 8, DeMille Archives, BYU.

28. D. F. Eldridge to C. B. DeMille, January 6, 1942, Box 1116, folder 8, DeMille Archives, BYU.

29. Memos of W. A. Gabrielson, Chief of Police, Honolulu, Hawaii, May 12, 1943, and Col. Kendall J. Fielder, Office of the Assistant Chief of Staff for Military Intelligence, in "Statements Regarding Rumors of Sabotage in Hawaii," July 6, 1943, Box 1121, folder 15, DeMille Archives, BYU.

30. Mrs. Maynard F. Thayer, acting chairman, Committee on American Principles and Fair Play, to C. B. DeMille, July 6, 1943, Box 1121, folder 15, DeMille Archives, BYU.

31. Corporal Frank Sacco to C. B. DeMille, July 12, 1943, Box 1121, folder 15, DeMille Archives, BYU.

32. "Salute to the Marines," *Lux Radio Theatre*, broadcast November 1, 1943.

33. Herbert Palmer to C. B. DeMille, Box 1128, folder 1, DeMille Archives, BYU.

34. Yumiko Kashiwagi to C. B. DeMille, November 16, 1943, Box 1121, folder 15, DeMille Collection, BYU.

35. "Jane" to C. B. DeMille, January 1, 1944, Box 1121, folder 15, DeMille Archives, BYU.

36. W. Roberts to Elmer Davis, February 15, 1943, NA 208-140-749, Records of the Clearance Section.

37. The Mac Family to C. B. DeMille, June 1943, Box 1122, folder 5, DeMille Archives, BYU.

38. Agnes Thurston to C. B. DeMille, n.d., Box 1122, folder 6, DeMille Archives, BYU.

39. Dunning, *On the Air*, 48.

40. According to Lawrence Deckinger, Biow's former research director, in telephone conversation with author, December 14, 1999.

41. Al Schaffer, interview by author, April 5, 2001.

42. H. William Fitelson, ed., *Theatre Guild on the Air* (New York: Rinehart, 1947) as quoted in Gerald Weales, "Arthur Miller Takes the Air," *American Drama* (Fall 1995): 7.

43. Miller, *Timebends*, 204–205.

44. Arthur Miller to Orson Welles, October 18, 1942, Boxes 1–4, Orson Welles Collection, courtesy of Lilly Library, Indiana University, Bloomington, Indiana.

45. Thomas Freebairn-Smith to Max Ehrlich, May 12, 1943, Ehrlich Collection, WISC.

46. This account is recalled in Dunning, *On the Air*, 145.

PRESENTING THE
U.S. ARMED FORCES

If what I am writing as propaganda will hurt my eventual reputation as a writer very well then, let it . . . I can't just sit on my integrity as a writer as a hen on a China egg, for the duration.

—Stephen Vincent Benét as quoted in *Atlantic Monthly*

You are "Mother." Two daughters and one son call you that. The oldest child, your nineteen-year-old son, was just drafted two months ago. You tried not to put on a fuss when he got his draft notice. He seemed proud to receive it. You cried. You remembered your brother and the day he went away to the first war. It was the last time you saw him. Once he used to tease you. But you barely remember that now. You are constantly haunted with the memory of the day that he took you to the park. You were seven then. He talked to you so sweetly. Afterward you told your mother that you wanted to marry a man just like your brother. She laughed. But you meant it.

    You now live daily with the fear that a telegram will come with bad news about your son. Two years ago you heard James Cagney in a frightening radio program that kept you thinking about the war in Europe.[1] It was about a man left blind, deaf, limbless, and voiceless as a result of injuries that he suffered in the first war. You usually accept the idea that the country had to go to war. That's what your head tells you. The pain in your heart tells you something else, however. It's with you constantly.

The radio show that "Mother" heard in March 1940 was Arch Oboler's adaptation of Dalton Trumbo's antiwar novel *Johnny Got His Gun*. Actor John Valentine, who played a role in the broadcast, was struck by James Cagney's intense focus and concentration.[2] Normally during rehearsals, when a radio actor finished his scene he would leave his microphone, sit down, and relax. Cagney took the role very seriously. Despite the hour-long-show's lengthy rehearsals he remained standing at the microphone even when he finished his lines. Valentine also recalled the time of the show's broadcast with visceral memory.

Valentine was a Communist Party member, and the antiwar theme of "Johnny Got His Gun" fit in well with the party's position on the war in 1940. Few radio actors could limit themselves to performing only on shows that reflected their own views, but this one echoed Valentine's own sentiments at the time.

Oboler's production was somewhat of an aberration, considering that he had gone on record as opposing appeasement of Hitler. According to Oboler, not long after the play's broadcast, antiwar activists approached him and asked him to lend them a recording of it to use at rallies against the draft and against further American armament.[3] By this point, Oboler realized the inconsistency implicit in his having produced such a play and he turned them down. "Johnny Got His Gun" was the last antiwar radio drama of the era.

"Mother" and all the other parents, wives, and siblings of servicemen needed reassurance about the military that took their loved ones away. So did the young men themselves. They needed to know that the Armed Forces were competent institutions that cared for the welfare of the young men who wore their uniforms. To this end, one of the main themes of U.S. war propaganda in the 1940s was the preparedness, courage, and high quality of America's armed forces. Of course, stories about the Armed Forces had potential to be very violent. In presenting them, radio needed to be cautious not to increase its listeners' anxiety. To this end, as early as August 1942, William B. Lewis, as chief of the Office of War Information's radio section, issued a warning about radio dramatization of violent scenes. "Beware of the horror angle when dramatizing adventures of the Merchant Marine. Shun any mention of blazing oil on the surface of the sea, or the agonies of dying men in drifting life boats. Unfortunately these things do happen, but they have no more place on the air than the description of a soldier having his leg blown off."[4]

Although this particular warning had specific reference to shows concerning the Merchant Marine, it was clearly an expression of general OWI policy. For shows broadcast under the aegis of other federal agencies including the military, there were censors who had to pass on scripts. When occasionally advice such as Lewis's was ignored, listeners reacted swiftly. Two months after Lewis's pronouncement, the OWI broadcast "Blood and Money," a fifteen-minute dramatization intended to garner support for the government's price control program. Ignoring the spirit of Lewis's edict, the show featured the agonized scream of an American soldier upon being shot. An angry Detroit mother, about to send her eighteen-year-old son off to war, responded. "Of all the assanine [*sic*] ways of getting people's attention on the radio. . . . This is the worst I have yet heard! Whoever is responsible . . . isn't worth his salt. And we could begin saving money right now by eliminating him from the government payroll. . . . I'd like to shake his teeth out!"[5]

The Armed Forces were the dominant topic of three of the plays in Corwin's *This Is War* series, most prominent among them Stephen Vincent Benét's "Your Army," a play in verse. It was also the theme of scores of other wartime radio plays. As was his wont, Benét worked on the script for "Your Army" in long four- and five-hour stretches from mid afternoon to early evening all through the second half of February 1942.[6] The show continued radio's prewar presentation of America as a multiethnic patchwork that despite its diversity was nevertheless united. "We know this is our army," says the play's narrator. "Our army. A people's army, raised and equipped and run by a free people, made up of Bill Jones and Bennie Cohen and Stan Woczinski, Burt Anderson and Charlie Pappas."[7] As the narrator presents it, "Money won't get you into West Point and neither will the Social Register." Benét also linked the Army of his day with its earlier incarnations. Again the narrator: "It's an old army and a new one. It goes back to the cross-belted Continentals and the farmers who held their fire at Bunker Hill." Corwin told Benét the play was the best in the series, and Benét's protégé, Norman Rosten, sixteen years his junior, seconded the motion, waxing enthusiastic in a postcard about it, "It was wonderful. It was. I tried to think of a less worn adjective but it was wonderful!"[8]

Three other programs dealing with the Armed Forces, *They Call Me Joe, Chaplain Jim*, and *Army Service Forces Presents,* had their origins within the military. *They Call Me Joe*, a short "Roots"-type series of dramatizations, was the product of the Educational Unit of the Armed Forces Radio Service (AFRS), a branch of the Army Morale Division. *They Call Me Joe* was the brainchild of Eric Barnouw, who besides being a former NBC script editor was director of the AFRS unit from the beginning of 1944. Barnouw had suggested a series to deal with the multiethnic nature of the Army.[9] NBC financed and broadcast the show for the domestic American audience and not, as most AFRS productions, just for the Armed Forces. The series consisted of family chronicles of a narrator, a fictional serviceman, speaking in the first person singular and opening the show with a standard format, "My name is Giuseppe—they call me Joe" or "My name is José—they call me Joe." One week an Irish-American soldier described how the potato famine in Ireland drove his ancestors to the United States in the 1840s. Another week it was a Scandinavian-American soldier from the Midwest. Among the show's writers were Norman Rosten and Morton Wishengrad.

They Call Me Joe was intended to improve intercultural understanding. But its fine objective notwithstanding, it ran into some problems. In one case, a member of a congressional committee summoned Major Paul Horgan of the War Department Information and Education Division to answer some questions. "What," demanded the congressman, "was the significance of the name Joe?" The major was puzzled. It took him some moments to realize; and when he did, it was with the effect of a staggering revelation, that the congressman was trying to unite the expression "G. I. Joe" with the name of Josef Stalin.[10] In addition, the congressman took issue with the show's theme song, which came from the song "The Ballad for Americans." John La Touche wrote the words and Earl Robinson wrote the music for the song, originally for the WPA Federal Theatre. The 1940 Republican National Convention featured it as its theme song, and singer Paul Robeson sang it twice on CBS, including once for Norman Corwin's 1940 series *Pursuit of Happiness*. But both Robeson's and Robinson's politics were on the left. Although the influence of the Dies Committee was beginning to gather momentum, it did not yet have enough to stop the show's use of the song.

Chaplain Jim was a product of the War Department. In 1940, Edward Kirby, Director of Public Relations of the National Association of Broadcasters (NAB), contacted Lt. Col. Ward Maris, the War Department's Chief of the Press Relations Section. With the imminent approach of America's entry into the war, broadcasters were nervous. Their anxiety went beyond what many Americans shared about the prospects of war. It stemmed from the fact that in the event of war, the Communications Act of 1934 gave the president the power to take over all licensed radio stations "upon just compensation to the owners."

Rumors were circulating that the government had a master plan, and Kirby's task was to determine whether they had any basis in fact. Did the War Department have any plan for utilizing commercial radio in the event of war? In any case, Kirby needed to find out whether it was possible to develop an industry modus operandi that might avoid a government takeover. Besides the obvious reasons for concern, broadcasters were aware that government takeover and operation of the railroads during World War I had been a disaster.

Col. Maris welcomed Kirby's inquiry and introduced him to the top echelon of those responsible for the military use of electronic communications in broadcasting. Kirby learned that not only was there no plan, there was not even provision for voluntary censorship. The United States in 1940 was unprepared for mobilization of radio communication for wartime.

As a result of Kirby's discovery, Maris called on him to make recommendations for the War Department's use of radio in the event of war. Soon Kirby himself was brought into the Department as the Secretary of War's Civilian Adviser for Radio. Now the War Department began to arrange to put the Army on a better communications footing if and when war came. A new two-star general, Robert Richardson, organized the War Department's first Bureau of Public Relations.

Prominent among its new subdivisions was a radio branch. Richardson appointed Kirby as its chief, despite the latter's civilian status. Among Kirby's responsibilities were maintaining liaison with both the military and the broadcasting industry as he set up the radio branch and prepared it for its likely wartime role.[11]

The new radio branch assumed a wide range of responsibilities. Most were irrelevant to the listening experience of the civilian population—and to this book. What is relevant, however, is the radio branch's role in producing *Chaplain Jim*. *Chaplain Jim* focused on a fictional religious chaplain, a kindly young man who served in both the European and Pacific theaters of the war. Louis Cowan, a consultant to the department's radio branch, took the initiative that created the series. Cowan, a graduate of the University of Chicago, came to the department having independently created a highly successful radio program, *The Quiz Kids*. In the postwar years he became president of the CBS Television Network. Soon after the war began, Cowan offered himself as a "dollar a year man" to Kirby.[12] With Kirby's backing, Cowan approached Ed Kovak, a vice president of the NBC Blue Network (which eventually became the American Broadcasting Company) with a proposal for a new show. Cowan suggested a military-related program with a religious orientation. But he proposed that instead of focusing on prayer or religiously oriented music, the show should be an entertaining, dramatic one that would assure parents that their sons had someone to turn to in the Army when they needed him.

To Cowan's surprise, Kovak loved the idea. "You've got a half-hour on the Blue Network. When do you want to start?" Kovak asked Cowan. Cowan and Kovak then turned the project over to Frank and Anne Hummert of the Blackett, Sample, and Hummert advertising agency. With a prewar record of two dozen soap operas on afternoon networks, the agency, or actually the Hummerts themselves, were the leading producers of radio serials in the 1930s and 1940s. Eventually the couple split off from the agency to concentrate on producing their shows. They "supervised" writers who filled in dialogue from broad sketches provided by Mrs. Hummert.

Frank was a tall, thin, slightly stoop-shouldered and solemn-looking man, and, as an actress recalled, Anne, twenty years his junior, was a small, slim, cheerful-looking woman with light brown hair. Except for a light trace of lipstick, she wore no makeup. She reminded the actress of a well-to-do Quaker lady.[13] Anne had been a journalist with the *International Herald Tribune* before coming to work at the agency, first as his editorial assistant and then as his writing partner.

The Hummerts were a very serious and demanding couple. Woe to any actor who came late to a rehearsal. They were also very reclusive and were seldom seen outside their Greenwich, Connecticut, home. Only one person in broadcasting, an assistant, was known to have ever been invited to see them there. Legend had it that the Hummerts' dining room had only three pieces of furniture: a long table with just one chair at either end.

Frank was so private that, according to one story, he once fired an employee for talking to him in the washroom; and Anne, for her part, once fired a writer on the spot when, after she told the woman, "I want you to put God into every plot that you write," the writer replied, apparently facetiously, "And who is going to play his role?" [14]

The Hummerts conceived of *Chaplain Jim* as a show for a special audience. They directed it at the little-educated, anxious ones who could not quite understand why "Uncle Sam" had taken their loved ones and sent them to faraway places. Most of the young soldiers whose families were the show's target audience had never been outside the limits of their home towns or counties before being drafted. *Chaplain Jim* was designed to put their loved ones at ease. The notion that there was someone else to whom a troubled soldier could turn besides an often-unsympathetic sergeant was a source of comfort to mothers and wives.

The premier broadcast of *Chaplain Jim* was a memorable one for Edward Kirby and his wife Marjorie. It took place in the spring of 1942 in NBC's large studio 8H at Radio City, which was often used for concerts. The Hummerts invited them to watch it and to have dinner with them afterwards. "I wonder where they'll take us," Mrs. Kirby said to her husband shortly before the show began. "Maybe it will be to Club 21 or the Stork Club."

When the show ended, the Hummerts met them at the studio exit and led them out to the street where a horse and carriage awaited them. "This is for us," Frank Hummert told them. "This way we don't have any problem with gas rationing. We hope you don't mind," he added, "if we have dinner at our place." "Our place" was an elegant apartment on Fifth Avenue. Although the Kirbys had also speculated about who might be joining them, it turned out that the dinner party was to consist of just the two couples.

The Hummerts' apartment was an immense one. As Frank Hummert led the Kirbys through it, he turned on the lights in the room ahead while Anne turned them off in the one they were leaving. "I hope you don't mind if we eat in the kitchen," Hummert told them just as they walked into and then quickly out of the dining room. In the kitchen, he opened up a can of Campbell's vegetable soup while Anne opened a can of peaches, which she served on a bed of lettuce. Later she commented, "I hope you don't mind if the cake has been here a little while. It's still good though."

Chaplain Jim, the character, became a real "Living Friend" in the minds of thousands. They were encouraged to write to him personally to tell him their problems. Many did so. They complained of not hearing from their loved one in the service—or of feeling stranded or deserted even if they were receiving letters. The Adjutant General's office answered each letter. It also frequently put a follow-up through to military channels. It is difficult to statistically calculate the show's success. But Edward Kirby claimed that the show and the follow-up prevented tens of thousands of homes from breaking up. He similarly credited it with preventing numerous soldiers from going AWOL or committing other acts of disobedience. There was one aspect of listener reaction that could be measured quite objectively. The "Chaplain" was so real to so many listeners each week that they sent him candy, homemade cookies, and donations of cash to carry on his work.[15]

The Army was also responsible for *Army Service Forces Presents*. This series featured dramatizations based on actual war incidents involving the Army engineers, medics, chaplains, and fifteen other departments of the Army, produced under the supervision of the War Department's Bureau of Public Relations.

Arthur Laurents, the most important writer for *Army Service Forces Presents*, was working at the Army's Astoria, New York, studios late in 1943 when he received a telegram ordering him to report the

next day to Rockefeller Center in Manhattan.[16] There was no explanation. Suspecting that there was a radio unit there, he checked a
newspaper, found the series listed in the daily progamming schedule,
and guessed correctly that he was going to write for it. At Rockefeller
Center he was assigned to work with a colonel who directed the show
and a captain who researched it.

To give Laurents a feeling for the subjects that he was going to
write about, he was put through some additional training. This included some short technical courses: one dealt with tanks and a second put him on a firing range. But when he took a third one that ne-
cessitated his flying in a dive bomber, the experience proved too much
for him and he vomited in his hat.

One day the colonel informed him that Laurents, the captain, and
he, himself, were going overseas to research conditions at the front
firsthand. But shortly afterward, to the disgruntlement of the other
two men, the Army canceled the trip. As a noncommissioned officer,
Laurents was not eligible to go, and without him, the key member of
the team, there was no point to it.

The Man Behind the Gun, another series about the military, premiered early in 1943, the second year of the war. A somber, innovative
CBS production about individual members of the Armed Forces, it was
the second collaboration between director William Robson and Ranald
MacDougall, its writer. The series had its roots in "Your Air Forces," a
program that MacDougall wrote for *This Is War*. "Your Air Forces" featured an eavesdropping technique in which the listener was more or
less placed in the position of a passenger aboard the plane, privy to the
conversations of a bomber crew on a mission. With this in mind, Mac-
Dougall planned a whole series of such programs.

From the very beginning, critics and the public recognized the special qualities of *"The Man Behind the Gun."* John Hutchens of the
New York Times praised MacDougall's solid characterizations and
skillful narration.[17] He lauded the writer's ability to tell the story in a
straight line and complimented his gift for creating nervous suspense
and wrote, "Above all he has a point of view. He knows that the men
of whom he writes are heroic. He knows also that to themselves they
are not heroes. Dying, they do not ask to have the Declaration of Independence read to them; they ask for a cigarette."

During the writing of the series' third program, MacDougall developed a new technique, writing in the second person singular, "you," effectively pulling the listener right into the story.[18] MacDougall, noted for his thorough research, spent at least three days of each week traveling up and down the Atlantic seaboard to various military bases. He wrote many of the shows on trains or airplanes and, even once, on board a PT boat racing at an incredible speed to New York.

When he was able to work at home or in the studio, MacDougall usually wrote a whole show in one sitting, often working about twenty hours straight, with the help of several cups of coffee. Periodically he would permit himself a little nap. But to prevent himself from falling asleep too long, he would prop a lighted cigarette between his fingers in such a way that he could not drop it. When the cigarette burnt down far enough, he would wake up. For long afterward he had calluses from the cigarette burns.[19]

An experience MacDougall had with censorship of a play that his cast already rehearsed illustrates a common problem of war writing. Navy censors, claiming that an incident portrayed in the script violated security, refused to clear it even after MacDougall offered to cut the offending section. They explained that if they showed him what to cut, they would be commiting a breach of security. With a broadcast scheduled and no script, MacDougall salvaged the situation, however, after finding a theme for a new one by chance in a small newspaper article about an emergency appendectomy performed aboard a submarine. Having spent a great deal of time on submarines while doing research, he had enough factual material to round out the script. He finished the writing less than an hour before the broadcast and was still making changes while it was going on.[20]

The Man Behind the Gun was notable for the development of a rich repertoire of realistic sound effects. As noted earlier, Robson had a profound understanding of the importance of sound. He made several unique sound discoveries.[21] To replicate the sound of a destroyer dropping depth charges he played a phonograph recording of a cement mixer at 33 1/3 RPM instead of the usual 78 RPM. Several hours of experimentation also showed that snapping a piece of silk in front of a microphone approximated the sound of a parachute opening. Perhaps the cleverest innovation in sound that developed during the production of

The Man Behind the Gun came about as the result of Robson's effort to re-create the noise of men in battle conditions. Robson understood the phenomenon of threshold of sound, that, for example, one's ability to be heard in any given place is relative to competing sounds. The louder the other sounds, the louder one must talk. To create uniquely credible sound effects, Robson produced the show with two speakers on the dead sides of a non-directional microphone that blared the sound effects of guns going off or PT motors running at full throttle into the ears of the actors standing in front of the microphones. As a result, the actors had to shout to hear themselves—exactly as they would have in an actual combat situation. Robson was delighted when military men would tell him "Well, you must have flown the plane," or "you must have been down in the submarine . . . ."

Robson was a memorable character to behold in his director's booth.[22] Allan Sloane who also wrote for *The Man Behind the Gun*, described Robson as belonging to the "Leonard Bernstein" school of directing, referring to the famed conductor's exuberant physical performance as he directed. "You were not safe in the booth with him," Sloane reminisced, "unless you were out of his arms' reach." In one rehearsal involving a lifeboat, Robson conducted a burial at sea, literally acting out the physical action of tossing a corpse from the boat into the sea. He grunted, strained, lifted, spread his arms as if he alone were holding the corpse—and with one last grunt, tossed the imaginary body of a seaman into the sea. But then he lost his balance, slipped, and cracked his forehead on the very real booth counter. Another time, Robson had his arm above his head, in a Statue of Liberty stance, waiting for the story to come to a high level of suspense. Then when the cue came, he threw his hand forward, bringing it down, in miscalculation, to the edge of the booth's window—at the cost of a forefinger nail. But the show went on.

In addition to *The Man Behind the Gun*'s quality sound effects, the series boasted a first-rate cast of actors, which included Jackson Beck, Larry Haines, Art Carney, and Frank Lovejoy. Of Beck, its ubiquitous narrator and a stalwart of Robson's stock company, Sloane said "His voice was an instrument and he had a narrative skill that was unmatchable." In appearance, Beck looked like what such a voice should emanate from. He was heavyset, and his voice was exactly tuned to his physique. He would drop the volume to a whisper—of which every syllable was heard no matter what sound pattern. Larry Haines, a soap opera star, had a baritone voice to Jackson Beck's bass.

Art Carney had an incredible talent for mimicry. But frequently inebriated in those years, he presented a special problem. In rehearsals for the show, someone had to be on hand to see that he did not wander away. Finally, there was Frank Lovejoy, the series's core actor about whom Sloane said "[Lovejoy] was always cast as a nice guy, even though he mostly played officers."

Frequently the writers included euphemisms in the scripts to give them what MacDougall called a "man to man" authenticity. But a phrase like "she was stacked up like a brick courthouse," sent the actors into fits of laughter.[23] So did a line that appeared in a show in a plaintive speech by a sailor aboard the aircraft carrier "Yorktown." Just back from shore leave, he returned with a grass skirt as a souvenir. He was thinking of his girlfriend back home and how she would look in it. "Boy! Imagine Consuela Schlepkiss in a grass skirt, walking down Flatbush Avenoo [sic]." Both in rehearsals and on the air, the actor failed to get past "Consuela Schlepkiss," so consumed was he with laughter. Several actors, particularly those who were notoriously susceptible to a "breakup" on the air, dreaded any of those white-washed lines. Often they would be transformed into helpless laughter and have to be carried way from the microphone. With Carney in the cast, given his drinking problem and his raucous sense of humor, the group did not need any encouragement to get into shenanigans.

Carney left *The Man Behind the Gun* in the spring of 1944 when he was drafted. In one of his last shows, he portrayed an Australian soldier.[24] After being tutored to get the accent right, to test its authenticity, one afternoon he visited a travel office where he was told an Australian was working. He passed the test when the Aussie took him for a fellow countryman. After he was drafted, Carney was sent for basic training to Camp Upton on Long Island, where one evening he had the experience of hearing a repeat of the same show. But now, Carney was truly the "Man Behind the Gun."

A letter from the wife of a physician gave some testimony to the effectiveness of *"The Man Behind the Gun."* A war industry worker, a slacker, came to her husband one day asking for a note for work so that he could take a few days off. "Go home and listen to *The Man Behind the Gun*," the doctor told him. "Afterwards, if you still feel that you want the note, come back and I'll write it."[25]

In 1943, the broadcasting industry recognized the quality of Mac-Dougall's and Robson's work on *The Man Behind the Gun*, granting it a coveted Peabody Award. Later that year, MacDougall left the show and Arthur Laurents replaced him. Although Laurents was still in the Army, now not only was he able to receive pay as a civilian, but the Army even acted as his agent in getting him the job.[26] As with MacDougall, work on the series gave him experience on the way to a successful career beyond radio.

Allan Sloane was the next and last writer for *The Man Behind the Gun*. Sloane continued his predecessors' concern for authenticity, traveling to Washington, D.C., once a month to talk to the Navy Department.[27] He also visited bars to talk to servicemen. He told them what he was doing and what he was seeking. "I got a story nobody knows," a man in the Air Force told him. "I was in the outfit that shot down that SOB Yamamoto." The man was a crew member of a P-38. "But that's a land based plane!" Sloane replied with a puzzled look. "That's right. That's how we got him. We knew exactly where he was going to be and when." Sloane then visited the library and researched the incident. As a result, the finished script contained a great deal of factual content that had not appeared in newspaper accounts of the incident. However, when Robson submitted the script to the censors, it was slapped down. "Eliminate all references to the P-38," he was told. "We would be extremely interested to find out where your writer got this confidential information." In the end, although neither he nor Sloane knew why, Robson had to discard the script. The reason for the censor's concern centered around the P-38 crew member's comment "We knew exactly where he was going to be and when." Sloane had stumbled onto the biggest story of his career. Had a Japanese spy heard the projected broadcast, he would have realized that the reason the Air Force knew this information was that American cryptographers had broken the Japanese code!

Sloane worked on the show until 1944, by which time CBS deemed it outdated and canceled it. Robson himself was somewhat tired of the show. "The time has been sold," he wrote MacDougall on the eve of its demise, "and the consensus seems to be that although the show is still good, its psychology is 1942 instead of 1944, although nobody can give me a definition of the 1944 psychology."[28]

NBC started another series on the military, *It's the Navy*, written mostly by Millard Lampell, in the spring of 1942. A typical episode "The Captain Comes Home," concerns a sailor on an American patrol boat ("The sailors call them rat poison, cause they're death on U-boats"), whose father, a former World War I German U-boat captain, had emigrated to America after the war.[29] Now, as captain of an American freighter, the father, played by Joseph Schildkraut, is caught by the Germans. He had seemingly been convinced to captain a submarine and try to land some Germans off the coast of North Carolina. But on reaching the coast, the captain signals the presence of the submarine to the Americans. The captain's own son, aboard the patrol boat, spots the signal and drops depth charges.

After catching the captain, his Nazi superior berates the not-well-turned "turncoat." "You were not very smart. It was a most stupid thing to do. One man against the Third Reich." "One man is all it takes, Herr Commandant," the captain tells his accuser. "One man at each trigger. . . . One man at the controls of every bombing plane. . . . That's what the United States is like . . . it's a nation of men . . . every one of them with guts and strength and dignity . . . . You and your nation are carbon copies."

The American Armed Forces were also the subject of a number of shows in the commercial radio series, *Cavalcade of America*, *We Deliver the Goods*, *Lux Radio Theatre*, *Service to the Front*, and *Words at War*. Three titles that were typical of *Cavalcade* shows dealing with the military are "Take Her Down," "Sky Nursemaid," a show about the Army Evacuation Service, and "The Sailor Takes a Wife."[30]

"Take Her Down" featured Clark Gable, who shortly before had served in the Air Force as a gunner and photographer in air raids over Europe.[31] He had attained the rank of major and earned an Air Medal. This, his first radio appearance since his release from active duty, was announced beforehand and there was a scramble for tickets. But the folks who received them were quite disappointed. Gable was playing the role of a submarine captain who sacrificed his life to save his crew. His and eight other roles required the sounds of men in a submarine. To achieve this, they spent most of the performance speaking from offstage in a 10 × 12-foot isolation booth. An actor who worked on the show remembered the broadcast clearly.[32] For all his fame, Gable was not particularly good at his craft, and on radio he had a special problem. Live radio broadcasts petrified him, and he read his lines too slowly. On top of this, one of the actors in the booth passed wind during the performance. But they could not open the door until the end of the broadcast. Somehow the group managed to suppress their laughter and complete the show without cracking up on air.

"The Sailor Takes a Wife," written by Allan Sloane, concerns the Merchant Marine, the "stepchild" of the World War II military. The Merchant Marine was under the supervision of the United States Maritime Commission, established in 1936 to develop a fleet capable of serving as a naval and military auxiliary in time of war. A part of its responsibility was to train personnel to operate merchant vessels. As we learn from the broadcast, in the first year of the war, the Merchant Marine experienced a greater percentage of casualties than any other branch of the Armed Forces.[33] In the story, Barry Arthur (played by Dick Powell) is a 4-F newspaperman who tries first to volunteer for the service. He wishes to impress a certain young woman who is accusing him of being a "shirker." After he is rejected, he successfully joins the Merchant Marine, the "civilian navy." The first time Barry ships out, a Japanese submarine sinks his ship. The portrayal of the sinking, with scarce detail concerning injuries and deaths of the men on board the ship, is interesting in how it typifies much of radio drama of the war era.

In the scene after the sinking, the young woman whose criticism drove him to join the service comes to interview him in the hospital—and they declare their love for each other. But Barry is not coming back to the newsroom right away. He is going back to sea, this time for the "right reason." "I am going back . . . this time," he says, " because there's fighting going on and there's all those guys over there who need this stuff."

"The Sailor Takes a Wife" is an interesting study of how war writing so frequently bumped against the anti-Communist mania. In this case, the writer was indeed a member of the Communist Party. In testimony before a congressional committee nine years after the end of the war,

Sloane told how he took advantage of his position to carry out the party's work.[34] He inserted a piece of "Communist propaganda" into the script. It was the one occasion in his career, he said, when he used his work to do anything other than tell the story. What was the insidious nature of the propaganda? Sloane explained that he tried to show that the men who served in the Armed Forces came from a wide variety of social, economic, and ethnic backgrounds. It was really a presentation of the same multiethnic patchwork painted in Stephen Vincent Benét's "Your Army" and the Armed Forces Radio Network's *They Call Me Joe*. But the *Cavalcade of America*; Du Pont, its sponsor; and Batten, Barton, Durstine and Osborn (BBD&O), the ad agency that produced *Cavalcade*, appeared to be even more conservative than the Armed Forces Radio Network.

What Sloane did was simply name one character "Pop Silverman." Instead of using "all-American" names such as "Tucker," "Rogers," "Shield," "Wiley," or "Brooks" (all of them used in the titles of various radio shows of the era), Sloane, who had changed his name from Silverman, named a character after his own Jewish father. Besides carrying out the party's work, he explained, his motivation was to honor his father. In the end, however, he failed. His attempt was spotted. "Ah ha! That old Communist line," commented the *Cavalcade*'s director, in the process of pointing out several changes that he wanted made. "Everybody has to have a Jewish name in the script, or an Italian name—why do you have to do that? Fix that." And Sloane did, converting "Pop Silverman" to "Pop."

In addition to the occasional show about the Merchant Marine on the *Cavalcade of America* and other commercial series, the United States Maritime Commission produced *We Deliver The Goods*, a weekly series on that topic during the summer of 1944. The show, produced for the West Coast at the Merchant Marine training station on Catalina Island, dramatized stories about those who performed acts of bravery and was broadcast weekly on Sundays. The actors had to take "the Big Red Steamer" from the Catalina Terminal to Catalina Island every week. The trip was often memorable, particularly in wintertime, because sometimes they took it in very rough weather. The cast enjoyed the experience immensely. Howard Culver, who played the lead role in the series, remembered how the servicemen on

Catalina, thrilled with having the show done where they could see it, treated them like kings. In fact, some of the merchant seamen were actually a part of the show. The casino out on the point in Catalina, overlooking the harbor, was one of the beautiful buildings that Wrigley, of chewing gum fame, built. On show night it was always bulging with an audience of merchant mariners![35]

A June 1945 broadcast of *We Deliver the Goods* features a theme similar to the one in "The Sailor Takes a Wife," in which the service-man undergoes a trauma and then as soon as he can tries to go right back into action. Here, too, it is a merchant mariner whose ship had been sunk. This time, however, he had been held in a German prisoner of war camp for three years. Now, on the very day of his return home, only minutes after reunion with his wife, he vows to return to the fray. "For three years, those of us in prison camps have been out of the fight," he says. "We've stored up a lot of hatred in that time. We've seen Fascism at first hand . . . we're going out there—to the Pacific—and send those dirty sons of heaven to hell!"

In the spring of 1944, Norman Corwin presented "Untitled," one of his best plays of the war, a poignant narrative about a soldier recently killed in battle. He wrote it in response to talk that was current about giving Germany a "soft peace." "Untitled" is an unequivocally antifascist production that condemned homefront apathy and the sometimes coddling of the enemy. The play, one of radio's more important statements on the war, received tremendous critical acclaim and more than 1,500 letters from listeners.

Words at War dealt with a wide variety of war themes. Among the show's programs dealing with the military was "Guys on the Ground," based on a book by Captain Alfred Friendly, better known in the post-war era as Fred Friendly, one of the most creative individuals to work in television broadcasting. The show, aired in December 1944, was "a tribute to the men of the Air Force who rarely if ever leave terra firma, whose job is to 'furnish and fix.'" It concerns a newspaper reporter who is trying to extract dramatic stories from some modest pilots who insist on telling her about the great ground crews that service their planes and about the planes themselves, that is, about "The Coughin' Coffin" that seems to have nine lives. "But it has a lucky name. And a very dedicated crew that takes care of it. Fifty missions . . . count 'em . . . no sir, they ain't buryin the Coffin! Nobody! We'll put her together again! She's got more lives than a barrel of pussycats! We'll put her together again, and she'll *fly*!" In the end the pilots convince the reporter that she's got a good story.[36]

Frank and Doris Hursley, a writing couple from the Midwest, were responsible for another show about the Armed Forces, *Service to the Front,* which concerned the experiences of soldiers in Army service departments such as the Army Engineering Corps and the Quarter-master Corps. Like the writers for *The Man Behind the Gun*, the Hursleys traveled to research their stories. In addition, on one occasion, they put themselves, at least slightly, into the shoes of the GI on the battlefront. They invited their neighbors to share an unusual meal with them, serving a limited fare of only 10-in-1 ration packs, a new type of K ration, and tap water. The 10-in-1 ration packs, so named because they fed either one meal for ten men or ten meals for one, had just come out. Polly, the Hursley's daughter, recalled how as a twelve-year-old she found the party to be a jolly experience. Afterward, the couple wrote a script about men eating at the front.[37]

Finally, between December 1944 and February of the following year, NBC produced a "documentary drama" series entitled *These Are Our Men,* which features "authentic live stories" of American military leaders. Episode #5 concerns Navy Admiral William F. Halsey.[38] The show's portrayal of Halsey is an interesting one.

> " . . . he's all Navy . . . the saltiest admiral of them all."
> " . . . a tough bulldog of a seadog."

We learn from the script that Halsey only met his father when he was two years old. "It's not strange in the Navy," Halsey's mother explains. "Bill's father was on a world cruise when Bill was born." We also find out that Halsey wears a tattoo, once owned a parrot ("as an old salt should"), and, macho hero that he is, does without sleep for extended periods of time. Even long before the attack on Pearl Harbor, shortly after the Russo-Japanese War, Halsey "didn't care much for Japs . . . because they conducted a sneak attack in Port Arthur against the Russians during that earlier war." Allegedly, during that early period, Halsey, then an ensign, gave a not-entirely-figurative slap in the face to Japanese Admiral Togo. As we hear, while Halsey was in Yokohama a Japanese officer informed him that the Japanese Navy wanted to honor Admiral Sperry in their traditional way, "Banzai," a ceremony in which sailors toss a person into the air. Sperry consented, Halsey arranged for the ceremony, and the Japanese tossed Sperry "a gentle two feet" into the air. Next, Halsey suggested a similar and reciprocal honoring of Admiral Togo. But with the young Halsey in the lead, the American sailors "bounced Admiral Togo off the ceiling," and Halsey was heard muttering "That's for Port Arthur, Togo."

It is virtually impossible to measure the effectiveness in achieving the aims of shows that were broadcast more than half a century ago. However, anecdotal evidence indicates that at least to some extent radio dramas about America's armed forces boosted civilian morale and helped recruiting efforts. Particularly when the shows were broadcast in conjunction with other strategies, they helped the nation to deal with a time of great national stress. Edward Kirby's claim that *Chaplain Jim* helped prevent soldiers from going AWOL was certainly a very subjective one. But the letters did pour in. Remember the doctor who chewed out his slacker patient and told him to go home and listen to *The Man Behind the Gun*? There is also the experience of the Writer's War Board (WWB) in sponsoring a number of plays dealing with the military. In compliance with a request from the Office of War Information, it assisted in a campaign to increase the number of applications for bombardiers. The WWB's articles, broadcasts, and plays were so successful that the Air Force was flooded with applications for airmen, and it finally asked the WWB to desist. Similarly, a letter to Frank and Doris Hursley from the Army Service Forces' Chief of Transportation credited a July 1945 broadcast about the Transportation Corps with attracting 1000 applications for positions with the western railroads.[39]

NOTES

1. Arch Oboler's "Johnny Got His Gun," broadcast March 9, 1940, a tape of which can be found in *Arch Oboler Remembers WWII*, Radio Spirits.

2. John Valentine (pseud.), interview by author, October 2, 1999.

3. Ira Skutch, ed., *Five Directors: The Golden Age of Radio* (Lanham, Md.: The Scarecrow Press, Inc., 1998), 159.

4. Memo from William B. Lewis, Chief, Radio Bureau, OWI, in OWI publication "The Radio Front" Subject: Men for Our Merchant Fleet, 2, August 15, 1942. Dick Dorrance Collection, Box 4, folder 8, Library of American Broadcasting, the University of Maryland.

5. Mrs. R. Conway Knapp to station WWJ (Detroit), October 18, 1942, NA 208-92-593, folder J.

6. Charles A. Fenton, *Stephen Vincent Benét, the Life and Times of an American Man of Letters, 1898–1943* (New Haven, Conn.: Yale University Press, 1958), 368.

7. This and the following two quotes from the play appear in its printed version in Norman Corwin, et al,, *This Is War: A Collection of Plays about America on the March, by Norman Corwin and others* (New York: Dodd, Mead, 1942), 72, 89, 90.

8. Corwin's comment appears in Fenton, *Stephen Vincent Benét,* 90. Rosten's can be found in Norman Rosten to Stephen Vincent Benét, March 8, 1942, Benét Collection, YALE.

9. For further discussion of *They Call Me Joe,* see Erik Barnouw, *The Golden Web: A History of Broadcasting in the United States, vol. 2, 1933–1953* (New York: Oxford University Press, 1968), 196, and Erik Barnouw, "Educational Unit in World War II," *Journal of Popular Culture*, XII:2 (Fall 1979).

10. Barnouw, *The Golden Web*, 196.

11. This account is based on Col. Edward Kirby, Public Relations Director, USO (unpublished), *References and Recollections of Historic Highlights: American Broadcasting in World War II*, 1964, Kirby Collection, WISC.

12. Barnouw, *The Golden Web*, 161.

13. Mary Jane Higby, *Tune in Tomorrow* (New York: Cowles, 1968), 129.

14. Barnouw, *The Golden Web*, 95.

15. Kirby, *References and Recollections of Historic Highlights.*

16. Arthur Laurents, *Original Story By: A Memoir of Broadway and Hollywood* (New York: Alfred A. Knopf, 2000), 28.

17. John K. Hutchens, "Man Behind the Gun," *New York Times*, March 21, 1943, II, 9:1.

18. Leonard Maltin, *The Great American Broadcast: A Celebration of Radio's Golden Age.* (New York: Dutton, 1997), 31.

19. Ranald MacDougall to E. Barnouw, May 2, 1945, Box 38, Barnouw Collection, COL-RB.

20. Ranald MacDougall to David Sievers, Acting Head of Radio Division, November 4, 1998, UCLA, MacDougall Collection, AMPAS.

21. The following accounts of Robson's innovations in sound effects are based on Maltin, *The Great American Broadcast*, 98.

22. I am grateful to the late Allan Sloane for his detailed recollections of production of *The Man Behind the Gun*, which he sent me in a lengthy undated letter in 1998. The following section (Allan Sloane who succeeded . . . you had a show) is based on Sloane's account.

23. MacDougall recalled the cast's shenanigans (i.e., regarding "brick courthouse" and "Consuela Schlepkiss") in Ranald MacDougall, "Documentaries for Civilians: The Man Behind the Man Behind the Gun," Jerome Lawrence, ed., *Off Mike: Radio Writing by the Nation's Top Radio Writers* (New York: Essential Books, 1944), 157.

24. Art Carney, telephone conversation with author, March 30, 2000.

25. Josephine H. MacLatchy, ed., *Education on the Air: Fourteenth Yearbook of the Institute for Education by Radio* (Columbus: Ohio State University, 1943), 61.

26. Arthur Laurents to author, June 12, 1996.

27. Allan Sloane, interview with author, New Canaan, Conn., May 13, 1999.

28. William Robson to Ranald MacDougall, February 6, 1944, MacDougall Collection, AMPAS.

29. The following summary and quotations are based on Millard Lampell, "The Captain Comes Home," August 14, 1942, from the *It's the Navy* series, Lampell Collection, WISC.

30. Tapes of these three shows are featured in the two-volume boxed set, *Cavalcade of America*, Radio Spirits. "Take Her Down," by Norman Rosten, was broadcast on October 25, 1943; "Sky Nursemaid," by Sue Taylor White, was broadcast on June 28, 1943; "The Sailor Takes a Wife," by Allan Sloane, was broadcast on January 31, 1944.

31. Most of this account ("Take Her Down" featured . . . isolation booth) is based on Martin Grams Jr., *The History of the Cavalcade of America* (Kearney, Neb.: Morris Publishing, 1998). For the greater part, the book is unpaginated.

32. The rest of this account of the broadcast of "Take Her Down," obtained during a telephone interview, is based on the recollections of the actor, who prefers to remain anonymous.

33. The following summary and quotation from "The Sailor Takes A Wife" are based on the taped version of the broadcast. See footnote 32.

34. Sloane's account of his testimony concerning "The Sailor Takes a Wife" can be found in U.S. House Committee on Un-American Activities, *Communist Methods of Infiltration (Entertainment–Part 1). Hearing*

before a subcommittee of the Committee on Un-American Activities, 83rd Cong., 2nd sess., January 13, 1954, 3873-3874.

35. This account is based on a March 15, 1999 E-mail message from Lois Culver, widow of actor Howard Culver, who participated in broadcasts of *We Deliver The Goods*.

36. Alfred Friendly, "Guys on the Ground," adapted by Peter Martin, episode 75, December 5, 1944, Box 500, folder 2, *Words at War,* NBC Collection, WISC.

37. Polly Keusink, telephone conversation with author, January 10, 2000.

38. Both the following summary of the show and the quotes are taken from a script located in Office of Public Relations, General Records of the Department of the Navy, NA 80-167-11, LL NARS-Al.

39. Major General C. P. Gross, Chief of Transportation, to Mr. and Mrs. Hursley, August 9, 1944, Box 22, Hursley Collection, WYO.

THE ENEMY

... we the people, can win neither our war nor our peace unless we understand whom we are fighting. . . . This is a program of cruel hard truth. Not for the squeamish, or the timid. This truth is ugly and at times horrible. This is the truth about our enemy.

—Introduction to *This Is Our Enemy*

Your name is Ernie. It is September 1942. When you first heard about Hitler, before the war began, you wondered for a while about him. You are not the most politically minded person. But you believe in hearing both sides of any issue. You listened to the broadcasts of Father Coughlin and read articles about Charles Lindbergh and his pro-German views. Both seemed to offset the growing negative image that the media generally was presenting of Hitler, portraying him as a leader who was trying to defend his country against the threat of communism. Much of what they said made sense to you. You told your wife and friends, "Hitler may use some tough talk. But that's not my problem." You also heard some German shortwave broadcasts. "Maybe the Germans did get a raw deal in Versailles," you said to yourself. As far as you could tell, Hitler was doing what he needed to do to rebuild Germany.

The war in Europe has been raging for three years. The United States has been involved only for the last nine months. Initially, you

did not have much interest in the war, at least not in a personal sense.
You have no children and you are thirty-eight, too old to be drafted.
But you resent President Roosevelt and what you saw as his attempts
before Pearl Harbor was attacked to get the country into the war. In
any case, you have misgivings about why American soldiers and
American taxes had to become involved. The Germans are a civilized
people. They produced great musicians: Bach, Mozart, Beethoven,
and Wagner. Sure they made the first steps in the war. But every
country gets involved in wars.

The questions "Who are our Nazi enemies?" and "Why are we fighting them?" were commonly the subject of propaganda radio dramas during the war. Many of these programs were written for the "Ernies" in the United States. In addition, radio dramas asked how much responsibility for the war should be laid at the feet of the German people and whether it was appropriate to hate the Germans. One reason that these topics were chosen for radio propaganda was a concern that although Americans were in a rage toward the Japanese, they had too mild a perception of their German enemy. The campaign also was linked with the Roosevelt administration's decision to pursue an "Atlantic-first" strategy.

In April 1942, the Office of Facts and Figures' (OFF) Intelligence Bureau surveyed public opinion about the Axis enemies. Three to one, respondees favored putting more effort into fighting Japan than Germany. Research showed two reasons for this attitude: the obvious one was the attack on Pearl Harbor; racism toward the Japanese was the other. As a consequence of these findings and the Roosevelt administration's decision to give the German enemy priority, OFF launched a "nature of the enemy" propaganda campaign. It featured so many radio plays in 1942 on this theme that the year deserves the appellation, "The year of the nature of the enemy campaign."

The Office of War Information (OWI) conducted another survey in July. This one showed that when asked to describe the Japanese, respondents most commonly selected the words "sly," "cruel," and "treacherous." In contrast, although the same people chose terms such as "warlike" and "cruel" to characterize the Germans, they also called them "hard-working." Even while they were fighting the Germans, Americans could still say good things about them.

Reflecting popular sentiment, World War II propaganda often portrayed the Japanese as subhuman. For example, in "A Lesson in Japanese," a *Treasury Star Parade* episode, Fredric March, the narrator, says "Listen! Have you ever watched a well-trained monkey at the zoo! Have you seen how carefully he imitates his trainer. . . . The monkey goes through so many human movements so well that he actually seems to *be* human! But under his fur, he's still a savage little beast! Now consider the imitative little Japanese . . . who for 75 years has built himself into something so closely resembling a civilized human being that he actually believes he is just that."[1]

Shortly after comparing the Japanese to monkeys, the narrator switches metaphors and describes them as reptiles. Commenting on the strong "S" sound in the Japanese language, he says "You know, snakes have the same characteristic—hissing! What a sharp similarity. . . . The Japanese—some of them painted green—some of them covered with green mosquito netting—wiggling their way across the ground on the plains of Luzon—through the jungles of Java—the hills of Burma—Listen! [A soft hissing, building under] Do you hear them . . . ! Do you hear the little green snakes!"[2]

Treasury Star Parade was hardly the only show that vented American hostility toward the Japanese. A 1943 broadcast of *The Man Behind the Gun* features a Gurkha jungle fighter behind the Japanese lines in Burma. Having just returned from a mission in which his patrol surprised a Japanese patrol and killed them with their knives, he shows a British and an American soldier a trophy that he has taken. "No more Jap—no Johnny kill, Hee Hai! Look, Sah'b," he tells them. "Trade him for boots, eh?"[3] When the American realizes what the Gurkha is showing them, he is shocked. The script doesn't say it outright, but it is clear that the Gurkha is holding the genitals of a Japanese soldier. "Well—your own Indians in America—" the British soldier starts to tell him, at which point the American interrupts him. "That was plain honest scalping, sonny—Whoo!" The message appears to be, "Look Yank, it's war and the Gurkhas have their ways—and after all these are only Japs. So don't be so shocked!"

Lux Radio Theatre also pulled no punches in its hostility toward the Japanese. One *Lux* show, "So Proudly We Hail," features Veronica Lake in the role of Olivia, a bitter and moody Army nurse who was evacuated from the island of Corregidor after its surrender to the Japanese. Olivia had already lost her fiancé, who had been killed at Pearl Harbor. Now, she learns that ten of her nurse colleagues have been left behind to fall into the hands of the Japanese because there was not enough room on the evacuation transports. When a colleague attempts to deal with Olivia's bitterness, Olivia responds angrily, "I know why I'm here and I know what I am going to do," she says. "I'm going to kill Japs—every bloodstained one I can get my hands on. . . . Doesn't sound nice coming from a nurse? Does it? We're supposed to be angels of mercy . . . we're supposed to serve humanity in the name of humanity. What humanity? Jap humanity?"[4]

Such shows that appealed to the public's baser sentiments received, of course, some letters expressing approbation. In October 1942, a listener to *Lux*'s "Wake Island" responded to the broadcast by writing to DeMille, "The nation should . . . put every penny they have in stamps and bonds to kill the yellow Japs."[5] However, two *Lux* shows with messages similar to "So Proudly We Hail," prompted critical reaction. A 1943 broadcast of "Salute to the Marines" inspired a listener to complain, "We resent being bombarded with racial hatreds, fictitious threats and fears. Give us realism. We can take it and Lord knows we need it. Only give us play selections that stick to the truth."[6] The following year, an official of the Missouri Council of Churches wrote in response to the airing of "Guadalcanal [Diary]" "I want to protest vigorously against including such statements as will develop more class and race bitterness. In the play . . . one of your principal characters said, in speaking of the Japanese people, 'Japs ain't people!'"[7]

In December 1942, during a broadcast of *Lights Out*, Arch Oboler articulated a candid view of the Japanese that was somewhat typical of the times. "A few weeks ago I started a game," he wrote around the time of the first anniversary of the attack on Pearl Harbor. "Perhaps you heard about it. It's called 'They're here for me.' It's a very simple game. You sit where you are and you think, 'The Japs, the Nazis— they're here for me. Not for someone in the newspapers, or someone in the town half-way across the world, someone I don't even know in this neighbourhood. But for me.' Yeah, a smirky little Jap is standing at the door. He's there for you—not in the headlines, not just an idea, but actually there for you. It can happen you know. Three million dead in Europe attest to that fact. Think about that Jap or that Nazi waiting for you and then remember that every War savings Stamp and every War Bond that you buy is a bullet, or a bomb, or a tank, or an airplane between you personally, and the horror of a Jap-Nazi world."[8]

Even shortly after the war ended, while trying to make a plea for tolerance of Japanese-Americans, Oboler could not restrain his anger. In September 1945, NBC aired his "The Family Nagashi," about a family who had spent the war in an American internment camp. Early in the broadcast, Oboler interrupts to say "I bring you this play not because I'm a lover of those slant-eyed individuals who raped Nanking . . . [and] . . . beat and murdered their . . . American prisoners. I bring it to you because . . . an injustice done to any of us is an injustice to all of us."[9]

Oboler played a particularly prominent, perhaps radical, role in the wartime propaganda campaign. His statements about the Japanese reflected views that he expressed months earlier when he caused a stir at the annual meeting of the Institute for Education by Radio at Ohio State University. He had argued that to successfully carry on the war, Americans needed to hate all that the enemy stood for. At the time he had specified "the Nazis," but given his later statements about the Japanese, he clearly applied the statement to both nations and their armies.

As part of his remarks, Oboler also attacked the networks' stalling and half-heartedness. Not a network representative spoke up during the whole two-and-a-half hours of the session during which Oboler made his remarks. The press picked up his statement, and Eleanor Roosevelt and writer Norman Cousins later debated the issue in the July 4th edition of the *Saturday Review*, with Cousins supporting Oboler's position and Roosevelt taking the position that "as dedicated to the struggle as we needed to be, hate is a destructive force."[10]

In addition to his comments about the enemy during the broadcasts and at the radio conference, Oboler presented his views in "Hate," a play in his first series of the war.[11] The series, *Plays for Americans*, premiered in April 1942, the same prolific month as Corwin's *"This Is War."* "Hate" depicts a Norwegian minister who attempts to mediate between his congregation and a Nazi force that occupies his town. He accepts the promise of the German commander, a major, not to harm any of the town's residents. The minister then advises his congregation not to resist and preaches that faith will ensure resolution of the town's problems. Afterward, on learning that the major deceived him and had six of his fellow townsmen hanged, the minister realizes his naïveté and winds up killing the major with his bare hands.

Although broadcasts concerning the Japanese were the most vituperative ones, the bulk of the nature of the enemy propaganda shows dealt with Germany. In an unfinished memoir, the late actor Arnold Moss recalled that this led to a demand for radio actors who were not in the service who could do dialects well. "Hardly a day went by," he wrote, "when I failed to play at least one of the despised Nazis on somebody's program." Frequently, two popular Nazi songs, "Deutschland Uber Alles" and the "Horst Wessel Song," were played as background for many of the roles that Moss assumed. As a result they became part of his subconscious. One lovely spring day, as Moss was marching along Madison Avenue, he noticed people stopping to stare at him in amazement. "Some few even started to follow me," wrote Moss, " I hadn't the remotest idea what there was about me that was attracting so much attention. It finally came to me. As I'd been walking at a brisk, almost military pace, I'd been singing. Not very loud, but loud enough to attract the crowds that had begun to stare. And what had I been singing as I stepped along . . . in my lively rhythm? A snappy little Nazi tune left over from the broadcast I'd just concluded. . . . From that moment on, I walked slowly, in dogged stony silence. The crowd dispersed."[12]

Bill Lipton, another actor who played the role of a Nazi, also got into some trouble. In one radio drama he so convincingly played the role of a German boy who turned in his father to the Gestapo that for a while afterward he experienced a genuine antagonism from some of the Jewish musicians in the show's orchestra.[13]

Oboler's 1942 *Treasury Star Parade* broadcast, "Chicago, Germany," is one of the war's best known "nature of the enemy" radio plays. Featuring Joan Blondell, it tells the story of the deterioration of a family in a Chicago conquered by Nazi invaders. One sister becomes a prostitute, a second one becomes a slave laborer. Marion, played by Blondell, categorizes the destruction of the American way of life:

Marion: . . . What is there in life for somebody just plain ordinary like me? To marry someone you love.

Voice: Verboten!

Marion: To have children.

Voice : Verboten!

Marion: To have a home.

Voice: Verboten! . . .

Marion: To—to go shopping on pay day—

Voice: Verboten!

Marion: If you haven't got the money—window shop.

Voice: Verboten!

Marion: And see the kids growin' up and going to school.

Voice: Verboten!

Marion: And getting smarter than you are—and they grow older and you grow older with the man you love—and just living like human beings! But now I wasn't a human being anymore—They said so! "Verboten"—everything verboten for me—for people *like* me who are just plain Americans! . . . This was *their* world—*they'd won* . . . there wasn't any place left on the world for us.[14]

At the end of the broadcast comes reprieve. "This has been a play," says the announcer, "of an America that must never happen—that *will* never happen!"

Another early show dealing with the Nazis was Norman Corwin's "The Enemy," broadcast on a Saturday night in April 1942 as number nine in *This Is War.* "The Enemy" dramatizes Axis attitudes in a bitter propagandistic mood. *Variety* reviewed it favorably, calling narrator Clifton Fadiman's reading of his part a "tour de force." "No doubt," wrote the reviewer, "we need such reminders of what the Nazis are like, such broad hints of what our fate will be if we fail to crush them. We are a good natured people. Willing to believe, a lot of us that under a more congenial economy a lot of rats might have grown up to be household pets. Only economic determinism doomed them to be vultures. The Nazis, so runs one all too familiar argument, have been merely obeying nature in seeking a more roomy rat run. We must not condemn them."[15]

"The Enemy" illustrates the naïveté of some U.S. wartime propaganda. In one scene, a teacher in Warsaw asks a young student named

Woczinski the seemingly unnecessary question of whether she is Polish. On the other hand, a scene of the forced draining of blood from that child illustrates the reality of a system that placed genocide on an equal footing with winning the war. If it sounded like a propaganda excess to an American radio audience of 1942, it is quite credible more than fifty more years after the war and the Holocaust to an American who has seen films such as *Sophie's Choice* and *Schindler's List*. In reality, the problem with wartime American radio was that it understated Nazi atrocities. Newspapers of the day featured articles about Nazi concentration camps. However, they fell far short of describing the mass slaughter that was taking place in the camps and elsewhere. By and large the radio dramatists were unaware that the horrors they were describing in their plays were minuscule compared with the actual murder of 12 million Jews and Gentiles in the death camps and by firing squads.

Rex Stout wrote only one radio play. But as head of the Writers War Board (WWB) he exerted immense influence on its decision to deal with the "hate the enemy" and "nature of the enemy" issues. Before the war, Stout read extensively about Germany and the Germans.[16] He developed a strong antipathy toward pan-Germanism, the notion of uniting all the German speaking people of central Europe under one rule. During the war he also directed this antipathy toward Germans in general in public lectures, radio programs, and magazines articles. During a visit with fourteen other writers, editors, and photographers to a war zone in Europe, Stout translated his aggressive feelings into direct action. One day the group found themselves in the German city of Aachen, which was still experiencing heavy fighting. While standing behind a tree, Stout took the opportunity to fire a shot at a distant enemy soldier.

Two weeks after the Lidice broadcast, Stout gave a talk about the work of the Lidice Committee at a P.E.N. dinner. During the course of the evening, he became involved in a shouting match with two members of the audience, among them the well-known civil libertarian lawyer Arthur Garfield Hayes. Hayes and the other man were incensed at what they perceived as a rabid anti-Germanism that was no more logical than the Nazi belief that Germans constituted a superior race.

Carl Friedrich, a Harvard University professor, joined the fray in an article in the *New York Times*. Friedrich and Stout were already antagonists from about a year or so earlier. Stout had been instrumental in ousting Friedrich from the Council for Democracy because of Friedrich's resistance to the council's growing involvement in the production of war propaganda. Friedrich took issue with the notion that one had to hate the enemy, contending that ". . . hate is a sign of weakness . . . it is a defeatist in disguise who preaches hate. For what he really says is this: We do not know whether what we are fighting for is right; therefore we must hate our enemies."[17] In addition, Friedrich warned about the undesirable effects on children of broadcasting hate. He acknowledged the need to tell the truth about the enemy but insisted that radio programming needed to do this without descending to the level of the enemy. As an illustration of how this could be done, Friedrich cited a recent *Treasury Star Parade* broadcast in which the leading character told about "his German born little grocer . . . in such a way as to warn the audience very effectively against the fifth column and yet at the same time arouse sympathy for this poor chap by having him turn over to the War Bond campaign funds which he had been holding for a Nazi relative of his."

By September, with the various elements of the "nature of the enemy" campaign having been put into operation, the networks, the WWB, the OWI, and the Roosevelt administration in general achieved their goal. The results of surveys by the OWI's Intelligence Bureau presented a pleasing picture to these groups. The public had changed its views on the question of which enemy needed to be defeated first. A majority now believed that it was Germany, not Japan. Carl Friedrich had not changed Stout's views, and Stout was still on the attack. That same month he told a radio audience "I am willing to grant to any grown German one right and one only, the right to a decent burial." He came to believe that the main obstacle to peace was an inherent antidemocratic trait of the German national character. For Stout, the German people as a whole, not just Hitler, were responsible for events in their country and for German aggression throughout Europe. The *Treasury Star Parade*'s view, for example, that differentiated the average German citizen from his Nazi leaders, was unacceptable. And Stout was convinced that the American people needed to be persuaded to see the rectitude of his view. First, using his formidable powers of persuasion, he convinced the WWB to adopt his view as its own. A significant part of the reason for the decision was the WWB's view that it had to assist the government to eliminate the possibility of a premature peace in order to achieve unconditional surrender.

Stout continued his attack in the following year. In January 1943, in an article in the *New York Times Magazine,* he propounded the theory that Hitler was the culmination of a deeply rooted mental and nervous disease afflicting the German people. "I hate all Germans who accept the doctrine of the German master race," he wrote, "and I hate all Germans who reluctant to join the Nazis, nevertheless, failed, through lack of courage . . . to prevent the Nazis from seizing power."[18]

Stout's article produced a storm of controversy, and the *Times* was inundated with letters condemning his views. One, from a New Jersey man, illustrated the type of thinking that may have inspired Stout to adopt such a radical view in the first place.[19] At least seven months before publication of the New Jersey man's letter, the *Times* had begun publishing stories about Hitler's firing squads having murdered hundreds of thousands of European civilians. Yet the writer likened Nazi crimes to "mean and brutish things" that he did as a child, despite which his mother maintained affection for him. He suggested that the Nazis, too, would eventually have to be forgiven.

Stout's WWB used the airwaves to affect the public's perception of Germany in a number of ways, including distributing recommendations that radio vocabulary be changed along "suitable lines." It advocated use of the word "German" instead of "Nazi," except where specific reference was made to the Nazi Party; it preferred "enslaved" to "occupied" when referring to territory held by the Germans; "murder" was to replace "execute" when referring to Germans killing civilians; and "Russians" was to be used rather than "Reds." The last suggestion reflected the WWB's conviction that U.S. hostility to the Soviet Union was a severe obstacle to Allied unity during the war and to the achievement of postwar objectives that the WWB endorsed.

The WWB also sponsored anti-Axis, particularly strong anti-German, propaganda, including two of the most important plays in the "nature of the enemy" campaign. One was Stephen Vincent Benét's

"They Burned the Books," a powerful piece linked to a nationwide event that had occurred in Nazi Germany in 1933.[20] The event, the public burning of books written by Jews and other alleged enemies of Germany, shocked the world but provoked only a mild outcry at the time. In fact, around the time of the incident, Lewis Mumford, the prominent social philosopher, speaking before the American Academy of the Arts, suggested that though the fascist enemy was ugly and despicable, burning books was not altogether a negative thing. There was too much being published all the time, so he told his audience. Access to the printed page was too easy.[21]

It took nine years from the time of the book burning, and several months into the war for the United States, before this horrific incident was depicted in a play on American radio. The impetus came from an OFF official, and the idea was passed on to the WWB, which then worked out a collaborative effort with the newly formed Council on Books in Wartime.[22] It was the resulting committee to coordinate commemorative efforts that contacted Stephen Vincent Benét and asked him to write a script.

At the time that Benét was asked to write "They Burned the Books," he was trying to complete a long poem, *Western Star*. But passionately dedicated to the war effort, he put it aside and began to work on the WWB project. The result was a stirring protest against the tyranny of the Nazis' "New Order." Benét reenacted the original incident by evoking voices of the authors whose books were burned. He then showed what the United States would be like under the Nazis. The events described in "They Burned the Books" signaled clearly the nature of Nazi attitudes toward freedom of expression. "They Burned the Books" proclaims that no fire can burn out the human spirit; fascism will go the way of all tyrannies.

"They Burned the Books" was one of the most influential radio plays of the war era. NBC broadcast it in May 1942 and again the following year. The WWB designated the play its first "Script of the Month" and distributed it widely for use by schools, local broadcasts, and Army camps, where it was used for "orientation." It was also translated into several languages, dispatched overseas, and published in book form and in an abbreviated version in *Scholastic Magazine*.

The occasion of its rebroadcast in 1942 was part of a widely coordinated and publicized campaign sponsored in part by the Council of Books in Wartime to commemorate the original book burning. The Council contacted 350 clergymen, asking them to mention the anniversary in their May 9 sermons, and Eleanor Roosevelt published an article about the book burning in her syndicated weekly newspaper column. The New York Public Library displayed its flag at half mast and asked librarians around the United States to do likewise. The library also distributed nationwide a list of books that the Nazis had banned.[23]

The WWB's second major radio drama in verse to promote its "nature of the enemy" campaign was Edna St. Vincent Millay's "The Murder of Lidice." This play was a response to a particularly heinous Nazi atrocity in the Czech town of Lidice. In May 1942, Czech partisans assassinated Deputy Chief of the Gestapo Reinhard Heydrich, known as "the Hangman of Europe" because of his role in the slaughter of conquered people. In retribution, shortly afterward, ten truckloads of German Security Police leveled the town, executed all male adult inhabitants, and deported the surviving women and children.

The savagery at Lidice horrified the world. In the United States, the WWB reacted by collaborating with Elmer Davis, newly appointed to his position at the OWI, to use the episode to unify the Allies against the Nazis. Although the WWB was to do all the work, the decision was made to establish a "front committee" that would appear to do it.

The WWB's first activity involved the renaming of an Illinois village with a substantial Czech population in memory of Lidice. The objective was to counter the Nazi intent to erase "Lidice" from the map. The effort, aided by the endorsement of an honorary committee containing 110 names, received widespread publicity. Among the members of the committee were Albert Einstein, Carl Sandburg, Justice William O. Douglas, and actress Tallulah Bankhead. A second abortive renaming of a town, in Canada, proved an embarrassment when somebody forgot to get the consent of the villagers. Hearing about the plan that had been made without their knowledge, they refused to go along with the idea.

The WWB's request that Edna St. Vincent Millay write a dramatized poem commemorating Lidice was fortunately more successful than the

Canadian effort. Like fellow poets Benét and Archibald MacLeish, Millay was also working in the service of war propaganda. Like MacLeish, she traveled the road from ardent pacifism to passionate advocacy of American participation in the war. The rise of fascism in Europe caused her not only to change her views but also to try to awaken people to the dangers of Nazism. The fall of Czechoslovakia and events in Spain inspired her to write strong poems, such as a sonnet, "Czechoslovakia," and "Say That We Saw Spain Die," which gave voice to her anguish.

Although not in very good health, Millay responded to the WWB's request, working all summer at a feverish pace. The result of her labor, "The Murder of Lidice," was broadcast on NBC in October with Alexander Woollcott acting as master of ceremonies. It was also beamed via shortwave to Australia, New Zealand, Brazil, and a variety of other countries. At the end of the broadcast, Millay assisted in auctioning the bound manuscript of the broadcast to benefit Czech War Relief. It sold for $1,000. Second to the broadcast of Benét's "They Burned the Books," this was the most prominent WWB sponsorship of a propaganda radio play.

Despite the publicity that attended "The Murder of Lidice" and despite some polite reviews, as the childish rhymes of the following excerpt illustrate, the play was far from being Millay's best work.

Good people all, from our graves we call
To you, so happy and free;
Whether ye live in a village small
Or in a city with buildings tall,
Or the sandy lonesome beach of the sea,
Or the woody hills, or the flat prairie
Hear us speak; oh hear what we say;
We are the people of Lidice![24]

A review of the Millay poem that appeared in the *New Republic* called it "a poor poem, full of unintentional comic lines such as "Heydrich the Hangman howls tonight. He howls for a bucket of bubbly blood.""[25] To the reviewer, Millay's play served only to reduce the very real and terrible tragedy of Lidice to embarrassing bathos.

Not content with just the one radio play about Lidice, the WWB sponsored a second, one month later, based on a short Paramount film and featuring Clifton Fadiman and actress Madeleine Carroll. If the radio version was anything like the filmed one, it would have been better not done. *The New Republic* described the former as suffering from "so much mawkishness, ineptness, and so many mock-heroic speeches, that it left Lidice half-drowned in grease paint and glycerine tears."[26]

In 1948, Millay repudiated what she called her "bad wartime poems" that she said were not warranted even to back up morale. She included in that category "The Murder of Lidice." Stephen Vincent Benét anticipated this kind of postwar perception of wartime propaganda. In this case, it was the poet herself who was unfairly applying the criteria of a different time to her own work.

The WWB also sponsored two other plays dealing with Germany. One, "The Nature of the Enemy," put great emphasis on the idea of collective guilt.[27] The other, "The Nazi," one of the WWB's two script selections for December 1942, told the story of a family in occupied France whose son joined the Nazis and denounced his father, a member of the French underground.

In December 1943, *Words at War* presented one of the most interesting portrayals of the German enemy. A play entitled "The Ninth Commandment" tells the story of a Dutch family who take in Johann, a malnourished German boy, shortly after the end of World War I.[28] Twice, Samuel, the Calvinist father who is so strict that he even locks the family's sugar bowl, catches Johann stealing from it and then lying when confronted. After the second incident, Samuel gives Johann a severe thrashing. Johann then musses his hair, pulls buttons off his shirt to exaggerate its effects, and visits the town's mayor. There he accuses Samuel of regularly beating and starving him. Shortly afterward, Johann returns to Germany. One day, several years later, Johann, now a strapping six-footer appears again in Holland. He visits Samuel, pretending to have come on a vacation, and Samuel puts him up for a week. In reality, Johann is spying for the Nazis, who by now have come to power. What makes the play so interesting is the implied origin of Johann's deceit and his willingness to do the Nazis' dirty work. At least in his early youth, there is no indication that this is a boy whom the Nazis have brainwashed. The earliest signs of his evil character appear to be rooted elsewhere, perhaps in his essential identity as a German. He is a liar and an opportunist from an early age. And he easily assumes the role of a spy who betrays those who had earlier taken him into the bosom of their family.

In addition to the individual shows, the OFF/OWI series *You Can't Do Business with Hitler* and *This Is Our Enemy* sought to mold public opinion concerning the nature of the enemy. *You Can't Do Business* was based on a book by the same name, by Douglas Miller, an ardent interventionist and a former commercial attaché at the American Embassy in Berlin. Miller's book stressed that Germany was using business as a weapon in its effort to achieve global domination, and the radio series hit on a broad variety of relevant themes with episodes bearing titles such as "Work or Die," "Money Talks with a German Accent," and "Swastikas Over the Equator."

"No American Goods Wanted" deals with an alleged Nazi conspiracy to destroy America's trade relations with Europe. "Broken Promises" dramatizes that Germans were not living up to their business contracts with international trading partners. But the series also went beyond its title with shows such as "The Anti-Christ" and "Pagan Gods," both of which demonstrate Hitler's campaign to destroy Christianity and replace it with a Nazi religion.

In a significant way, *You Can't Do Business* misrepresented the relationship between the German people and their government. The series shows a gulf between the German people and the Nazi Party, distinguishing the people from their leadership. [29] In fact it was inaccurate. By and large, the Germans supported their government both before and during the war, at least until it became obvious that Germany was about to lose the war. Many Americans then—and decades later—were oblivious to the fact that the Nazis came to power initially because of the popular support at the ballot box. Running against Kurt von Hindenburg in the 1932 presidential elections, Hitler won 38 percent of the vote, which was hardly a majority but sufficient to prompt Hindenburg to bring Hitler into the government, giving him a base to gather the rest of his power through extraconstitutional means. However, *You Can't Do Business* made it appear that the Germans were just as much victims of the Nazis as were people in the occupied countries. For example, according to a show entitled "Work or Die," as the result of an eight-year process, the average German worker was enslaved. Similarly, according to two other installments, "Beast of Burden" and "The Sell Out," the Gestapo had turned German businessmen into beasts of burden whose role was to serve the "New Order."

Unfortunately, the record of listener reaction to *You Can't Do Business* is quite weak. At least one listener, a Philadelphia resident, objected in March 1943 to the show's attempt to present the Germans as victims of the Nazis: "I heard your #54 broadcast of the hardships undergone by the German people . . . have you heard by any chance how they DO treat their slave labor—women brought in from other countries? Now who under the sun wrote that dribble for you anyway. The only time I or other Americans wish to hear propaganda with regards to germans, is when two german (sic) lives are taken for each of our dear lads that will perish in this world catastrophe the Germans brought on. . . . We had enough propaganda after the last war in favor of germany and its authorities and the poor, poor, poor people. . . . That sort of dribble that was handed out Sunday reeks too much of Senators Wheeler and Nye, who would isolate us to the advantage of the Germans."[30] On the other hand, another listener, a Chicagoan, representing a smaller group of listeners who heard a German language version of one of the shows, wrote:

> In every German American home one will hear "'do you listen to that filthy propaganda 'You can't do business with Hitler?'" Well and the answer always is Pfui Teufel [yuck, affirmative]: any good and decent German American will not listen and as soon as that phrase is announced they will turn off the German hour program! The listeners will boycott such storekeepers who advertise such broadcasts. And your Jewish outfit will not benefit by that. What German American people expect is good music and not filthy propaganda, otherwise we do not need a German Hour! . . . Must everything be as filthy as the Hollywood Films they are showing all over? Everybody knows that it is nothing else but war propaganda and filth and the people are fed up on that kind of mudslinging and you do likewise!
> Disgusted,
> American-born German![31]

Like *You Can't Do Business with Hitler, This Is Our Enemy* continued to emphasize Nazi Germany as the chief enemy. If the characters in *This Is Our Enemy* were often unidimensional, they were also often placed into telling plots. In one show, a ten-year-old boy dies of a burst appendix because the adult head of his Hitler Youth group refuses to heed his cries of pain. Later, the same man, distorting the circumstances of the boy's death, presents the boy's parents with a scroll honoring their son for having given his life for the Führer. In another installment, a young lawyer, a dedicated Nazi, is forbidden to marry his sweetheart because a required medical examination reveals that she will not be able to conceive a child. In both shows, the Nazis come off as caricatures of themselves. One wonders if the series's failure to humanize the villains sabotaged its ability to persuade listeners to accept as true its descriptions of the Third Reich. Unfortunately, perhaps because of the many similar shows that flooded the airwaves, it is virtually impossible to identify anyone who even remembered the series, let alone any of its individual shows.

How did wartime radio drama depict America's enemies and to what extent did these radio plays achieve their objectives? In general, wartime radio had carte blanche in portraying the Japanese enemy as it wished. It often employed racist epithets for a listening audience that needed little encouragement in expressing its hostility toward its culturally alien Asian enemy. Few Americans were inclined to give the Japanese the benefit of the doubt. Thus, OWI surveys conducted in the late spring of 1944 revealed that only 13 percent of them thought that the Japanese people would like to get rid of their leadership.

In contrast to the weak challenge that American radio drama faced in presenting the Japanese foe, in depicting the German enemy it had its job cut out for it. Many Americans, including Dwight Eisenhower, Supreme Commander of the Allied Forces in Europe, traced at least part of their ancestry back to Germany. Adding to this, a powerful streak of isolationism ran through recent American history; and, as the popularity of Father Coughlin demonstrates, some elements of American society subscribed to the reactionary philosophies that underlay the German and Italian political systems. Finally, many Americans felt antagonistic toward Germany's enemy, the Soviet Union. This sometimes translated into the notion that the enemy of my enemy is my friend.

With all these obstacles to a unified anti-German sentiment, American radio had to forcefully detail why Americans should mount an all-out effort against the Third Reich. Government radio drama often took a moderate approach, mainly targeting Germany's leadership and stressing how the Nazis abused their own citizens. In contrast, the WWB, under the influence of Rex Stout, sponsored shows that often fostered attitudes of hatred not only toward the Nazis but also against Germany as a whole. Partly as a consequence of thousands of "nature of the enemy" broadcasts, the American public developed increasing hostility toward Germany. In 1942, the earliest of these programs helped convince Americans that the war against Germany deserved a higher priority than the fight against Japan. And toward the end of the war, increased enmity toward Germany helped diminish sentiment for a negotiated peace and lent support for prosecution of accused war criminals. It would be a mistake to overstate the influence of these broadcasts, however. Exaggerated portrayal of the victimization of the German people in the *You Can't Do Business with Hitler* series and *This Is Our Enemy* helped restrain the capacity to vilify the German populace to the American public.

Massive numbers of Germans voted the Nazis into the Reichstag and scores—or perhaps thousands—of Germans served as support staff for the secret police and concentration camp apparatus. But to many Americans the Germans appeared to be blameless victims of their "masters" right up to and beyond the end of the war. The same OWI survey that showed most Americans believing that the Japanese were satisfied with their wartime leadership indicated that 65 percent of them believed that the German people wanted to get rid of their Nazi leadership. These attitudes contributed to the climate that resulted in the U.S. government's moderate treatment of the German enemy at the end of the war. Thus, the United States supported a policy whereby the war crimes tribunals focused primarily on senior Nazi officials responsible for human rights violations. In addition, U.S. occupation forces employed many Germans whose wartime roles were highly questionable. Furthermore, the U.S. government's failure to establish appropriate statutes permitted some sixty Nazi war criminals to enter the United States.

NOTES

1. Neal Hopkins, "A Lesson in Japanese," in William Bacher, ed., *The Treasury Star Parade* (New York: Farrar & Rinehart, 1945), 359.

2. Hopkins, "Lesson in Japanese," in Bacher, *Treasury Star Parade*, 363.

3. Allan Sloane, *The Man Behind the Gun*, October 11, 1943, private collection.

4. "So Proudly We Hail," *Lux Radio Theatre*, November 1, 1943.

5. E. Frank Morgan to C. B. DeMille, October 26, 1942, Box 1116, folder 9, DeMille Archives, BYU.

6. Herbert Palmer to C. B. DeMille, November 8, 1943, Box 1128, folder 1, DeMille Archives, BYU.

7. Mr. Beck, General Secretary of the Missouri Council of Churches, to C. B. DeMille, March 2, 1944, Box 1129, folder 2, DeMille Archives, BYU.

8. J. Fred MacDonald, *Don't Touch That Dial: Radio Programming in American Life, 1920–1960* (Chicago: Nelson Hall, 1979), 67–68.

9. Arch Oboler's "The Family Nagashi," broadcast September 27, 1945, a tape of which can be found in *Arch Oboler Remembers WWII*, Radio Spirits.

10. Eleanor Roosevelt, "Must We Hate to Fight," *Saturday Review of Literature* 25, no. 13 (July 4, 1942).

11. Arch Oboler, *Plays for Americans* (New York: Farrar & Rinehart, 1942), 25–41.

12. From an unpublished memoir, personal papers of Arnold Moss, private collection.

13. Bill Lipton to author, October 6, 1999.

14. Arch Oboler, "Chicago Germany," in Oboler, *Plays for Americans,* 65–83.

15. *Variety*, April 15, 1942, vol. 146, no. 6, 32.

16. Except where otherwise indicated, this discussion of Stout's attitude toward the Germans is based on John McAleer, *Rex Stout: A Biography* (Boston: Little, Brown, 1977).

17. C. J. Friedrich, "Case Against Hate," *New York Times*, August 30, 1942, VIII, 8:5.

18. Rex Stout, "We Shall Hate or We Shall Fail," *New York Times Magazine,* January 17, 1943, VII, 29.

19. George C. Vincent, letter to the editor, *New York Times*, January 21, 1943, 20:6.

20. Stephen Vincent Benét, *We Stand United and Other Radio Scripts* (New York: Farrar & Rinehart, 1945), 99–117.

21. Norman Corwin, "Radio and Morale," *Saturday Review of Literature* 25 (July 4, 1942): 6–7.

22. Thomas Howell, "The Writers War Board: Writers and World War II" (Ph.D. diss., Louisiana State University, 1971), 219.

23. *Bulletin*, May 20, 1943, Council of Books in Wartime, 2.

24. Edna St. Vincent Millay, *The Murder of Lidice* (New York: Harper, 1942), 30.

25. "Lidice Lives by Committee," *New Republic* 107, no. 19 (November 9, 1942): 593.

26. "Lidice Lives," *New Republic*, 593.

27. McAleer, *Rex Stout,* 314–315.

28. Hendrick Willem Van Loon, "The Ninth Commandment," episode 29, adapted by Richard McDonough, December 28, 1943, *Words at War*, Box 499, folder 3, NBC Collection, WISC.

29. Gerhard Horten, "Radio Goes to War: The Cultural Politics of Propaganda during World War II" (Ph.D. diss., University of California at Berkeley, 1994), 97.

30. Name illegible, to Office of War Information, March 5, 1943, NA.

31. Listener response to Chicago station WGES, February 24, 1942; NA 208-233-1119 as quoted in Horten, "Radio Goes to War," 140.

"Programs such as yours are a wonderful thing for morale," sailor Milard King Roper (c. 1943) wrote to Stephen Vincent Benét after hearing a broadcast of Letters from Adolph *on a car radio while hitching back to base. (Courtesy of Betty Roper.)*

(L. to R.) Cecil B. DeMille, Ruth Hussey, Cary Grant, Katharine Hepburn, unidentified man, and Virginia Weidler admire James Stewart's Army Air Corps uniform in the studio of the Lux Radio Theatre in July 1942. Stewart, one of Hollywood's most popular actors, narrated Norman Corwin's December 1941 four-network broadcast "We Hold These Truths" and participated in a number of other war-era radio plays. DeMille, the enormously successful film director and producer, hosted the Lux show and was its pseudo-producer for a seven-year period ending in early 1945. (Courtesy of National Archives.)

Joseph Julian, c. 1947, popular radio actor in the 1940s through the 1970s, narrated Norman Corwin's 1942 series This Is War *from England. Julian unsuccessfully sued the blacklisters in the 1950s. (Courtesy of Allan Sloane.)*

Joseph Liss, radio writer and wartime head of the Editorial Division of the Office of War Information's Domestic Radio Bureau. (Courtesy of Emily Liss Nixon.)

William B. Lewis (c. 1943). As a vice president of CBS, Lewis was Norman Corwin's mentor. Later he served as an executive with the Office of Facts and Figures and the Office of War Information, which produced the Uncle Sam series and numerous other war-related shows. (Courtesy of Lucille Lewis Johnson.)

Frank and Doris Hursley (on left) with unidentified interviewer (c.1943). The Hursleys lived on a Wisconsin farm while they produced American Women and Service to the Front, two wartime morale-boosting shows. (Photo by Howard Greeter; courtesy of Deborah Hardy.)

(L. to R.) Canada Lee, Dorothy Maynor, Fredi Washington, and Fredric March in a New York studio of the Mutual Broadcasting System during rehearsals in 1943 for "Beyond the Call of Duty." (Courtesy of Frances Lee Pearson.)

William Robson, talented director of CBS's The Man Behind the Gun *and other shows. Robson, who also wrote and directed "An Open Letter on Racism," the 1943 antiracist show that won a Peabody Award, was blacklisted in the postwar era. (Courtesy of Allan Sloane.)*

(L. to R.) Carl Sandburg, writer Norman Rosten, and Orson Welles in the famous NBC Studio 8H during the occasion of the August 29, 1942, broadcast of Rosten's Ballad of Bataan. (Photo by Mary Morris; courtesy of Patricia Rosten Filan. All reasonable efforts have been made to locate the copyright holder.)

Allan Sloane (second from right in rear) and fellow soldiers at Ft. Bragg, North Carolina, in 1941, from which he smuggled out articles criticizing segregation in the Armed Forces. One of radio's most skilled writers, Sloane wrote for Green Valley, USA, The Man Behind the Gun, *and many other shows. (Courtesy of Allan Sloane.)*

During the war, Morton Wishengrad, shown here with actress Siobhan McKenna, wrote for NBC's Labor for Victory series, the American Red Cross, as well as the Cavalcade of America. After the war, he helped develop the popular Jewish program The Eternal Light. (Courtesy of Tess Wishengrad Siegel.)

Arnold Moss (c. 1950), one of radio's most proficient actors, frequently played German roles in World War II era radio broadcasts. (Courtesy of Andrea End.)

(L. to R.) Norman Corwin, Elliot Lewis, Fletcher Markle, and Arch Oboler, four of radio's great directors, in later years (c. 1985). Corwin and Oboler produced hundreds of war-related plays; Lewis acted in many of Oboler's wartime shows before becoming a director; Markle produced wartime documentaries for the Royal Canadian Air Force, before emigrating to the United States. (Courtesy of Thousand Oaks Library.)

Together with her husband, Frank, Anne Hummert (c. 1940) was the creator of numerous radio soap operas. During the war, at government request, the Hummerts created Chaplain Jim, *a popular show that provided reassurance for the families of GIs. (Courtesy of Lincoln Center Library for the Performing Arts.)*

British-born Violet Atkins Klein (shown with her husband c. 1950) wrote for Treasury Star Parade. *(Courtesy of Gilda Block.)*

College professor, broadcast historian, and former script director Erik Barnouw helped develop the NBC series Words at War. (Courtesy of Erik Barnouw.)

Actor Larry Haines was a regular on CBS's The Man Behind the Gun, *a program known for first-rate writing and a rich repertoire of sound effects. (Courtesy of Larry Haines.)*

11

AMERICA'S ALLIES: THE BRITISH

I could rather see the Germans in England than those damned aristocratic, horse riding snobs there now. The English have done nothing in this war thus far except borrow money, planes, and men from the United States.

—Theodore Dreiser, in Richard Lingemann, *Theodore Dreiser*

Your name is Peter Conlon. You live in Boston but you were born in Belfast, Northern Ireland. Five years ago, in 1937, you left your family and emigrated to America. You were twenty-four. Two years later, war broke out in Europe. Shortly afterward, your older brother was one of sixty-five persons whom the British arrested on suspicion of being Irish Republicans.[1] Without benefit of a trial, they interned him and the others in Londonderry for the duration of the war. More recently, a cousin with whom you grew up died, also in connection with the struggle against the British. He had been arrested after allegedly taking part in raids on a post office and a bank in Northern Ireland. He was tried, convicted, and given a lengthy prison sentence. When he and two others took part in a hunger strike, the British allowed the three of them to die.

It is now March 1942. America's entry into the war weighs heavily on you. You don't know quite what to make of it. You read in the papers and you hear Edward R. Murrow on the radio from London about the heroism of the British during Nazi bombings of their cities. At the same time, you and your family have little love for the British. The Irish-American newspapers that you read report that the British helped to bring on the war and expected the United States to bail them out as it had during the Great War a couple of decades ago. You still have some clippings from before Pearl Harbor. "England Disregards Neutrals, Seizes U.S. Ships and Mail," says one headline. "England Suppresses and Manipulates War News," says another. After the United States entered the war, the Irish papers unhesitatingly backed the war against Japan. But you still read articles that make you question the U.S. alliance with Britain. One, published a month after Pearl Harbor, shrieked "U.S. Army in Ulster To Bolster British Forces There—As MacArthur Fights Alone!"

Your brother-in-law has a shortwave radio, and he has told you about several reports that he heard about the British. According to one, although tires and gasoline are being rationed in America, the British are joyriding using scarce resources provided by the United States. Another broadcast claimed that 120,000 British agents are operating in the United States and that some are sabotaging American industry so that the damage can provoke anti-Axis hysteria. Finally, a third report alleged that large numbers of British sailors who deserted their ships in American ports are applying for jobs on ships sailing on the Great Lakes. Someone told you that the broadcasts actually come from a Nazi shortwave transmitter as part of Hitler's propaganda effort. But you are not certain if this is true.

Many Americans shared Peter's uncertainty about what was true concerning the British. If American wartime propaganda concerning Britain was effectively to eliminate this uncertainty and reduce the level of American anglophobia, it had at least three tasks. First, it needed to address American resentment of Britain's rigid and snobbish class system. Second, it had to try to deal with the matter of British imperialism, which many Americans resented. Finally, it needed as much as possible to portray an identity of interests between Americans and Britons in their need to win the war.

In early 1942, Germany was broadcasting fifteen hours a day to the Western Hemisphere. Although the actual listening audience for

these shortwave broadcasts was small, some American newspaper re-
porters and broadcasters, caught up in their daily competition with
colleagues, used Axis radio as a source of news. This repetition gave a
semblance of credibility to stories emanating from the enemy. The in-
decision that Axis news helped foster was clearly an obstacle to the
American people giving full support to the war effort.

The British came into the war at its start. They had managed to de-
lay their involvement after a string of German acts of aggression and
broken promises of peace. However, within three days of Germany's
September 1939 attack on Poland, Britain and France, bound by
treaty to defend Poland, declared war. France capitulated within less
than a year, and for many months the British fought Germany virtually alone. The German bombardment of Britain threatened to figu-
ratively sink the island into the sea.

Many Britons and sympathizers in America feared for Britain's future. In the United States this was reflected in public pronouncements. In August 1940, a group of interventionists placed a large advertisement in the *New York Times* that asked dramatically, "If Hitler
Gets the British Fleet—Can He Take the United States?"[2] The ad
pointed out that Germany was manufacturing more airplanes in a
month than the United States was making in a year and observed that
the American Atlantic fleet was too weak to help prevent a German
conquest of Britain. The ad also recommended that the United States
lend Britain fleets of destroyers and airplanes. Finally, signaling the
desperation that its sponsors felt, the ad made the radical and rather
naïve suggestion that the United States, Britain, Canada, and Ireland
form a political union. That way, it continued, if the British Isles were
lost, the British fleet could be sent to the United States.

Although Britain's situation early in the war was a precarious one,
there were strong expressions of anti-British sentiment in the United
States, particularly from conservative elements in American society
such as the America First Committee and the Hearst press. But some
also came from the Popular Front. In 1940, the America First Committee hired Batten, Barton, Durstine and Osborn (BBD&O), the same
advertising agency that produced the *Cavalcade of America* series, to
produce a series of recorded programs opposing aid to Britain.[3] The

America First Committee was the organization around which the leading isolationist sentiment coalesced. A statement in the Hearst newspapers, in this case in January 1942, *after* Pearl Harbor, also expressed
anti-British sentiment. According to the article, "She [England] has sys-
tematically sacrificed her Allies to her safety and her own immediate
objectives. She sacrificed Norway—She sacrificed Belgium in identi-
cally the same manner—England abandoned France at Dunkirk—In a
word, England's plain policy seems to HAVE Allies, but not to BE an
Ally."[4] Finally, in 1942, the prominent American writer and Popular
Fronter Theodore Dreiser, another anglophobe, publicly made the anti-
British comment at the beginning of this chapter, for which the Writer's
War Board attacked him in the newspapers.

The hostility of some Americans toward Britain stemmed partly
from a critical view of British colonial policy. Since 1930 when Mo-
handas Gandhi carried out his celebrated salt march to the sea, newsreels and other news media reported on his leadership of the struggle
for the Indian peoples' freedom. This coverage resulted in a wave of
sympathy for the anti-British campaign among many American liberals and blacks. Americans also resented the British agents whose
propaganda had played a major role in getting the United States into
World War I. Among the driving forces of anti-British sentiment were
Senators Rush Holt, an isolationist Democrat from West Virginia, and
Gerald Nye of North Dakota. In the summer of 1940, Holt delivered
a speech against "British propaganda." About 100,000 "interested persons" got copies of it through the *Congressional Record,* and Holt let
it be known that he could arrange to have an additional 250,000 copies
printed.

Nye, a strong critic of the interventionist movement, cosponsored Senate hearings in September 1941 to investigate allegations
that certain filmmakers and radio shows were producing and disseminating propaganda as part of an attempt to bring the United
States into the war. The group sponsoring the hearings was actually
an ad hoc "noncommittee"; the Senate never authorized its work,
and Nye and company operated in kangaroo court fashion. Nye and
the America First group also vehemently opposed the Lend-Lease
Act of March 1941 that provided Britain with much needed military
equipment.

The various expressions of anglophobia among students struck visiting professor Louis MacNeice, a British poet, while he was at Cornell University in 1940. When he returned home at the end of the year, he started writing propaganda radio drama for the BBC. Given all these anti-British utterances, there was clearly a broad need to put the British in the best light.

Even before the attack on Pearl Harbor, American radio tried to respond to attacks on Britain and enhance American understanding of our soon-to-be closest ally. In the summer of 1940, while the Luftwaffe's bombs rained down on London and there was fear that the Nazis might invade any day, Norman Corwin produced "To Tim at Twenty." The very day of the broadcast, the front page of the *Times* featured a lengthy headline that began: "600 NAZI PLANES RAID LONDON AREA AGAIN."[5]

"To Tim at Twenty" concerns an RAF gunner who is about to go off on a fatal mission. Before leaving, he writes a letter to his young son to be read only when the boy reaches the age of twenty. Corwin dedicated the play to his friends actors Charles Laughton and Laughton's wife Elsa Lanchester, both of whom performed in its broadcast.[6] The Laughtons were both Britons who had moved to Hollywood. During the Blitz they were worried about friends and relatives back in England concerning whom they were receiving frequent reports of casualties.

"Welcome to Glory," a short dramatic fantasy, was another pre–Pearl Harbor piece. Produced in the summer of 1941, it concerns Alf Jenkins, an English fishmonger who is killed by falling debris while taking shelter in Westminster Abbey during the Blitz. Immediately after his death he encounters the ghost of Queen Elizabeth I. She tells him that Germany will fail in its effort to take over England just as the Spanish Armada failed to defeat England in the seventeenth century. "Today civilians stand as bravely as any warrior of the past," the queen says, "you and the thousands who have died as you did." She continues, "In my day, too, another would-be conqueror attempted an invasion. His ships, a bold armada, were scattered to the winds . . . the snow-like cliffs of Dover are potent magic 'gainst a madman's fury. Those dear cliffs are bulwarks, standing to defend our way of living. No tyrant, no oppressor, no dictator can ever pass those sentinels of freedom. In every age, when England needs a man, she doesn't call in vain."[7]

On January 1, 1942, three weeks after the Japanese attack on Pearl Harbor, the United States, Great Britain, and twenty-four other nations entered into a wartime alliance, the United Nations. Now, with the United States engaged in a collective fight against the Axis powers, the need for a positive orientation toward the British intensified. During the first full year of American involvement in the war, a number of shows pursued this objective. The *Keep 'Em Rolling* variety series broadcast two of them, "Anthem in the Sky" and "The Snow Goose."

"Anthem in the Sky" was one of the most unusual dramatizations of the war era. The notion that a nation has God on its side is a common one in wartime. But "Anthem in the Sky" presents a literal interpretation of this concept. It features the appearance of a mysterious RAF pilot (played by Tyrone Power) who bails out of his plane after it is shot down. After a bombing raid, in which her fellow townspeople are almost wiped out, a young woman climbs a hill overlooking her town. She happens upon the pilot, whose plane had been the only one to take on the attackers. His hands are bleeding, but his spirits are high in contrast to hers. He selflessly expresses his desire to go down into the valley and help the villagers. She has lost all faith, however, and she balks. "Why should it mean so much to you," she asks him, "Do you have someone in the village?" "Yes . . . yes, I have," the pilot replies. "But you're not English!" she remarks, to which he says "N-n-n-not . . . exactly." She cries out to him, "Show us, that we may believe! . . . Give us a sign," Soon another squadron of planes appears in the sky. After an initial fright, she realizes that this time it is not the Luftwaffe. The planes are American bombers. This is the sign for which she asked. When the pilot suddenly disappears, she returns to his burnt plane. There she finds three strange spikes "of crude and ancient make." And she remembers that . . . "His hands had bled . . . and that His plane and all those others from America had been like Crosses In the Sky . . . !"[8]

"The Snow Goose" is a romantic, even saccharine story set against the background of events of the spring of 1940.[9] In late May, the Germans conquered Belgium, trapping 338,000 Allied troops, mostly British, with their backs to the English Channel. In the five or six weeks that followed, the British Navy with the help of hundreds of

British civilians employed 800 vessels including fishing boats and even rowboats to successfully evacuate the trapped soldiers from the French port city of Dunkirk. The British government succeeded in turning a terrible defeat into a propaganda victory, the so-called "Miracle of Dunkerque." "The Snow Goose," continuing that process, tells the story of Flita, a young woman who brings an injured snow goose to Philip, a hunchbacked painter who lives alone in an abandoned lighthouse. Philip nurses the bird back to health. Later when he takes his boat to participate in the Dunkirk rescue, the snow goose follows him in the air. Philip is mortally wounded by German gunfire as he approaches the Belgian shore. But the bird manages to warn some other rescuers away from a nearby German mine.

Lux Radio Theatre also tried to build American support for the British. In July 1942, during a break in a broadcast, Cary Grant, one of its stars, announced "I was born in England. I'm an American citizen now. But even if I had been born in this great country, I would still wish that I could persuade my fellow countrymen not to criticize our allies in England. They have been fighting a great fight for more than three years. For a while they had to do it by themselves—in fact they held out alone for more than a year. Let's cheer 'em on right now."[10]

In September, *Lux* broadcast "This Above All," another show starring Tyrone Power. It concerns Clive, a troubled deserter, who survived the evacuation of Dunkirk only to realize that he can find no reason to rejoin his unit and resume fighting. However, Prudence, an upper class woman who defied tradition and joined the WACS, falls in love with him and helps him pick up the pieces of his shattered existence. Considering that the show features bombs falling on Britain during the telling of the story, its premise about Clive's mental state is difficult to accept. The first half of the show stresses Pru's determination to ignore the class boundaries that have separated her aristocratic parents from commoners. They are angry with her for joining the WACs not as an officer but in the ranks. "For generations the Cathaways have been leaders, not followers," they tell her. "In joining this women's army you're deliberately throwing aside certain rules, certain traditions." Pru responds by blasting her family in a way that would have made Theodore Dreiser cheer. "I'm in 1940 and you're in 1880," she tells them angrily. "Your kind of thinking is more dangerous to us than Hitler is. . . . You believe that forty million people exist in England to make you comfortable. You hate this war because you knock your shins in a blackout. . . . You fear it because the common men who are doing the fighting may suddenly begin to doubt the importance of risking their lives to keep you an immortal part of England."[11]

Later, after Clive and Pru meet and fall in love, he asks her why a soldier should risk his life for Britain and she replies, "It's not the time to doubt and argue when your country's fighting for its life. "We're fighting to survive." She then pulls out all the stops with an outpouring of patriotic reasons. "You're fighting for England," she reminds him. "England is speakers in Hyde Park free to say what they wish. It's polite bobbies at the corner and it's the New Forest in ferns and holly trees." As she goes on, violins begin to play in the background. "It's the ring and the shine and the green of our blessed land. It's the shout of a newsboy on the corner or the sound of a taxi horn or the age and dignity of our cities."[12] The violins get louder. In the end of course, Clive rediscovers the deep well of his own patriotism and nearly loses his life while rescuing a man in a bombed-out building.

In addition to occasional shows that dealt with Britain as part of a wider series that also concerned other topics, there was an important series in a special program of cooperation between the BBC and American networks. The series, an ambitious Norman Corwin/CBS project titled *An American in England,* developed following a visit to London by William Paley of CBS and began to take shape in the spring of 1942. CBS invited Corwin to do it, probably at the suggestion of American war correspondent Edward R. Murrow. The main part of the series began that summer, and although Murrow was designated the producer, he acted almost solely as liaison for the BBC that provided facilities for the broadcasts. Corwin himself ran the whole show, conferring occasionally with Murrow. Benjamin Britten, the conductor and composer, was assigned to lead the RAF orchestra that played the score for the series.

Corwin, who had just finished his difficult work on *This Is War,* was determined now to avoid the bureaucratic snafus that he had just experienced. As a consequence, he prepared a memorandum that laid out the precise conditions under which he would work. It guaranteed his independence on the project from "American or British governmental" interference, once general agreement was reached on the directives, scope, and form of the series. Both CBS and the BBC accepted the memorandum. This done, Corwin left New York for England.

After his plane landed in Bristol, Corwin began to research his scripts even as he rode by train to London. During the journey he had a memorable conversation with a Flying Officer Smith. As Corwin later reproduced it in one of his radio series's segments, Smith (whom he called "Hill" in the broadcast) looked beyond the war and predicted that when it ended Britain would experience great political, economic, and social change. Of course neither of them knew it, but the man was anticipating actual reforms that a postwar socialist government would make. Smith criticized his country's class system and sniped at how it had provided incompetent management of British affairs. He believed that the same energy and expenditures that had been spent on waging war would be used to create a real peace. "It staggers the mind," he said, "to think of what could be done in the way of housing and health and education for the cost of what it takes to run a week of this war."[13]

As Corwin wrote about the experience some time later, "It was this hot, crowded train with dirty windows, no drinking water, and flushless toilets, that presented me with the ending to my script, and I was most grateful. Not so much to the train itself, but to . . . Smith . . . a remarkable man."[14] When they arrived in London, before they parted, Smith said to Corwin, "When you're looking about the country, don't judge us by the . . . lobbies of a few hotels in London. See us as we are—see us in the streets and in the factories and pubs and army camps and aerodromes and schools."[15]

Corwin's American narrator for *An American in England,* Joe Julian, had an encounter soon after his arrival in England that proved equally informative to him, but for different reasons. On arriving, Julian went into a little restaurant near the airport. Months earlier, the war had forced the British government to institute rationing of ham, bacon, eggs, sugar, and other food products. Unaware of this, Julian ordered ham and eggs. "Anything else, sir?" asked the waitress, who thought he was joking. Yes, replied Julian, quite seriously. "Bring me some tea with lemon." After that, Julian learned fairly quickly the reality of conditions in wartime Britain.

For the series to be received at the proper time in the United States, the live broadcast had to be performed at 4:00 A.M. "double summer time" in London. This meant that everyone connected with the production: cast, engineers, orchestra members, sound technicians, Murrow, Britten, and Corwin had to leave central London at 2 A.M. and travel in a procession to the suburbs. Shortly before the war, fearing the possibility of bombing, the BBC had moved the broadcasting studios to the countryside, almost emptying Broadcasting House in London in the process. Features and Drama, the department that produced radio drama, wound up in a mansion outside Evesham, which had once been the home of an exiled Duc d'Orleans and that was now given the code name "Hogsnorton." The location was supposed to have been an official secret, but even before the outbreak of war the Nazis knew where it was. During the summer of 1941, while a BBC engineer was visiting a radio exhibition in Berlin, an official of the Reich asked, "By the way, how is your little secret hideout in the vale of Evesham getting along?"[16]

The first segment of *An American in England,* "London by Clipper," was a fictionalized account of Corwin's own flight to Britain. It related his first impressions of Britain at war. One notable passage from the play demonstrated how despite his being an American, Joe, Corwin's persona, was able to empathize with what the British experienced from the damage that German bombs had done to them: "right in front of your eyes . . . are the first bomb ruins you have ever seen," says Joe, "It's an ordinary suburban house such as you'd find in Chevy Chase, Oak Park, Glendale—any of ten thousand towns in the states. But the roof of this one is burnt away and the insides blasted out . . . and now you're passing a church, a little church like the one in Winthrop, Massachusetts, or Kent, Ohio, or Pleasantville, Mississippi. Only this one is just four hollow walls."[17]

Unfortunately a communications problem linked with the play's opening lines turned the attempted broadcast into a disaster. Corwin began the play with a literary device intended to attract the radio listener. The first words of the play simulated trouble with a telephone connection ("Hello! . . . hello! What's the matter with this line?") It was in theory a wonderful idea, but the device backfired because nobody had notified the engineers in New York that the opening was just a simulation. Apparently, when they heard the voice's irritation about a disconnection, they assumed that the circuit routing was faulty and they pulled the plug. A week after the abortive broadcast, Corwin tried again and this time it went off well. The *New York Times* said of the program: "a poet's vision, a good reporter's clarity and a technician's precise knowledge of his craft. . . . Everything done in little touches, but the cumulative effect is profoundly stirring . . . a distinguished program . . . major work in a minor key."[18]

Even after rebroadcast of "London by Clipper," *An American in England* encountered problems. Atmospheric disturbances and distorted shortwave transmission totally sabotaged transmission in early September of "An Anglo-American Angle," the last of its nine plays. Also, because the series was scheduled to appear against Bob Hope on another network, its domestic rating was low. Nevertheless, CBS was pleased with it and extended it by four more shows in December. To avoid the transmission problems, however, Corwin produced the rest of the series from the United States. It included a repeat broadcast of "An Anglo-American Angle."

Probably the best of Corwin's plays about Britain was "Cromer," the first one in the extended series. The show documents small details of a typical English village during the war. In it, Corwin gets the listeners' attention with an understated beginning. "Cromer is a town on the east coast of England," says the announcer, "and this is a program about it. The program has to do with bombs and a postmaster and a rescue squad and an old church and a Spitfire and several other matters, and it takes a half hour."[19]

Both listeners and reviewers greeted the program enthusiastically. "I remember the incident . . . ," wrote one listener, "when you hear the organ coming through the shattered church, suddenly contrasted with the hard thrilling gunfire practice of the airplane. That little bit cemented my Anglo American relations plenty. It gave you the feeling that here are the British doing BOTH now, the organ music, I mean, and the gun practice."[20]

The *New York Times* reviewer, equally impressed, wrote "Corwin . . . is looking at a foreign land with that special perception a stranger brings to a scene that is new to him. A broken clock, a doll's head in the rubble after an air raid; an old man's voice in a pub; the smell of the weather on the North Sea coast, sixteen and a half minutes fly-ing time from a Nazi base. As you listen, a village comes suddenly alive, and with it a nation. Mr. Corwin had done more ambitious and perhaps more enduring work than this, but nothing that in its way was finer."[21]

In addition to attempting to improve American attitudes about Britain, *An American in England* was also broadcast in Britain. Here the objective was to be of a reciprocal nature, but a radio series was not sufficient to eradicate the hard-bitten attitudes of at least one British listener. In one of the broadcasts, the commander of a com-pany of young women in the British Army complained that many of her charges were practically illiterate. The episode upset this listener. You have sought "to demonstrate to your American listeners the great inferiority of British education to that of America," he complained. "You cannot go on for more than a minute without boasting in true American style that you are the most wonderful people in the world."[22] But apart from this one letter, the vast majority of letters from Britons indicated that the series achieved its objective. The co-operation between the BBC and the American networks led by the end of the war to an impressive number of dramatizations made in Britain being broadcast in the United States.

Another Norman Corwin production dealing with Britain, "Unti-tled," deserves mention once more. His protagonist, "Hank Peters," gives voice to the commonality of experience that bound Americans and their allies during the war, "I am very dead, but no deader than the British who struck at Alamein, the Reds who crossed the Dnieper go-ing west," says Hank.[23] But the play also gives a faint hint of Corwin's critical view of British colonialism, a hope that after the Allies defeat their enemies, Western Europe would emancipate its colonies. "Will someone give my best to Marian the day that Palestine is taken up?"[24] he says quickly and cryptically. Only the most astute listeners could have picked up on the comment, a prodding of the British to grant indepen-dence to Palestine (meaning Israel). The reference was subtle enough that Corwin found it necessary to add an explanatory footnote to a pub-lished version of the play that appeared in an anthology.

By January 1945, with many Americans confident that the war was all but won, the *Words at War* series presented a play about Britain

that differed markedly from its predecessors, expressing as it did a critique, albeit a bit indirect, of British colonial policy. Many wartime radio plays promoted the idea that the war was fought to defend democracy. But by implication, this one, "It's Always Tomorrow," also
pushed the idea that it was a war to promote national self-determina-
tion. The play tells of Dave Sedgewick, an American journalist whose
newspaper sends him to England.[25] On arrival, Dave encounters the
worst of British upper-class snobbery and procolonial arrogance, far
worse than that of Pru's parents in Lux Radio Theatre's "This Above
All." For one thing he hears people criticizing him for bringing Polly,
his new working-class girlfriend, to the posh Savoy Restaurant, a bas-
tion of the upper class. In addition, Thornsby, a man from the British
Foreign Office, bad-mouths U.S. Vice President Henry Wallace and
other officials of the FDR administration: "a menace with their clap-
trap of brave new worlds" and "remaking the universe," says
Thornsby. "Socialism, that's what it is." Wallace, a left-wing politician,
was frequently the target of political conservatives and reactionaries.
Speaking of the British colonies, Thornsby says, "How would Africa or
India—or even America have developed if it hadn't been for the
British? . . . Why should we turn them over to backward nations?"

From the opposite side, Polly detests the upper class and has difficulty supporting the war effort. "I hate this war which is being fought
to save them and their precious skins," she tells Dave. "Let the Germans win." But Dave replies "Sure there's injustice in England and
America too. But do you honestly think you can wipe out those injustices if Hitler, Himmler and that gang get the upper hand?" Eventually he persuades her to support the war effort. She accepts his argument that the war is a people's war and that when it ends, the "little
people" will see to it that the upper crust listens to them.

At least in regard to the plays just cited, American radio drama
made serious inroads in trying to counter both Axis and domestic
anti-British propaganda. In regard to the first objective, to try to reduce resentment of the British class system, radio drama sought particularly to achieve it by conveying the notion that class distinctions
were fading. The conversation between the ghost of Elizabeth I and
a recently killed English fishmonger in "Welcome to Glory" may have
been too pallid a piece of evidence that British class boundaries were

becoming less significant. However, the willingness of Pru, the upper class woman in *Lux's* "This Above All" to join the WACs and marry a soldier from a lower class sent a stronger message that Britain was a nation in transition. So did Corwin's Flying Officer Hill in "London by Clipper" when he predicted that the British people would insist on major social reforms after the war. Similarly, Dave Sedgewick in *Words at War's* "It's Always Tomorrow" described the war as one that would end with the "little people" securing the social changes they needed.

Domestic American propaganda's second objective in regard to Britain, to address American resentment of British imperialism, was more difficult to deal with than the social class issue. Under the influence of the Office of War Information, members of the American media were reluctant to offend an ally with outright attacks on British colonial policy. As a consequence, radio drama rarely criticized it. The negative portrayal of the loud-mouthed Thornsby of the British Foreign Office, who defended British rule in Africa and India, was about as strong a statement as American radio drama made on the topic.

The third task, to convey an identity of interests between Americans and Britons in fighting the war, was much easier. The first step here, to demonstrate British courage in the face of enemy attack, was child's play. Consider the heroism of Philip, the hunchbacked artist, in "The Snow Goose," or of Clive in "This Above All," who at great risk to his life rescues the man in the bombed-out building. The next step was to put the lives and struggles of Allied soldiers and civilians (and frequently their deaths) in the same context. As demonstrated in relation to Corwin's "Untitled" and "London by Clipper," he was able to do this eloquently. In so many words, he said, "We must stand by our British ally. He—and we—each of us—is Everyman. Or as the Popular Front would put it, he, meaning the little guy, the worker or the farmer, not the aristocrat, is our brother."

NOTES

1. "Threats Are Made to Kill DeValera," *New York Times*, November 11, 1939, 4:8.

2. Advertisement: "If Hitler Gets the British Fleet . . . Can He Take the United States?" *New York Times*, August 19, 1940, 11.

3. Erik Barnouw, *The Golden Web: A History of Broadcasting in the United States, vol. 2, 1933–1953* (New York: Oxford University Press, 1968), 138.

4. Hearst newspapers, January 28, 1942, as quoted in Gerhard Horten, "Radio Goes to War: The Cultural Politics of Propaganda during World War II" (Ph.D. diss., University of California at Berkeley, 1994), 78.

5. James Reston, "600 NAZI PLANES RAID LONDON AREA AGAIN," *New York Times*, August 19, 1940, 1.

6. Norman Corwin, *Thirteen by Corwin: Radio Dramas by Norman Corwin* (New York: Henry Holt, 1942), 249–257.

7. Kenneth Webb, "Welcome to Glory," in Norman Weiser, *The Writer's Radio Theater* (New York: Harper & Row, 1941), 126.

8. Milton Geiger, "Anthem in the Sky," in the *Keep 'Em Rolling* series, April 5, 1942, from Great American Radio, Genesee, MI 48437.

9. Paul Gallico, "The Snow Goose," in the *Keep 'Em Rolling* series, May 10, 1942, from Schmidco Golden Age of Radio.

10. The show, broadcast on July 20, 1942, was "The Philadelphia Story," *Lux Radio Theatre* NA Box 5 LA boxes—Lux Folder, Lux show, July 20, 1942.

11. "This Above All," *Lux Radio Theatre*, September 14, 1942.

12. "This Above All," *Lux Radio Theatre*.

13. Norman Corwin, "London by Clipper," in Norman Corwin, *Untitled and Other Radio Dramas* (New York: Henry Holt, 1945), 153.

14. Corwin, *Untitled and Other Radio Dramas*, 163.

15. Corwin, "London by Clipper," in Corwin, *Untitled and Other Radio Dramas*, 154.

16. Val Gielgud, *Years of the Locust* (London: Nicholson and Watson, 1947), 167.

17. Corwin, "London by Clipper," in Corwin, *Untitled and Other Radio Dramas*, 151–152.

18. John K. Hutchen, "That Realm, That England," *New York Times*, August 16, 1942, VIII, 8:1.

19. Norman Corwin, "Cromer" (aired December 1, 1942), in *Thirteen by Corwin*, from LodesTone (audiotapes).

20. Irvin Shapiro to CBS, December 26, 1942, Corwin Collection, TOL.

21. John Hutchens, "Several Matters," *New York Times*, December 6, 1942, VIII, 12.

22. M. Paterson to Norman Corwin, September 1, 1942, COR 00024, Corwin Collection, TOL.

23. Norman Corwin, "Untitled," in Corwin, *Untitled and Other Radio Dramas,* 62.

24. Corwin, "Untitled," in Corwin, *Untitled and Other Radio Dramas,* 62.

25. Robert St. John, "It's Always Tomorrow," episode 79, adapted by Martin Sterne, January 2, 1945, *Words at War,* Box 500, folder 5, NBC Collection, WISC.

12

AMERICA'S ALLIES: THE SOVIETS

Distrust and hatred of Russia was the triumph of a long and calculated propaganda of suspicion and wishful thinking. The Reds were inept, lackadaisical, unholy . . . their air force was pitiful and their planes not much better than kites. The Bolsheviks . . . were purgers, liquidators, unremitting enemies of the individual.

—Norman Corwin, *Untitled and Other Radio Dramas*

Your name is Irina.[1] You were born in the late 1930s in a small Ukrainian town, the youngest of three sisters. In June 1941, two and a half years after the Germans conquered western Poland, they suddenly invaded eastern Poland and the Soviet Union. Your town was one of the first into which they marched. With no time to pack anything, your family fled immediately, to the southeast. The journey was a horror; the Germans bombed the road on which you were traveling. Your father was one of the first to be killed. When the bombs fell close to horses that were pulling carriages, they reared up on their back legs, spilling people into roadside ditches. Afterward, the survivors quickly gathered their horses, mourned a few minutes for those who were killed, and then continued on their way. It went on like this day after day. Always you were just one small step ahead of the Germans.

Eventually, you reached the city of Stalingrad. It was a tragic place to land, the scene a year and a half later of one of the most terrible battles of the war. Although in the end the Red Army was victorious, almost the whole city was destroyed. Shortly after the battle, your mother became seriously ill and died. Two things kept you and your sisters going. You survived physically by scavenging and spiritually by periodically hearing the radio in the street, reassuring the population that in the end Russia would prevail. Partly the scavenging involved gathering unharvested wheat from the fields. While your sisters collected the few stalks that were left, you guarded what they found from the birds. With no means of processing the wheat, you ground it and ate it raw. Occasionally you had some fish from the Volga River. Usually they were dead ones that you found lying on the shore, sometimes contaminated by the blood of soldiers whose bodies had fallen into the river. But once one of your sisters caught one with her bare hands from a dented boat that she found.

At the end of the war, a great uncle in Moscow learned through the Red Cross where you were and paid for the four of you to take a train back home. But when you arrived, there was no one to take care of you there. The uncle and his wife, childless, sent for you; your sisters were sent to an orphanage. You grew up in Moscow, married, and had a daughter.

In the 1990s, you and your family emigrated to Brooklyn, New York, where you settled in the Russian community of Brighton Beach. One day several years later, as you were sitting on a bench on the boardwalk, three American teenagers approached you and handed you a questionnaire. You looked at them suspiciously. With some difficulty, you finally understood what they wanted. They were on a school visit to the community. One question asked "Which of the following was the best Soviet leader?" The choices were Lenin, Stalin, Khrushchev, Brezhnev, and Gorbachev. You replied unhesitatingly: "Stalin." "Why Stalin?" one of them asked you. "Because he defeated Hitler and he made our streets safe," you replied.

It is difficult to say how many Russians would agree with Irina's estimation of Stalin's rule. Despite the fact that her answer would surprise most Americans, the boardwalk incident really occurred. To a multitude of Soviet citizens, despite the enormity of Stalin's crimes, he was their savior during the war, and many still regard him that way.

The June 1941 German attack on Russia that so affected Irina's family was followed six months later by America's entry into the war. Like Britain, the Soviet Union, too, signed the United Nations declaration. Now the United States, the world's greatest democracy, was allied with a totalitarian communist power in a common cause. For many Americans the alliance was a source of great discomfort. And just as Nazi shortwave radio propaganda tried to stir up anti-British sentiment, it also tried to fan anti-Soviet attitudes. It claimed, for example, that America had promised to feed the Russians even if its own babies had to starve. In addition, American isolationists targeted the Soviet Union more vehemently than they did Britain. They even criticized the Soviets in the spring of 1942 when Russia was under heavy German attack and it was not certain that the Red Army would be able to survive. Again, as this March 1942 report shows, the Hearst newspapers helped lead the attack. "Matters seem to be progressing very favorably in Russia—for Russia," said the editorial. "Of course, Russia is not a full partner of the United States. . . . She is a semi-partner of the Axis. She is making friendly treaties with Japan—protecting Japan on her Siberian frontier. There is always in the Russian mental process the suggestion of the brutal selfishness and utter untrustworthiness of this wild animal which is her symbol."[2]

Roman Catholic Bishop Fulton Sheen was in the forefront of those who blasted America's Soviet ally. He did so routinely before Pearl Harbor during frequent radio appearances. For a while after the United States entered into the war he let up. But on Good Friday, in April 1942, despite an NBC request to delete his remarks about the Soviet Union on a special event program, he resumed his attack. NBC took no retaliatory action.

Until the war, American radio drama, even educational programs, avoided dealing with the Soviet Union. It was too hot a topic to handle. After all, only two decades earlier, the United States sent a small expeditionary force to Russia to aid counterrevolutionaries trying to overthrow Bolshevism in Russia. But now, with the Soviets allied with the United States, especially during the last two years of the war, American radio broadcast a number of plays about the Soviet Union. The Writers War Board (WWB) and the Council for Democracy promoted such broadcasts. "World conquest, or anything approaching it," proclaimed a council publication, "has never gained the support of Russian leaders or peoples."[3]

Norman Corwin articulated the perception of anti-Soviet attitudes that was common among liberals, much, but not all, of it based on good evidence. "No country, certainly not Germany or Japan, has been so vilified by the majority of the American press. . . ," claimed Corwin. "One can draw a line down through the middle of a fairly fat 'Who's Who' and divide artists, scientists, statesmen into camps of anti and pro Soviet sympathy."[4] Corwin also blamed the anti-Soviet mind-set among the Western democracies for several major international problems. He attributed to it the hands-off policy that left the Soviet government as the only one to come to the aid of the Spanish loyalists. He also characterized it as the dominant force responsible for Britain's and France's failure to invite the Soviet Union, a cosigner of a military treaty with France and Czechoslovakia, to the Munich Conference.

The burden under which Corwin and his colleagues were laboring was that to a great extent Soviet censorship and poor reporting in the 1930s masked the extent of Stalinist human rights abuses. The strength of the nativist and neofascist threat in the United States also distracted many on the left from perceiving the Soviet system for what it really was. A story in the *Washington Post* illustrates some of this bias. In April 1943, the German government announced that a site had been found in the Katyn forest near Smolensk where three years earlier Soviets had allegedly massacred 12,000 Polish officers. Subsequently, the Polish government-in-exile based in London had severed relations with the Soviet government. In an April 1943 newspaper column, journalist William Shirer discussed the Polish government-in-exile's reaction to the Nazi claim. Shirer scoffed at the report, commenting that "the Polish government-in-exile should make [relations between the Soviet and Polish governments] worse by deliberately playing into the hands of Nazi propaganda . . . will surprise many friends of Poland in this country."[5] The problem is that the Nazi announcement was true. Shirer had put aside the crucial quality that any good journalist needs: a determination to examine the facts.

From a vantage point of fifty years after the war, it may not be fair to judge the treatment that Corwin, Shirer, and their colleagues gave the Soviets. In reaction to a general American bias against all things Soviet, more than just Corwin and Shirer developed skewed perceptions. In the early decades of the Soviet Union's existence, some in the West saw how it was attempting to give the masses access to decent health care and education, and how it was fighting racism. These attractive qualities blinded many foreign observers to gross Soviet human rights violations. Thus, Langston Hughes signed a statement by American progressives that supported the conduct of the infamous Moscow purge trials, which the document hailed as the Soviet Union's effort to free itself from "insidious internal dangers" that threatened peace and democracy.

The *Treasury Star Parade* series produced some of the earliest and most frequent broadcasts about the Soviet war effort. Film star John Garfield, a highly visible Popular Fronter, took part in a number of the series's shows. As William Bacher, its director, recalled, in March 1942, shortly after the program was brought to Hollywood, Garfield burst into Bacher's room at the Beverly Hills Hotel holding a script entitled "A Letter from a Red Army Man." The script extolled Soviet–American friendship and detailed the protagonist's determination to see the Nazis defeated. "No use, Bacher, you couldn't find a better guy to do this piece than me and I'm gonna do it anyway, see?"[6] Garfield, told the startled director. And Garfield had his way.

Another *Treasury Star Parade* play about the Soviet Union concerns a Russian high-school girl, a guerrilla fighter, whom the Nazis capture and torture. "Comrades, comrades, hear me," she yells just as she is about to be hanged, "Do not grieve, I am happy to die. Do as I have done. Kill them! Destroy them! Burn them! . . . You German soldiers, surrender. Surrender before it is too late. Victory will be ours! *VICTORY!! VIC . . . (agh) . . . (agh)*."[7]

Danish born Sandra Michael, recipient of a prestigious Peabody Award, also focused on the Soviet Union. Michael's unique soap opera *Against the Storm* premiered a month after the war broke out in Europe. It quickly established in its theme a resistance to the war and to war in general. Its first broadcast called on U.S. officials to admit refugees from the Nazis. Even President Roosevelt accepted a speaking engagement on the show. But the attack on Pearl Harbor canceled the segment on which he was to appear.

In March 1943, the WWB sponsored Michael's "My Brother Lives in Stalingrad," one of the first plays about the Soviet Union to be heard on an American network. The script, which details the wartime suffering of the Soviets, features an announcer, a Russian, and a crudely ethnocentrist American. "Of course these Russians are a peculiar people," the American says early in the broadcast, "They haven't had the advantages of real culture, and they're brought up to fight, I guess; that must be why they can stand it so well. Anyway, I thank heaven that the war is as far away from the United States as it is."[8]

Afterward, the narrator takes the American on a fantasy visit to the Russian, a woman. Like the American, she, too, has a young child. On seeing the horrible impact the Battle of Stalingrad has on the woman and her family, the American becomes embarrassed by his initial insensitivity and comments "God forgive me. And God help me to do my part before it is too late."

In September 1943, CBS produced "Moscow" as the third part of Norman Corwin's *"Passport for Adams."* Like Sandra Michael's play, "Moscow" clearly shows a liberal bias toward the Soviets. In the program, Corwin dealt with the matter of German prisoners of war. At one point, Quiz, the photographer, comes to blows with an arrogant German prisoner in a Soviet prisoner of war camp. The prisoner is taken away, and Quiz and Adams are brought to the Soviet prison's commandant. The man expresses sympathy for Quiz's feelings about the German but reminds him that he must treat his prisoners humanely. When Quiz challenges him, the commandant replies. "We hate them worse than you . . . [but] we believe in human dignity, Mr. Quisenberry, and in international law."[9] Somewhere in the Soviet Union during World War II there may have been such a prison commandant, but his attitude was hardly typical in a nation that carried out a forced famine in Ukraine, shot thousands during the purges, and carried out the Katyn Forest executions.

In July 1944, on the 26th anniversary of the establishment of the Red Army, Russian Relief and the WWB cosponsored a broadcast of "Concerning the Red Army," written by Norman Rosten at the request of Norman Corwin, who directed the program. The play starred Will Geer, who once went on record as saying that he preferred roles in plays whose themes he supported, even if the particular character that he played did not necessarily express his sentiments. Given that statement, Geer's earlier support of fund-raising events to benefit Russian Aid, and his interest in the Soviet Union after his 1935 visit there, his participation in the broadcast was clearly an expression of his own views.

The author of "Concerning the Red Army," Rosten was impressed by the Soviet Union's early stand against fascism during the Spanish Civil War. He wrote the script at a point when the war had already months before turned in the Allies' favor. "Concerning the Red Army" pays tribute to the valiant efforts of the Soviet people but gives short shrift to the totalitarian nature of their government. At one point a narrator takes on a group of critics, saying

> The Red Army reaps what it has sown. It has sown strength. At the beginning there were the doubters. The Red Army? One sentence each, please, for the poll.
> Voice 1. Three weeks and it'll all be over . . .
> Voice 4. They're tough people, but they can't handle machines . . .
> Voice 7. Didn't the Russians shoot their generals?
> Narrator. Hear that? The famous and terrible rocket guns which went into action at Stalingrad . . . while the well-meaning or best-paid brains of the world were preparing the last rites, the Red Army was building these rocket guns by the thousands. Just one of the surprises among many.[10]

The narrator never answers the quickly asked question about the Russians shooting their generals. In fact, during the purges of the 1930s, about 800,000 people were executed and the Red Army lost perhaps half of its officer corps. The oversight was a typical product of the era. Inaccurate reporting in the American media, and a preoccupation with and total distrust of Nazi propaganda, contributed to a myopia among many progressives concerning criticism of the Soviets.

Arch Oboler's politics were a bit to the right of many of his wartime radio colleagues. He did not appear to share the fascination with the Soviet experiment that intrigued many of them. Yet for his *Free World Theatre* he chose to include a show, by another contributor, that fit into the mold of those discussed here. In April 1943, the series broadcast "The Fountain of Dancing Children," a play in verse starring Claudette Colbert that celebrated the Soviet victory over the Nazis at Stalingrad.

By the fall of 1944, the WWB was disturbed at the results of public opinion polls that revealed that most Americans still thoroughly distrusted the Soviet Union and that they identified Russians with communism. Some six months later the WWB's script of the month was "Death to Dr. Burdenko." Through a person of peasant background, the play gave a highly favorable presentation of the Soviet Union from the days of the last czar to World War II.

Finally, a short presentation in May 1945, soon after Germany's surrender, presented a Joseph Stalin whom many Soviets might have had difficulty recognizing. The piece, from the popular *March of Time* series, accurately stated that Stalin was viewed almost with veneration by much of the population. As Irina, in Brighton Beach, confirmed, he was. Soviet propaganda had presented him as the great wartime savior of the nation, and many citizens subscribed to this view. However, in this broadcast, a moderator, Richard Lauterbach, who had just published a book about the Soviets, stated "On the rare occasions when Stalin doesn't get his own way, he evidently can accept the verdict with good grace."[11] The historical record that paints Stalin as a man who murdered his own wife hardly supports such a statement. The broadcast then goes on with a dramatized vignette showing how on hearing that a Soviet airplane designer could not accept Stalin's own recommendations to increase the range of the "LAGG," a Soviet fighter, the dictator meekly replies "Now, what can I do with you? You don't want to. So we'll drop the matter there." Give Stalin credit for the moment and assume he really said that. Lauterbach comments now, after the dialogue between Stalin and the designer ends: "The new model of the LAGG does not incorporate Stalin's ideas, and nothing dire has happened to Lavochkin." What has Lauterbach proved? A later vignette shows a conversation the day after a Kremlin dinner in honor of the members of the Union of Polish Patriots. During the dinner, a Polish professor seated next to Stalin kept arguing on the need to nationalize Polish industries. The next day, Stalin is talking to Wanda Wasilewska, the organization's chairman whom he had summoned.

Stalin: You'd better quiet down that mathematics professor of yours. . . .
Last night he spent two hours trying to convert me to communism for
Poland.
Wanda: (HUMORLESS) Did he?
Stalin: *He did not.*

The point is that, of course, in the postwar period the Soviets did
exactly what the mathematics professor called on Stalin to do. Lauterbach's whitewashing of Stalin was exactly that.

There is no debating the fact that wartime radio made a huge pitch to
present the Soviets in a positive light, occasionally with distortions. This
did not go unnoticed by the political right, which deemed the fact that
the Soviets were America's ally during the war to be irrelevant. Corwin,
Shirer, Rosten, Garfield, and Geer were among those who were called
on in one way or another to account for their wartime-expressed support
for the Soviets. It needs to be pointed out, however, that the instances of
bold whitewashing of the Soviets that were presented here were rare,
not typical of the plays that dealt with the Soviet Union. For the most
part, they conveyed quite accurately the heroism and courage of the Soviets during the war. The vast bulk of the war-related dramas on the topic
were credible. Soviet citizens did rally round the flag. They did fight to
the last man or woman. The political right missed that, however.

NOTES

1. The following account is based on an unpublished biographical account of the life of Ida Shlain by Leo Raikhman of Sydney, Australia.

2. As quoted in Gerhard Horten, "Radio Goes to War: The Cultural Politics of Propaganda during World War II" (Ph.D. diss., University of California at Berkeley, 1994), 78.

3. Bulletin #28, the Council for Democracy.

4. Norman Corwin, *Untitled and Other Radio Dramas* (New York: Henry
Holt, 1945), 399.

5. William Shirer, "Propaganda Front: Poles Play into Nazi's Hands in
Treatment of 'Massacre' Story," *Washington Post*, April 25, 1943, 2b:7.

6. Boris Grabatov, "A Letter from a Red Army Man," in William Bacher,
ed., *The Treasury Star Parade* (New York: Farrar & Rinehart), 169.

7. Violet Atkins, "The Silent Women," in Bacher, *The Treasury Star Parade*, 250.

8. Sandra Michael, "My Brother Lives in Stalingrad," Writers [War] Board, War Scripts, no. 35, March 1943, NYPL-LC.

9. Norman Corwin, "Moscow," in Corwin, *Untitled and Other Radio Dramas*, 391–392.

10. Norman Rosten, "Concerning the Red Army," in Erik Barnouw, *Radio Drama in Action* (New York: Farrar & Rinehart, 1945), 171.

11. *March of Time*, May 24, 1945, NA 80-167LL-6, folder: March of Time.

⓭

THE HOME FRONT

I heard "This Is War" Saturday night. The query "What are you doing?" is one that I have been trying to answer for myself. . . . I am
serving as a Senior Air Warden. Yet I feel that what I am doing is
entirely inadequate for my share of the stupendous job that confronts us collectively.

—R. L. Haas in a letter to Archibald MacLeish

*Your name is Trudy. You are 27, the mother of two young children. You
live in Kingston, Pennsylvania. The bombing of Pearl Harbor woke
you up. You had been out of touch with the events that led up to the
start of the war. You never considered yourself a political person and
the children keep you so busy that you rarely listen to reporting of
news on the radio. Once, somebody mentioned Lowell Thomas's name
and you said "Who's he?"*

*When the war began, it quickly impacted. First your younger
brother was drafted. Then your husband, who is thirty-four, started
wondering out loud if he should enlist. Most recently, the rationing program has grabbed your attention. Your widowed mother lives forty
miles away. Two and sometimes three Sundays a month, your husband
used to drive you and the kids to visit her. Now because of gas rationing, your husband tells you that the trips along the hilly route in*

*your family's gas-guzzler have to be cut back to once a month. This gets
you angry. On the way to the post office every day, you walk past the
home of your congressman. He gets the X ration coupon that entitles
him to unlimited gasoline. You see this as grossly unfair, and it makes
you question the whole rationing program.*

The Trudys of America resented that some people had to make more
sacrifices than others during the war. Partly out of concern for this resentment, radio dealt with relevant home-front issues. Government
agencies, particularly the Office of War Information (OWI), produced
most of the dramas dealing with these topics. A June 1942 survey, conducted shortly after the creation of the OWI, identified two deter-
rents to civilian morale: the public's failure to comprehend the seriousness of the war and its inability to see the personal benefits of
victory. As a consequence of this type of learning, government propaganda tried to convince people that it was in their best interest to cooperate with programs such as rationing. It also urged them to avoid
black market trading and hoarding.

Government propaganda also focused on ways in which civilians, often people in particular trades and occupations such as doctors, farmers, and workers, and even children, could help achieve victory in their
daily lives. Dramatic propaganda broadcasts dealt with nutrition, home
canning, victory gardens, car pooling, commodity shortages, and fifth-
column groups that sought to spread Nazi beliefs to Americans. There
were even plays telling how pets could help in the war effort. Owners
of dogs and even unneeded typewriters were the targets of some
dramatizations. The government asked the owners of certain breeds of
dogs to donate them for use as message carriers, and it asked those
with unneeded typewriters to sell them to the government.

RATIONING

Government agencies often used public opinion surveys to determine
what themes to include in propaganda broadcasts. However, one important theme was apparent without any survey. Within days of the attack on Pearl Harbor it was evident that something needed to be done

to regulate domestic consumption of scarce resources needed to support the troops and fight the enemy.

On December 10, 1941, the government announced a ban on the sale of new automobile tires. Tires used up some 75 percent of America's crude rubber, and it was immediately apparent that rubber was going to be in short supply.[1] All of the country's rubber was imported, and just at this time the Japanese were clearly about to take over Malaysia and Indonesia, the source of much of the country's rubber.[2] The government also established the first war rationing plan only a few weeks after Pearl Harbor, limiting each person to a half pound of sugar per week for the first eight weeks following the plan's adoption.

In February 1942, a ban was announced on civilian purchase of automobiles and pickup trucks. March saw the appearance of the first ration books, distributed at elementary schools.[3] Each person received a book of stamps to be used over a six-month period for buying meat, butter, sugar, shoes, and canned vegetables.

In mid May, gasoline rationing was established on the East Coast. In fact there were sufficient supplies of gasoline; the rationale was to save rubber.[4] If you could not drive because of inadequate fuel supplies, your tires would last longer. Consumers received ration cards based on their perceived need. Holders of an A card received a mere five gallons a week for their 1930s or early 1940s gas guzzler. Doctors and others thought to need some extra fuel received B cards. Those believed to need unlimited gasoline received the most valuable X card.[5] Rationing continued throughout the war. In 1943, shoes and various foods (including cheeses, processed food, and meats) were added to the list. To help deal with scarcity, Tuesdays and Fridays became "meatless days."

Within days, if not hours, of the attack on Pearl Harbor the vast majority of those who had wavered about the idea of America fighting in the war put aside their reservations. After all, the enemy had struck the first blow. Americans recognized that rationing was required to preserve supplies for the war effort. Housewives made substitutions when possible, such as corn syrup and saccharin, for sugar, when making cakes and cookies. People pitched in to save scrap.

Among those who took part in the latter effort was the family of OWI official William B. Lewis. In 1942, Lewis gave his two children, ages four and seven, a talk about the country's need for metal scrap. He promised them a gift of war stamps if they would collect a sizable heap of scrap from their farm in Maryland. A day or two later, Lewis discovered them lugging the family's fireplace andirons out of the house. He did not have the heart to stop them, and the andirons, family heirlooms, wound up being melted down for their iron content.[6]

Restrictions on gasoline use and the encouragement to conserve it proved to be perhaps the most controversial part of the effort to conserve resources. Some joined the effort with gusto out of a strong sense of patriotic duty. "We toed the line strictly," said John Milton Kennedy, announcer for the *Lux Radio Theatre*.[7] Kennedy, who lived about a mile and a half from the Music Box Theater from which the show was broadcast, generally walked to work to conserve fuel. When occasionally he did drive, he would roll his car out of his driveway, close the garage door, and then coast downhill to work. At the bottom of the first street, because the entire route was downhill, he was even able to make the first of several turns while still driving sans engine, until finally he coasted to a stop in the parking lot near the theater.

Kennedy's reaction notwithstanding, the rationing program opened up a Pandora's box. In many ways, commodity shortages and rationing raised the ire of many Americans. Rationing of sugar and rubber was done in such a way that everyone was treated fairly. Not so with gasoline rationing, which, along with tire rationing, asked Americans to cool their love affair with the automobile. Consumers perceived the way that gasoline rationing in particular was conducted as being unfair, and they responded accordingly. Initially it was implemented only on the East Coast. So while their cousins in Colorado and California were free to take Sunday drives, easterners had to sit on the front porch. In addition, most people resented the inclusion of members of Congress among the groups receiving the coveted X cards.

There were other sources of resentment, too. Woe to the family whose ration books or stamps were lost or destroyed, recalled Sheila Hanson, who grew up in a small town in Illinois, more than five decades later.

I remember being in church. It was a Catholic mass . . . my mother was kneeling and praying, I was sitting . . . right next to her . . . but sort of behind her so she couldn't see me. I opened her purse, took out the ration book and the stamps. The stamps were different colors as I recall. The colors were kind of an orangie color and some were blue. . . . I was being very quiet because she never, ever let me near the stamps or book. She looked around to see what I was doing. She didn't say anything, and she went back to praying. I proceeded to lick the stamps and stick them into the book. When she turned around again, she moved like lightning and grabbed those stamps and the books away from me. I knew she wanted to throttle me, but since it was church, she contained herself—somewhat. She swore like a mule skinner on the way home she was so mad at me.[8]

Not long afterward, Sheila was standing at the cash register with her mother in a grocery store. When her mother pulled out her ration book with the stamps already glued to the pages, with Sheila standing next to her crying, she began to explain what had happened. The clerk who had maintained a skeptical look on her face "with her lip curled as if in better judgment she shouldn't," accepted the stamps prelicked. But as Sheila and her mother were leaving, the woman commented within their earshot, "Some people will do anything, including make their kid cry, to cheat on the rationing!"

In fact there was widespread cheating. One form it took was the growth of a black market for gasoline and other commodities. Its magnitude was evident in a story in *Colliers* about a Texas journalist who drove from the Rio Grande to the Canadian border without a single gasoline coupon, purchasing the 123 gallons needed during the journey on the black market.[9] Everybody had his favorite source of black market gasoline. John Eisenhower, stationed at the Infantry School, Fort Benning, Georgia, recalled that he and his fellow officers liked to drive up to Atlanta after duty on Saturdays. It was simply a matter of buying gasoline from a gas station willing to sell it for double the legal price.[10]

Arthur Miller had a different view. In his autobiography he noted how the wartime cheaters affected his morale. "Psychologically situated as I was," wrote Miller, who was twice turned down for the Army when he tried to enlist, "a young fit man barred from a war others were dying in . . . it was probably inevitable that the selfishness, cheating and economic rapacity on the home front should have cut into me with its contrast to the soldiers' sacrifices and the holiness of the Allied cause."[11]

A number of government-made plays dealt with the black market, hoarding, and commodity shortages. Two of them stressed the need for responsible use of gasoline. A *Treasury Star Parade* show featured Robert Montgomery as a truck driver whose speeding wasted that one gallon of gasoline that might have saved the lives of two American pilots whose plane crashed just a few miles from their destination when they ran out of fuel.[12] "Hoarding," a December 1942 segment from a series entitled *Consumer Time*, depicted a clash between eighteen-year-old Joan and her parents who were hoarding 100 gallons of black market gasoline and seventy-two pounds of coffee.[13] "The fact that we have all that gas in our garage," Joan argues "may mean that some war workers can't get to the factory on time." Accentuating the issue, the mother of Paul, Joan's boyfriend, a soldier at the battle front, arrives to share a letter from him with Joan's family. Paul's letter rips into home-front hoarders. After reading it, his mother dramatically announces that on this very day she has also received word of his death. The problem with both of these plays is that they were both based on the false premise that there was a gasoline shortage. To the extent that that fact was known, this type of emotional blackmail may have backfired, creating more distrust rather than motivating the public to comply with the rationing program.

A third program dealing with rationing was more honest in its theme if not its dialogue. In mid April 1943, the *Uncle Sam* series featured a show about the rubber shortage.[14] In this one, Stella Morton prevails over the initial objection of her husband, Wilbur, in her desire to ride out to an antique sale in the countryside. Wilbur would prefer that they help the war effort by avoiding unnecessary wear to their tires. While riding in the countryside, their car develops a flat tire. Shortly afterward, a hitchhiking soldier comes along and helps them change it. While assisting them, he tells them that he is on his way home, having been wounded in action and he relates how vital rubber is to the war effort. "If we ever run out of it," he tells the Mortons, "we might just as well throw away our guns." That does it for the Mortons. Never again will they waste rubber.

Another *Uncle Sam* show, "Black Market," depicts the trial and conviction of a black marketeer specializing in meat.[15] The prosecutor in the play characterizes the trial as "perhaps the most important case to come before this court," and adds, "on the decision of this court depend the lives of our fighting men in every corner of the globe. . . . The people . . . will not tolerate the new crop of Benedict Arnolds, the blitz bootleggers." According to Uncle Sam, the narrator, the illegal sales of meat cause meat shortages and "are now endangering the very course of the war." Uncle Sam, as propagandist at least, was not known for understatement.

The trial reveals that the defendant, Mr. Cross, and his cohort, Dixon, not only engaged in black marketeering but also wasted war materials:

> Prosecutor (to Cross's partner): What did you do with the insides, Mr. Dixon? The hearts, the livers and other edible meats?
> Dixon: Well, we didn't do anything with that. We threw that away.
> Prosecutor: Did you know that these insides that you threw away are used for surgical sutures, adrenaline, insulin and gelatin for military photographic film?

During the course of the trial, the farmer who sold him two steers and the butcher whom Cross forced to buy his meat testify against him. "I'm not running a peanut route, bud," the butcher quotes Cross as having told him, "You take this stuff or else!" In the end, Cross is convicted.

WORKERS

The theme of the valiant working man or the noble trade union appeared in, among others, two wartime plays in the *This Is War* series. "You want to know how the winning of the war is up to you?" asks a character in the first play, "Well for one thing it . . . depends on . . . whether you fight the government instead of Germany, or the labor unions instead of the Japs."[16]

In the second play, a working man played by John Garfield says, "If a few of the people includin' some radio commentators and some stuffed shirts, who been screamin' their heads off about labor—if they only put all that wind and energy into some little job that would help lick Hitler . . . then we'd be *gettin'* somewhere."[17]

The most important dramatic series concerning the working man's role in the war effort was *Labor for Victory,* which began in 1942. The show was an indirect consequence of a series of attacks on organized labor that the networks had permitted in the name of "free speech" while at the same time denying to labor the right to respond.[18] Among those participating in the attacks were newscasters H. V. Kaltenborn and Fulton Lewis Jr., both of whom accused unions of "unpatriotic strikes."[19]

Lewis's attacks were at least partly motivated by self-interest. In May 1941, the National Association of Manufacturers hired him to present a series of testimonials concerning big business and its effort to help national defense.[20] Kaltenborn's criticism grew out of the fact that, after the country entered the war, American war production was slow in getting under way. In a fall 1943 broadcast, he claimed that more airplanes were being made by nonunion labor than in unionized factories.[21] However, unlike Lewis, Kaltenborn criticized not only labor but also management and the government for not working together to maximize war production.

Lewis's and Kaltenborn's criticisms clearly angered and frightened organized labor. When in response in early 1939 some Midwest unions threatened boycotts, General Mills, Kaltenborn's sponsor, refused to renew his contract. Kaltenborn managed to pick up a new one, Pure Oil Company, even though Pure Oil, too, was vulnerable to union protests. In addition to membership boycotts, engineers and master mechanics were in a position to recommend to their employers which brand of fuel and oil their companies should use. Still, Pure Oil stood by Kaltenborn.

At least one of Kaltenborn's attacks was directed at *This Is War,* which he suggested could be more appropriately called "This Is How to Lose the War." Following Kaltenborn's lead, two people wrote letters to the government about the prolabor sentiment in *This Is War.* Both letter writers acknowledged hearing his commentary on it and echoed his views of both the series and of labor's role in the war effort. "If you let the labor leaders and wasteful politicians ruin this country's chance of winning this war," wrote a woman from New York State, "no radio programs can make up for this threat."[22] The second writer, a salesman from Chicago, apparently repeating comments by Kaltenborn, claimed, somewhat obliquely, that an Indiana steel mill was facing a shutdown because the union was behind in dues collection.[23] He also charged that labor unions were being unfairly exempted from the draft.

In 1941, clearly influenced by the attacks on them, unions began to press for regular air time to respond to the attacks. Finally, in 1942, NBC gave them air time in the form of a weekly fifteen-minute slot, *Labor for Victory,* presented alternately by the American Federation of Labor (AFL) and the Congress of Industrial Organizations (CIO).

Initially, *Labor for Victory* was supposed to avoid controversial issues. However, by the very nature of the concerns of unions, this proved impossible. Although the AFL preferred to stress good relationships, the CIO, particularly, took a more aggressive stance, presenting grievances, often via dramatic presentations. One concern addressed by the CIO was its opposition to racial discrimination, which it argued was essential to the war effort.

An August 1942 broadcast featuring several stories about the courage and devotion to the war effort of three workers, one British, one Chinese, and one Russian, typifies some of the CIO-sponsored scripts. We learn that, at times, British workers even stayed on the job through bombing raids. Harry Bryson, for instance, a member of the steel workers' union in Newcastle, volunteers to work an extra shift because the factory is short of workers. At one point the workers are taking a tea break courtesy of a mobile kitchen that the CIO contributed to the British. Suddenly an alarm bell warns of an air raid. Harry does not head for the shelter, however. "Shelter? Who's going to the shelter?" he asks, "I'm going back to work!"[24]

Gradually, NBC came around to viewing *Labor for Victory* as labor's forum for opinions. The resulting series often dealt with proposed legislation on the grounds of its importance to labor and to war production. Besides dramatizations concerning unions and the war effort, it also included interviews, speeches, roundtable discussions, and music.

Millard Lampell was prominent among *Labor for Victory* writers. Composer Marc Blitzstein also wrote several episodes. Both were members of the Communist Party, and their writings reflected their orientation. However, despite the perception of the witch hunters of the era, this meant a concern for social justice, not an interest in revolution. Blitzstein's first program dealt with the controversial issue of how to come up with the $8 billion needed to finance the war effort. The U.S. House Ways and Means Committee had decided after closed-door sessions to use sales taxes to finance the war while Progressives and others on the left strongly preferred taxing business profits and higher income brackets. President Roosevelt favored limiting personal income to $25,000 a year.

Blitzstein's play attacks the secrecy of the House committee's deliberations. It features an interchange between Johnny, a Montana miner, and Mary, his wife. Mary encourages him to see the proposal for a sales tax as a "plot" that he should help defeat by supporting a resolution in his union supporting the president's proposal. In one song in the show, Johnny, played by actor José Ferrer, tells of a dream in which money is growing on trees and the government does away with taxes.

> It seems the big shots
> paid every penny,
> whatever the demands,
> We little guys watched
> them win the war,
> while we sat on our hands,
> They did it with one toy sabre—
> no use at all for labor—
> Boy, oh boy, that was some dream.

To a slow waltz, Johnny then tells Mary not to worry: "On twenty-five thousand a year, we'll get along."[25]

A War Production Fund to Conserve Manpower produced *Men, Machines and Victory,* another show concerning the working man. Devoted to safety in the workplace, it was created out of concern that, according to a script in the series, 1.5 million war workers were killed or injured in accidents[26] in the eleven months since Pearl Harbor. An

October 1942 episode concerns Joe Sklarsky, a miner with 25 years' experience, who claims "Every time I dig coal, I also dig a grave for Hitler." Unfortunately, one day, Sklarsky's supervisor and Sklarsky himself make two serious errors in the mine. In violation of regulations, the supervisor leaves Sklarsky to work alone and Sklarsky, ignoring the rule to put up two props for each one knocked down, begins to remove two of them to make room for workers who will soon come to lay down track in the shaft. His action brings about a cave-in, which kills him.

FARMERS

The *Treasury Star Parade* and *Uncle Sam* series both featured shows about the importance of farmers. *Treasury Star Parade's* show No. 11, "The Average American," which featured Fredric March, stressed that the nation's first duty is to produce food.[27] Such shows were fairly bland and likely forgotten a week or so after their broadcast. But Millard Lampell's "Farmers at War," a July 1943 *Uncle Sam* broadcast that attempted to encourage farmers to give their all for the war effort, backfired and made the newspapers.[28] The show concerns a family from North Dakota's Red River Valley who have to abandon their farm because of drought and become migrant workers in California. After Pearl Harbor, the son joins the Army and the father, by now both too old to enlist and too old to continue as a migrant worker, becomes a teacher of farming. "We need farm hands so bad," a clerk in a government employment office tells him, "we're letting men out of the army to bring in the crops."

Apparently Lampell's information about the North Dakota drought was at least in part faulty. The broadcast engendered a flurry of complaints about his references to "dead land, cracked and dried under six inches of dust." "It is a down right libel on this fertile valley," a North Dakota radio station manager wrote to his congressman. Eventually the issue was brought to the attention of North Dakota Senator Gerald Nye. As noted previously, Nye was a Roosevelt adversary who opposed anything that smacked of interventionist propaganda. He seized the opportunity to denounce the OWI for "smearing the fair

name of North Dakota." In the end, although many of the facts concerning conditions in the Red River Valley were supported by documentation, the OWI issued a partial apology to Nye.

Uncle Sam also featured a spring 1943 show entitled "U.S. Crop
Corps,"[29] the source of the quotation at the beginning of chapter 1. It
concerns a family arguing about how to spend the weekend: some
members want to go to the lake in the country; others want to stay in
town. The argument is settled when a call comes in for volunteers to
help local farmers bring in the tomato crop.

AIRPLANE SPOTTERS

Some plays told the story of the folks in the coastal states who kept their
eyes glued to the sky watching for enemy aircraft flying over their respective areas. In the World War II days before radar, this was the only
early warning system. From their observation towers these volunteers
phoned in their reports to a filter center that kept track of aviation movements through the use of model aircraft on a huge horizontal map; the
models were pushed around by long rods.

Bruce Hunt, a retired teacher and a native of Bridgewater, Massachusetts, recalled that when he was eleven he and some friends joined
their local Aircraft Warning Crew. After studying outlines of airplanes
and their characteristics, for about a year-and-a-half they stood watch in
the town's College Tower, on top of the main administration building in
the center of Bridgewater, looking and listening for enemy aircraft.
More than half-a-century later, Hunt remembered the details about
one of the planes: "the XXYY—Italian Trainer, speed 150 MPH, range
200 miles." From Bridgewater, spotters had a direct line to Floyd Ben-
nett Field on Long Island. Initially, they were required to report anything that they saw or heard that was out of the ordinary. But after a few
months their responsibility was narrowed to reporting only what they
had seen; 90 percent of the "heards" had turned out to be beer trucks
grinding their gears as they made a tough corner a block away.[30]

The West Coast series *Eyes Aloft* specialized in shows about the
150,000 volunteer airplane spotters of the Ground Observer Corps in
the Pacific coastal states. The corps was founded in the summer of

1941 and was supposed to commence work on December 11 in connection with war games that the Army Air Force planned for that date. However, within hours of the attack on Pearl Harbor, the observers were called to take their posts. The shows, which featured actor Henry Fonda, among others, reflect the fervor of volunteerism and patriotism during the first years of the war. One hears an Army officer reporting to West Coasters: "It's not a matter of IF the Japanese attack us; it's a matter of When."

One broadcast in the series concerns a town that is having problems staffing two observation posts high in the mountains where trails are often impassable because of winter conditions. Suddenly, town resident Ed Bushnell volunteers to go and live at the post on Dutchman Butte. Others, too, volunteer for week-long stints to assist or spell him. Then another resident, Mrs. Phillip Stanley, agrees to staff the other post, Live Oak Mountain. Later, Mrs. Stanley and a group of people who are carrying provisions for her, ascend Live Oak Mountain. As she looks into the valley below, she says in a teary voice, "It's beautiful down there, isn't it? It's little enough we can do coming up here to keep watch over land like that, down below us." "There, there mother," her daughter responds. "You mustn't cry."[31]

By Christmas eve, Mrs. Stanley and her family have served sixteen days on the icy mountain. Recognizing their dedication, a group of townspeople call her on the telephone and sing Christmas carols, with musical accompaniment, to the lonely watchers. Later we also learn that Mrs. Stanley, her family, and five neighbors spent a total of "72 long days and nights."

At the show's conclusion, the narrator notes that during all the time that they were up at their post, they did not spot a single airplane. "Discouraging?" he asks. "They say not. Useless? No! They were ready, waiting, watching. On duty. Ready to do their part to help warn the nation of the possible approach of the enemy by air."

LOOSE LIPS

"Loose Lips Sink Ships," was one of the most widely publicized slogans of the war era. Out of concern for the need for security of military information, a few plays dealt with the need for the public to heed its advice. The issue of careless gossip received widespread publicity in January 1942 when the *New York Times* carried an article about Allan Harvie, a British steward, who survived the sinking of four ships.[32] Harvie's last such experience resulted in his being adrift in an open boat for 21 days.

Harvie charged that in one of those instances it was careless talk that brought about a ship's sinking when it was only thirty miles out of a British port. It started, so he claimed, when a barmaid overheard a garrulous sailor saying goodbye to his girlfriend. The sailor revealed where he was shipping off to, his ship's name and even what its cargo was. The barmaid innocently repeated the conversation to the cashier, and eventually the details reached a Nazi agent, who passed it on to a German submarine that sank the ship at a cost of eighteen lives and a valuable cargo. Although Harvie's story was impressive, his credibility is questionable. One must wonder how he acquired the details concerning the path traveled by the sailor's revelations.

In May 1943, the *American Women* series aired two plays on the topic of careless talk. One told of two soldiers, one of whom wrote to his family after they were both decorated for bravery in a heroic battle. Because the battle was a military secret, vital information was kept from the enemy. In the other, a major grumbles that the American people talk too freely about things that can reach the enemy. Women's Air Corps Lt. Ferris agrees with him, but citing the 100,000 people in Schenectady, New York, who were involved in the manufacture of a new gun motor carriage and kept its development a secret, she insists that people have also learned to keep secrets. When the cannon was used in a North African battle, the Allies achieved a victory.

The following month the *Cavalcade of America* broadcast "The Enemy Is Listening," the story of two sailors home on a brief leave whose seemingly innocuous remarks in public lead eventually to their and their ship's doom. The play is narrated by Everett Sloane, an "enemy spy" who describes a chain of careless remarks by the two sailors and several others, similar to the one that Harvie recited that leads to the sinking of the ship. At the end of the broadcast Sloane addresses the audience. "See how simple it was," he says in a cynical tone. "How easy. These people could have stopped it. How lucky

for me that they didn't. Ha, ha, ha! They were all nice people too—
and everyday people. Not one of them would have told me anything
if they'd known I was listening."[33]

ANIMALS

A spring 1943 *Uncle Sam* broadcast that apparently dealt with the
Armed Forces' use of animals elicited a response that showed radio's
power to motivate. "I have been listening to your program for many
days," wrote Gloria Branesky, a fifteen-year-old girl from North
Dakota, "I also have taken your advice of many things. But there is
one thing that puzzles me. What can horses and dogs do in the winning of this war? . . . I love horses and dogs. When I work for my country I want my pets to help me. Now what can they do?"[34]

"Horses are used by the U.S. Cavalry," Joseph Liss of the OWI's radio bureau wrote back to Gloria. "Dogs are secured by a patriotic organization called 'Dogs for Defense.' . . . These dogs are trained to
serve as pack dogs, sledge dogs, sentry dogs . . . as well as messengers
or "runners."[35] Three plays on the theme, Arthur Miller's "Canine
Joe," a light-hearted *Cavalcade of America* show, two *Service to the
Front* shows, and one in the *American Women* series were all part of
the OWI's Special Assignment Plan. Perhaps reflecting a high mortal-
ity rate in the canine corps, all three featured dogs that wound up being shot while in action. Two survived, however. Although a good part
of the Miller play takes place overseas in the Pacific where Joe and his
trainer, Private "Pottsy," have been assigned to action, the message is
clear to listeners: "The army needs your dog."

FAMILIAL DISRUPTIONS

The disruption of families brought about by the wartime housing
shortage and the need for women to take jobs and for people to move
around were common themes of wartime propaganda. The main
story line of *Hasten the Day* was built around the wartime life of the
Tucker family, who, unable to find better housing in crowded

wartime Harristown, had to live in a gas station. Episode eleven typifies the style of the series.[36] In the absence of the Tuckers' regular milkman, who has gone off to war, the milkman's wife assumes responsibility for doing the milk route. But one day, when she collapses from exhaustion, Mr. Tucker and his son Dave finish her deliveries. The simple message is "Everybody must pitch in and make whatever sacrifice is necessary."

"Child Care," an *Uncle Sam* show, touched on two social problems that presented major obstacles to the war effort: juvenile delinquency and absenteeism from work. With a good part of the male workforce away at the battlefront, hundreds of thousands of women had to work in their place. Especially in the war's latter years, this included mothers of preschool- and school-age children. Because of inadequate day care, these mothers' employment was often characterized by absenteeism. One working mother dramatically articulates her concerns to her factory's manager: "I'll have to find me somebody that'll take care of my child," she tells him, "a woman or a place where she won't be scared, where she won't feel so awful alone, eight years old and against the world, where somebody will smile at her sometime and maybe give her a little love and see she eats right and helps when she bumps her knee and gives her back to me each night with a little of words [sic] and laughing."[37] Later, the testimony of several mothers in the factory helps management realize that they have to become involved in providing day care.

One common phenomenon during the war was that many relatively newly married women wound up living with their parents or in-laws. A summer 1942 broadcast, "A War Bride's Sister," part of the series *Children in Wartime,* tells the story of Donna, a fourteen-year-old girl, and Rachel, her pregnant older sister. When Rachel moves back home after her husband is sent overseas, Donna suddenly has to give up her room and move into a bedroom with an elderly aunt. She does not take the change well. At one point when Rachel asks, "What's the matter, Donna?" Donna responds "It's *you*! . . . Why couldn't you have it somewhere else, instead of *my* room?"[38]

"Camp Followers," a *Words at War* show, had some interesting things to say about the situation of war wives who relocated to the bases where their men were stationed to be with them. At the start of the broadcast, a female voice hints at the attitudes with which these women have to deal. "I started out feeling sorry for Army wives," says the voice, "but if you could see what I've seen, if you could see what they've done in this town—They'll cheat ya and leave ya' holdin' the bag every time. They're rotten. Just plain rotten. I have no use for any one of 'em. They're nothin' but *camp followers!*"[39]

The show depicts "Bobbi," a young wife from New York, who travels a great distance to a town near an Army base and immediately suffers the first of numerous indignities when she meets a rude hotel clerk. Subsequently, she also has to deal with a snooping landlady, who eventually evicts her for a minor infraction of the house rules. She also encounters difficulty when potential employers, claiming that her dependence on her husband's location gives her a too-transient status, reject her job applications.

DISASTERS

Some shows, such as the thirteen-week government series *Not For Glory*, attempted to reinforce civilian confidence in the government and its agencies. *Not For Glory* sang the praises of various civil defense organizations and how they were helping their communities in times of crisis. A June 1943 broadcast, for example, told how the citizens of Wheeling, West Virginia, and their local civil defense organization managed to salvage materials in a war plant that was in the path of a severe flood of the Ohio River. In the process, members of the community forgot whatever differences they may have had. "I'm an air raid warden by right," said a volunteer who lost his armband during a rescue mission and was wearing a substitute one instead. "But that's the insignia of a Jewish Chaplain!" a colleague pointed out, "It doesn't belong on an Irish air raid warden," to which the first man replies, "If it's all right with the Jewish Chaplain, it's all right with me."[40]

In case a listener might miss the show's relevance to the war, beyond talking just about the saving of the war plant the scriptwriter dragged it in further, saying "we set up this organization to take care of air raids. That's our job. But . . . the river's going to get here before the enemy planes. . . . It can . . . kill as many people as block busters. . . . As far as I'm concerned, this is war, and it doesn't matter whether its Heinkel Bombers or the Ohio River."

TREASON

A few plays dealt with internal threat to the nation. At times before the war, anti-interventionists such as the America Firsters and Father Coughlin made statements that came close to treason. Some of this behavior continued after the United States became involved in the war. In the spring of 1942, FBI agents arrested more than thirty American fascists in various places around the country and charged them with sedition. Among those arrested were Robert Noble and Ellis Jones, coleaders of a California group called the National Copperheads, and William Pelley, who headed the Silver Shirts, a North Carolina organization. Noble, who once served in the Navy, was dishonorably discharged for desertion in 1917. Pelley, a short man with a goatee who claimed to have had a "clairaudient" conversation with Hitler, was convicted in 1935 of fraudulently selling stock in an insolvent company.

The charges against the arrestees were based on written statements they had earlier made. Noble and Jones had characterized General Douglas MacArthur as having "just run out in the dead of night" when MacArthur made his retreat from Bataan.[41] The government also cited a letter that a third man sent to soldiers that stated, concerning President Roosevelt, "Some neck—for a rope" and asked "Does our Commander in Chief have ideas or is he just the world's greatest humbug?"[42]

You Can't Do Business with Hitler presented two plays, neither particularly inspired or inspiring, concerning these fascist leaders. An episode entitled "The Sixth Column" showed Jones and Noble as direct agents of the Nazis who were involved in transcribing and then disseminating Nazi propaganda that was shortwaved to America.[43] It also showed another man, a member of Francis P. Moran's "Christian Front" organization, trying to stir up anti-Communist and anti-Semitic sentiment among Irish Americans.

In 1944 a trial of the fascist group opened in Washington. However, the prosecution made a poor case, and, as one newspaper commented editorially, the government made a giant mistake in bringing it to trial. During the proceedings the judge died, and some time later the entire case fell apart.[44]

CONCLUSION

How effective was radio in achieving its goals in regard to the war on the home front? It is virtually impossible, especially more than fifty years after the war ended, to provide any objective answer. One reason is that other media were also used to carry out the same campaigns for which radio was used. Also, the survey techniques of the time were still rather primitive. But radio was by far the most pervasive medium. No single newspaper or magazine article could claim an audience in the same millions that some of the radio shows could claim.

In any case, Chester J. LaRoche, chairman of the War Advertising Council, testified that the combined efforts of the council, the OWI, and various federal agencies were successful in persuading the American public to help the war effort. LaRoche stated that, as of June 1943, the public had turned in enough scrap metal to create a national stockpile. They had saved 50 million pounds of fat, oversubscribed two great war loans, and planted 20 million victory gardens. In addition, hundreds of thousands had volunteered for part-time work as ration board members, auxiliary helpers on farms, and workers in food processing plants.[45]

Listener response can theoretically be used to try to evaluate the efficacy of radio programs. As was often the case with government series, there is only a meager record of such reaction to most of the shows just described. There is no relevant record, for example, of listener response to the *Uncle Sam* shows that dealt with rationing. However, judging from letters sent in reaction to the *Consumer Time* shows, including some that dealt with rationing, the series was a hit, both generally and in relation to its treatment of the rationing issue. "I'm certain," wrote a woman from Georgia regarding one broadcast, "that if every housewife could have heard the playlet she would have been ready then if not before to ration meat of her own free will."[46] "Let me congratulate you on your propaganda program on sugar rationing," wrote another listener.[47] Yet these responses still say nothing about the extent to which the shows affected people's behavior.

NOTES

1. Paul Casdorph, *Let the Good Times Roll* (New York: Paragon House, 1989), 14.

2. Doris Kearns Goodwin, *No Ordinary Time* (New York: Simon & Schuster, 1994), 356.

3. Casdorph, *Good Times Roll*, 14.

4. Goodwin, *No Ordinary Time*, 357.

5. Goodwin, *No Ordinary Time*, 356.

6. *Radio Daily*, October 6, 1942, Vol. XXI, No. 4, 7.

7. John Milton Kennedy, telephone conversation with author, November 8, 1999.

8. Sheila Hanson to the author, September 8, 2000.

9. Casdorph, *Good Times Roll*, 126-127.

10. John Eisenhower, interview with author, College Park, Md., October, 6, 1999.

11. Arthur Miller, *Timebends* (New York: Grove Press, 1987), 223.

12. J. Fred MacDonald, "Government Propaganda in Commercial Radio: The Case of Treasury Star Parade, 1942–1943," *Journal of Popular Culture*, Vol. XII, no. 2 (Fall 1979), 285-304.

13. Jane Ashman, "Hoarding," *Consumer Time,* December 26, 1942, NA 208-140-773.

14. Home Forces: "Rubber," *Uncle Sam*, week of April 12, 1943, NA-132-744.

15. Home Forces: "Black Market," *Uncle Sam*, week of April 26, 1943, NA-132-744.

16. Philip Wylie, "You're On Your Own," in Norman Corwin et al., *This Is War: A Collection of Plays about America on the March, by Norman Corwin and others* (New York: Dodd, Mead, 1942), 128.

17. Norman Corwin, "It's in the Works," in Corwin et al., *This Is War*, 151.

18. Erik Barnouw, *Radio Drama in Action* (New York: Farrar & Rinehart, 1945), 80.

19. The following account is taken from David G. Clark, "H. V. Kaltenborn and His Sponsors," *Journal of Broadcasting* (Fall 1968): 313-316, and David Culbert, *News for Everyman: Radio and Foreign Affairs in Thirties America* (Westport, Conn.: Greenwood Press, 1976), 115.

20. Culbert, *News for Everyman*, 160.

21. Minerva Pious, "Report to the Union: AFRA's Own Office of War Information," *Stand By*, V, no. 1 (November 1943): 4.

22. Helen Gail to Franklin Delano Roosevelt, February 22, 1942, NA 208-5-22, folder 370 "Radio and Television," March 1942.

23. F. T. Benjamin to Archibald MacLeish, February 23, 1942, NA 208-5-22, folder 370 "Radio and Television," March 1942.

24. *Labor for Victory*, August 15, 1942, NBC Collection, WISC.

25. Scripts of the *Labor for Victory* series are contained in the NBC Collection at WISC. The following discussion and quotes from Blitzstein's first *Labor for Victory* script are based on Eric Gordon, *Mark the Music: The Life and Work of Mark Blitzstein* (New York: St. Martin's Press, 1989), 222.

26. "Men, Machines and Victory," October 9, 1942, Joseph Liss Collection, BU.

27. MacDonald, "Government Propaganda in Commercial Radio," 292.

28. Millard Lampell, "Farmers at War," *Uncle Sam*, week of July 5, 1943, NA-132-745.

29. Home Forces: "U.S. Crop Corps," *Uncle Sam*, week of May 3, 1943, NA-132-744.

30. Bruce Hunt, interview by author, Skiathos, Greece, April 26, 2000.

31. *Eyes Aloft*, n.d., private collection.

32. "Condemns Loose Talk by US Seamen," *New York Times*, 10:6, January 23, 1942.

33. Mignon G. Eberhart, "The Enemy Is Listening," June 7, 1943, *Cavalcade of America*, Radio Spirits.

34. Gloria Branesky to Joseph Liss, June 23, 1943, NA 208-140-749.

35. Joseph Liss to Gloria Branesky, August 3, 1943.

36. *Hasten the Day*, episode 1, NA 208-145-759.

37. Harry Granick, Home Forces: "Child Care," *Uncle Sam*, week of July 26, 1943, NA-132-745.

38. "A Warbride's Sister," Script No. 17, *Children in Wartime*, July 28, 1942, NA 208-97-634, folder "Labor, Department of, Radio."

39. Barbara Klaw, "Camp Followers," adapted by Priscilla Kent, *Words at War*, Box 500, folder 4, November 28, 1944, NBC Collection, WISC.

40. "Wheeling Story," Program 1, *Not for Glory*, June 26, 1943, NA 171-95-35.

41. "Milquetoast Gets Muscles" *Time,* April 13, 1942, 20.

42. "Milquetoast Gets Muscles" *Time,* 20

43. Episode 19, "The Sixth Column," *You Can't Do Business with Hitler,* NYPL-LC.

44. "Trial's End," *Time*, December 11, 1944, 44:24.

45. David Kress, "The Office of War Information During World War II." (Master's thesis, Bowling Green University, 1952), 121–122.

46. *Consumer Time Mail Response,* 9 OWI, NA.

47. *Consumer Time Mail Response,* 14.

14

FIGHTING INTOLERANCE

I was shocked to hear the comments of an Irish maid in this hotel: when she received word that her son had been captured in Tunisia, she went into a diatribe against the Jews. Although the Germans had captured her son, she was not mad at the Germans because she believed the Jews had caused the war.

—William Robson in *Education on the Air: Fourteenth Yearbook of the Institute for Education by Radio*

You are nineteen years old. You are black—"Negro" in the parlance of the era. It is February 1942. Your country has been at war for two months. You tried to enlist right at the start. First you tried the Marines. They rejected you. Then you tried the Navy. "We can only take you as a mess man," the recruiter told you. "No thanks," you replied. "I guess Uncle Sam doesn't really want me." A few days later you found out that, adding insult to injury, the War Department had a requirement that black recruits have a higher minimum intelligence score than whites. Then the Army drafted you. You were assigned to basic training in North Carolina. On your way to North Carolina, a sergeant appeared at the end of your car on the troop train. "Colored to the rear," he called out. You're now at the base—in a segregated unit. Daily, you face all the ugliness that is Jim Crow. Not that you had to come south. You saw and heard enough racism in the north to know what it means to be black in America in 1942. Only yesterday your father wrote to you about how he and your uncle were turned away when they tried to apply for a job in a defense plant. Even if you just stayed in your house, you couldn't escape it. Sometimes your mother used to listen to a program featuring white male minstrel comics purporting to play the roles of black women. They spoke an octave above their normal voice. "Mama," you chided her. "Why do you listen to these shows? They're insulting Negroes. Just listen to the names they give the Colored characters. Do you know any Negroes named "Anesthetic," "Cerebellum," or "Cantaloupe." Why don't you turn off that garbage?"

Now you are seeing the picture even more fully. One day in basic training you saw a sign. The Red Cross was calling for blood donors. You volunteered. Then you learned that they segregated the blood of black donors from the blood of whites.[1]

The day before you reported for induction, you heard a radio speech to the National Urban League by a Mr. MacLeish, a government official.[2] He mentioned a letter that he received that argued that "American Negroes aren't sure they want to fight this war at all." You nodded your head knowingly. MacLeish went on to try to convince the audience that the letter writer was wrong. You realized that he was trying to reassure whites. Asserting that "the choice is freedom on one side, slavery on the other," he claimed that no war had ever been fought for such a simple and clear reason. He declared that American Negroes had a special understanding of what the war was about because "[they] . . . have given their blood also in the great choice between freedom and slavery—much blood and very often." Later you read a magazine article that explained how the Nazis believed that "Aryans" were superior to Jews and other "non-Aryans" and that their very blood was superior. "What am I fighting for?" you asked yourself. "Who's fooling who? I'm not even sure whether a concentration camp is worse than a Georgia chain gang or whether Nazi storm troopers are worse than a red-neck mob in Sykeston, Missouri.

In 1943, in the middle of American involvement in the war, Americans seemed to all have a common set of enemies. Yet, as the nineteen-year-old black soldier realized, in many ways the nation was divided. Two of the major culprits were anti-Semitism and racism.

Sometimes the anti-Semitism was expressed in direct and even violent ways. At the outset of the war, anti-Semitic street gangs were regularly beating Jews on the streets of Boston, Philadelphia, and New York. More often, however, the hatred was expressed through words. "Christians Only," said many newspaper want ads during the Depression.

In addition to the anti-Semitic public pronouncements of Father Coughlin and aviator Charles Lindbergh, right-wing publications including the *Brooklyn Tablet*, the borough's diocese newspaper, made their impact. In one editorial, the *Tablet* claimed that "in the professions, civil service, schools and public life [Jews] are represented out of proportion to their numbers."

More shocking than the *Tablet*'s editorial was publication of an article in the mainstream *Saturday Evening Post* early in 1942 whose thesis was that the Jews themselves were responsible for anti-Semitism.[3] Such an argument, moving responsibility from the perpetrators of hate as it did, is an old ploy that bigots continue to use. The article caused a furor, and the *Post* felt the need to publish an apology for it in a newspaper, although curiously not in its own pages! Expressed as it was in such an important nationwide forum, it was clear that anti-Semitism was a mainstream sentiment.

Much of the most damaging anti-Semitism was expressed by means that often could not be documented. In the interwar years, the nation's best private colleges limited Jewish enrollment to about 10 percent. New York City's five medical schools also had a quota for Jews. None of these institutions openly acknowledged such practices, however. Similarly, in New York City many banks, insurance agencies, law offices, as well as the city's gas and telephone companies routinely rejected job applications from persons with Jewish sounding names. Adding fuel to the fire of home-grown hatred, Nazi shortwave propaganda did its best to fan the flames of intolerance. These broadcasts claimed that the Jews had started the war, either in their capacity as international capitalists who were exploiting the masses or as communists who were trying to destroy capitalism.

For blacks, things were worse. The Scottsboro case, which began in 1931, shocked fair-minded people throughout the United States. It began when two white officers dragged nine black youths off a train in a small town in Alabama and charged them with raping two white girls. One of the girls later recanted her testimony for the prosecution.

Still the case dragged on through the decade, highlighting the severe racial injustice of the south. Langston Hughes was so bothered about it that he even visited the boys in prison. While the NAACP hesitated to act, the Communist Party saw the case as an opportunity to increase its success in recruiting blacks. It became the leading group to try to mobilize public support for the accused boys.[4] Hughes and fellow writers Abe Polonsky, Millard Lampell, Arthur Laurents, and Allan Sloane noticed this. So did many other progressives. The party's courageous stand attracted them. Hughes and some of his progressive colleagues either joined the party or participated in activities that it sponsored.

The injustice of "Jim Crow" struck Allan Sloane when he first arrived at Fort Bragg, North Carolina, early in 1941 after he volunteered for the Army.[5] The first things that caught his attention were the "White" and "Colored" signs. Immediately adjacent to Sloane's all-white unit was an all-black one of truck drivers, gun carriage haulers, personnel chauffeurs, and bridge builders. From Fort Bragg, under a pseudonym, Sloane sent stories about what he called "our new army" via a cousin in New York to *Colliers* and *PM Daily,* a liberal New York newspaper. He focused on the irony of "Jim Crow" in a service dedicated to freedom and equality.

One day, Sloane was called to company headquarters to report to Colonel Alexander M. Patch. Patch liked to go around and ask soldiers, "How do you like the army? Any complaints, don't write to Mrs. Roosevelt. Come see me." Patch was troubled, he told Sloane off the record. Someone was sending stories about the base to the newspapers. To deal with the problem, headquarters was setting up a divisional public relations unit and staffing it with people with backgrounds in journalism. Sloane was transferred to headquarters, where, among other things, he was assigned to find out who was sending the stories. Of course he was never able to tell Patch who the culprit was, but the ploy stopped him from sending out any more.

The war also opened Joe Julian's eyes to how racism was affecting black soldiers. One evening, while he was in London in connection with his work on Corwin's series *An American in England,* he took a stroll.[6] At Piccadilly Circus he got into a discussion with an American GI, a black corporal. The corporal described the dilemma of a black soldier, far from home, in the company of racist white countrymen who harassed him. The British, in contrast, treated black GIs with dignity. As if to underscore the soldier's point, as the two were talking, two white GIs interrupted their conversation and made disparaging remarks to the black soldier.

In response to Julian's question "How do most Negro soldiers feel about the war?" the GI told Julian "I think we feel it don' matter much what happens. We just know we have to fight so we fight." Julian returned to his hotel in an agitated state. Quickly, while it was still fresh in his mind, he wrote down the conversation. He then called Corwin, who came over to the hotel to read what he had written. The black corporal's statements affected Corwin, too. Corwin agreed with Julian both that the soldier seemed to speak for a wider group of black American GIs stationed in England and that the dialogue merited inclusion in Corwin's next script.

The following morning Corwin and Julian met with Edward R. Murrow in the latter's office. Julian was impressed with his first look at the famed war correspondent. There he sat, tall and thin, with a knifelike crease in his trousers and his Savile Row look. Murrow reacted with great enthusiasm to the dialogue. "Let's do it! Let's raise a little hell back home!" Murrow exclaimed. But the following day, Murrow had second thoughts. "This is the wrong time to be raising hell back home," he told Julian. "We need a united front. That has to take precedence over an issue that's likely to be divisive." The matter was dropped there.

Ed Murrow was not the only one who feared "rocking the boat." Only weeks later, the radio division of the Office of Facts and Figures (OFF) took up the question of producing a special series devoted to minority groups. By the meeting's end, the decision was "no." The rationale was that such a program might do more to emphasize minority groups than to unify them with the rest of the country.[7] In fact, radio did pick up the theme of blacks and the war. Despite the reluctance to change the status quo, a variety of radio dramas made a stand against racism, weak though it generally was. In an effort to unify the nation and ameliorate the racial climate, the networks and the various agencies worked with writers such as Arch Oboler, Norman Corwin, Erik Barnouw, Arthur Laurents, Millard Lampell, and

Langston Hughes to tackle these problems. The anti-Nazi rhetoric of fighting for democracy molded a small coalition of black actors and liberal whites in broadcasting who sought to speak out against domestic racism.[8] In some cases, interracial friendships were forged. Roz Leader, widow of NBC director Anton Leader, recalled years later her and her husband's friendship with Roi Ottley, producer of an innovative radio drama series about blacks. But particularly for the blacks, such a friendship came at a cost. Ottley suffered the indignity on at least one occasion of being denied access to the elevator in the Leaders' building by the elevator operator.[9]

If individual writers and actors were willing to speak out against racism, the government was not. Federal officials were blind to the connection between domestic racism and blacks' attitudes about the war. Initially, they even refused to believe that black Americans were ambiguous about the war effort. Vice President Wallace and Archibald MacLeish, for example, saw the war as a revolutionary struggle, and MacLeish expected blacks to support the war effort with enthusiasm. After all, they were descended from slaves. Federal radio programming about race relations was very limited during the war. Government officials knew that something needed to be broadcast about and to blacks. But they had anxiety about how to break the silence about blacks' rightful role in American life, preferring to build up black morale without endorsing radical reforms.

After MacLeish's previously referred to radio speech to the National Urban League, a white listener wrote to him complaining that his misperception of black thinking scared her. She described the way Negroes were thinking according to her maid and according to "several other colored people who are my friends." She continued. "I learn that all Negroes, from menial laborers to professional people, are unconvinced they have in fact a stake in this country. They wonder whether living under the domination of the Japanese, or even under Hitler, could be worse than living under the fascism as practiced in the southern states. . . .They compare the Red Cross's attitude toward Negro blood donors to the unscientific racial theories advanced by Hitler. They wonder if the ghettoes in which they are forced to live, as exemplified by Harlem, could be any better than the ghettoes of Europe into which Hitler has forced the Jews. They compared their inability to exercise the right to ballot in some sections of our land to Hitler's depriving the Jews of their citizenship rights."[10]

Civilian and military intelligence reports also provided warnings about low black morale. But administration officials interpreted them as evidence to feed fears that blacks were vulnerable to foreign propaganda. *PM Daily* and other leftist sources, reacting that MacLeish's point about slavery was not a sufficient one to convince blacks to support the war effort, chastised him for underestimating the extent of Negro doubt about the war effort.[11]

Particularly in the early months of the war, in trying to build enthusiasm for the war effort, federal officials relied heavily on the argument that the war was a fight against slavery. MacLeish's speech to the National Urban League was not the only time that the argument was made. A month after that speech, OFF officials met with representatives of black organizations to discuss the wartime problems of Negro citizens. The majority of the conferees stated that they could not help build morale among blacks until the government took some concrete steps to reduce the mistreatment of blacks "throughout the whole war effort." Two months later, OFF conducted a survey of blacks' attitudes toward the military and toward the enemy. Its findings, published in a pamphlet *The Negro Looks at the War*, disturbed government officials. Forty-two percent of those surveyed believed it was more important to make democracy work at home than to defeat the Axis powers. Blacks complained particularly about segregation in the military and about their exclusion from positions of command in black military units. A third of the respondents believed that blacks would be treated about the same under Japanese rule and 20 percent thought that they would be treated "better." The results were interpreted as evidence of the success of Japanese propaganda efforts. Responding to a similar questionnaire about German versus American rule, the overwhelming response was that blacks would be worse off under the Germans. But 20 percent thought life would be the same. Other federal surveys of the time showed similar results.

After MacLeish read the findings, he sent secret memoranda to various federal officials, recommending a plan to raise Negro morale. First he suggested that whites—white employers particularly, be informed of the Negroes' contribution to industry. Second, he proposed that the federal government collaborate with black organizations to offset Axis propaganda that portrayed the war as a racial struggle. Finally, MacLeish argued that the best way to improve Negro morale would be to reduce discrimination. The message had finally gotten through to him.

There is no record of the responses to MacLeish's proposals. But by June, his authority was greatly reduced when the Office of War Information (OWI) superseded OFF and MacLeish himself was made subordinate to OWI's new head, Elmer Davis. For the rest of 1942 and the following year, OWI struggled to develop a policy on how to respond to a growing black anger about racial injustice and anti-black violence. OWI refused to attack segregation, afraid it might antagonize white southern congressmen.

Among the sources of conflict at OWI about how to deal with low Negro morale was the employment of two very disparate consultants: Theodore Berry, a black lawyer from Ohio, and Milton Starr, the white owner of a chain of black movie theaters in the South. Berry championed an aggressive OWI effort to build morale among blacks and simultaneously try to change white racial attitudes and practices. He argued that without the latter, any campaign to raise morale among blacks would consist of empty rhetoric.

In bold contrast, Starr, whose views came to prevail in the OWI, claimed in a report in the summer of 1942 that the black masses actually accepted current racial conditions. He charged that it was black leaders and the black press, neither of whom he believed accurately represented the masses, who were responsible for the weak support for the war effort among blacks. Starr claimed that it would be sufficient to counteract black leaders and Japanese propaganda to publish favorable news about the achievements of Negro soldiers in the black press, radio, and other media.

Given Starr's influence, it should be no surprise to hear that government-sponsored radio dramas made the weakest commentary on the race issue. The OWI and the War Department carried out a limited public campaign to increase racial tolerance and bolster Negro morale. One of the earliest signs of this on radio was the broadcast of "The Battle of Henry Johnson," the fourth program in the series *Freedom's People.* The series, produced by the U.S. Office of Education beginning in October 1941, dramatized black contributions to American life in music, drama, sports, science, industry, education, and national defense.[12]

"The Battle of Henry Johnson," aired two weeks after Pearl Harbor, actually dealt with an incident that occurred during World War I. But by implication it made a statement concerning blacks in relation to the war that had just begun. It concerned two heroic, wounded black soldiers who, despite their injuries, dispersed twenty-four Germans with at least eight casualties. Its relevance to America's new situation was quite clear.

Langston Hughes encountered the obtuseness and racism of federal officials barely more than a month after American entry into the war. Hughes had no doubt that the defeat of Nazi Germany was as much in the interest of American blacks as it was for whites. In January 1942, he was asked to write a *Keep 'Em Rolling* script for a Lincoln's Birthday program that was being broadcast on the Mutual Radio Network.[13] He agreed to do so, but only reluctantly; he had already had one unhappy experience with network executives. When he sought payment, a bureaucrat flew from Washington, D.C., treated him to a whiskey sour, and explained that the writers were not paid for this sort of work. The government, the bureaucrat explained, viewed the contribution of writers to the war effort as an expression of their patriotism. Later, Hughes learned that this was not true. He protested to the Office of Civilian Defense that while white writers had opportunities to earn money, blacks were shut out from such possibilities. He agreed to do the script but wrote to his agent, "Negroes were never asked to write anything except when a segregated all-Negro program was coming up.[14]

Initially, Bernard Schoenfeld, a government official, told Hughes "I need not tell you what to write since you have always written truth, and that is what counts at all times." Hughes then sent him an eight-page script, "Brothers," about "Charlie," a black sailor coming home from duty at sea.[15] President Roosevelt had recently made a pronouncement to Congress on the Four Freedoms for which the United States was fighting: freedom of speech and worship and freedom from want and fear. Hughes's script developed these themes but applied them to race. On coming home, Charlie finds his younger brother bitter about the treatment of blacks in America and reluctant to support the war effort.

Charlie appeals to him, and to blacks in general, saying "Why Hitler'd make a doublebarreled padlocked ghetto out of Harlem so quick you couldn't say 'Flat Foot Floogie.'" But he then concedes in a way not heard on American radio that his brother does have some arguments on his side, commenting "We got a few Hitlers at home to lick." When his mother comments that "they ain't using bombing planes," He replies "They got lynch mobs, though, and Jim Crow cars for Negroes."

To Hughes's dismay and fury, the government rejected his script. "Too controversial," they said. His characterization of proponents of segregation and lynch mobs scared them off. As he explained, he wrote the script boldly because "so far the programs seemingly aimed at colored people have hedged miserably." He denounced the radio industry as "a most reactionary and difficult medium in which to put forward any decent or progressive ideas regarding Negro life." Re-garding the networks, he added, "I, personally, have lost all interest in dealing with them." "God knows we better win before Hitler comes over here to aid in the lynchings," he told a friend.

Later, he put his bitterness aside and sent some song scripts to a Defense Bond Drive. To help the government sell war bonds through the radio series *Treasury Star Parade*, he also sent a radio drama about American folk heroes. He also tried once more to have his pre-viously rejected "Brothers" accepted. Again it was greeted as too rad-ical. Eventually, in September 1942, the Writers War Board (WWB) accepted it, but not as a regular script. Instead they sent it out for use as a "War Script of the Month Extra."

Government-produced plays continued for the most part to present a tepid message concerning the race issue for the duration of the war. Nobody wanted to incur Senator Bilbo's wrath. Thus "Negroes in the War," an *Uncle Sam* production, presents the theme of Nazi race ha-tred toward blacks that the government liked to emphasize.[16] It told listeners at one point, "The German people have been told by their Fuehrer [*sic*] that the Negro has neither a soul nor an intellect." The play features a mother helping her eight-year-old son deal with accu-sations that he is "no good" because he is colored. She tells him about a great role model, George Washington Carver, the Negro scientist. Listeners then hear a historical flashback, a conversation between a young Carver, about to enroll in Iowa State College, and a professor at the college. "Most people seem to think that the likes of me has no place in college," Carver tells the professor. "They say we're meant to use . . . only our hands." "What rot . . . ," the professor replies. Then to refute the notion of black intellectual inferiority, he cites the example of the black who manufactured the first clock made in the United States. "Sure he was a Negro," the professor says, "but because of his accomplishments he was admired and respected by everybody. That's all you need to get along, Carver . . . brains and work."

From a racially conservative viewpoint, Carver was an ideal model for blacks. We learn that he rejected an offer from Henry Ford to head up Ford's chemical laboratories: "the Doctor didn't want money and he didn't want power. He wanted understanding for himself as a colored man and for his people." However, "Negroes in the War" presents a very tame model for blacks oppressed by a system riddled with segregation and violence. As it deals with the very real problem of low perception of black intellect, the issue functions as a straw man, allowing listeners to ignore the lynch mobs and other manifestations of racial hatred. No threat here to white society!

It took a crisis to produce a really candid radio play about blacks, and it came from a white writer. As Langston Hughes noted, when it came to dealing with black themes, the networks were generally no greater risk-takers than the government, preferring shows with themes that were nice and safe. In June 1943, race riots erupted in Detroit, leaving thirty-four people, twenty-five blacks and nine whites, dead on the streets. Thirteen hundred people were arrested. The event alarmed authorities around the nation and inspired them to take steps to pacify black communities. One of those steps was the use of radio drama. This is the origin of one of the great radio classics: William Robson's "An Open Letter on Racial Hatred." There are conflicting accounts regarding the origin of this broadcast. According to one, the initiative for the program came from Walter White of the National Association for the Advancement of Colored People (NAACP). This may have been through an organization called the Entertainment Emergency Committee. Not long after the riots, White contacted Wendell Willkie, former Republican candidate for president in the 1940 elections, and sought Willkie's help. After the election, Willkie undertook a journey around the world as President Roosevelt's personal representative. The experience produced a great change in Willkie, and he developed a new concern for race relations and a determination to liberalize the Republican Party. Following White's approach to Willkie, the two decided to promote a dramatization of the riots and then contacted either CBS or possibly Bill Robson directly.

The result of the contacts was that the omnipresent Robson was asked to write a script about the riots themselves. Recalling the time two years later, Robson wrote "We were extremely careful in the preparation of the script, since the country was pockmarked with tension areas where it was feared new race riots might break out. Our problem was to throw the light of truth on the Detroit incident, without inciting either Whites or Negroes to riot elsewhere. Therefore it was necessary to show the positive aspects of person helping person, rather than the destructive aspects of the disturbance."[17]

The project was considered such a delicate one that CBS President William Paley took a personal interest in its production, frequently asking Robson to make changes in the script. At one point, Paley told Robson, "I have a report from our man in Washington that the FBI had definite proof that the Negroes started the riot in Detroit. How about that? You don't say it in your script." Robson replied that he had no evidence to make such a claim. "Are you certain of your facts?" Paley asked. And Robson replied that he was.[18]

What Robson did say in his script and what helped set it apart from other scripts on race relations, particularly government ones, was that at least part of the reason for the riots was white racism. He pointed to one particular factor: job discrimination.

> Mr. Reason: Why are you recruiting labor in the South, when you've already got a big pool of labor in Detroit? . . .
> Mr. Detroit: Listen, bud we're not hirin' any Negroes.
> Mr. Reason: But the War Manpower Commission has ordered that local labor had to be exhausted before you could—
> Mr. Detroit: Maybe they did, but they're not enforcin' the order and we don't want any black—[19]

Robson also made a not very oblique comment about the Detroit police—decades before racial profiling of blacks exploded as a national issue in the United States.

Second voice: Six hundred injured. The majority Negroes.
Voice: Thirty-five dead.
Voice: Twenty-nine Negroes.
Voice: Seventeen of them shot by the police.[20]

CBS broadcast the entire program over a closed circuit to all the stations the day of the show, giving them the opportunity of refusing to carry it if they so wished. Several southern stations were incensed about the program. Otherwise, very few turned it down. However, a statement from a representative of a Detroit station reveals that even the management of some stations that did air the show felt that they were walking on eggshells in doing so. Radio was not yet comfortable with advocacy. "We carried Mr. Robson's program," wrote the representative, "[but] we did it with some misgivings, because, having heard it previously, we realized that the setting he painted was of West Woodward Avenue—certainly not East Woodward Avenue. The Whites were as badly treated on the east side . . . as the Negroes were on the west side. [Also] we were afraid some late-tuners-in, Negroes especially, might hear the exclamation that the Whites were throwing a Negro woman off the bridge. You can realize what that might have led to if some Negro had just tuned in and thought that the revolt had started all over again, and said to his neighbor, 'Let's get going.' Although Mr. Robson thought his program was a fair picture, and it was for the most part, it gave a biased picture in the opinion of those of us who knew conditions inside Detroit."[21]

The claim that the show presented a distorted view deserves some skepticism. The extremely high percentage of blacks killed, arrested, and injured needs to be set against the percentage of blacks in the total population of Detroit. Blacks were a minority in the city! *Time* called the program "One of the most eloquent and outspoken programs in radio history."[22] The reactions were as varied and violent as the point of view of the listener.

In July 1943, soon after the riots in Detroit, New York Mayor Fiorello LaGuardia asked Hughes to assist in developing a series of radio programs, *Unity at Home, Victory Abroad.* Its objective would be to show "what New York is, how it came into its present being, and why there is no reason that the peace and neighborliness that does exist should ever be disturbed." The WWB, supporting LaGuardia's campaign, also wrote Hughes seeking programs stressing racial harmony "so that there will be no danger of race riots in New York."

Hughes agreed to produce a few scripts. But first he blasted the racist policies of radio that failed to depict the real problems of Negroes. "Personally I do not like radio," he complained, "and I feel that it is almost as far from being a free medium of expression for Negro writers as Hitler's airplanes are for the Jews."[23] Shortly after Hughes sent his letter to the WWB, on August 1, a white policeman shot and seriously wounded a black soldier in New York. The incident led to racial violence resulting in the deaths of five and injuries to 400. Hughes declared that such disturbances usually brought racial progress and expressed a longing to be on the streets. "All the best colored people declare they have been set back fifty years," he wrote to a friend. "I don't know exactly from what."

With the outbreak of violence, pressure increased on Hughes to help pacify the black community. In response, he sent the WWB some songs and two short plays. The first play, "In the Service of My Country," was broadcast in early September on station WNYC. It had been inspired by pictures of blacks and whites working side by side building the Alaska–Canada Highway. The WWB praised it, calling it "the finest job that has been done on this subject."

The WWB also commented favorably on Hughes's second play, "Private Jim Crow," a show about segregation in the armed forces. "Private Jim Crow" was based on the ordinary experiences of black soldiers, particularly in the South.[24] It showed small but significant instances of humiliation. A black soldier, for example, could buy cigarettes and chocolate bars in a store but not ice cream or bottled soda. If he consumed ice cream or drinks in a public place with whites present, he might be seen as violating the segregationist laws that prohibited the races from eating together. "Delicate nuance of the color line," Hughes noted: "A chocolate bar but not an ice cream bar." Despite the significance of "Private Jim Crow," the WWB decided it was too hot for them. Years later, Hughes recalled his work for the WWB with some bitterness. "During the war I did a number of requested scripts for the Writers' War Board, used throughout the country," he wrote. "Most of the white writers serving this committee also got any number of paying jobs to do patriotic scripts. Not one chance to do a commercial script was offered me."

Apart from Robson, virtually none of the writers of plays dealing with blacks presented shows that really threatened the status quo. Norman Corwin came close to doing so with his "Dorie Got A Medal," which CBS broadcast in the spring of 1944. The show concerns Dorie Miller, a black Navy mess man who was on board the *U.S.S. Arizona* in Pearl Harbor at the time of the Japanese attack. A racist policy in the navy had denied weapons training to him and other blacks. Yet during the attack, Miller seized a machine gun and shot down several Japanese planes. Subsequently, he was awarded the Navy Cross. But he continued as a mess man until his death in action two years later in the Pacific.[25]

The Miller case was a cause célèbre within the black community. News of his heroism was confined to the black press and black newsreels, for fear of offending the Navy, because his story showed the stupidity of segregation in the military. Hughes would have loved to do a radio play about Miller, but the most he could do was write a poem about him.

Norman Corwin's play about Miller received some approbation. "If we could have more of this sort of thing on the radio," wrote one listener, "I think it would not be long before we would begin to make some inroads on poll taxes, lynchings and other forms of racial discrimination."[26] But Corwin himself was not pleased with the show, and a black columnist in a Pennsylvania newspaper faulted it "for the absence of even 'a single note of protest' in the entire thing. . . . Anybody listening . . . would have thought Dorie . . . was just a nice colored boy from down South who wanted to fight Hitler. . . . He didn't seem to be particularly angry or disturbed that he had to get his training in machine gun in a penny arcade." The reviewer concluded, "if he had any inner tension or resentments, they didn't come out in that radio program."[27]

Corwin apparently saw through the hypocrisy of a black man fighting to defend a democracy whose fruits he could not fully share. But just as Ed Murrow had backed off from approving Joe Julian's pitch for a hard-hitting program about bias against blacks in the spring of 1942, Corwin appeared not to want to offend the Navy.

Another well-intentioned but weak-hitting play dealing with race was Arch Oboler's "Strange Morning."[28] Although it was broadcast the month before Germany's defeat, the show dealt with Germany's capitulation as though it had already occurred. The play featured Ingrid Bergman as a nurse who was visiting a chronic care hospital ward to inform the men that Germany had surrendered. Through her discussions with the patients, Oboler showed that after the war ended, America would still have to deal with the phenomenon of the permanently disabled GIs and a variety of other social problems. But ignoring the racism that permeated the military during the war, Oboler somewhat glorified the situation of blacks in the military. Thus, a black soldier told the nurse of his reluctance to return to civilian life. In the military hospital, the GI claimed, "Nobody said 'Get out black boy, One side nigger.' Somebody said 'Nice going fella' and the guy next to me stuck a cigarette in my lips and somebody else lit it. . . . They talk to me." "Strange Morning" followed reality to a small extent. Two years earlier, during a visit to troops in Alaska, Bergman had visited a hospital. "The worst part is going around the wards talking," she wrote subsequently in a letter: "sometimes I sing, sometimes I tell a story. I started to cry for the first time. I felt so lost for words."[29] In the play, too, the nurse breaks down crying after visiting the ward.

Probably the most candid series to discuss blacks, *New World A-Coming*, was done on WMCA, a local New York radio station. The series premiered in 1944 "to portray by radio the contributions of the Negro race to American life, 'his country and ours,'" according to the station's new president, Nathan Straus. Its cast was primarily black: Canada Lee was its narrator. But some white performers also appeared, including Alexander Scourby, Will Geer, and Joseph Julian.

Straus was a wealthy New Yorker who had worked as a newspaper journalist and served in the state senate, where he gained a reputation as an expert on the problems of housing for the poor. In 1937, President Roosevelt appointed Straus as the first head of the Federal Housing Authority. Straus and his staff were committed to the idea of racial harmony in pursuing their objectives. But by 1942, this provoked severe criticism from Southern Democrats in the House of Representatives. Amidst the pressures, Roosevelt accepted Straus's resignation, despite his high regard for the New Yorker, in order to placate the Southern Democrats.

Returning to New York, Straus bought WMCA with the intention of carrying on his social activism in a different venue. The station already had a reputation for being independent and gutsy and for having a strong relationship with the city's black community. As early as 1938 it was broadcasting *Tales from Harlem,* a weekly review of news and notes of interest to black citizens.

Straus's wife Helen joined him in his determination to use radio to carry out a mission of public service. In 1943, Roi Ottley, a black New York editor, journalist, and social worker, published a book entitled *New World A-Coming.* The book discussed discrimination in housing and employment and other socioeconomic problems that blacks, particularly in Harlem, were experiencing. Helen Straus read Ottley's book and recommended it to her husband, and the station began to work toward the goal of adapting the book into a dramatic series.

Each week *New World A-Coming* presented vignettes demonstrating the advancement of civil rights and discussing the many obstacles yet to be overcome. In form, the series owed a debt to the *March of Time* series. The sketches were short, punchy, and well acted and were tied each week into a selected theme: "The Negro," "Fascism and Democracy," "The Negro in Early America," "The Story behind the Headlines in the Negro Press," "White Folks Do Some Funny Things," and many others.

New World A-Coming was an extraordinary program for its time. While it was not a "militant" show, neither was it complacent. At its heart was the message that blacks had the power to change an oppressive system—and in fact that it was their responsibility to challenge that system. This contrasted sharply to the message in "Negroes in the War" and similar government productions. Furthermore, no network could have dared to broadcast such a series, a sad commentary on the times.

New World A-Coming was presented by the City-Wide Citizens Committee of Harlem, a coalition of black and white leaders dedicated to the advancement of racial equality in New York. Leaders from the committee often gave talks on the program. In addition to the committee, the WWB and the Radio Directors Guild cooperated with the project. It premiered in March 1944 and was heard on Sunday afternoons "at three past three."

Like *Lux Radio Theatre* and the *Cavalcade of America, New World A-Coming* dealt with a variety of themes unrelated to the war. But a number of its shows, such as "Parachutes for Democracy," "Furlough Home," "Report from the Front," "Tribute to a Hero," and "Heroes of the Skies" were clearly war related. "Parachutes for Democracy," a November 1944 drama, was another show that touched on the heroism of Dorie Miller. It told the true story of Skippy Smith, a black businessman. With the financial help of actor Eddie Anderson, Smith founded a parachute company in California during the war that employed an integrated work force. Anderson played the role of Rochester on the Jack Benny Show. Dorie Miller's name came into play in the context of the period when Skippy was first working in a parachute factory, several years before he founded his own. "They told this . . . this guy to report for work here. In this department, one white employee complained to a white colleague, 'How do you like that?'"

But his colleague replied, "Listen. Did you hear about a colored fellow at Pearl Harbor last week?. . . . Dorie Miller . . . when the Japs flew in and started pasting us, this Miller guy runs to a gun and shoots at the Jap planes just like everybody else. . . . If a colored boy can help to fight the war there's no reason why one of them can't work here."[30]

"Heroes of the Skies," airing in December 1944, told the story of another Smith, Eddie, a young pilot from New York.[31] Eddie's group of twelve black flyers took on sixteen German fighters and shot down eight of them with no losses. But early in the drama, the narrator informed the audience of how Eddie subsequently was shot down. "I saw his plane plummeting to the earth," he recalled, "and I saw his grave. . . . It was marked only by smoke and seared grass somewhere in Italy. I'd like to tell you about Eddie, because I think you ought to know what he died for. You see, Eddie and I are Negroes . . . and we were buddies together from the first day in training school."

The narrator then explained that Eddie was part of the famed group of black pilots who were trained in a segregated squadron in Tuskegee, Alabama. The squadron was "a test of whether or not the Negro can fly as combat fighters in this war." Unlike a number of simplistic shows about blacks, "Heroes of the Skies" challenged the treatment of blacks by even well-meaning but patronizing liberals. One character complained, "Why do we Negroes have to be singled out and called an 'experiment'? . . . They don't call white flyers 'experiments.' . . . Fellows go to training school and they either make it or get washed out. . . . They're not made to feel that they're in a cage with a burning spotlight on them."

Like a number of wartime shows about blacks, this one carried a double message. Part of it was for black listeners. "If the fascists win this war," Eddie argues, "then everything our people have ever gained will be lost—just like that—in a snap of the fingers. . . . What this war is all about . . . [is] to bring the freedom of Chicago and New York not only to Germany and the Far East, but to our own southland, as well."

The other message, about segregation in the Armed Forces, also from Eddie, was for both blacks and whites. "The planes we fly all have the same white stars on them," he explained, "the winged emblems on our shoulders are the same, . . . the brass markers on our collars are the same—US—United States—there's no difference, white or colored, in any of those things. . . . It shouldn't be different at training schools, flying fields, or in combat against the enemy. If it is different—then it's like a Jim Crow train—where a white man sits in one place and a Negro sits somewhere else—separated—apart."

Toward the end of the war two powerful plays about blacks were written for *Assignment Home*, a CBS series intended as propaganda for the home front. Arthur Laurents wrote one entitled "The Knife" that dealt with the position of the black soldier in the Army. As Laurents recalled, the script was received with great excitement until it got to Washington, where it was initially vetoed.[32] Somehow, according to Laurents, it reached the desk of Secretary of War Henry Stimson who not only made sure the program was aired but also gave the production unit a letter of commendation for it.

A second play for the series had even rougher sledding. This script, entitled "The Glass," originated in June 1945 with a suggestion in a letter from Truman Gibson to CBS vice president Robert Heller.[33] Gibson was concerned about the reception that civilians would give the 850,000 returning black GIs. Most blacks entered the service illiterate and uneducated. Now they would return home having seen societies where blacks were greeted with a respect never accorded them at home. As Gibson emphasized, even in the middle of the war when harmonious race relations were needed to maximize the nation's attention to the enemy, racism against black soldiers had been a serious problem. He expressed concern that on the conclusion of the war, an even greater resurgence of hostility from many whites would greet the mass return of black GIs. Gibson suggested that CBS do a show about the returning black soldiers. CBS was impressed by Gibson's letter, and Arnold Perl, an Army corporal, was assigned to work on a script dealing with the issues that Gibson raised. The script told about two soldiers, one black and one white, who worked side by side, were both wounded at the Battle of the Bulge, and recuperated in hospital beds next to each other. After their discharge from the Army, the two continued their friendship. When the black soldier encountered racial discrimination in his first attempt to find a job, his white friend helped him get a job with his own employer.

Plans for broadcast of "The Glass" got as far as rehearsals at CBS. Then, suddenly they came to a grinding halt. The Army Department, uncomfortable with the script's blunt attack on racism, withdrew its support and CBS in turn canceled the show. The decision infuriated a variety of blacks and white liberals, and some of them, including the editor of a black newspaper chain and The Hollywood Independent Citizens Committee of the Arts, Sciences and Professions, which included among its members Norman Corwin, wrote to the Army demanding explanation. Gibson's assistant, Louis Lautier, replied, saying that the War Department had not wanted to become involved in a controversial subject concerning civilian life. On learning of this rationale for the cancellation, the NAACP complained to Secretary of War Stimson himself. But the matter was dead.

In the course of outlining the history of the whole episode, author Barbara Savage wrote, "The War Department decision . . . demonstrates how narrow had been the expansion of the permissible political boundaries on race by the war's end. While it was acceptable for a federal agency to show the Negro's contribution to the war effort, the Department was not willing to present the corollary argument that military service qualified black 'civilians' for anything akin to equal treatment from the white civilian world they were destined to reenter."[34]

The War Department's failure to proceed with broadcast of "The Glass" symbolized the entire problem of the government's attitude toward the race relations issue. Although writers such as Corwin, Oboler, Robson, and Wishengrad produced programs showing the heroism and abilities of blacks and women, that failure combined with the general timidity of the networks to limit the effectiveness of wartime radio as a vehicle for social change. Then, when the war ended, programs promoting tolerance disappeared altogether from the airwaves. They only reemerged in commercial broadcasting with the beginning of the civil rights and women's liberation movements of the 1960s and 1970s.[35]

NOTES

1. Arnold Rampersad, *The Life of Langston Hughes: Volume II: 1941–1967, I Dream A World* (New York: Oxford University Press, 1988), 36.

2. Barbara Savage, "Broadcasting Freedom: Radio, War and the Roots of Civil Rights Liberalism 1938–1948." (Ph.D. diss., Yale University, 1995), 212.

3. Milton Mayer, "The Case Against the Jew," *Saturday Evening Post,* 214, March 28, 1942, 18–19.

4. Arnold Rampersad, *The Life of Langston Hughes: Volume I: 1902–1941, I Too Sing America* (New York: Oxford University Press, 1988), 216–217.

5. Sloane recalled this, his first encounter with Jim Crow, in a letter (undated) to the author.

6. The description of the following incident is based on an account in Joseph Julian, *This Was Radio: A Personal Memoir* (New York: Viking Press, 1975), 96–100.

7. William B. Lewis to Douglas Meservey, April 25, 1942, NA 208-5-21, folder 370 "Radio and Television."

8. J. Fred MacDonald, *Don't Touch That Dial: Radio Programming in American Life, 1920–1960* (Chicago: Nelson Hall, 1979), 346.

9. Roz Leader, interview by author, Los Angeles, August 17, 1999.

10. Caroline Blake to Archibald MacLeish, February 14, 1942, as quoted in Barbara Savage, *Broadcasting Freedom: Radio, War and the Politics of Race, 1938–1948* (Chapel Hill: University of North Carolina Press, 1999), 110. The book is based on Savage's dissertation. See note 2.

11. Savage, *Broadcasting Freedom,* 214.

12. William Barlow, *Voice Over: The Making of Black Radio* (Philadelphia: Temple University Press, 1999), 70.

13. Rampersad, *I Dream A World,* 38.

14. This quote and much of the following discussion concerning Hughes's difficulties in writing for radio, including the following additional quotes: "Negroes were never . . . coming up"; "I need not . . . at all times"; "so far . . . hedged miserably"; and "God knows . . . in the lynchings," are based on Rampersad, *I Dream A World,* 39.

15. Langston Hughes, "Brothers," August 16, 1943, JWJ, MSS Hughes, Box 214, YALE.

16. "Negroes in the War," *Uncle Sam*, week of February 8–12, 1943, NA-132-744.

17. As quoted in Erik Barnouw, *Radio Drama in Action* (New York: Farrar & Rinehart, 1945), 60.

18. Erik Barnouw, *The Golden Web: A History of Broadcasting in the United States. Volume 2, 1933–1953* (New York: Oxford University Press, 1968), 182–183.

19. William N. Robson, "Open Letter on Race Hatred," in Barnouw, *Radio Drama in Action,* 66.

20. Robson, "Open Letter on Race Hatred," in Barnouw, *Radio Drama in Action,* 71.

21. Josephine H. MacLatchy, ed., *Education on the Air: Fifteenth Yearbook of the Institute for Education by Radio* (Columbus: Ohio State University, 1944), 33.

22. "Outspoken Broadcast," *Time*, August 9, 1943, Vol. XLII, no. 6, 62.

23. Langston Hughes, letter to Erik Barnouw, March 27, 1945, Hughes Collection, YALE.

24. Langston Hughes, "Private Jim Crow," August 16, 1943, YALE.

25. Rampersad, *I Dream A World,* 35.

26. Dr. Sam Ritvo to CBS, n.d., COR 00956, Corwin Collection, TOL.

27. Horace Clayton, in *The Courier,* May 13, 1944, in Norman Corwin's scrapbook #4, Corwin Collection, TOL.

28. Arch Oboler, "Strange Morning," in *Arch Oboler Remembers World War II,* Radio Spirits.

29. Laurence Leamer, *As Time Goes By: The Life of Ingrid Bergman* (New York: Harper & Row, 1986), 106.

30. Joseph Gottlieb and Mitchell Grayson, "Parachutes for Democracy," aired November 26, 1944 in the *New World A-Coming* series, Radio Script Collection, NYPL-S, Astor, Lenox and Tilden Foundations.

31. Mitchell Grayson, "Heroes of the Skies," aired December 3, 1944 in the *New World A-Coming* series, Radio Script Collection, NYPL-S.

32. Arthur Laurents, *Original Story By: A Memoir of Broadway and Hollywood* (New York: Alfred A. Knopf, 2000), 29.

33. The following account concerning "The Glass" is based on Savage, *Broadcasting Freedom*, 149-152.

34. Savage, *Broadcasting Freedom*, 152.

35. Robert Hilliard and Michael Keith, *The Broadcast Century: A Biography of American Broadcasting* (Boston: Focal Press, 1992), 101.

ⓕ

WOMEN

Mr. Johnson, I feel I should tell you—I may be leaving you. I'm thinking of joining the WAVES. . . . Perhaps I can do clerical work at some Naval base. You see, sir, every woman who is trained to do Navy work releases a man for active service. That's what I want to do.

—"Fighting Forces—The Waves," *Uncle Sam*

Your name is Jeannie. You live in Detroit, Michigan. It is February 1943. You are the oldest of four sisters. From your early childhood you were given a great deal of responsibility in your family, helping your mother take care of the house and even assisting more than most oldest sisters to raise your younger ones. Somehow your lot in life became quite different from that of your sisters and your girlfriends. "Jeannie is going to take care of me in my old age," your father constantly tells people. You've never had a boyfriend, although all of your sisters have. Your next oldest sister even got engaged a few months ago.

Your life has not changed much from before the war. Right after high school you started working in the local library as a library assistant, and you're still there. Usually your father drives you to work in the morning and you take the bus home after work. Last week, Agnes, your best friend, told you that she was taking a job in a war plant. You were shocked. "Aren't you afraid that people will tell you that that's not a very feminine place for a woman?" you asked her. But she threw a whole bunch of reasons back at you and got you thinking.

One day at dinner time, you told your family about Agnes's decision. The announcement started a heated debate. "A factory is no place for a woman," your father proclaimed loudly. Although your mother nodded her head silently in agreement, your youngest sister, particularly, challenged him as she often does. "Papa," she yelled, "Everybody has to do their share, including girls." "And women," another sister chimed in. "You're just too old fashioned to understand," the youngest added. "If it were up to you, women would still not be able to vote." You sat quietly, taking it all in. You didn't dare tell your father that Agnes was nagging you to leave the library and join her in the factory.

In December 1940, in reaction to the mounting world crisis, President Roosevelt spoke to the nation of the need to "build with all possible speed every machine, every arsenal, every factory that we need to manufacture our defense material."[1] From the very beginning Roosevelt recognized the importance of industrial production to a successful prosecution of the war. In April 1942, five months after the nation joined the war effort as a belligerent, he created the War Manpower Commission (WMC). Its purpose was to direct the flow of workers into war industries.[2] Roosevelt appointed former Indiana governor Paul McNutt to head the new agency.

A June 1942 survey spotlighted the failure of Americans to comprehend the seriousness of the war and to see the personal benefits of victory. As a consequence, in addition to concentrating on ways people in the various trades and occupations could help the war effort, government propaganda also focused on how the Jeannies of America could help.

Despite FDR's efforts, by the end of 1943 the manpower shortage was so bad that he decided on a desperate strategy. Early in the new year he announced to the nation his intention to request that the Congress pass a new law that would provide the government with the power to draft workers into the defense industry.[3] Months later, the House of Representatives acted on the request. Fortunately, Germany's surrender in May 1945 obviated the Senate's need to follow suit.

Given the urgency of the manpower question, it should not seem surprising that the government put forth a major effort to recruit women to join the wartime workforce. In various ways the government made it clear that more than just Armed Forces personnel were needed to help win the war. The process required the coordinated assistance of every segment of society, from both men and women: workers, farmers, housewives, physicians, nurses, and people in occupations far removed from the military.

To help maximize the efforts of both sexes to bring about defeat of the Axis powers, the WMC launched various campaigns. Its first, inaugurated in December 1942, was aimed at both women and men. Its second, three months later, employed the slogan "The More Women at Work, the Sooner We'll Win" and introduced the idea that by taking jobs women could save lives.[4]

By the fall of 1943 there were shortages of labor in the service, trade, and supply industries. At least part of the reason for this was that women had left poorly paid jobs in restaurants and laundries for better-paying ones in manufacturing plants. As a result, the WMC and the Office of War Information (OWI) conducted a major campaign, "Women in Necessary Services." Its main goal was to convince women that much of the work outside war industries was important to enable the nation to prosecute the war. In other words, women were needed to keep the civilian economy working during the war.[5]

In January 1944, as plans were underway for the D-Day invasion of Europe, government planners realized that more WACS would be needed to help replace men at desk jobs. For this reason, in March, the WMC, the OWI, and the Armed Forces launched a new campaign to recruit women into the military services and into civilian work.[6] This was the first time that both recruiters of civilian and military woman power made such a joint effort. The campaign was based on the assumption that women were reluctant to take war jobs. Also in early 1944, the OWI became involved in establishing a national Women in the War program, which focused on trying to get more workers into labor-short local economies and into the Armed Forces and to keep on the job those women already working.[7] Partly as a result of the WMC's efforts, the number of women in the industrial labor force rose from 13 million in 1940 to more than 19 million in 1944.[8]

Most of the war-related radio series dealt with the issue of women and the war in one way or another, but one in particular was devoted solely to that topic. In July 1943, CBS launched *American Women*, a series of fifteen-minute shows written by Frank and Doris Hursley, the husband and wife team who wrote *Service to the Front*. Frank Hursley was a professor at the University of Wisconsin. Doris, a lawyer, was the daughter of Victor Berger, a congressman whose socialist and pacifist views led to his indictment during World War I for "obstructing the war effort." Despite the indictment, he was reelected.

The Hursleys broke into radio in 1937 when they won first prize in a scriptwriting contest.[9] After their entry was produced in a five-day test run, they were offered a permanent job producing *Aunt Jenny*, a soap opera. Both Doris and Frank gave up their earlier careers to write for radio full time. Like the Hummerts, radio's best known husband and wife team, the Hursleys were also relatively uninvolved politically compared at least to writers such as Millard Lampell, Arthur Miller, Allan Sloane, and Langston Hughes. They lived on a farm in a small town near Milwaukee, far from the country's political centers, and did not even know many other writers. Before the war began they leased their land to a dairy farmer. Their lives changed, however, after a government call for people to grow soybeans and flax. Although the Hursleys lacked any experience, they decided to farm their land themselves, even as they were also writing for radio and raising a family.

The word "feminist" was not in vogue in the 1940s. Yet, by all common contemporary standards, Doris Hursley deserved the appellation. She was just the right candidate to write a series that promoted women entering the workforce to assume nontraditional roles. As she demonstrated in the way she raised her own daughters, Hursley believed that women needed to break down some of the traditional boundaries that put illogical strictures on them. Once during a particularly cold Wisconsin winter, she sent her daughters off to school in long pants rather than skirts. But to help them adjust to the notion of what at the time was still considered strictly male attire, she sewed some very feminine looking suspenders with flowers on them. The girls grew up benefiting from their mother's influence, and one of them became a professor at the University of Wyoming.

In *American Women,* sponsored by the William Wrigley Jr. Company, the Hursleys depicted the war-related activities of women: the jobs they held in factories, the WAVES and other female military services, their volunteer activities, and war-related problems of various institutions such as the USO and the National Education Association. *American Women* began its broadcasts shortly before the WMC and the OWI started their fall 1943 major campaign, "Women in Necessary Services." Thus a number of its first shows appear to have been produced as a result of that campaign. A mid-September broadcast told how one woman helps out the economy by working in a bakery. She "persuades her husband to let her take [the] job" after he finds out how short-handed all the stores are.[10] Another show presented the story of a young woman who helps out on her aunt and uncle's farm. And in two others, soon afterward, Granny Jackson, age 60, runs a farm with the help of her granddaughters, and Grandmother Brown, aged 61, takes a job as a restaurant cook.

In the process of trying to bring women into the war effort, *American Women* also addressed contemporary attitudes about women. Often the Hursleys' scripts reflect something of a tug of war about how assertive women should be, sometimes challenging contemporary attitudes and sometimes largely just reflecting them. Among those tending mostly to reflect contemporary attitudes were two that promoted the idea that taking a job to help the war effort just might give a woman the chance to meet the man of her dreams. In one show, a woman takes a job as a welder and she and an inspector at the plant fall in love. In another one, "Aunt Amy," a forty-five-year-old spinster takes a job as a clerk in a pharmacy after learning that the pharmacist desperately needs help. While working there, Aunt Amy not only begins to achieve self-fulfillment, she also meets a tall, slim widower and gets herself a beau. Heard today, the script is campy. But the push to get women into the mainstream workforce was a radical thing for the times.

Some *American Women* scripts emphasize the need for women to make sacrifices, in accord with their traditional role. One promotes the example of Shirley Henderson, who passes up a chance to go to Officers Training School because she likes her job as a secretary to a colonel in Washington. Two others stress the civic virtues of young women who put aside their college careers for the war effort. In the first one, Lucille leaves the state university in her sophomore year to take a job at the Douglas Aircraft factory. In the second one, Iris decides to stay on the farm to help out her family and delays using a college scholarship until after the war ends. A December 1943 show tells the story of Ginny, a devoted daughter, who volunteers to give up the coveted part of the heroine in her high school play. She is needed at home to prepare dinner for her father because her mother is working the 3 to 11 P.M. shift in a war job. Fortunately, the rest of the cast agrees to hold early morning rehearsals, making Ginny's sacrifice unnecessary.

Of course, these occasional scripts from *American Women* were not the only ones to reflect a traditional view of women. "The Bullet That's Going to Kill Hitler," an August 1942 play in the *Labor for Victory* series, stresses the importance of even the seemingly least important occupation in relation to achieving victory.[11] The first scene features a wise young soldier home on furlough to whom a naïve young woman who works in a factory says, "Gee! I wish I were a man—and in the army." A few minutes later, the soldier comments how she is "mixed up because she doesn't know she is helping to win the war." He then takes her and another woman to a munitions plant where he explains the steps by which a bullet is made. Even white collar workers, the soldier points out, are involved in its production. When one woman challenges him to show how her job in a doughnut shop is helping the war effort, he points out that the munitions worker eats her doughnuts. As the first woman challenges him to show how her job as a switchboard operator is helping, she herself suddenly remembers that she helped locate a doctor when the same munitions worker injured himself. She realizes that in a small way she helped to speed his return to work. "The point is," says the soldier, "this is total war, just like the President said." Fortunately, there were more sophisticated plays than this one.

In their *American Women* scripts showing more assertive women, the Hursleys continued to maintain a moderate tone and present quite plausible situations. Several of them show women successfully replacing men who go off to war: one woman taking on her husband's mail route; another proving how she can be a good fire lookout on

"Sable Mountain"; and a third, crippled, who successfully takes on a job at a drug store. In one story a woman proves to men who thought that women can't handle an overhead crane that they are wrong. In another, a crew of female airplane mechanics dispel the doubts of Johnny, a test pilot, about their ability to reassemble a plane. And in a third one, two WACs overcome the preconceptions of two soldiers at Army headquarters in Naples, Italy, that women cannot satisfactorily handle their office jobs.

It would be interesting to know the extent to which *American Women* and other radio shows influenced Americans to heed messages such as "join the Armed Forces" that were contained in the broadcasts. However, the challenge to people's long-term memory concerning these shows has proved too much for interviewees. Nevertheless, even without claiming a causal relationship between radio and, say, the extent to which women joined the war effort, it is worth noting the experiences of some of the women who became war plant workers or women who joined the Armed Forces.

Of course, many women who moved out of protective environments to help the war effort still stuck in many ways to the social norms of the times, often maintaining passive or unassertive behavior typical of many women of the era. However, some grabbed at the opportunity to assert themselves. The late Margaret Burns, of Long Island, for example, might have been Marge the Meek before she joined the WACs in February 1943.[12] Her boyfriend had just jilted her and she was not feeling very good about herself. She was working in a glue factory at the time in Gloucester, Massachusetts, and living with her parents in a house without any hot water or indoor plumbing. Then one day she decided to join up. Ms. Burns was sent to Ft. Riley, Kansas, where she became the dispatch boss in a motor pool. With time, the men who at first mocked her because she was a WAC learned to step warily around her. In the Army, she developed a tart tongue. "The men thought I was just a stupid woman," she used to say. "They expected me to jump through a hoop. Well not me. If a general tried to play me for a fool, I'd make sure he got a crappy Jeep." Another woman, whose name was not recorded, also showed that women involved in the war effort were not shrinking violets. This woman, an Army nurse who took part in the North African invasion, finding the hospitals in which she was working under fire from snipers, became so incensed about the risk to her patients that several GIs had to forcibly restrain her from going outside to "give them a piece of her mind."

One of the most common uses of radio drama vis-à-vis the home front was to promote the recruitment of nurses. Because in the 1940s the ranks of nurses were filled almost entirely by women, it was clear that special appeals had to be made to them. The need for nurses fluctuated during the war. Initially, the Army was caught quite short-handed. At the time of the attack on Pearl Harbor, the Army Nurse Corps had fewer than 1,000 nurses. Within two years, the War Department announced that it had sufficient numbers for both existing and anticipated Army needs. Because the Red Cross assumed responsibility for recruitment of the Army Nurse Corps, the Army asked the organization to stop recruiting. In compliance, the Red Cross sent telegrams to local volunteer committees in every state advising them to discontinue their drive.

In the spring of 1944, when the Army was involved in intensive planning for the Allied invasion of France and an anticipated high casualty rate, the situation changed. In late April, the War Department revised its earlier decision and established a new quota for the Army Nurse Corps. Now the Army needed an additional 10,000 more nurses, and soon. Unfortunately, local Red Cross recruiting networks had been disbanded and nurses who responded to the latest drive had difficulty enlisting.

Because of the Army's planning error, and under the mistaken impression that American nurses were shirking their duty, in January 1945 President Roosevelt announced in his annual State of the Union address that he was asking Congress to pass a bill to draft nurses. The bill passed in the House and came within one vote in the Senate before the surrender of Germany. In the interim, the enrollment of over 10,000 nurses in the Army Nurse Corps early in 1945 rendered the measure superfluous.

To aid in the ongoing effort to help recruit nurses, during the war the *American Women* series featured 18 broadcasts, among its total of 230, dealing with the need for Army and home nurses and nurse's aides. One such show was a May 1944 broadcast about a young woman named Mary who decides to join the Cadet Nurse Corps after learning that a hand-grenade wound has left her boyfriend with amnesia. Her goal, we learn, is to help all the men who came back from the war in need of help.

Nurse recruitment was not the sole province of shows that focused particularly on women. *Lux Radio Theatre*'s 1943 presentation of "So Proudly We Hail" paid tribute to women of the Army Nurse Corps and received the thanks from at least two listeners. "I am glad that you paid the nurses such well deserved tribute tonight," wrote one.[13] "I am sure since every one else has heard . . . 'So Proudly We Hail,'" wrote another, "[they] will buy more stamps and bonds."[14] But at least one person perceived the show quite differently. "I didn't appreciate . . . "So Proudly We Hail," wrote a New Jersey resident with five sons in the service. "So Proudly We Hail what? A group of hysterical women depicting our nurses. I for one wouldn't like any of them taking care of my boys."[15]

The Red Cross produced most of the wartime programs designed to promote nurse recruitment. Possibly the earliest such show was *They Live Forever*. Among its episodes was a March 1942 broadcast about Dorothy Morse, a Red Cross nurse who lost her life six months before Pearl Harbor while aboard a ship that was torpedoed enroute to the Red Cross–Harvard Hospital in England.

Perhaps the most important Red Cross series was *That They Might Live*, which began in January 1943 on NBC as a thirteen-week series. Helen Hayes, Tallulah Bankhead, and Gertrude Lawrence were among its prominent stars. The show sought to recruit graduate nurses for the Army and Navy, volunteer nurse's aides for hospitals, and women to study home nursing for the Red Cross. But its success resulted in renewals that extended it to a full year's run. By January 1944 when it ended, 300,000 graduate nurses had been enrolled for war duty and tens of thousands of women were recruited for the other two programs.

As with many wartime shows, announcements containing direct pitches related to the more subtle messages contained in the plays accompanied broadcasts of *That They Might Live*. The middle announcement of a December 1943 broadcast contained a message from a staff sergeant from West Virginia. "I was wounded on a combat mission over Guadalcanal. As a result I lost both of my legs. Life looked grim when I landed in an Army hospital in New Zealand. An Army nurse there gave me a puppy dog to play with and she let me take care of it. What that nurse did changed my whole future. As soon as I get out I'm going to raise dogs. I've got that nurse to thank for giving me something to live for."[16]

Occasionally, Red Cross shows, or at least the accompanying announcements, departed from their essential purpose of promoting support for its humanitarian work. In such cases they sometimes sounded more like the most blatantly propagandistic shows promoting the overall war effort. When, for example, the narrator of an announcement during one episode of *They Live Forever* asked, "Do you want your wife fondled by a Nazi storm trooper or your daughter outraged by a foot soldier?" he was rather unlikely to inspire any women to sign up for nursing school.[17]

A typical program promoting the need for nurse's aides appeared in a series entitled *The March of Mercy* early in 1943. This story concerned "Edna Cooper," a stenographer who helps out at the local hospital one evening a week and on Saturday afternoons. One night a neighbor rouses Edna out of her sleep to help his ailing father. "Mom's tried the doctor," the neighbor explains. "He can't come on account he's in the Army." On arrival at the neighbor's house, Edna realizes that the ailing man has symptoms of peritonitis that she had overheard a doctor describing to an intern. She has the man rushed to the hospital in the milkman's horse-drawn wagon, thus saving his life. "Edna Cooper was only a Nurse's Aide," listeners are told at the program's end. "But . . . what would we do without her and the 68,000 Ladies in Blue like her? The war has taken our doctors, our nurses, our trained personnel. . . . Without volunteers like Edna, there is hardly a hospital in America that could continue to function efficiently."[18]

Besides addressing the question of women and work, some plays dealt with women as soldiers, as a source of morale problems, or as victims of the Nazis. "Since You Went Away," a September 1943 program in the *Words at War* series, deals with a concern that had been articulated even before American involvement in the war. A year earlier, two months before Pearl Harbor, a representative of the Washington office of the Council for Democracy reported the Army Department's anxiety about the problem of Army morale. "While the army can work on the morale of the soldiers," the Council's representative said, "it would be necessary for outside organizations, without any governmental connections, to work on the families of draftees, who are responsible for the discontent and weak morale in the army which had been aroused through letters from home." In "Since You Went Away," Anne, an insecure woman, initially has trouble adapting to her husband's departure for the military, partly because a "friend" suggests that he may be involved in extramarital affairs.[19] But in the end, Anne overcomes her anxieties and assures her husband during a long distance phone conversation that she has come to terms with his being away.

With two types of exception, American radio avoided treating the notion of American women as battlefield soldiers. Two plays in the *Treasury Star Parade* series by English-born Violet Atkins Klein illustrate that it applauded the idea of women fighting on the battlefield in foreign countries, particularly in the Soviet Union. In a September 1942 recording of "Diary of a Red Army Woman," Tania, a Russian aviatrix, refuses to let motherhood shield her from the stern necessities of duty.[20] Tania is so devoted to fighting the enemy that she even flies a mission in her ninth month of pregnancy and while in flight she apparently goes into labor. The script also presents the amazing claim that Tania, a bomber pilot, successfully shoots down more than fifteen enemy planes, an achievement more commonly the province of fighter pilots.

Treasury Star Parade also told the story of Molly Pitcher, the legendary heroine of the American Revolution who claimed her place in the history books after taking her wounded husband's place firing a cannon. Apparently, as with the female Soviet soldiers, Molly was sufficiently remote from American women of the World War II era for listeners to understand that the plays were not meant as literal pieces of advocacy. American radio had to be careful about the type of female role that it held up as a model. Thus, in January 1943, the OWI rejected an Agricultural Department script in which a mother leaves her children without lunch to go to work in a war plant. The WMC did not encourage mothers with children under fourteen to leave them to work in war plants.[21]

In June 1944, forces under the command of Supreme Allied Commander Dwight D. Eisenhower landed in Normandy to begin the liberation of Europe. The success of the Normandy invasion made it clear that the war had turned. Germany was doomed. And so was the idea of continuing to rely on women as anything approaching equal partners in the war effort. As a consequence, radio drama began to de-emphasize the role of women in the war effort.

Only ten days after Normandy, although the war was still more than a year from ending, the *American Women* series broadcast its last show. Six months later, another series, *America in the Air* produced "Salute to the WASPS," in conjunction with the deactivation of the "Women's Air Force Service Pilots." The message was "Thanks ladies, it's time to get back to normalcy."

A poll of women workers in 1944 showed that more than 70 percent wished to keep their jobs. However, the demands of "full employment" and the push to give jobs to returning GIs quickly pushed the women aside. In the mid-war period, when some layoffs had occurred in the war industries, women had been only 40 to 50 percent of those let go. However, between June and August 1945, while men were being laid off at a rate of 42 per 1000, "Rosie the Riveters" were being fired at 72 per 1,000, almost twice the rate of men. Furthermore, during the summer of 1945, three fourths of the women in the aircraft and shipbuilding industries lost their jobs.[22] Mary Ann Kutner, who worked at a Grumman Aircraft war plant on Long Island, remembered the process. "We had a choice," she said, "Give up our jobs to the returning veterans or stay. We had to sign a statement indicating which we preferred. Most of us gave up our jobs. It was the right thing to do. But I had to go out and get another job. It was meant to be."[23]

There was one voice of protest. A 1944 broadcast of Hi Brown's *Green Valley* featured Carol Thorne, a fictional character dedicated to getting fair play for women. One of her goals was equal pay with men for equal work. "I hope women don't quit their jobs when the men get back from the war," she tells her landlord. "The more of us who work, the more we'll produce." When he replies, "What are you, a Communist?" she answers him "If I am, Henry Kaiser [the industrialist] is too. He said the same thing."[24]

The nation, the military, and apparently radio, too, never had a consistent view about the proper role of women in the war. As various broadcasts show, sometimes radio presented women as competent, mature people in whom total confidence could be invested. Many female war workers found that their presence in defense plants was appreciated. But as Mildred Leipzig, who worked in a Long Island war plant, recalled, the idea of women in overalls working in factories disturbed some men. Leipzig remembered some male colleagues using obscenities to try to intimidate the women who dared intrude into "their domain."[25]

Wartime radio drama had a job to do to support the war effort. Part of it had been to boost the nation's readiness to accept women in nontraditional roles. But the networks were never comfortable running ahead of the nation to promote social change. When the war ended, radio considered it had done its job. The Army, war plants, and radio sent women back home, "where they belonged."

NOTES

1. Franklin D. Roosevelt, *The Public Papers of Franklin D. Roosevelt*, comp. Sam Rosenman (New York: Random House, 1950), 642–643.

2. The following account is based on Arthur Link, *American Epoch: A History of the United States since the 1890's* (New York: Knopf, 1967), 532–533.

3. Link, *American Epoch*, 532–533, or John H. Crider, "President Asks Civilian Draft to Bar Strikes, . . . [Service Act Urged]," *New York Times*, January 11, 1944, 1:8.

4. Leila J. Rupp, *Mobilizing Women for War: German and American Propaganda, 1939–1945* (Princeton, N.J.: Princeton University Press, 1978), 94.

5. Maureen Honey, *Creating Rosie the Riveter* (Amherst: University of Massachusetts Press, 1984), 39.

6. Rupp, *Mobilizing Women*, 94.

7. Honey, *Creating Rosie the Riveter*, 34.

8. Eleanor Straub, "Government Policy toward Civilian Women during World War II" (Ph.D. diss., Emory University, 1973), 23.

9. Polly Keusink, telephone interview by the author, January 10, 2000.

10. The scripts of the *American Women* series are contained in the Hursley collection, WYO.

11. Marc Blitzstein, "The Bullet That's Going to Kill Hitler," *Labor for Victory*, box 442, folder 8, NBC Collection, WISC.

12. The following account is taken from Donald P. Myers, "A Woman in the War," *Newsday*, March 20, 2000.

13. Carolyn Lyons to C. B. DeMille, November 1, 1943, Box 1121, folder 16, BYU.

14. Joyce Kallinicos to C. B. DeMille, November 3, 1943, Box 1121, folder 16, BYU.

15. Margaret E. Regan to C. B. DeMille, November 16, 1943, Box 1121, folder 16, BYU.

16. Elsworth R. Day speaking during the broadcast of December 4, 1943, RG 200 Records of the American Red Cross, 1935–1946, Box 40, folder 020.32 Radio Scripts Gen F-That, NA.

17. "Program Reviews," *Radio Daily*, Vol. 20, no. 20, July 28, 1942, 6:3.

18. Morton Wishengrad, "March of Mercy," Episode #13, February 9, 1943, American Red Cross Central File, 1935–1946, Group 3, NA 200, Box 32, folder 020.32, NA.

19. Margaret Buell Wilder, "Since You Went Away," adapted by Nora Stirling, *Words at War* series, September 1943, NBC Collection, WISC.

20. Violet Atkins Klein, "Diary of a Red Army Women," Box 5, Violet Atkins Klein Collection, Special Collections Library, California State University at Northridge.

21. Joe Liss (memo) to Douglas Meservey, February 2, 1943, NA 208-140-750.

22. Karen Anderson, *Wartime Women: Sex Roles, Family Relations, and the Status of Women* (Westport, Conn.: Greenwood Press, 1981), 164.

23. Mary Ann Kutner, Telephone conversation with author, March 14, 2000.

24. Carol Hughes, "Soap Opera with Social Significance," *Magazine Digest,* Vol. XXIX, no. 2 (August 1944): 31–35.

25. Mildred Leipzig, interview by author, Sea Cliff, N.Y., October 21, 1999.

16

THE WAR AGAINST THE JEWS

So I began. The average script takes me from ten to fifteen hours
of steady writing. "Warsaw Ghetto" took nearly ten days. I wrote,
rewrote, discarded, began again a dozen times. I hardly knew what
I wanted. I neglected to shave, found myself unable to sleep, and
littered the floor with paper.

—Morton Wishengrad, *Radio Drama in Action*

*Your name is Rachel. You were born in eastern Poland, the oldest of
seven children. In the mid 1920s, prompted by terrible poverty, your
parents sent you and your younger sister Leah to the United States.
Your mother's brother and his family, who had emigrated a dozen years
earlier, took you in. Throughout the 1930s as the war clouds gathered,
you corresponded with your parents. At one point, in mid 1939, another
sister in Poland was on the verge of joining you. Then after the outbreak
of war, the letters suddenly stopped. You could only follow in the newspapers what was happening. You took some comfort in the fact that although the Nazis invaded western Poland, it was the Soviets, not the
Nazis who invaded eastern Poland where most of your family lived. But
you did have a married sister who was now living in Warsaw, which the
Nazis had occupied. You were very worried about her.*

In October you read in the New York Post *that Jews were being targeted as had never occurred before. Only two months after the war*

began, The Post *claimed that "The complete ruin and physical destruction of Polish Jewry under Adolf Hitler is a question of months if not weeks."¹ You read in horror a little more than a year and a half later of the sudden German attack on the Soviet Union. It included the Soviet-occupied part of Poland. At first you read of German attacks on Jews. Then the reports became more ominous. You became aware that the Nazis had established many concentration camps and that they were herding Jews from all over Europe into them. You were glad when the United States entered the war six months after the Germans occupied your village. "Now my family will have a chance," you said. But in the first several years of the war, your hopes were not well fulfilled. For one thing, you came to realize that President Roosevelt was not giving the situation of the Jews a high priority.*

In addition, as the war continued you realized that newspapers and the radio were not treating the situation of the Jews as a major story. Often it seemed that they were just one group among many—Catholics, trade unionists, and others—that the Nazis were targeting. You wondered why this was so. "Are they intentionally downplaying stories about atrocities against Jews?" you once asked your husband. "Don't be silly," he told you. "I know you are worried about your family," he added. "That's where that idea is coming from. And I know it's been hard on you not hearing from them for so long. But they'll make it." That was a year or so ago. In the summer of 1944, you read an article in the New York Times *that 400,000 Hungarian Jews had been deported to their deaths and that another 350,000 were to be killed in the next three weeks.² The article was only four inches long and you found it on page 12. The words jumped off the page at you. But many people could easily have overlooked it. "Page 12," you said to yourself. "Is this a small story? Why is it being hidden?" You looked at page 1. Among other things, it carried a story about Fourth of July holiday crowds!*

When the war ended you waited nervously for word from your family? Had they survived? Once a month you scoured the lists of survivors that your synagogue received from the Red Cross. Then, one day you saw the name of your brother Benjamin. You cried for joy, but as the tears streamed down your cheeks, you realized that the omission of your parents' names and those of your other two brothers and two sisters probably meant that they were dead. In fact, they were.

Historian Lucy Davidowicz published her book *The War Against the Jews* in 1975, thirty years after the end of World War II. Her central thesis was that the Nazis were simultaneously carrying out two wars: one against the Allies; the other, with no less priority, against the Jews.[3] Davidowicz's contention was a new one, and it had little currency during the war. That so few radio plays were written in both the United States and Britain during the war on the topic of the Jewish Holocaust reflects both this and the level of influence of anti-Semitism in both countries. Nevertheless, it should be understood, as Rachel realized during the war, that there was early evidence, available not only to the molders of opinion but also to the reader of the tabloids, that Jews were being targeted as had never occurred before.

Given all the evidence that accumulated throughout the more than five years of the war, it should have made sense to publicize the special nature of the Nazi campaign against the Jews. There were other articles in addition to the one that Rachel read in the *New York Post*, and there were radio reports. In December 1942, in his broadcast from London, Edward R. Murrow stated "The phrase 'concentration camps' is obsolete. . . . It is now possible to speak only of extermination camps." But by and large the Holocaust was grossly underreported. Part of the explanation is that the full dimensions of Nazi genocide were too difficult to grasp. The reality of what was happening in the gas chambers in Auschwitz and other death camps from 1941 was poorly understood by even the most sophisticated among America's molders of public opinion. Many progressive writers of the era were characterized by a socialist mind set. Arthur Miller recalled that even the Jews among them believed that the emphasis had to be put on winning the war for everyone and that it would have been wrong to single out the Jews as a special class of victims.

In the case of the Office of War Information (OWI), it appears that failure to publicize the Holocaust was part of a deliberate policy. When late in 1944 the War Refugee Board made public a report about the killings at Auschwitz, OWI director Elmer Davis attempted to have it suppressed.[4] Davis feared that such news would hurt the agency's credibility. He believed that it would be too much for the public to believe. Given the efforts of Holocaust deniers years after it became as well documented as any phenomenon in history, one might understand (although not necessarily agree with) his viewpoint. It is easy to imagine John Taber or other right-wing OWI critics charging Davis with exaggerating the evidence. Only in the last few months of the war, by which time the first death camps were being liberated, did the OWI take the lead in getting the news out. But there appears not to have been a single government-sponsored radio drama on the subject.

In one major instance in the private sector, a Jew's reaction to anti-Semitism was a major factor in a decision to downplay any references to persecution of Jews. Arthur Sulzberger, publisher of the *New York Times*, had sufficient experience with anti-Semitism that it pushed him into being an accomodationist, a route that many Jews took. He so feared the *Times* being viewed as a "Jewish paper" that at his direction the *Times* permitted printed ads for businesses that used words like "restricted" or "selected clientele," indicating that Jews were not allowed. Like an OWI radio series, *This Is Our Enemy,* that focused on the impact of Nazism on women, youth, Catholics, doctors, and other groups, but never on Jews, the *Times*'s opinion page concentrated its attention on all victims of Nazi aggression, only occasionally referring to Jews as a group. Even *Times* editorials concerning the Warsaw ghetto uprising that involved virtually 100 percent only Jews, referred to "the Poles" and "Warsaw patriots."[5]

Perhaps the earliest dramatization that touched on the Holocaust was a short piece by Arch Oboler entitled "Suffer the Little Children," which described bias against a group of refugee children en route to the United States aboard a ship.[6] The play, which featured Katharine Hepburn, was inspired by an attempt in 1939 to pass the Wagner-Rogers Bill, which would have allowed 20,000 children from Germany to come to the United States for temporary refuge from Nazism.[7] The bill's roots trace back to Kristallnacht, the November 1938 nationwide pogrom in Germany and Austria.[8] That infamous incident finally made clear to many the intentions of the Hitler regime to accelerate the process of persecution of Jews. As a result of Kristallnacht, the Netherlands, Belgium, and Britain had each opened their borders to thousands of children whose parents in Germany had seen the handwriting on the wall. In the United States, several months after Kristallnacht, New York Senator Robert F. Wagner, a German-born Christian, tried in cooperation with Edith Nourse Rogers, a congresswoman from Massachusetts, to secure passage by the Congress of a bill to bring the United States into the rescue effort.

Among the supporters of the Wagner-Rogers Bill was the American Friends Service Committee (AFSC), a Quaker organization. The AFSC prepared an elaborate plan to implement the Wagner proposal if it passed. It also assisted in planning the broadcast of the Oboler play, hoping the play would help drum up support for the bill. But the American Legion and other opponents of the bill scuttled the bill, and Wagner was forced to withdraw it. It was perhaps a sign of the times that even though most of the children whom the bill would have affected were Jews, the play avoided even using the word "Jew."

Another early play that touched on the Holocaust was "Mass Murder," a show in the government series *You Can't Do Business with Hitler.*[9] The broadcast, heard throughout the country, described Hitler's *Lebensraum* (Living Space) concept. The policy, which he first promoted in his book *Mein Kampf,* in 1924, provided for the expansion of Germany into Eastern Europe. As the Nazis decided at a conference in a Berlin suburb in January 1942, partly to carry this out they established a policy of genocide to eliminate the Jews from Europe. They also established a de facto policy to eliminate certain other groups. For example, they sought to "cut off the head of Poland," meaning to kill the Catholic clergy, intellectuals, and political leaders who comprised Poland's cultural and political leadership. They also targeted all Gypsies and homosexuals. However, except for their policy regarding the Gypsies, a far smaller group than the Jews of Europe, they never had any plan that approached the scope of their "Final Solution," which aimed at killing all Jews regardless of their age and their religious devotion.

"Mass Murder" exaggerated Hitler's policy. It attributed a wide variety of killings to the Lebensraum policy, not just of Jews and not only in Eastern Europe but also of Norwegians and Frenchmen. In the play, the Nazis shoot 350 Norwegians for participating in a strike, as well as a larger number of Frenchmen, perhaps 13,000. In reality, there is no evidence that they had any design on Norway as a place for German settlement; they perceived Norwegians, a Germanic people, as fellow Aryans. The significance of these errors is heightened by the fact that the play only briefly mentions the experience of the Jewish populations of the nations that the Nazis conquered. In each case, once the Nazis defeated the local military opposition, the Jews were the first people the Nazis pursued. In addition, some elements in the local Gentile population often aided the Nazis in this process.

The producers of *You Can't Do Business with Hitler* repeated their underestimation of the severity of the Nazis' treatment of the Jews in at least one other show in the series. In introducing Episode Nine, Douglas Miller, the former diplomat who wrote the book on which the series was based, refers to the Nazis' unceasing campaign "to destroy all faiths—the Jewish, the Protestant, the Catholic."[10] He adds "We know what happened to the Jews in Germany." Later he comments "The Protestants as well as Catholics and Jews are denied freedom of worship in Germany." Both Miller and the show's producer appear to be ignorant of how far beyond the denial of freedom of religion of German, Polish, and French Jews the problem really was. At the very time when Polish Jewish mothers were being herded into gas chambers carrying their infants, Miller was more or less equating the fate of Europe's Jews with that of religious German Christians, some of whose pastors and priests were being harassed. There is no record of Miller's level of understanding of the true situation. He apparently left his diplomatic post even before Auschwitz was built. With no reason to assume that he knew the extent of the Final Solution, even though he had established himself as an expert on the policies of the Nazis, one can give him the benefit of any doubt. However, even if it was out of his ignorance, it is worth noting that he contributed to a false picture of the Nazis. For Europe's Jews, the problem was not simply(!) one of denied religious freedom. It was one of sheer physical survival. *You Can't Do Business with Hitler* missed the boat by a mile.

Two plays that did deal directly with the Holocaust were Irving Ravetch's "The Second Battle of Warsaw" and Morton Wishengrad's "The Battle of the Warsaw Ghetto." Ravetch's play was broadcast in June 1943 as part of *Free World Theatre*. The story of the Warsaw ghetto and of the Jewish partisans who fought against overwhelming odds is one of the most dramatic ones of the era. The ghetto uprising was the first and largest armed rebellion by any civilian group in occupied Europe. By the time it occurred, 90 percent of the half million

Jews who had been in the ghetto were gone, deported to Auschwitz, Treblinka, and other death camps. Of the 60,000 left in the beginning of 1943, most were able-bodied workers, The rising began in January when the SS entered the ghetto to round up another group to deport to the camps. Instead, they encountered armed Jewish resistance that killed twenty of them. Miraculously, for even the Polish resistance refused at first to supply them with arms, the ghetto residents held the Nazis at bay for three months. It took 3,000 German troops, encirclement of the ghetto by tanks and artillery, plus the use of search dogs, fire, and bombers to finally subdue the ghetto fighters. In a heavy battle, the Nazis liquidated the estimated 40,000 Jews who were left, and the Red Army found only about 200 when it liberated the ghetto in January 1945.

"The Battle of the Warsaw Ghetto" originated in the summer of 1943, when Milton Krents of the American Jewish Committee asked Wishengrad to write a special program on the topic. To assist him, Krents sent Wishengrad a fat folder of newspaper clippings and other materials from its files.[11] The project put Wishengrad under tremendous emotional strain, and the writing proceeded with great difficulty. At times he was mumbling to himself. He invented all sorts of pretexts to get out of the commitment. He told Krents that he was moving, that his apartment was a jungle of packing cases, and that his daughter was sick. But Krents was persistent. Finally Wishengrad's wife sat down with him and had him talk to her. For nearly three hours he poured out his heart about the Warsaw ghetto. After that, the writing came more smoothly. NBC presented "Battle" three times, beginning on Yom Kippur, the Jewish Day of Atonement, in 1943. It starred Raymond Massey, who, moved by the subject of the drama, gave his services gratis in lieu of his usual fee of $3,000 for a one half-hour broadcast. The three performances drew a response of 12,000 letters.

Other than these few plays, wartime radio drama, particularly commercial shows such as the *Cavalcade of America,* either totally ignored or only briefly referred to the Holocaust. Given the political composition of the ad agency and sponsor behind the *Cavalcade of America,* Batten, Barton, Durstine and Osborn (BBD&O) and Du Pont, respectively, it should not be surprising that the series never mentioned the Holocaust. In fact, it appears that, like

Oboler's play, the entire series rarely or never even mentioned the existence of Jews, despite the fact that they were the Nazis' prime scapegoat. Possibly the only *Cavalcade* show that even acknowledged their existence, let alone their persecution by the Nazis, was the previously mentioned April 1943 Arthur Miller play about Pastor Martin Niemoller.[12] Blink, however, and you can miss the allusion to the Jews. "Holy Week, the year of our lord 1943," says Paul Lucas, the narrator, as he begins the broadcast, "Out over the American land, . . . under the sign of the cross and under the six pointed star of Israel, men and women of good will are reaffirming . . . the right of every man to worship after the manner of his believing. But in Nazi Germany this right no longer exists."

At least one other American radio play also dealt with Niemoller as a symbol of conscientious opposition to Nazism. Ironically, however, the American media's hailing him as a model of a man of conscience turned out to be controversial. In July 1945, Alan Green of the Writers War Board wrote a WWB editorial challenging Niemoller's status as a symbol of democracy. Niemoller had been a Nazi and had championed the cause of German expansionism. Green charged that he appeared to leave the Nazi Party only because Hitler broke with the church. Finally, after Germany's surrender and his release from prison, Niemoller told the press that American style democracy was not suitable for the Germans. "They like to feel authority," he claimed.[13]

Radio's failure to properly focus on the Holocaust was taken to task in a letter to Norman Corwin after broadcast in January 1947 of the first program of his documentary series *One World*. The previous year the Willkie Memorial of Freedom House honored Corwin as the first recipient of the One World Award, an all expenses-paid, around-the-world trip modeled after the one that Willkie had made in 1942. The 1947 series was based on Corwin's gleanings from his experiences and observations abroad. "My disappointment was very keen and intense," the writer noted "I feel very let down. To think that in your opening program there wasn't even an iota of space for 6,000,000 Jewish dead."[14]

Apparently it was not until the war was over for many months that a radio play dealt very directly with the death camps themselves. In

January 1947, a little more than a year and a half after the conclusion of the war in Europe, there were some 256,000 Jews in displaced persons camps. Four months later, the United Jewish Appeal produced "Barbed Wire Sky" by Ranald MacDougall. The play, starring John Garfield, Edward G. Robinson, and Paul Muni, was intended to encourage financial contribution to assist the 170,000 children who survived the death camps. It shows how so many of the Jews who survived them met with hostility from local Gentile populations ("Go back to the gas chambers, Jew!") when they tried to return to their homes in eastern Europe. Also, unlike the other plays described here, none of which discussed the actual mass murders of civilians, "Barbed Wire Sky" surveyed the horrors of the camps."The mound at Belsen was three hundred feet long, one hundred feet high," says the narrator. " It consisted of thirty thousand human bodies, stacked up like cordwood."[15]

Why did radio fail to seize on the events of the Holocaust as they were occurring and publicize them? The answer is linked to many factors. For one thing, as illustrated earlier, sponsors and broadcasting and advertising agency executives often refused to deal with Jewish themes. In addition, anti-Semites then and still now argue that the stories of persecution of Jews were often exaggerated. The radio writers often obtained their material from newspapers that, as shown, downplayed the severity and extent of atrocities against Jews.

Another reason for radio drama's scant treatment of the Holocaust is that many American Jews and Jewish organizations were hobbled by the "don't make waves" mentality. "What is anti-Semitism?" begins a dark-humored joke that some Jews tell. "Being against Jews more than is necessary," is the answer. So the *Times*'s Sulzberger, and some other Jews, tolerated and even played along with "necessary" anti-Semitism. Perhaps even the anglicization of many first generation Jews' names illustrates this. Norman Rosenstein became Norman Rosten. Allan Silverman became Allan Sloane; Julius Garfinkle became John Garfield, and Julian Schwartz became Joe Julian. Hide your ethnic identity, become less Jewish, and anti-Semitism will go away. This is a harsh judgment that does not take into account the pressures of the times. After all, giving in to the pressures implied with the statement "You're not going to get a job here with that name," isn't necessarily cowardice. In any case, if one goes to the trouble of hiding his ethnic identity it also makes sense not to yell, "Look what they're doing to those Jews!" But there's a danger in throwing rocks at these Jewish writers. Less so than the Jews of Europe, they were still victims of the plague of anti-Semitism.

NOTES

1. Mendel Mozes, "Jew Executed in Each Family in Polish Town," *New York Post*, October 30, 1939, 6:1.

2. "350,000 More Jews Believed Doomed," *New York Times*, July 2, 1944, 112:7.

3. Lucy Davidowicz, *The War Against the Jews: 1933–1945* (New York: Holt, Rinehart and Winston, 1975).

4. This account of Davis's role in censoring the War Refugee Report is based on Clayton Laurie, *The Propaganda Warriors: America's Crusade against Nazi Germany* (Lawrence: University Press of Kansas, 1996), 180.

5. See Susan E. Tifft and Alex S. Jones, "The Times and the Holocaust," *Moment Magazine*, 25, no. 2 (April 2000): 58–60.

6. Arch Oboler, *This Freedom: Thirteen New Radio Plays* (New York: Random House, 1942), 5–12.

7. Oboler, *This Freedom*, 2–4.

8. This account is based on Arthur Morse, *While Six Million Died* (New York: Random House, 1968), 252–269.

9. Episode 5, "Mass Murder," *You Can't Do Business with Hitler*, NYPL-LC.

10. Episode 9, *You Can't Do Business with Hitler.*

11. The following account is based on Erik Barnouw, *Radio Drama in Action* (New York: Farrar & Rinehart), 32–33.

12. Arthur Miller, "Listen to the Sound of Wings," *Cavalcade of America,* vol. I, Radio Spirits.

13. John McAleer, *Rex Stout: A Biography* (Boston: Little Brown, 1977), 345.

14. Simon S. Silverman to Norman Corwin, January 14, 1947, COR 00447, Corwin Collection, TOL.

15. Ranald MacDougall, "Barbed Wire Sky," broadcast May 6, 1947, "Miscellaneous Radio Writing," MacDougall Collection, ACAD.

17

LOOKING TOWARD THE POSTWAR ERA

The road home isn't just a quick one-way trip from the battlefield to the front door. Home isn't just coming in past the city limits. It isn't just a certain house on a certain street. Home is a way of life. Home is fitting into a community again, feeling a dignity and an understanding with the people around you. It takes time. It comes slowly. After combat comes the readjustment to peace, the changing of values.

—Millard Lampell, *The Long Way Home*

Your name in Megan. It is December 1944. Last September you learned that Larry, your husband, was coming home from the war. But it is not quite as you had wished. You received a telegram that he was in a hospital in France. He was not physically wounded. He was shell shocked. You learned in September that he had taken part in the D-Day invasion of the Normandy Peninsula. Then his unit was part of the forces that pushed the Germans out of France. Much of the fighting was house to house, and the strain that started amid the slaughter that took place in Normandy got to be too much for him. He cracked.

When Larry came home he was brought to a Veterans Administration hospital in another state, far from where you live. When the doctors told you that he would need hospitalization for at least six more months, you

*decided to move near him. You gave up your nice apartment and a good
secretarial job to move into a tiny rented room in a stranger's house and
work as a poorly paid clerk in a variety store. You now see Larry every
day. But he's still not the Larry you married and whom you saw march
off to war several years ago. Gradually, you have seen some improve-
ment. At first he wore a blank look on his face every time you went to
see him. Lately you see more evidence that he is glad to see you. Once in
a while there's even a thin smile. At nighttime, especially in the beginning, you used to push your face into the pillow so that the landlady
wouldn't hear you as you cried yourself to sleep. Once a week you call
your sister back home. In the beginning you repeated to her everything
that the doctors told you. They warned you that even after they released
him from the hospital, it would take many months before he would be
anything like himself. She sympathizes with you tremendously, but she
doesn't understand. "Just ignore what the doctors tell you," she said.
"He'll be fine in a few weeks. Just act like nothing happened."*

Long before the war ended, a number of radio plays focused attention on the social ills that had been neglected during the war and on
some that arose because of it. In broad terms, radio plays as far back
as Norman Corwin's program on the Bill of Rights sometimes tried to
define the positive aspects of the American system to clarify what
were the goals of the war effort. In addition, some tried to address
problems such as unemployment. Most serious among problems that
arose because of the war were returning soldiers like Larry who had
been crippled physically or psychologically.

The question of how to deal with returning veterans was a controversial one. The Hearst press and some popular magazines portrayed
the issue as one created by hysterical writers. Both preached a static
view that the United States did not need to change and that the boys
will be the same. It is unlikely that the copywriters were blacks who
had ever dealt with Jim Crow. In June 1943, a fictional letter from an
American prisoner of war preached to readers of *Life*. "Home—
where I want unchanged, just as I remember them now, all the things
that I hold dear. . . . Don't *ever* let these be lost. Keep everything just
as it is until I come back."[1] Two years later, an article in the *Reader's
Digest* quoted Major General Norman T. Kirk, the Surgeon General
of the Army, who recommended to civilians, "welcome the boys

home naturally as what they are—that is fundamentally the same boys who went away.[2] In Kirk's view (and apparently the *Digest's* too), "The average soldier returning to civilian life is basically the same man he was when he went away." No post-traumatic stress syndrome in this scheme of thinking.

On the other hand, late in the war, popular fiction did acknowledge that some GIs would return home bearing psychological wounds. But it proposed simplistic solutions, many of them characterized by the romantic theme that the love and understanding of a pretty girl was all that a wounded soldier needed after his release from the hospital.

Aligned against the naïve viewpoints of Hearst papers, the *Reader's Digest,* and other publications was an interesting group of leftists, among them Millard Lampell, Arthur Laurents, and some West Coast writers. All of them focused on the problems of the returning soldiers. "Any man who is in the army for even one year," wrote Laurents, "is going to change a great deal. The country has changed. The whole world has."[3] The West Coast writers shared the view of Laurents that soldiers would need to make major adjustments as the result of demobilization. They also emphasized that civilians, too, would need to make adjustments.

In the middle of 1944, starting with the Normandy invasion, the number of returning casualties began to mount. Partly with this realization, Major Ed Byron and Robert Heller of CBS conceived of a program to help condition the civilian population to the men who were returning, often missing a leg or an arm. The Army asked Laurents to develop the series *Assignment Home,* and the Canadian Broadcasting Corporation cosponsored it.

At one point, Laurents was assigned to Pilgrim State Mental Hospital on Long Island where he posed as a patient to research a script concerning shell-shocked veterans.[4] To prepare for the visit, Laurents met with Dr. William Menninger, the head of Army Psychiatry. Laurents was so highly impressed by Menninger's humanistic view of patient care that during their conversation he confided that he was a homosexual. The admission was a risky one. Had Menninger divulged that information, Laurents faced immediate court-martial or worse. But Menninger said, "That's the Army's problem, not yours."

For several days, Laurents slept in barracks with other patients and stood on line with them to receive medication. Instead of swallowing the pills he received, however, he palmed them and then threw them away. One evening in the barracks, Laurents had a big scare. Lights had long been turned out and most patients were asleep, when a large blond man quietly slipped out of his bunk, came over to Laurents, and crept his hand toward Laurents's crotch. Terrified of being at the mercy of a mentally disturbed patient, Laurents looked at the man in the dim light that came in through the window and mouthed the word "Tomorrow." The man withdrew and returned to his bunk.

The next morning the man tagged along after Laurents and they began to talk. Laurents learned that the patient was not mentally ill. Throughout his several years in uniform, the man was so fearful that his homosexuality would be found out that the strain finally got to him. This man, too, only pretended to take his medication and then threw it away. Shortly afterward, Laurents began to feel panicky about being in the hospital. Only two top officers knew his real status in the hospital, and he began to feel that he would never get out. Fortunately he was able to call Menninger from a telephone booth and Menninger calmed his anxieties.

Laurents was present one evening when the USO put on *Blithe Spirit*, a Noel Coward show, for the patients. It featured a scene with a ghost, however, that proved to be too much for patients who had witnessed numerous deaths of numerous fellow soldiers, and it had to be halted when a number of them began to have emotional outbursts.

The first show in the *Assignment Home* series, "No Confetti," was produced in December 1944. It concerns a disabled serviceman who sets up psychological defenses against seeking aid from the Veterans Administration and other war agencies and resists contacting his peacetime employer because he can not fill his old job as a result of his disabilities. But with his wife's support and persistence and help from the Veterans Administration and his employer, he takes on a new job in which his disability is not a problem.[5] Another show, "The Face," tells the story of two soldiers who undergo extensive plastic surgery on their faces.

In another broadcast, "Primer for Civilians," a disabled soldier recovers enough to be discharged from the Army in time to get home for Christmas dinner. However, he quickly experiences a number of painful incidents in his new role as a civilian: one with a work-weary waitress, another with a well-meaning but thoughtless barber, and a third with a family member. In this show, Laurents used a device in which the narrator addresses the offending civilians, pointing out where they erred in the way they treated the returned soldier.

In a 1999 interview, Laurents recalled working on *Assignment Home*. The Army was cautious that nothing "untoward" crept into his scripts. Working on a rotating basis, several censors, lieutenants, were on hand in the studio to look over the scripts as Laurents developed them. The censor of the day would sit at the table with Laurents and the cast while they did a reading. Laurents recollected. "He would sit there making 'no, no, no' pencil marks. Then we would go into consultation. I was always very rebellious. I had no fear. I wasn't writing propaganda. I was writing what I believed about the human race. I also wrote the way people talked. I wanted to show people's real reactions. In those scripts I always had somebody who resented authority. And the censor would reject that, of course. 'Oh, you can't denigrate the brass,' he would tell me. Sometimes we would yell. Sometimes he'd win. Sometimes he wouldn't. It was sort of a game."[6]

As the war began to wind down, Laurents noticed a change in the attitude of the War Department. Earlier it had been concerned about presenting shows that stressed those areas in which the Army was racially integrated. But cancellation of broadcast of "The Glass," Arnold Perl's play dealing with racism, symbolized that now, after D-Day, things were different. It was clear that the Allies were going to win the war and the service of blacks to the war effort would soon be terminated. The subject of racism no longer had a place on the airwaves. *Assignment Home* ran until September 1946, when it was canceled.

In the summer of 1944, Millard Lampell also did first-hand research concerning the experience of injured veterans, living with them, going through processing lines with them, and sitting in on psychiatric treatment and physical therapy sessions. On completing his research, he wrote and produced a series for the Army Air Forces program *First in the Air* and directed their broadcast for CBS. In one of the shows, "Welcome the Traveler Home," Joe Topinka, a recently discharged veteran returning home aboard a train, is reading from his hometown paper to another GI about the "returned veteran problem." He comes across an article that claims that "After years of killings, our soldiers will have lost all regard for human life." He also finds a "throaty ad" put out by the big manufacturers that claims, "All our boys want is to return to the simple things they left behind. A piece of Mom's blueberry pie and a coke at the corner drugstore. . . ." Joe adds his own comment: "Don't worry. Every time I feel like splitting my grandmother's head with an ax, I'll grab another piece of Mom's blueberry pie and count to ten."[7]

Another story, "The Empty Sleeve," concerns "Pete Seeger," a soldier who lost an arm over the Italian Alps on the way to Munich behind the waist gun of a B-17. "Seeger" had been hit by a German 30-mm shell. After his release from a military hospital, "Seeger" develops a bitter attitude, partly because of stares and questions from strangers. In one instance he replies to a nosy man's inquiry "How'd it happen Sergeant?" with "I got it caught in a pencil sharpener."[8]

The West Coast radio contribution concerning the problems of the returning soldier, the radio series *Reunion, USA,* came about as the result of the Hollywood Writers Mobilization's (HWM's) series of seminars in 1944. Psychologists and others from the helping professions held discussions with radio and film writers and directors. At the conclusion of the talks, a consensus was reached that something had to be done to counter the simplistic view that the media was presenting concerning such problems as the psychologically wounded soldier. The HWM decided that the answer was to produce a radio series.

Reunion, USA ran between May and November 1945. Its first few shows focused on the broad problems of adjustment that both soldiers and civilians would need to make as a result of the demobilization that would soon occur. However, beginning with the fifth one, the series shifted to a more political perspective, away from the problems of individuals and to those of society in general. These later shows dealt with the need for jobs for veterans, the broad need for international cooperation, and the problems of anti-Semitism and the nature of the threat of subversion from the right.[9]

One of the most interesting broadcasts in this series was its last one, "The Case of David Smith" by Abraham Polonsky. Polonsky was one of the most political radio writers in a field that attracted very political people. "I came of age in a country that had come to a standstill, with fifty million people unemployed and the banks closed," Polonsky told an interviewer in 1997.[10] Like many of his colleagues, he wrote for the *Columbia Workshop* early in his radio career. During the war he produced "black programs," broadcasts from undercover stations that purportedly came from the Office of Strategic Services and the Free French Forces.

"The Case of David Smith," about a former prisoner of war of the Japanese, appears on the surface to be about a soldier in a catatonic-like state who suffers from post-traumatic stress syndrome.[11] A veteran's hospital's board of inquiry is trying to decided how to close the case of the patient, Lt. Smith. During the war, Smith had been sent on a mission to organize guerrilla bands of natives against the Japanese. "You are fighting to be free," he told them, intending his words to be a promise that, after the war, their nation would indeed be free. For this was one of the deeply held beliefs that motivated Smith himself. Smith finds out after his liberation, however, that the unidentified Asian people, for whose liberation he had fought, were being recolonized as the war was ending. His fatal ailment is not a psychoneurotic problem; it's an existential one. He cannot reconcile himself to the fact that the purpose for which he fought was a lie, and he has lost the will to live. However, the board of inquiry chooses to ignore the one board member who understands the essence of Smith's malady.

Two other plays on the theme of postwar adjustment are *Words at War's* "The Veteran Comes Back" and "Soldier to Civilian." "The Veteran Comes Back," heard in the fall of 1944, describes politicians so involved in political process that they ignore the voice of "GI Joe."[12] Finally "Joe," raising his voice above the din, berates them: "during any war in history, nothing is too good for the veteran. After the war nobody gives a damn." Several flashbacks then show how veterans of previous wars (including an American Civil War veteran and American, French, and German veterans of World War I) took destructive paths as the result of inadequate efforts by government to assist them to reintegrate into society.

It was disgruntled veterans, we are told, who established both the Ku Klux Klan and the German Nazi Party. The speakers all agree that unless the returning veteran can be successfully reintegrated into society he will be a threat to it. And what did the returning

American veteran of World War II want? A better America: jobs for all, decent housing, social security, human rights, a better educational system, a rehabilitation program, and better health care for his family and himself.

"Soldier to Civilian," an adaptation of a book by George Pratt, a psychiatrist, was broadcast in the spring of the following year.[13] In this show, Corporal Russ Richards is being discharged. "Uhh . . . Corporal," a doctor says to Richards, ". . . don't take this wrong . . . but . . . two and a half years is a long, long time. I mean . . . when you do go home, keep remembering that a lot of things've happened to you. And a lot of things have happened to that girl and your folks too, you know?" The script then goes on to show Russ's well-meaning hometown folks planning for the veterans' return. But the planners have little understanding of the veterans' needs. "How about giving everyone of 'em a nice, big American flag?" suggests one man. Others suggest a parade, a bronze plaque, or $5 worth of groceries. There are other problems, too. Soon after his return, Russ becomes upset that his girlfriend, Christine, is working when he would like to spend time with her, and that his parents keep pressing on him their expectations. "Get this straight . . . both of you," he finally explodes, "I'm running my own life."

As the two previously mentioned shows illustrate, *Words at War* stood out for its effort to tackle hard social questions. In April 1945, one other *Words at War* show, "Full Employment in a Free Society," addressed the question of the conditions to which veterans were returning. This one, based on a book by Sir William Beveridge, dealing with the question of how the nation could achieve full employment, turned out to be the beginning of the series's end.

Beveridge, a member of the British Parliament, had published his book (with the same title as the broadcast) five months earlier. He was already well known for a controversial 1942 report with which he was associated that detailed plans for a comprehensive social security scheme for Britain.[14] Now, his 1944 book argued in favor of a method of achieving postwar full employment and prosperity. Part of his proposal called for the British government to buy surplus supplies of essential goods to increase demand and therefore provide jobs. Such supplies, he maintained, could be sold at a later date. Beveridge believed that unemployment may stem from a misdirection of demand and by failure to organize the labor market.

The *New York Times* blasted Beveridge's proposals in an editorial, claiming that government purchase of surplus supplies would create new problems "without eliminating or correcting the old ones."[15] The *Times* also warned that Beveridge's idea would inevitably get government involved in the sticky business of controlling production.

Words at War's broadcast of an adaptation of Beveridge's book caused a furor.[16] Immediately, the National Association of Manufacturers and other spokesmen for big business descended "like a ton of bricks" on NBC, claiming foul. Industrialists wanted the counter side projected, against full employment and social security plans. NBC started to hedge on the air, disclaiming responsibility for the books dramatized.

As a consequence of the controversy, the Council for Books in Wartime, which initiated the *Words at War* series, became agitated. The council, unhappy about apologizing for contents of books made into a show, voted not to permit such action in future and not to permit use of its name behind any books that it did not consider as "weapons" in war. The result was that following a broadcast in the first week of June 1945, NBC dropped the program.

The termination of *Words at War* just a month after Germany's surrender, but while the country was still fighting Japan, bore similarity to the cancellation or discontinuation of other broadcasts that proposed social change, such as the *American Women* series and programs promoting tolerance, particularly toward blacks. There seemed little reason for doubt. The end of the war meant a political and social swing to conservatism in American life.

NOTES

1. *Life*, June 14, 1943.

2. Don Wharton, "The Soldiers Say 'Don't Do It,'" *Readers Digest*, March 1945, 15–18.

3. Arthur Laurents to Erik Barnouw, n.d., Box 38, Barnouw collection, COL-RB.

4. This account of Laurents's visit to the hospital is based on Arthur Laurents, *Original Story By: A Memoir of Broadway and Hollywood* (New York: Alfred A. Knopf, 2000), 55–57.

5. As described in Minerva Pious, "Report to the Union: AFRA's Own Office of War Information," *Stand By*, VI, no. 3 (January 1945): 4.

6. Arthur Laurents, interview by author, Quogue, N.Y., August 12, 1999.

7. Millard Lampell, *The Long Way Home* (New York: Julian Messner, 1946), 25–27.

8. Lampell, *The Long Way Home*, 109–121.

9. Larry Ceplair and Steven Englund, *The Inquisition in Hollywood: Politics in the Film Community, 1930–1960* (Garden City, N.Y.: Anchor Press/Doubleday, 1980), 193.

10. Abraham Polonsky, telephone conversation with author, August 29, 1998.

11. Abraham Polonsky, "The Case of David Smith," *Hollywood Quarterly* 1, no. 2 (January 1946): 185–198.

12. Willard Waller, "The Veteran Comes Back," adapted by Ben Kagan, *Words at War*, Box 500, folder 2, NBC Collection, Sept. 5, 1944, WISC.

13. George K. Pratt, "Soldier to Civilian," adapted by Bafe Blau, *Words at War*, Box 501, folder 1, May 29, 1945, NBC Collection, WISC.

14. Ralph Robey, "The Beveridge Report and America," *Newsweek*, January 11, 1943, 56.

15. "Another Beveridge Plan," *New York Times*, November 17, 1944, 18:2.

16. This account is based on Robert Ballou, *A History of the Council on Books in Wartime 1942–1946* (New York: Country Life Press, 1946), 37–38.

THE WAR ENDS

Three of us listened in our darkened living room as the program came with clarity over our FM station. I was glad the lights were out, for tears were there and I don't think I was the only person who shed them. After the broadcast had been on for about ten minutes, I had switched the lights out for fear some friend would knock on the door and break the spell. I can recall no other occasion when radio had been able to sustain a mood for such a length of time.

—A listener to "On a Note of Triumph," in R. LeRoy Bannerman, *On a Note of Triumph: Norman Corwin and the Golden Years of Radio.*

Your name is Elly.[1] Early in the war, shortly after your marriage, Arty, your husband, was sent to an Army base in Greenland. It seemed an odd place for a guy from Brooklyn to be located. But there was no fighting in Greenland, and it seemed a safe place for him. Two years later, when your father-in-law had a heart attack, the Red Cross arranged for a furlough so that Arty could return home to see his father. While he was still at home, the Battle of the Bulge took place. You followed newspaper reports about it. Thousands of Americans were killed, and you were glad that he missed it. You hoped at the time that perhaps the Army might give him a permanent assignment in the States. But after a few weeks, Arty was sent overseas to Europe. Week and after week you prayed for his safety. You knew that with the Allied armies moving closer and closer to Germany, the end was in sight. Then, one morning early in May 1945, Freda, your neighbor in the apartment below yours, came running upstairs and banged on the door. "Elly," she said, "your husband's going to come home soon. The war in Europe is over. Germany surrendered."

At first you didn't let yourself believe Freda. Ten days earlier there had been a premature report that the fighting had ended in Europe. Now you had to find out for yourself. You turned on the radio and immediately heard the excited voice of someone reading a bulletin. It was true. Arty was coming home!

By late 1944 there was no doubt that German defeat was now within sight. CBS asked Norman Corwin to prepare an hour-long commemorative script for the forthcoming Allied victory in Europe.[2] The assignment proved to be a difficult one. Corwin was weary of war-related writing. It was hard for him to get up steam for the new project. But he did, working on it everywhere, even in barber shops and taxicabs. Early in May 1945 Corwin was in San Francisco at the founding conference of the United Nations when word of Hitler's suicide reached him. He rushed to Los Angeles. Just as he began rehearsals of his completed script, he received word of an armistice. CBS scheduled a broadcast; then learning that the reported armistice was false, they canceled it.

Finally on May 7, Germany capitulated. The following day, Corwin's program, "On a Note of Triumph," went on the air. It was his masterpiece, and newspapers in Philadelphia, Milwaukee, Knoxville, and many other cities hailed it as such. Corwin's "Bill of Rights" show had opened the war, and now "On a Note of Triumph" closed it, at least its main part. The broadcast attracted a flood of response: 4,278 letters, cards, and wires; a thousand calls at CBS in New York; and some 1,600 at CBS in Hollywood. Carl Sandburg wrote, calling it "a vast announcement, a terrific interrogatory, and certainly one of the all-time great American poems."[3] In a surrealist touch, the Army decided to require every German prisoner of war to listen to a German translation of the program. Ironically, in one such camp, the person charged with arranging for them to hear it was Corwin's own brother,

Al. "You can imagine my elation and pride," he later wrote to Norman, "when I read the order and you can imagine my zeal in carrying out those orders. . . . He continued, "A year ago, a show of this sort would have created riots and perhaps sabotage within the compound. They'd have yelled 'propaganda,' 'violation of the Geneva Convention.' But last night they listened silently. . . . Playing my brother's show to 1,250 POWs is an experience I shall never forget."[4]

"On a Note of Triumph" was so popular that a recording of it sold widely. Once, more than two decades after the war, Corwin was aboard a transatlantic flight in the first class compartment. About 1:00 A.M., as the pilot was walking down the aisle, he spotted Corwin's name pinned to the back of the writer's seat. "Are you Norman Corwin?" the pilot asked in awe. "Yes, I am," Corwin replied, at which the pilot began to recite some lines from "On a Note of Triumph." "I have a recording of it," he explained. " I play it to my kids at least once a year so that they'll remember an important lesson of the past."[5]

As the certainty of Allied victory became apparent in the last year of the war, attention began to focus on an important issue of the forthcoming postwar era. How should the Allies deal with Nazi war criminals and with Germany in general? The same right-wing forces that opposed American involvement in what they called "a foreign war that was none of our business" were calling for a soft peace with Germany.

The topic of Nazi war crimes had first been presented as early as the spring of 1943, in at least one show in an NBC series, *Day of Reckoning*, that the Council for Democracy had helped sponsor. Initially, the Writers War Board (WWB) was asked to sponsor it, too, but it rejected the offer. Each play in the series concerned some aspect of Axis war crimes. Norman Rosten's "The Unholy Three," for example, the series's final broadcast, deals with the crimes against humanity of Deputy Führer Herman Goering, Propaganda Minister Paul Joseph Goebbels, and Gestapo Chief Heinrich Himmler. Written partly in blank verse and partly in dialogue, it features a climax in which the three Nazi leaders are brought to a quiet, attractive town where they feel they have found a sanctuary, only to find out that they are in a restored Lidice. Rosten himself was pleased with the effort, "I took care of Goebbels, Goering and Himmler. But good," he reported in a newspaper interview. The critics liked Rosten's contribution, too. The *New York Times* called it "a bitter and stirring recital of the crimes" of the Nazis and *Variety* praised it as "a forceful, moving portrayal of the evidence of heinous crimes."[6] *Variety* also praised its theme of justice rather than revenge.[7] The radio critic for *PM Daily* agreed, calling the broadcast the most effective one in the series. "It meted out punishment without hysteria," she wrote. "It stated clearly 'our theme is not revenge but justice.' . . . The script . . . studied the disease of fascism, [and] searched out its guilt."[8]

In the spring of 1944, the matter of Nazi war crimes arose again, this time in connection with the WWB and the "hate the Germans" issue. The WWB had developed a hard-line anti-German stance that included open advocacy of hatred for the Germans. As Clifton Fadiman and Rex Stout articulated it, the board also believed in the collective guilt of the German people for their nation's wartime activities. It was for this reason that the WWB rejected the idea of sponsoring the *Day of Reckoning* series. The WWB wanted the Allies to hold responsible for Nazi war crimes not just the top Nazi leadership but also a wide section of the German population. This policy proved to involve the WWB in its greatest controversy when it sponsored a petition calling for a hard-line peace treaty. In a letter to his fellow board members, Fadiman noted that after World War I there had been an attempt to blame Germany's aggression solely on the Kaiser.[9] He argued that there was a similar faulty perception that all the blame for the recent war in Europe should be placed just on the Nazis, and that it was this notion that was behind growing sentiment in the United States for a soft peace. Fadiman wrote that he believed that the board needed to take action to counter these misperceptions. One board member, Langston Hughes, responded negatively to the proposal. "Man, I can't sign that German statement. . . ," he wrote. "It just strikes me as absurd for a Negro who can't even vote in almost half the USA to be telling the whole German nation where to get off!" He added "I'm willing to howl at the Nazis and I do."[10]

Fadiman's and Stout's views on the subject were heard at the highest levels. In October 1944, President Roosevelt sent Stout a telegram inviting him to the White House to discuss the topic of the postwar treatment of Germany. Stout willingly accepted, but the record only shows that the White House meeting was subsequently scheduled for after the 1944 election. The point is, however, that the WWB's influence was widespread.

In both August and October 1944, NBC broadcast *Words at War*'s "War Criminals and Punishment," a later dramatization on the theme of war crimes, adapted from a book by George Creel. Using a narrator and several unidentified voices, all of whom were speaking to Adolf Hitler, the program predicted that unless special efforts were made, Nazi war criminals were likely to escape justice. "And don't let me hear that bull about the democratic decent Germans making another dictator impossible over there!" warned the narrator. "You've killed or banished most of the decent Germans. And democracy has never stood a chance in Germany anyway. Three times in seventy years the German people have banded like robots under a dictator and have marched out to ravage the world. . . . The German people don't even know what the word means!"[11]

In February 1945, only three months before the defeat of Germany, *Words at War* also featured "What To Do with Germany," a prophetic dramatization of famed lawyer Louis Nizer's book of the same name. It started with a harsh premise that "World conquest by rape and murder had been bred in the bone of the German people . . . ," and that "The Germans have been the scavengers and the scourge of civilization." From there it proceeded to the question of how to treat Germany in general. Nizer recommended for punishment, meaning death or imprisonment, "Every German officer above the rank of Colonel, [and] every member of the Reichstag."[12]

"What To Do with Germany" cites alleged German plans soon after their defeat in World War I to violate the Versailles Treaty and go to war again. Listeners heard Nizer's claim that before the ink had dried on the Versailles Treaty the Germans were engaged in planning to convert lipstick factories to make cartridges for guns and use glider clubs to train military pilots. The program then predicts similar behavior after Germany loses World War II and bolsters the claim by citing a warning attributed to British Foreign Secretary Anthony Eden that a nucleus of high-ranking officers had already created a secret organization to continue resistance in Germany after the Allied occupation to prepare for a third World War.

Nizer's solution was to put Germany "on probation like a criminal." "If Germany is to be really disarmed," listeners heard, "she must be disarmed industrially too. . . . All industries which made possible the reconstruction of the war machine . . . metals, chemicals, machine tools . . . these industries must be completely removed from German management. Only a hard peace will bring a peaceful world."

With the conclusion of the fighting in Europe in May, of course, the war was still not over. On August 6, the United States dropped an atomic bomb on Hiroshima. It was clear that the end was days away. This time, the honor of producing a show for broadcast immediately on the heels of a historic event went to two writers quite less known than Corwin: Doris and Frank Hursley.[13] The Hursleys were sitting in their farmhouse in rural Wisconsin when they heard the announcement about the bomb.[14] Their regular program, a show in their *Service to the Front* series, scheduled for broadcast the next day, was being rehearsed in Chicago. However, realizing that the occasion called for something special, they set to work trying to get information by telephone from Army headquarters in Washington, D.C. They were unsuccessful. What the Army was unwilling to tell the Hursleys or anyone else for that matter, was that the United States was going to drop a second bomb in three days, this one on Nagasaki. The only sources available to the writing couple were what had been printed in the newspapers.

By now it was early evening and they knew that Ted Robertson, their producer in Chicago, was done with rehearsals for the show that was scheduled for the next day. They phoned him. "Ted, you heard the news about the bomb that was dropped on Japan, didn't you?" they asked. They then outlined their plan to do an "all nighter" to prepare a documentary about the bomb for the next day's broadcast. Robertson agreed to gather up all the newspapers that he could and take the first train to Milwaukee. He reached the Hursleys at 9:30 P.M. and they began to put a script together. By morning, with the script still incomplete, they all headed for Chicago, continuing to work on the train and later in the studio where new information was coming through on the news wires. Once the script was finished, they had to read it long distance over the telephone to nervous War Department officials in Washington, D.C.

The Hursleys' play "Atomic Bombs" traces the history of the Allied efforts to win the race against the Nazis to develop the bomb. "When was your atomic bomb to be ready?" a British interrogator asks a Nazi scientist in the play. "It was scheduled for use in October. And it would have been ready," is his reply. In the wake of the first bomb and with Japanese surrender still not certain, the play does not and could not anticipate the wider questions that eventually had to be discussed about atomic weapons and atomic energy. But as a hastily conceived effort to report on a startling historical event, it filled the bill well.

In November 1945, war crimes trials began in Nuremberg, Germany. Eleven months later, on the day of the hangings of Julius Streicher, Ernst Kaltenbrunner, Wilhelm Keitel, and seven other top Nazis at Nuremberg, CBS made the first of two broadcasts of "The Empty Noose," by Arnold Perl. Perl wrote the play as an antidote to catharsis, complacency, and the notion that once these men were dead the world would be safe from racism and hatred.

> Eyewitness: . . . I kept asking the questions: did they really die—all they stood for? You see, I've got a natural right to ask. I fought my way into Nuremberg; without me they wouldn't have got theirs this morning. As those traps were sprung, I kept seeing something, not something I imagine, but something real, . . . to me anyway—an empty noose still waiting for its final victim, . . . the foulest thing we'll ever know—Fascism—that. Did that thing die. . . . I don't think so. . . . In Germany there were those beginnings and . . . they weren't recognized, or fought against. Sometimes we don't want to see them; we brush them off. . . . Still that empty noose keeps coming back when I think of a guy like Joe up the block. A union man, Joe, going on fifty. For all I know he's a Republican. "I don't know, Joe says to me the other day, "guess what they're calling me now—a Red,". . . somebody's out to smash his union. . . . Is a thing like that dead, can you call it dead. . . . They died, but I can't help seeing that empty noose.[15]

Like Corwin's "On a Note of Triumph," "The Empty Noose" was planned long in advance of its actual broadcast. Its title and content were decided soon after the Allied Control Commission set an approximate date for the executions, but Perl wrote certain passages at the last minute, based on broadcast dispatches from eyewitneses. An incident shortly before the scheduled hangings gave selection of the play's title an ironic meaning. One of the condemned men, Herman Goering, cheated the hangman's noose by committing suicide.

With the end of the war, the execution of top war criminals and broadcast of "The Empty Noose," the vast bulk of wartime radio drama had run its course. There is no measurable evidence that radio had helped to shorten the war by so much as one day. As one radio writer, Abe Polonsky, told the author, "Wars are won by bullets, not by radio programs." Yet radio did help to sell war bonds, which in turn helped finance the war effort, and it also helped mobilize the country. A letter from fifty-four-year-old, R. L. Haas of New Jersey lends support to this point. "I heard *This Is War* Saturday night," he wrote in February 1942 to the Office of Facts and Figures. "The query 'What are you doing?' is one that I have been trying to answer for myself. . . . I am serving as a Senior Air Raid Warden. Yet I feel that what I am doing is entirely inadequate for my share of the stupendous job that confronts us collectively."[16]

As anecdotal evidence cited earlier indicates, radio drama also helped recruiting efforts for the Armed Forces, for nurses, and for home-front positions with the railroads and other public services. It also helped influence attitudes toward the enemy in ways that helped the government prosecute the war. Finally, radio drama illuminated the need for progress in racial relations and publicized the need for the United Nations, which was about to be founded.

Given the quantity alone of Norman Corwin's and Arch Oboler's radio work, most of which appeared during the war, it is appropriate here to consider its impact, reviewing what critics and peers had to say about the authors. A few critics faulted Corwin for sentimental common-man populism. For example, in *Radio and Television Writing*, Max Wylie wrote that Corwin's "comprehension of . . . [his] . . . fellow man is detached." He claimed that Corwin lacked warmth and was "unable to be in ready contact with others while at the same time . . . [he] . . . can be eloquent in the defense of others." He also criticized Corwin for a "lack of affinity or feeling of active kinship" with his fellows and for "not having much of a sense of humor." Finally, Wylie charged that Corwin "does not participate and that he is too much to one side of the happening and reflective about it . . . ; [his] . . . sympathy is not for the child under [his] hand but for nameless and countless children everywhere."[17]

For the most part, however, critics and fellow writers have accorded Corwin a rare and honored place in broadcasting history. In 1945, four months after the end of the war, one critic claimed "it is because Corwin as a writer went beyond being a master technician in his own medium . . . to become a fine artist: developing a unique individual form, scaling the heights of poetic diction with startling metaphors and similes, and unlike other script writers, writing with sincerity and a conviction, that gives his plays literary value. . . . If we judge all writing, radio or otherwise, on the basis of its literary value, it is the work of a man such as Corwin, with telescopic powers, that combines and creates new horizons stretching far beyond the limitations of his field, which shall become a landmark in the literary as well as the radio world."[18]

In 1947, two years after the end of the war, *The New Yorker* hailed Corwin as "America's most prominent playwright."[19] Decades later, in 1985, a group of friends honored him on the occasion of his seventy-fifth birthday at a dinner at the Beverly Hills Hotel. They also published a book with their comments about Corwin. Ray Bradbury, who as a young man read each of Corwin's anthologies of radio plays as they were published, claimed a huge debt to him. "He gave me the greatest gift any man can give another, to dare to speak in great tongues, hoping to find, along the way, a perhaps dilapidated but great notion." Bradbury wrote also that "When it came time for me to write for radio . . . you could hear Corwin's poetry warping and woofing all the way through my first half hour for the *World Security Workshop*."[20] Charles Kuralt also remembered reading a volume of Corwin's plays in his school library in North Carolina. "I read it at thirteen and knew what I wanted to try to do with my life."[21] Television writer Norman Lear credited Corwin for exemplifying "the virtues of honing a personal vision, taking risks with new techniques, and trying to find something fresh in a familiar yet malleable medium."[22]

There were much more mixed perceptions of Oboler's work, which by the end of his radio career comprised at least 850 radio dramas. He deserves credit for his efforts long before the attack on Pearl Harbor as a "premature antifascist" for calling attention to the horrors of

Nazism. It would be a terrible mistake to overlook his foresight. The quality of his work is perhaps a different matter. Despite its popularity, some early criticism of his serious plays hinted that, in the long run, his reputation would suffer.

Those who liked Oboler's work praised it for its stream-of-consciousness technique, terse dialogue, precise timing, and unusual sound effects. Playwright Jerome Lawrence recommended the inclusion of two of Oboler's radio plays, among them his adaptation of Dalton Trumbo's *Johnny Got His Gun,* in a list of radio's best. But Oboler's critics were many, and in the long run his work has become dated. Even as far back as 1941 they had some harsh things to say about its artistic merit. In that year, critic Dawn Powell reviewed *Fourteen Radio Plays,* an anthology of some of his works, in the *Partisan Review.* Criticizing their lack of subtlety, she wrote that "Oboler is for peace, the flag, motherhood, boyhood, mankind and above all, the underdog."[23] In her view the dilemmas of his characters are as profound as those of a comic strip character such as Popeye. It is not totally fair to judge radio plays without sound and music. But for one familiar with the taped versions of the plays, for the most part, these reviews are correct.

The same critic who praised Corwin's work in the *New York Daily News* in 1945 contrasted it to Oboler's. Where Corwin's plays contained startling metaphors and similes, sincerity, and conviction, he faulted Oboler's for overuse of the stream-of-consciousness technique, which he called "a lazy device." Like the *Partisan Review,* the *Daily News* also faulted Oboler for trite situations—complaining that his characters "suffer from an acute attack of syrupy melodrama."

Initially, as the war's end was approaching, a number of the radio dramatists were exhilarated by broadcasting's wartime achievements. Having felt that they had made important contributions during the war, many radio dramatists shared the belief that afterward they would be able to continue to serve the public interest. This was not to be. For one thing, a new and rapidly growing commercialism in radio helped push Corwin, Bill Robson, and a number of their colleagues who also wrote for noncommercial radio out of the medium. Second, with the war over, television began to come into its own. Although it began in the late 1930s, the war prolonged its infancy. By 1947, however, television programming began to expand and the American consumer began to develop a passion for the new electronic marvel.

Besides the expansion of television and the growth of commercialism, another, in some ways more profound, phenomenon shared responsibility for terminating the network careers of Corwin and many of his colleagues. In the last days of the war, four leaders in the field of wartime drama, William Robson, Anton Leader, Robert Shayon, and Frank Telford, a writer for the government, were taken on a War Department junket to Europe. The group received a front-line tour and were briefed by high-ranking Army officers. But during their tour they began to hear disturbing reports, first from military leaders, and in Italy from religious leaders. Once the Axis powers were defeated, so they were told, the United States would have to "deal with" the Soviets. In other words, in the minds of influential people, before one war had ended, another was beginning. Anti-Nazism had yielded to anti-Communism as major policy. So what was this last phenomenon that drove the radio writers from the networks? A relentless search for Communists and "fellow travelers" in broadcasting.

NOTES

1. This account is based on the author's interview of Eleanor Blustein, West Hempstead, N.Y., May 13, 2000.

2. Erik Barnouw, *The Golden Web: A History of Broadcasting in the United States, vol. 2, 1933–1953* (New York: Oxford University Press, 1968), 211.

3. Barnouw, *The Golden Web*, 212. As the book jacket to the printed version acknowledges (see Norman Corwin, *On a Note of Triumph* [New York: Simon& Schuster, 1945]), it was not a play, although it had important dramatic elements. The author pleads guilty to exercising his right to arbitarily include discussion of the broadcast here. It was perhaps Corwin's proudest moment, and the power of the script that captivated novelist Philip Roth (see his novel *I Married a Communist*), among others, argued convincingly that it could not be ignored here.

4. Alfred Corwin to Norman Corwin, September 18, 1945, COR 00644, TOL.

5. Norman Corwin to Mrs. Flora Schreiber, October 30, 1966, in Norman Corwin, *Norman Corwin's Letters*, ed. A. J. Langguth (New York: Barricade Books, 1994), 254.

6. John. K. Hutchens, "For the Record," *New York Times,* April 18, 1943, 9:2.

7. "Follow up Comment," *Variety,* April, 14, 1943, vol. 150, no. 5.

8. Judy Depuy, "Heard and Overheard," *PM Daily,* July 12, 1943, 23:4.

9. Clifton Fadiman to Langston Hughes, June 27, 1944, Hughes Collection, YALE.

10. Langston Hughes to Clifton Fadiman, July 17, 1944, Hughes Collection, YALE.

11. Richard McDonagh, "War Criminals and Punishment," Writers [War] Board, War Scripts, no. 59, August 1944, NYPL-LC.

12. Louis Nizer, "What to do with Germany," episode 84, adapted by Edward Jurist, February 14, 1945, *Words at War*, Box 500, folder 5. NBC Collection, WISC.

13. On the very day of the surrender of Japan, August 14, Norman Corwin produced a program to celebrate the occasion. It was a narrative poem, however, not a play. It was well received, inspiring a thousand letters from listeners, virtually all of them complimentary.

14. The following account is based on Margaret Mayorga, ed., *The Best of One-Act Plays of 1945* (New York: Dodd, Mead, 1946), 3–4. The quotations from the play are from Frank Hursley and Doris Hursley, *Atomic Bombs,* on page 15 in Mayorga's book.

15. Arnold Perl, "The Empty Noose," in Joseph Liss, *Radio's Best Plays* (New York: Greenberg, 1947), 121–130.

16. R. L. Haas to Archibald MacLeish, February 16, 1942, NA 208-5-21, folder 370 "Radio and Television."

17. Max Wylie, *Radio and Television Writing* (New York: Rinehart, 1950), 132.

18. The article "A Dash of Pepper," by Harriet Pepper Stark, is in a scrapbook that Corwin kept (now in his collection in the TOL). A notation indicates that it appeared on December 5, 1945 in the *News.* A search of the microfilmed copy of the New York *Daily News* failed to locate the article, however.

19. Philip Hamburger, "Profiles: The Odyssey of the Oblong Blur" *The New Yorker,* April 5, 1947, 36.

20. Ray Bradbury, "Introduction," in Columbia School of Journalism, *13 for Corwin* (New Jersey: Barricade Books, 1985), 8.

21. Charles Kuralt, "The Spoken Word," in Columbia School of Journalism, *13 for Corwin,* 15.

22. Norman Lear, "Letter to the World,"Columbia School of Journalism, *13 for Corwin,* 21.

23. Dawn Powell, "Radio's Gift to Art," *Partisan Review*, vol. VIII, no. 3, May-June 1941, 251.

19

THE POSTWAR ERA:
A CHANGE OF ENEMIES

Pal, You're dead. I submitted your name for a show and they told me I couldn't touch you with a barge pole. Don't quote me pal, because I'll deny I said it.

—A "friend" to Millard Lampell, *New York Times*

Your name is Michael. You live in Los Angeles, where you own an automobile distributorship. In church last Sunday, the priest was railing at the spread of communism across the country. During the war, you sometimes heard people say that we were fighting the wrong enemy, meaning we should have been allied with Germany against the Reds and not vice versa. A few times, with close friends, you even repeated the idea. You were never happy about the New Deal. You felt that Roosevelt was flirting with communism. You believe that as a result of it, the power of unions grew. And, as you see it, they have been riddled with communists. You are not happy about the increase that has occurred in government spending. You read in the diocese newspaper that communists are all over the place, especially in Hollywood and in the broadcasting industry. You remember the way that certain actors seemed to have a romance with Russia and never missed an opportunity to praise it.

A few years ago, you heard Robert Young, Lauren Bacall, Burl Ives, Gene Kelly, and other show business people denounce the work of the

House Un-American Activities Committee on a radio program called "Hollywood Fights Back."[1] They quoted various newspapers around the country that commented on the committee and its work. One, a Detroit paper, called for the committee's abolition. One actor attacked what he called the committee's "fascism in action." You heard that Norman Corwin wrote the script for the program. Now, in 1951, the United States is actually fighting communism on the battlefield—in Korea. You also know that the Russians have the atomic bomb, which they were able to develop with the assistance of the Rosenbergs, who were convicted just last week of giving the Russians atomic secrets. Since the end of the war, communism has spread into most of Eastern Europe. You are scared. Something needs to be done to stop the Reds before it's too late.

Throughout the war period, long before Bill Robson's and his colleagues' trip to Europe, there were forebodings in the United States of the political purge that would develop at the conclusion of the war: the activities of the Dies Committee, the Red-baiting of Orson Welles after broadcast of his *Free Company* production of "His Honor the Mayor," the attacks on Archibald MacLeish and the Office of Facts and Figures, and similar later ones on Elmer Davis and the Office of War Information.

As Robson, Welles, MacLeish, and their colleagues learned, after the war, not only abroad but in the United States itself, anticommunism replaced anti-Nazism as a dominant outlook. Michael and many other Americans were scared, and their fear manifested itself in a search for scapegoats. One of the earliest signs of this in radio was an incident involving Erik Barnouw.[2] In addition to having worked as a network script editor, Barnouw taught radio production at Columbia University, wrote a widely used book on the subject, and, with a number of other talented writers, wrote for the *Cavalcade of America*.

In 1945, the BBD&O advertising agency hired Barnouw as the *Cavalcade*'s editor. Two years later, when Columbia offered him a full-time teaching position, he resigned the editing job but continued to work occasionally as a contributor to the series. In 1949, Barnouw accepted the task of writing a show about President Millard Fillmore. Because Fillmore was born in Buffalo, New York, where the Du Pont Company, *Cavalcade*'s sponsor, had a factory, the company decided to take advantage of the occasion and turn the broadcast into a big public relations event. For this reason they asked Barnouw to join William A. Hart, Du Pont's advertising director, and travel to Buffalo. After agreeing to the trip, Barnouw ran into a conflict. He learned that he was being nominated as president of the Radio Writers Guild. He would be able to go to Buffalo but not stay for the full program of events. On the evening that he had to return to New York, Hart drove him to the railroad station. Hart had a terrible reputation at BBD&O, where he was sometimes referred to as "that bastard." But Barnouw found him pleasant enough to talk to. When they arrived at the station, Barnouw got out. However, before he could say goodbye, Hart suddenly blurted out, "Remember me to your communist friends" and slammed the door shut. Whether Hart was referring to the Radio Writers Guild in general or perhaps more specifically to a smaller group who worked for the *Cavalcade* was unclear. In any case, the Fillmore script proved to be Barnouw's last for the *Cavalcade*. It was house-cleaning time at BBD&O.

In October 1947, the House Un-American Activities Committee (HUAC) opened a series of hearings in the Old House Office Building in Washington, D.C., to investigate communist influence in the film industry. The chairman of the committee was Representative J. Parnell Thomas, a Republican from New Jersey. Two other committee members were John Rankin (D-Miss.), a vigorous racist and anti-Semite and HUAC's dominant figure in the mid 1940s, and a young California congressman, Richard M. Nixon. Rankin, who had vigorously opposed the New Deal and fought against a bill designed to give teeth to federal efforts to stop the practice of lynching blacks, once declared "Slavery was the greatest blessing the Negro people ever had."[3] During the course of the hearings, Rankin accused Hollywood movies of having sent coded messages about German air raids in order that communist spies and sympathizers in Europe could take cover.[4] The committee summoned a variety of writers, actors, and producers to the hearings, most of them people on the political left. In front of the dozens of journalists present, they were asked to name those whom they knew to be Communists. Thomas and his cronies informed them that if they cooperated, they might be able to save their own careers.

Actually, by the 1950s when the Red hunt was in full spring, the American Communist Party was a rather insignificant force in

American life. The height of its popularity was during the Depression when some Americans were looking for an alternative to the capitalist system that seemed to have failed. The party's attraction continued for those inclined to support it during the war, when the United States was allied with the Soviet Union. At that time, perhaps it had 75,000 members, still less than 1 percent of the population of the United States. As one writer put it, the party was "a flea on the dog's back." By 1950, its membership was down to only 10,000. Among these a substantial number were undercover FBI agents.[5] But the Red-baiters were never inclined to let the facts stand in the way of their obsession.

It is also worth noting that the nature of Communist Party membership and the extent of the party's influence were hardly what the Red hunters perceived. Like the overwhelming majority of members of the Republican and Democratic Parties, the overwhelming majority of Communist Party members had no intention of overthrowing the government or engaging in any other criminal activity. Folk singers Pete Seeger and Woody Guthrie and their friends often ignored or even laughed at the party's dogma. It was the party's opposition to racism and its support of various progressive causes that attracted them. Many shared with Frances Chaney, a radio actress, her reasons for joining the party. "It made me feel free. We wanted to make a difference in those troubled times and the Party gave us a chance."[6]

To fight the witch hunt that Congressman Thomas's committee initiated, Katharine Hepburn, Fredric March, and other entertainers met at the home of lyricist Ira Gershwin and founded a Committee for the First Amendment.[7] One week after the HUAC hearings started, the committee sponsored the broadcast on ABC of "Hollywood Fights Back," a radio rebuttal. The show aired from both Hollywood and New York. Norman Corwin produced the principal part of the program and directed the broadcast from Hollywood. Bill Robson directed the one in New York. The show featured a series of Hollywood stars voicing their opposition to the hearings. Fredric March said, "Who do you think they're really after? Who's next? Is it your minister who will be told what he can say in his pulpit? Is it your children's school teacher who will be told what she can say in classrooms?

Is it you who will have to look around nervously before you can say what is on your mind? Who are they after? They're after more than Hollywood. This reaches into every American city and town."[8]

Complementing the activities of HUAC, on the evening of November 24, 1947, fifty film executives met at the Waldorf Astoria Hotel. They were engaged in an action that would give ironic reward to various writers and actors, many of whom had often worked for nothing on war-related projects: the creation of a blacklist. The search was on for writers and others who had refused, many of them on grounds of conscience, to cooperate with investigations of "alleged subversives or disloyal elements in Hollywood."

In addition to the Washington hearings and the decision of the film executives, two years later, California State Senator Jack Tenney, a large, pasty-faced man, got into the act, conducting hearings in Los Angeles. A racist and anti-Semite, he was initially a radical left-wing politician.[9] In August 1938, in a speech at a rally of the Hollywood Anti-Nazi League, Tenney had demanded abolition of the Dies Committee. Later in the year, the Dies Committee heard testimony that Tenney was a Communist. But a year later, he suddenly saw the light and started doing his own Red-baiting. By 1941, Tenney was head of the State Senate's own "Fact Finding Committee on Un-American Activities."[10]

Just as Martin Dies had targeted actor Fredric March and March's wife Florence Eldredge, so did Tenney. In a report about the actor in the spring of 1949, Tenney accused him of fraternizing with communists. As evidence of this, he cited March's previously noted attendance at the "United Nations in America" dinner at the Hotel Biltmore.[11] Apparently along with March and the hundreds of others in attendance, some Communists may have been there, too.

As further "proof" of March's "improper politics," Tenney pointed to the actor's involvement with two "tainted" radio plays. One was written by Norman Corwin, one of the right-wing's favorite whipping boys.[12] "We know Corwin was not a communist, never was a communist," said Hollywood actor Ward Bond, who was heavily enmeshed in the blacklisting process. "But he'll do until one comes along."[13] With no official position, Bond had nevertheless assumed responsibility for "clearing" people for the whole motion picture industry. Apparently,

Tenney never identified the Corwin play by name. In his mind it was
sufficiently damning to mention Corwin's authorship.

Tenney singled out the second play, one in which March costarred
with Canada Lee, apparently because, to the witch hunters, Lee, too,
was a dangerous character, one of Stalin's agents with whom presumably any association produced some sort of contamination. Here, too,
the record does not indicate the specific show that Tenney had in
mind. Most likely it was "Beyond the Call of Duty," a 1943 broadcast
that dealt with race relations.[14] To what might Tenney have objected?
Surely it was not its sponsorship by the National Council of the Young
Men's Christian Association. The YMCA was hardly a radical organization. It is likely that the very theme, racial harmony, rubbed Tenney
the wrong way. In one scene from the script, "French," a black Navy
messman, puts himself in harm's way to save a group of four white
sailors. By itself the theme would not necessarily offend a die-hard
racist. Wasn't that the job of blacks, to serve whites and sacrifice for
them? But one of the white sailors in the scene speculates whether
given that both he and "French" are from New Jersey, the two of them
will ever go swimming together at the Jersey shore. The concept of interracial socializing was enough to prompt many a Red-baiter to cry
"Commie."

Tenney's questioning of Florence Eldridge showed further his
bizarre nature. At one point he asked her if she believed she was living in a democracy. When Eldridge replied that she did, Tenney
asked, "Did it ever occur to you that the word democracy does not appear in the Constitution of the United States?" He then explained, "it
does not . . . ours is a republic. Under a democratic society the major
party can vote the minority party out of power. They can put them into
slavery or take them out and shoot them, so our founding fathers felt
it would be better to have a republic so that all would be protected. I
think the word should be clarified so that we understand what it
means."[15]

The terror that affected the Marches and some other actors also
spread from Hollywood to other areas of entertainment, including radio and television. The large majority of the writers, actors, and directors affected were non-Communists who may have participated in
progressive activities. A smaller group were, in fact, Communists, but

their party membership had a quite different meaning than that which the blacklisters ascribed to it. The terror also affected government employees, but it sometimes suspiciously took on overtones of having more than a political coloration. In November 1947, Norman Corwin wrote to a friend, "There seems to be a new atrocity everyday. The latest item in this direction, the report that thirty-three of thirty-five people cashiered from the State Department since the recent purges turn out to be Jews. If this is correct, it is just something too close to official anti-Semitism to be merely coincidental."[16]

Contributing to the witch hunt on the government level, besides the work of congressional investigating committees, the FBI took action. J. Edgar Hoover sent a report to the Federal Communications Commission suggesting that Communist influence was achieving growing influence in the broadcasting industry.[17] In addition, the FBI expanded its surveillance of anyone whose name it received, even on anonymous tips, with any allegation of disloyalty or Communist affiliations. One of America's worst episodes of government and private persecution, a witch hunt for Communists and so-called "fellow travelers," was under way.

Even people like writer Violet Atkins Klein, who had no organizational affiliations, lived in fear of the witch hunters. Klein's daughter, Gilda Block, remembered her mother's anxiety during that era. Klein's own parents had emigrated from Russia and Poland, before the Russian Revolution. Her father left after a pogrom in Russia. In their new lives, first in England and later in the United States, Klein's mother, especially, developed an admiration for the Soviets who had successfully overthrown the hated czarist regime. Her leftist inclinations mainly expressed themselves in her subscribing to *People's World*, a leftist publication. Now, in the 1950s, Klein feared that someone might find her copies of the magazine. Block remembered her mother hiding them deep under the pillows of the living room window seat.[18]

At least three other groups besides the FBI, private ones, gave huge impetus to the anticommunist purge and promoted the blacklist. Each was actually composed of a minuscule membership, although they attempted to present an image of having a wider one. In 1947, three former FBI agents with access to both FBI and HUAC records founded the first of these, American Business Consultants, which came into the blacklist business by publishing *Counterattack—The Newsletter of Facts on Communism*. The new publication listed the names of writers and performers in broadcasting who had links with organizations or events that the editors considered unpatriotic. It even identified individuals whose only link with an alleged Communist organization, event, or publication was to have been praised by it.

In 1948, the American Broadcasting Company aired a drama entitled "Communism, US Brand," a fiercely anticommunist broadcast. The broadcast lent some weight to the allegations that HUAC, Tenney, and American Business Consultants were making about the infiltration of communism in the United States. Its author, however, was Morton Wishengrad, a moderate liberal but hardly a Red-baiter. As he told his friend Erik Barnouw, Wishengrad had a special sensitivity to communism ever since he witnessed an attempt by communist unionists to take over the International Ladies Garment Workers Union.[19]

Wishengrad received the first commentary about the show several weeks before its broadcast. He had described the project in some detail to his good friend Anton Leader, who was now living in Los Angeles. Like many on the left, Leader was alarmed at the growth of power of fanatical anticommunists in the few years after the war. "[Why have you] . . . joined the ranks of active cranks, neo-fascists, sensation seekers and red-baiters,"[20] Leader asked his friend? In fact, Wishengrad had no intention of assisting the Red-baiters. "I have only one object in mind," he replied in early July in a two-and-a-half page letter, "I want to demonstrate that the Communists are guilty of a lie. That they are not liberals. That liberals must never confuse the outward appearance of Soviet slogans with the inner reality of Soviet dictatorship. If I can get the liberals to stop fighting redbaiting and to start fighting the menace of fascism . . . to start actively working for the world they believe in, instead of defending a world they hate, then I will have done something, won't I."[21] The Red-baiters had not yet moved into high gear, however. Wishengrad could not anticipate that soon they would drive his friend Leader out of the country to seek work abroad!

The day after the show's broadcast, in mid summer, Norman Rosten sent Wishengrad a short note. "Heard your opus last night . . . you're too good a writer to go for soap opera. It ain't worth it—not even your picture in the *Sunday Times*."[22] The comment stung Wishengrad. "I met my wife while I was distributing leaflets . . . [and] I have spent at least two days on a picket line for every day I have spent writing," he replied in defense. "I have weathered every change in the party line since 1930, and . . . I have worked against Communists, with Communists, and apart from Communists in labor and liberal organizations since 1933." Wishengrad added, "I find myself wondering about your feeling as an artist to the daily de-secularization of art, music, literature, and science in the Soviet Union . . . you once wrote a piece attacking the Nazi book burnings . . . do you condemn Soviet book burnings?"[23]

In his follow-up letter, Rosten detailed his reactions to the show and to Wishengrad's letter. "It was loaded with half-truths, incompletions, out-of-context scenes, and a heavy handed sense of villainy . . . it was a failure as I heard it. Not without an ironic moral: the Communist uses the liberal, the corporation (ABC) uses Wishengrad, and everybody is happy including J. Parnell Thomas."[24] The exchange was unfortunate. These were two good men with much in common. But at the very least, Wishengrad misjudged the timing of his show. Without meaning to, he had lent ammunition to HUAC and a host of allied private witch-hunting groups. And these groups were becoming increasingly dangerous. The correspondence between Wishengrad and his colleagues revealed an ever-growing fissure in the broadcasting industry.

In June 1950, American Business Consultants came out with a new publication, *Red Channels: The Report of Communist Influence in Radio and Television.* In the spirit of *Counterattack,* its earlier publication, the 215-page report listed 151 performers, editors, and writers with "subversive" views whom it accused of furthering the Communist cause. Among the listees were Norman Corwin, Burgess Meredith, Joseph Julian, Norman Rosten, Langston Hughes, Arthur Laurents, Millard Lampell, and Edward G. Robinson. The basis for accusations that broadcasting accepted as proof of a procommunist attitude or affiliation included opposition to Franco during the Spanish Civil War, having aided refugees from Hitler, or having supported repeal of the poll tax on blacks. Opposition to racial discrimination, advocacy of civil rights, and favoring improved relations between the United States and the Soviet Union also qualified one for the "subversive" label. Key to the success of the witch hunt was a small group of right-wing journalists who frequently attacked alleged Communists and alleged communist sympathizers: George Sokolsky, Ed Sullivan, Victor Riesel, and Walter Winchell. Sullivan, who wrote for the New York *Daily News*, gave instant publicity to the new publication in his column. And *Red Channels* came to be found in the desk drawer of a number of broadcasting executives.

Many of the accusations against the alleged subversives were totally inaccurate. Norman Corwin's name wound up on the *Hollywood Writer's Blacklist* as well as in *Red Channels*. In typical Red-baiting fashion, the former cited him as toastmaster of an American Youth for Democracy dinner in San Francisco on a certain date in the fall of 1945, when in fact Corwin was in New York.[25] Stephen Vincent Benét's name appeared on a list similar to that in *Red Channels*, published by the staff of Wisconsin Senator Joseph McCarthy.[26] Here one essential error was that Benét was already long since dead.

Two typical accusations concerned Joseph Julian. Julian's first "crime" was participating in the 1942 meeting at Carnegie Hall. But *Red Channels* promoted him from his actual role as reader of a poem at the meeting to "speaker." The second notation referred to his attendance at a 1949 rally that was held by the National Committee of Arts, Sciences, and Professions to abolish HUAC.[27] The next major step in the escalation of the witch hunt involved Vincent Hartnett, a graduate of Notre Dame and a former naval intelligence officer, who also wrote the introduction to *Red Channels*. In 1951, while voluntarily testifying to a Senate subcommittee investigating "subversive infiltration of the entertainment industry," Hartnett urged that law enforcement agencies carry on an intensive investigation of Millard Lampell and implied that Peter Lyon deserved the same scrutiny.[28] A year later, Hartnett and a group of actors established Aware, Inc., an organization somewhat similar to American Business Consultants.

Hartnett, a frail, timid little man, established himself as a one-man clearance agency. He published and distributed to advertising agencies and other groups associated with broadcasting a third hate newsletter, *Aware, Incorporated*. Networks submitted lists of names of performers and others to him that he then labeled as "acceptable," "questionable," or "politically unreliable." Handling 100 names a day at $5 per name, or more if he could get it, Hartnett found that as well as being "virtuous," superpatriotism was also profitable. In one case, that of Arthur Miller, he charged $300.[29] Hartnett also assumed for himself the power to decide whether someone he had earlier judged less than acceptable had purged himself sufficiently to change his status. A Catholic, he had ties with *The Tablet*, a Catholic ultraconservative and anticommunist newspaper in Brooklyn whose editorial policies lent him much valued support.

Laurence Johnson, the silver-haired owner of a Syracuse, New York–based supermarket chain and an officer in the National Association of Supermarkets used his position to imply that he had influence over thousands of stores around the country. Johnson, who looked like a stereotypical film version of an elderly southern senator, worked hand in glove with both Hartnett and the American Legion. Hartnett fed names of alleged disloyal Americans to Johnson, who then visited manufacturers and informed them that his stores and those of his fellow supermarket owners would refuse to carry their products if they sponsored shows featuring those "disloyal" actors. At various times, persons accused of being Communists or fellow travelers sought out both Hartnett and Johnson. One of them, producer Hi Brown, was the subject of three references in *Red Channels*. In the fall of 1952, when he heard through the grapevine that Johnson was gunning for him, he went to see Johnson in the latter's New York hotel room.[30] For three hours, Brown, normally a very proud man, argued his case, among other things pointing out as a sign of his patriotism that he had worked for the Treasury Department.

In addition to the groups mentioned earlier, the Chamber of Commerce, some Roman Catholic groups, and even the Republican Party contributed to the atmosphere that enabled them to do their work. In 1946, the Chamber of Commerce published a thirty-eight-page pamphlet entitled *Communist Infiltration in the United States: Its Nature and How to Combat It*. The pamphlet identified the New Deal as preparing the way for communist ideology. Prior to the 1946 elections, the Republican Party distributed 683,000 copies of it.[31]

More significantly, the Roman Catholic hierarchy led by Francis Cardinal Spellman periodically warned American Catholics that the

United States was infected with the germs of communist slavery. Before the war, it was Father Charles Coughlin, on the lunatic fringe of the church, who spewed out his rabid anti-Semitic, antiliberal, and Red-baiting rhetoric on the air. Now others picked up his mantle. Besides the Brooklyn *Tablet*, the Los Angeles *Tidings*, another Roman Catholic publication, did its part to continue the Coughlin tradition, albeit with the anti-Semitic strains somewhat muted. In addition, in March 1947, the national commander of the Catholic War Veterans gave particularly shrill voice to the anti-Red mania when he called for deportation of all Communists, including U.S. citizens.[32]

The broadcasting industry also actively contributed to the blacklisting mania. A few of its executives initially protested the witch hunt. But, subsequently, it caved in to the threats and fully cooperated. In 1950, to reassure advertisers and the Communist hunters of the political correctness of his network's employees, CBS President Frank Stanton approved of a "loyalty oath" to be taken by all company employees.[33] Both the industry and a number of the advertising agencies hired "security officers." The security officer's job was two-pronged. He implemented the blacklist, but he could also clear a person. If information reached him that someone connected with a show was "politically questionable," he had to decide whether that person could be retained.

Jack Wren, a former Naval Intelligence officer, was BBD&O's "security" officer. Wren, considered the key liaison man between the ad agencies and *Counterattack*, was also the most commonly mentioned person when the subject of clearing an actor's name came up.[34] According to a retired BBD&O executive, Ben Duffy, another executive, a man who was close to Cardinal Spellman, one of the church's most vociferous anti-Communists, brought Wren into the agency.

Curiously, Wren's position in the company was an ambiguous one. His name was prominently listed on the ground-floor directory of BBD&O executives. Yet he occupied a small, plainly furnished office tucked off in a corner that had only one phone that more often than not he answered himself.[35]

The security officer for CBS was Dan O'Shea, a large, cigar-smoking vice president. Joe Julian, Bill Robson, and Allan Sloane all had dealings with O'Shea. After Julian learned that he was being blacklisted, he went to see O'Shea to clear his name.[36] Several months after it appeared in *Red Channels*, demand for Julian's acting services suddenly began to plummet. By 1953 his income was a measly $1,630, a fraction of what it had been a few years earlier.[37] Julian's experience illustrates part of O'Shea's modus operandi. O'Shea listened sympathetically as Julian told him that he was not a Communist. In turn, O'Shea told him that he believed him but he suggested that Julian drop a lawsuit that he had initiated against Vincent Hartnett and Laurence Johnson. He also asked why Julian had spoken only of what he had not done. How, O'Shea asked, had Julian contributed actively to the fight against communism? He pressed Julian to help his own case by attending some American Legion rallies or by aiding General Lucius Clay's anticommunist Crusade for Freedom. Clay's organization was raising funds to help the work of Radio Free Europe, which conducted broadcasts to Iron Curtain countries.

Soon afterward, Julian attended a Crusade for Freedom rally in Times Square, where, using a loudspeaker, he asked for contributions to further its work. But after a while he left, disgusted with himself. From the beginning, his attendance was an unlikely thing for him to do. As Julian wrote in his memoir, "My conscience would not allow me to go on, in view of my aversion to the hard-core sponsorship of the Crusade. The extreme right was just as unpalatable to me as the extreme left."[38] For one thing, Julian was Jewish and the anti-Semitic tinge of the supporters of groups such as the Crusade for Freedom was likely difficult to ignore.

After CBS removed Bill Robson from all positions of responsibility, Robson also tried to see O'Shea, who kept him waiting ten days.[39] When they finally met, O'Shea told him that he had information that in 1943 Robson had presented "a known communist" over a radio station in Pittsburgh. Apparently O'Shea had obtained this information from *Red Channels*. Robson replied that the citation was a case of mistaken identity. He explained that some years earlier, William Robson Sr., his father, as a secretary to the mayor of Pittsburgh, had arranged for a Soviet representative who was a guest of the mayor to take part in a discussion on the radio. O'Shea backed off and seemed to change his attitude, saying in the end, "anything I can do for you, here is my private telephone number. Please feel free to call me any time, collect." Several weeks later, still without any work, Robson called O'Shea. But speaking as though their previous conversation had never happened, O'Shea insisted to Robson that he had nothing to say to him. When Robson complained that O'Shea was standing in the way of his livelihood, O'Shea answered "You've not presented *any* evidence." Robson also tried unsuccessfully to get "cleared" at BBD&O.

At some point, most likely in late 1951, Robson found himself in California looking for a job in the motion picture industry. One day he went to see Ward Bond. Bond called Lawrence Johnson. "Do you have a guy named Robson on your list?" Bond inquired. Johnson, so he told Bond, had nothing on Robson. Robson left Bond hoping that this would clinch it for him. It did not. For some reason, and Robson never was able to find out why, nothing would budge O'Shea. Subsequently, O'Shea, referring to Robson, explained to Edward R. Murrow, an unabashed opponent of the blacklist, "He cannot un-accuse himself. He's been accused."

Allan Sloane had a totally different relationship with O'Shea than did Robson. Sloane's involvement with the CBS executive began one day in 1950 when O'Shea called him into his office.[40] Sloane's politics were much farther to the left than either Julian's or Robson's. O'Shea began to play cat and mouse with him in a way that can best be likened to how the detective in Dostoevesky's *Crime and Punishment* dealt with Rodion Raskolnikov, the novel's protagonist who had killed his landlady. The detective, who knew he had the goods on Raskolnikov, preferred to get a confession out of him rather than prove his case by other means. In pursuit of the same objective with Sloane, O'Shea badgered the harried writer, asking if there was something Sloane wanted to tell him and promising at the same time to help him with his problems. Initially, Sloane denied knowing what O'Shea was talking about. But eventually he gave in to O'Shea's promises, admitted that he had once been a member of the Communist Party, and agreed to testify to HUAC.

Subsequently, O'Shea became Sloane's mentor, helping him get work and, in one instance, even renegotiating a contract for Sloane. Sloane felt so indebted that one day he told O'Shea's secretary that he wanted to buy O'Shea a gift. She told him that O'Shea liked him very much but tried to dissuade him. It might, she suggested, disturb the relationship and make it look like payment for O'Shea's assistance. But on his way home from the office, Sloane spotted a silver carving of the Last Supper in a shop window. O'Shea had mentioned with pride his membership in both the Church's Knights of Malta, whose "Grand Protector" was the reactionary Cardinal Spellman, and the Knights of the Holy Sepulcher. Sloane knew that O'Shea could not turn this gift down. A few days after buying it, Sloane visited his mentor's office and laid a package on his desk. "What's this," O'Shea asked, pushing it aside. "It's for you." Sloane replied, at which O'Shea warned, "You're going to spoil our relationship." "Open it," Sloane told him. O'Shea finally succumbed to temptation and opened it. O'Shea cursed Sloane, in an affectionate tone, telling him that O'Shea's wife had admired the sculpture in the store window and acknowledged that he could not get himself to decline the gift.

The effect of publication of the names of many of the writers and actors took on a pattern. Millard Lampell and many others first learned of their new status only with the quiet cessation of job offers.[41] Lampell started having difficulty in getting calls through to producers he had known for years. His income dropped from five figures to $2,000 a year. He sold his car, moved his family into a cramped apartment in a cheap neighborhood, and lived on small loans from friends and earnings from occasional poorly paid assignments. Friends he had known for years passed him on the street with no more than a nod, and social invitations stopped coming. After three months of this, one day his agent called him in, locked her door, and announced in a tragic whisper, "You're on the list." Yet there was no way to get proof.

The cases of Canada Lee, Peter Lyon, Norman Rosten, and Norman Corwin also illustrate how the combined effects of the FBI and various other groups impacted accused persons. One day, in 1949, Lee's wife Frances heard a knock at the door. On opening it, she found two agents demanding to talk to Lee, *alone,* they insisted. Within a few minutes, from the next room she heard Lee uncharacteristically cursing and screaming. When they left, she was panic stricken because he had very high blood pressure and she tried to calm him down. Why had Lee become so emotional? The agents tried to pressure him to denounce, as a communist, Lee's friend, singer and fellow actor Paul Robeson. Lee refused.[42]

In subsequent months, a whispering campaign was carried out among broadcasting and advertising executives. The message was that because of Lee's appearance at benefits for organizations "purportedly" fighting race prejudice, he had subsequently been placed on the Attorney General's "subversive list" because he was "too controversial."

In the fall of 1949, Walter Winchell repeated some of the allegations in his New York *Daily Mirror* newspaper column. In one column in mid October, Winchell printed a brief item: "Canada Lee, the Negro star, will address a Vets' rally near Peekskill, Nov. 6th. He will wallop P. Robeson's 'line.'"[43] The comment enraged Lee, who immediately attempted to discover who sent it to Winchell. Somehow, Lee found out the answer. It was two advertising men, apparently hangers-on in the theater world who periodically sent tidbits to Winchell and other gossip columnists in exchange for a few dollars.[44] Lee told them that he had no intention of denouncing Robeson, and he wrote a retraction that he asked them to send to Winchell. They refused. Subsequently, Lee wrote directly to Winchell, explaining the facts of the case. After waiting in vain for Winchell's retraction, Lee finally wrote to the editor of the *Mirror*.[45] In addition to denying that he planned to attend a meeting to denounce Robeson, Lee set the record straight, first that he himself was a patriot and second that Negroes, in general, were, too. "As everyone must know by now, I am for complete democracy," he explained. "This is a great nation, and at no time in its history had there been any doubt of the Negroes' love, loyalty, and contribution to this nation's safety and culture." But no one could condemn Lee as a cop-out. He added, "I am against all isms, including that kind of Americanism which permits Jim Crow, Klanism, prejudice, lynching—and all other indignities and lack of opportunities that keep the Negro from being a first-class Citizen in this America for which so many have fought and died."

Later, apparently in response to a column in which Ed Sullivan slandered Lee, Lee wrote to Sullivan. "Ed, I am as much a communist as an Eskimo," he proclaimed. "Nor have I ever belonged to any subversive group."[46] Lee also called a press conference in which he denied that he was a Communist.

Peter Lyon and Norman Rosten were equally as innocent of any crime as Lee. Yet the FBI opened files on both of them, in 1944 on

Lyon and in 1950 on Rosten. Both files remained active for approximately ten years, the men's names appeared in *Red Channels*, and informants advised the FBI that the two were members of the Communist Party. In Rosten's case the bureau eventually had to acknowledge that it could not confirm that he had ever been a member.[47] In Lyon's, on the other hand, the agency continued to maintain that at least in the 1940s he was an active member. It made special mention of a report that in the summer of 1943, Lyon spoke at a meeting of the National Negro Congress in New York City. There, so an informer alleged, he stated that since CBS had taken the initiative to air William Robson's *Open Letter on Racism,* "there is every reason to hope for better cooperation from radio in such matters now."[48] Optimistic statements about improving race relations warranted notation in an FBI file! Another statement in the file shows that the bureau considered his 1951 invocation of the Fifth Amendment "properly an overt act" to warrant their maintaining his name on the security index.

Occasionally, the bureau subjected the two writers to "spot surveillance," trying to determine if there was any routine to their travels around the city. The bureau hoped to enlist them in its "security informant program." In 1952 they considered stopping Rosten on the street to do an interview, but they abandoned the idea, "in view of his journalistic employment," as a document in Rosten's file cryptically noted.[49] They did stop Lyon one day in the spring of 1954 as a document in his file relates: "Subject stated he was interested in continuing conversation, but had doctor's appointment. Agents agreed to drive subject to doctor's [sic]. Subject stated also wished to take dog to veterinarian. Subject with his dog joined agents in bureau car and conversation continued."[50] A later entry showed that Lyon declined the agency's request to become an informer. His file also contains statements alleging that the bureau was committed to discretion in its attempts to speak to him, that agents were under instructions not to attempt to visit him at home or to contact his employers. The notation is odd for two reasons. First, if it was policy to maintain such discretion, the notation was redundant. Second, Lyon's wife Jane recalled that in fact the bureau sent two agents to her office.[51]

Both Rosten and Lyon suffered financially from the blacklist. Rosten's situation appeared to stem primarily from being listed in *Red*

Channels. He lost his steady job with an advertising agency in 1950 and was forced to make his way in the freelance radio and television market. His name was withheld, however, from the shows that he wrote, and his income dropped by a third. In addition, regular free-lance shows that took his work in the past became evasive.[52] Lyon's loss of work occurred after he appeared before a Senate subcommit-tee and invoked the Fifth Amendment. On his return to New York, apparently feeling that candor was to his advantage, he told his em-ployers about the hearing. All of them, except *Holiday Magazine*, re-sponded by blacklisting him.[53]

The inclusion of Rosten's name in *Red Channels* impacted another person, too, in a case of mistaken identity. In 1948, actor Norman Rose was featured in "Communism, U.S. Brand," a program that most communist sympathizers and many noncommunist liberals would have given wide berth. Two years later, Rose was employed as narra-tor for an NBC science fiction show called *Dimension X*. "Norman, you can't do the show any more," the show's director said to him out of the blue. You're listed in *Red Channels*." The network had ordered Rose's dismissal. "Well between you and me, I wouldn't be surprised if it would be [listed]," Rose replied. "But I'm not listed in *Red Chan-nels*." Rose was correct. The network's brass had misread Norman Rosten's name. Rose retained his job.[54]

Norman Corwin saw the handwriting on the wall after a discussion late in 1948 with William Paley. The CBS president told Corwin that he was not oblivious to the Red scare. "There is going to be a terrible wave of reaction in this country," said Paley. "No place will be safe for a liberal. Why, when I went to a board meeting on Wall Street a little while ago . . . I found myself congratulated on all sides for getting rid of Bill Shirer." Afterward, Corwin realized that his own fate was clear. No one, himself included, could doubt that he was a liberal.[55]

In the same year, CBS offered Corwin a contract far inferior to previous ones, which would have enabled the network to claim half of all his subsidiary earnings such as income from film adaptations of his work. Corwin rejected it and, early in 1949, accepted a part-time job as Chief of Special Projects at United Nations Radio. Three months later, he learned that the FBI had included his name, Fredric March's, and those of a number of other prominent persons on a well-publicized list of alleged communist sympathizers. The basis for the appearance of Corwin's name was his authorship of "Set Your Clock at U235," a single-voiced narration that urged caution in the use of nuclear power. March had read it four years earlier at a meeting at Madison Square Garden whose topic was "Crisis Coming, Atom Bomb—for Peace or War?" When CBS learned that his name was on the list, it hurriedly issued a statement that he had not been on staff for more than a year.

Still further harassment came a few months later when Senator Pat McCarran attacked Corwin from the floor of the United States Senate, pointing him out as an example of how the United Nations had become infiltrated with communists. As "proof" of his claim, he cited Corwin's affiliation with organizations on the Attorney General's list of subversive organizations.[56]

Late in 1949, United Nations Radio agreed to collaborate with the Mutual Broadcasting System," with Corwin as series supervisor, to produce *The Pursuit of Peace*, a six-part documentary series.[57] This time, a month before the start of the series, a spokesman for Mutual's Baltimore affiliate announced that because of the involvement of Corwin, whom he called "a self admitted leftist," the affiliate would not accept the program. Although later the station's owner overruled the spokesman, Corwin was increasingly finding it difficult to avoid bumping into harassment. Finally, in November 1952, Senator McCarran's Internal Security Committee, which was investigating alleged communist infiltration of the United Nations, summoned him to appear before it. Corwin was questioned for a mere fifteen minutes and never recalled.

Arthur Laurents and Arthur Miller were less devastated than many of the others pursued by the witch-hunters. Yet they were far from unscathed. Laurents first learned that he was blacklisted when choreographer Jerome Robbins asked him to write a screenplay. After Laurents agreed to do it, Swifty Lazar, his agent, went about trying to conclude a contract. Later Lazar called Laurents. "You're out," he told Laurents. "They say you want too much money." "How much did you ask for?" Laurents asked. Lazar replied, "I didn't ask for anything yet."[58]

In 1949, by which time he had turned his back on radio, Arthur Miller won a Pulitzer prize for his stage play *Death of a Salesman*.

Miller was fortunate for more than one reason that he achieved this success. Theater actors and writers were much more insulated from political attacks than were those who worked in Hollywood or for radio. However, in 1954, when Miller attempted to renew his passport to attend the opening of one of his plays in Brussels, the State Department rejected his application. The decision was based on regulations denying passports to persons deemed to be supporting the Communist movement, regardless of whether or not they were proved to be party members. It took two years before the government finally relented and sent him a new passport. Even then, it was valid for only a six-month period.[59]

In 1951, the snowballing of opinion against perceived communist influence led to revived HUAC hearings in Washington. In addition, the Senate Judiciary Committee's Internal Security Subcommittee got into the act.

Broadcasting, like the nation at large, was divided on the issue of whether domestic communism posed a real threat to the nation. Both the Radio Writers Guild (RWG) and the newly merged union of radio and television performers, the American Federation of Television and Radio Artists (AFTRA), reflected this. The strongest resistance to blacklisting among the unions representing radio and television artists came from the leadership of the RWG. In 1952, an anticommunist faction in the guild published a blacklist that recorded alleged Communist-front activities of their colleagues.[60] This set off a storm within the guild, with Millard Lampell and Peter Lyon active in the group opposing the right wing.

AFTRA also experienced a civil war in its ranks. On one side was a group of anticommunists who dominated AFTRA's first board and actively cooperated with the blacklist. The group centered around Bud Collyer. Once Collyer inadvertently revealed how closely he was tied in with the *Red Channels* folks. On the day that the booklet appeared, he ran into fellow actor Ken Roberts, who had just learned that *Red Channels* had labeled him as a procommunist. "Kenny, Kenny," Collyer said in a consoling voice. "You weren't supposed to be in the book." Only hours later did Roberts realize what Collyer's remark signified.[61]

One day Frank Reel, AFTRA's former national executive secretary, was having words with Collyer about *Red Channels*. "Frank, this thing will only get worse," Collyer told him. "It's unfortunate, but a lot of innocent people are going to be hurt." Reel was stopped for a second. Then he replied "But Bud, the protection of the innocent is one of the most important things in the Bill of Rights." Collyer answered somberly, "Yes, I know." But his attitude and actions remained, "Whatever happened couldn't be helped. We have to protect America."[62]

In August 1955, two days before a round of HUAC hearings on the broadcast industry opened in the Federal Building on Foley Square in New York, Collyer and two other AFTRA board members sent telegrams to subpoenaed actors informing them that if they declined to answer any questions on grounds that their answers might incriminate them, AFTRA would expel them.[63] The targets of the witchhunters faced attack not only from external forces, the Congress, the FBI, and some journalists but also from their own brethren.

The radio work per se of the witch-hunt targets was never itself the prime focus of the committee's attention. Usually it was their political views, as expressed by their associations and the types of meetings they attended. But, as in the cases of Fredric March and Florence Eldredge, periodically an actor's or writer's radio work came under scrutiny. In 1951, radio writer Ruth Adams Knight appeared as a "friendly" witness before a Senate subcommittee that was investigating alleged communist infiltration of the broadcasting/entertainment industry.[64]

Knight testified that Lyon, Norman Corwin, and others, whom she called "pro-Communist," inserted communist propaganda into their radio scripts. To illustrate what she meant by "communist propaganda," she explained, "You would find, I am sure if you examined the work of these people, a constant derision of the average citizen. . . . There is no such thing in their scripts as a decent banker and a decent lawyer. The thing is subtle . . . it is scorn and contempt. . . . It is that attitude expressed that is the undermining thing with the simple people who later listen to radio [but] who would turn off outright Communist propaganda."[65]

In Knight's world the ordinary people were bankers and lawyers. One cannot help but wonder what place she ascribed to factory workers and others in the working class. In additional testimony, Knight

further demonstrated the typically flimsy evidence behind the purgers' allegations. She testified that "the group who work on certain
shows consistently are people who are sympathizers with an extremely
left wing view." A committee member then sought specifics.

> Senator Watkins: You have made that rather vague, "certain shows."
> Can you make it more definite?"
> Knight: That is not part of my evidence.
> Watkins: Can you point to anything in the programs that these left
> wingers write of the slanting of the program in such a way that it aids
> the foreign government and foreign ideology as against our own?
> Knight: . . . there was a script written by Peter Lyon for *Cavalcade* and
> I think it was called the swamp folk [*sic*] dealing with the Communist
> situation in Yugoslavia.

Knight went on to argue that in allegorical fashion the script
spoke of the brave partisans in Yugoslavia. In fact, there was no
script entitled "Swamp Folk." There was, however, a 1944 broadcast, "The First Commando," that featured a song called "Swamp
Fox."[66] It concerned General Francis Marion, the famed "swamp
fox," whose daring guerrilla raids helped the colonists defeat the
British during the American Revolution. It was part of the American history series which that year also produced plays concerning
Thomas Paine and Valley Forge. Even if her interpretation that it
touted the Yugoslav partisans who were fighting the Nazis were correct, the play would fit alongside others that glorified both regular
Allied armies such as the British and the Chinese and irregular
forces such as the French underground, which were also the subject of radio drama. However, a careful hearing of the play offers no
evidence supporting Knight's interpretion. In addition to attacking
Lyon, Knight attempted to go after Norman Corwin. However, the
committee asked her to hold off on those comments and, for whatever reason, it never returned to the topic.

Soon after Knight testified, the subcommittee summoned Lyon and
Millard Lampell. During the course of Lyon's testimony, its staff director and interrogator, Richard Arens, asked him a question concerning Corwin's series *Passport for Adams*. Presumably it was the
show's internationalist-minded character that disturbed the commit-

tee. "Do you recall," Arens asked Lyon, "making a speech to certain persons in which you said in effect 'If the CBS had received merely a thousand of your letters, this the best and most significant program on the air, could have been saved?'"[67]

It should be noted that Arens, a short man with a shaved head and a square pug face, was cut from the same cloth as Parnell Thomas and some of the other principals of the witch-hunting committees. In 1949, as counsel to the Senate Subcommittee on Immigration, he had helped defeat a proposal to admit 25,000 displaced Jews from Germany.[68] Later, he was fired after it was reported that he was on a retainer from a racist "foundation" as an expert on the genetic inferiority of blacks.[69]

REACTIONS

The individuals whom the combined forces of Red-baiting politicians, journalists, and American Legionnaire and other types targeted displayed a variety of reactions to the attacks. On one end of the spectrum were those who capitulated to the demands of the Red-baiters. It is difficult from a vantage point of fifty or more years after the fact to imagine the climate of fear that permeated the very air that people were breathing in the era. For a few tragic ones the attacks were so devastating that they contributed to their premature deaths. Others took flight, to London, for example. Finally, at the opposite pole from the capitulators were many who stood and fought.

Writers Bernard Schoenfeld, Langston Hughes, Allan Sloane, and film director (and former radio actor) Elia Kazan were among those who capitulated. During the war, Schoenfeld oversaw the writing and production of 275 special programs that were either dramatic or documentary in style. In 1952, after a friendly witness named Schoenfeld as having belonged to the Communist Party, he appeared before the committee, provided it with names, and urged Congress to outlaw the party.

In contrast to Schoenfeld, Hughes's capitulation to a Senate Committee harmed no one except perhaps himself. *Life*, J. Edgar Hoover, and other sources had smeared his name, calling him a danger to the country. There was nothing in Hughes's writing to warrant these accusations. But Roy Cohn, the vicious assistant to Senator Joseph McCarthy, forced Hughes to humiliate himself, nevertheless. Hughes provided no names to the committee. But he publicly repudiated his earlier expressed and strongly felt sympathies for the Soviet Union. Despite this treatment, when asked at the end of his testimony, "Were you treated in any whatsoever improper manner by this committee or any of its staff?" Hughes gave the committee a clean bill of health. Subsequently, despite his cooperation with the committee, Hughes's literary agency dropped him like a hot potato.[70]

After Allan Sloane admitted to Daniel O'Shea of CBS that he had once been a member of the Communist Party, through an intermediary, O'Shea contacted HUAC. In January 1954, Sloane came before the committee as a friendly witness. In words clearly designed to curry its favor, a repentant Sloane declared that his conscience had driven him to testify.[71] Sloane detailed his personal history, emphasizing what the committee was most interested in hearing, how he came to join the party and what his membership entailed. He also implicated his former friend Millard Lampell. The two had had a falling out in the fall of 1950 after Lampell ripped into Sloane for assisting an anticommunist Estonian refugee immigrant come to the United States.

Sloane's denunciation of Millard Lampell went beyond just identifying Lampell as a Communist. "[Would you] identify your relationship with Millard Lampell as being the controlling factor in bringing you into the Communist Party?" the counsel for the committee asked Sloane "Yes," Sloane replied, much to the committee's delight. "He was the trigger to my perhaps emotional or humanitarian outlook or attitude." In addition to naming Lampell, Sloane also brought up the name of Norman Rosten. When asked whether he had received propaganda materials from Communist front organizations in recent years, Sloane identified Rosten as the individual who had asked him to subscribe to *The National Guardian*, a newspaper that Sloane implied was filled with communist propaganda.

Elia Kazan's appearance before the committee proved to be the most controversial one. Kazan acted in one of the plays of the early 1941 *Free Company* series. But, of course, he became much better known as a stage and film director. A party member for a year and a half in the 1930s before he quit in disgust, Kazan was named in *Counterattack*. Like Schoenfeld, he cooperated with HUAC, providing it with the names of other party members. But Kazan went about it with a vengeance, even placing a statement in the *New York Times* outlining his views.[72] Also, he made it clear even decades later that he gave his testimony totally voluntarily. Kazan, too, believed that the committee was doing the country a service in attempting to root out communist influence.

As a black man, Canada Lee already had one strike against him in his pursuit of acting roles. Now, the blacklist and related government harassment put him under tremendous strain. The State Department gave Lee problems following his return to the United States to publicize the film *Cry, the Beloved Country*. Shortly after his return, realizing that his passport had to be renewed, he submitted a renewal application. But in the weeks that followed, the government dragged its feet in processing the application.

Lee had just begun to get out of the $18,000 debt that the blacklist had originally caused. Now, still unable to get work in the United States and unable to return to Europe to resume work on another film for which he was cast, he fell deeper into debt. To help Lee with the passport problem, in February, NAACP official Walter White traveled to Washington. But the State Department just stalled him, saying "The matter is still under review," and White returned to New York empty handed.[73] The cumulative pressures finally killed Lee. He died in May 1952 at the age of 45. The *New York Times* wrote that the cause of death was a heart attack. In fact, it was political persecution.

After Lee's death, even the politically conservative Ed Sullivan acknowledged that Lee was not a Communist. Sullivan referred to Lee in his column as "a warm hearted kid" who had more or less been duped by the Communists to aid their cause even if he had not joined the party.[74] Another column, most likely from the New York *Daily Worker*, the Communist newspaper, repeating the rumor of Lee's alleged denunciation of Paul Robeson, faulted Lee for caving in to the witch hunters.[75] Even in death, Canada Lee was hounded.

John Garfield died within a few days of his friend Canada Lee, of some of the same causes. In April 1951, Garfield testified before the HUAC committee. Although he appeared as a so-called friendly

witness, his answers, often evasive, did not really satisfy the committee. Without its bill of clean health, Garfield saw that his career was
in danger. Consequently, he met with two people whom he hoped
might help him achieve the clearance that he felt he needed. Ten days
before his death, he visited anticommunist labor columnist Victor
Riesel and told Riesel that he was preparing a document that would
describe his total political involvement, and that if necessary he would
reveal names. Garfield was under tremendous pressure, and he had
reason to believe that such cooperation would remove the threats to
his career that had been gathering. He also met with Arnold Forster
of the Anti-Defamation League of B'nai B'rith, which had the reputation of functioning as an intermediary between Red hunters and Jewish targets of the investigations. Garfield's friend Abe Polonsky, the
late writer-director, argued that Garfield had no intentions of naming
names. "He said he hated Communists, hated Communism, he was an
American," Polonsky claimed. "He told the Committee what it
wanted to hear. But he wouldn't say the one thing that would keep
him from walking down his old neighborhood block. Nobody could
say, 'Hey, there's the fucking stool pigeon' . . . in the street where he
comes from . . . you're not a stool pigeon. That's the ultimate horror."[76]

As a result of the blacklist, in order to keep working, some of the
writers worked under assumed names and sometimes hired front
men. Using the names of his two sons, Bill Robson became "Christopher Anthony." X became Y. At one time Millard Lampell was working under four different pseudonyms. For a four-month period he also
wrote material for a writer who was experiencing major writer's block.
Altogether in this way, Lampell authored a dozen television scripts,
two film scripts, and some radio broadcasts.

Writers working under aliases lived in a never-never land if, for example, a producer called for a script conference. To deal with such
problems, a blacklisted writer might hire a person to pretend to be the
actual writer. This was the theme of *The Front*, a 1976 film that
starred Woody Allen. Sometimes writers wound up getting a double
fee. If, after purchasing a script from a front man, a producer decided
that it needed revision, sometimes, rather than go to the person whom
he believed was the author, he would approach the blacklisted writer
on the sly, unaware that that person was the original author.

Joseph Losey, Anton Leader, Arthur Laurents, and, as mentioned, Canada Lee, were among a number of writers, actors, and directors who dealt with the blacklist by going abroad. Losey and Leader wound up in London, remaining there from 1962 to 1965. Losey developed a distinguished career as a film director, and Leader worked on television shows for M-G-M and directed a film, *Children of the Damned*. Laurents spent some time in France writing a film script and in Morocco where he survived by speculating on currency.

Fight

Norman Corwin and a number of other victims of broadcasting came at the attackers with bared fists. Among the approximately twenty-five writers, entertainers, and directors discussed here, at least fifteen were blacklisted. In addition, eleven of them were called to testify before witch-hunting legislative committees. An incomplete survey showed that although they were not called to testify, at least several others were the subjects of FBI investigations. Arthur Miller, Millard Lampell, Peter Lyon, and three others among them earned the distinction of being labeled "unfriendly witnesses." Either they cited the Fifth Amendment as justification for refusal to answer questions, or they even challenged the legitimacy of a committee to conduct its hearings.

Miller's appearance before the HUAC was connected with its 1956 investigation into "fraudulent procurement and misuse of passports by persons allegedly in the service of a communist conspiracy." He answered the committee's questions about himself without claiming any constitutional protection.[77] However, on conscientious grounds, he refused to name others present at a 1947 meeting of writers sponsored by a Communist front organization. The committee consequently charged him with contempt of Congress, a charge that was upheld in a 1957 federal trial, and Miller was fined $500 and given a thirty-day suspended sentence. The conviction was reversed on a technicality the following year.

Millard Lampell, Cliff Carpenter, Will Geer, and Peter Lyon were some of the witnesses who refused to answer questions on the grounds that their testimony might incriminate them. One of the questions Lampell refused to answer was whether he had signed an appeal on behalf of Willie McGee, a black man later executed for raping a white woman.[78] In an era in which a black man could be convicted in North Carolina for leering at a girl, liberals viewed a charge of rape against a southern black man with great skepticism. In turn, the political right perceived Lampell and other "premature civil rights advocates" as criminals just because they signed such a petition.

Although the Fifth Amendment protects one from self-incrimination, committee members took the fact of witnesses citing it as personal affronts that they treated as de facto admissions of guilt. Thus, when interrogator Richard Arens asked Lampell about organizations to which he belonged and Lampell refused on constitutional grounds to answer the question, Arens asked, "Would you kindly express for the purpose of the record how you feel in your heart that the answer to that question might incriminate you?"[79] When Will Geer appeared, he not only pled the Fifth, he also did battle with his interrogator. Geer was one of a number of witnesses to be asked, "In the event of an armed conflict in which the U.S. would find itself opposed to Soviet Russia, would you be willing to fight on the side of the United States?" Geer, who was then forty-nine, refused to play the questioner's game. "I would grow vegetables and perform in hospitals, like I did during World War II," he replied. "It would be a wonderful idea if they put every man my age in the front lines. . . . I think wars would be negotiated immediately."[80]

Three blacklisted people, Fredric March, Florence Eldridge, and Joseph Julian brought suit against the American Business Consultants, their blacklisters. It was *Counterattack*, American Business Consultants' first publication, that alleged that March was a Communist. Subsequently, for at least a six-month interval, job offers shriveled up. In a panic from the threat of the Marches' lawsuit, American Business Consultants sent its vice president to Hollywood in search of evidence to support their allegations. But there was none to be found, and they made an offer to settle out of court. The Marches accepted an agreement whereby *Counterattack* printed a retraction story, "Fredric March and his Wife Eldridge Condemn Communist Despotism in Stalinist Russia." American Business Consultants did not act in good faith, however. Although the original charges against the couple appeared on *Counterattack*'s front page, the retraction was buried in the publication's back pages.[81]

Even after the "clearing" of their names, the Marches still felt repercussions from their experience. In addition to losing income during the period when they were blacklisted, they incurred $50,000 in legal fees. Yet the settlement with American Business Consultants did not give them so much as a penny to reimburse them. As a result of their financial problems, as happened in the families of more than one blacklistee, the experience created a bitter barrier between the couple. Eldridge appeared to believe that she and March would have won the case had it gone to court. Considering the circumstances that prompted the defendants' initiative to offer the out-of-court settlement, such a conclusion seems justified. Complaining that March was not very staunch during the crisis, she told Elia Kazan "How hard it is to be a mother of someone your own age!"[82]

Joseph Julian's lawsuit started out badly. The judge who was to hear the case, Irving Saypol, had presided over the espionage trial of Julius and Ethel Rosenberg and had a long history of disagreements with Julian's lawyer. In addition, the defense counsel had once been Saypol's executive assistant. When Saypol himself asked if Julian's lawyer wished, therefore, for a change of judge, the lawyer said "Yes." Astoundingly, Saypol rejected it.

Julian's case dragged on for four years. Among the people who came to testify for him was Morton Wishengrad, author of the program "Communism, U.S. Brand" and clearly an anticommunist. Wishengrad told the court that Julian, too, was an anticommunist. However, Saypol, consistent in his bias from the very beginning, ruled such testimony as inadmissible and in the end granted a defense motion to dismiss the lawsuit. Several months later, an actor friend of Julian got into a conversation with one of the jurors in the case. "Julian sure got a raw deal," the man said, "Everyone on the jury was for him."

END OF THE BLACKLIST

The blacklist era that began in the late 1940s finally came to an end, more or less, in the mid 1960s when liberals and progressives were elected to the leadership in all major entertainment industry unions. The death blow involved a successful lawsuit by talk show personality

John Henry Faulk against Vincent Hartnett, Lawrence Johnson, and Aware, Inc. Faulk had fought being blacklisted for six years. Finally, in 1965, the jury, amazed at the viciousness of the defendants' behavior, awarded Faulk a $3.5 million combined compensatory and punitive judgment, a half-million more than he had asked.[83]

Faulk collected only a small portion of the award. In a bizarre ending to his role in the era, Lawrence Johnson died in his motel room shortly before the trial ended. The cause was ruled a medical one. However, rumors circulated throughout the broadcasting industry that he committed suicide.[84] As a result of Johnson's death, the jury could not assess punitive damages against him. Faced with the remaining assessment that exceeded the value of Johnson's estate, lawyers for the estate negotiated with Faulk and reached a settlement of $175,000.[85]

Aware, Inc. and Hartnett appealed the decision to the State Appellate Division. The Appellate Court upheld the jury's findings of culpability, in the process describing Hartnett's behavior as venal and characterized by deliberate malice. It did, however, reduce the amount of the award. It found Hartnett twice as culpable as Aware, Inc., which had virtually no assets anyway. Thus it lowered the compensatory damages that Aware, Inc. and Hartnett had to pay, to $50,000 and $100,000, respectively. It also lowered total punitive damages to $400,000.[86]

In defending himself against Faulk's lawsuit, Hartnett had tried to defend his personal integrity. He lost, and left New York with his tail between his legs. Faulk, on the other hand, had fought the blacklisters on behalf of scores of people who had suffered loss of employment, strains in familial and personal relationships, inability to make rent or mortgage payments, taunting of their children by classmates, threats to self-respect, and, in the case of Canada Lee, a friend of Faulk, the loss of his life. Faulk won, and the blacklist was over.

NOTES

1. This discussion is based on a taped copy of Norman Corwin, "Hollywood Fights Back," which aired on October 26, 1947. Copies are available from the Department of Communications, University of Memphis.

2. Erik Barnouw, *Media Marathon* (Durham, N.C.: Duke University Press, 1996), 78–79.

3. David Caute, *The Great Fear: The Anti-Communist Purge under Truman and Eisenhower* (New York: Simon & Schuster, 1978), 166.

4. Larry Ceplair, "SAG and the Motion Picture Blacklist," *Screen Actor*, January 1998, 20.

5. Victor Navasky, *Naming Names* (New York: Penguin Books, 1981), 25–26.

6. Frances Chaney, interviewed by author, New York City, September 2, 1999.

7. Larry Ceplair and Steven Englund, *The Inquisition in Hollywood: Politics in the Film Community, 1930–1960* (Garden City, N.Y.: Anchor Press/Doubleday, 1980), 275.

8. John Cogley, *Report on Blacklisting: II. Radio-Television.* (New York: Fund for the Republic, 1956), 4.

9. Nancy Lynn Schwartz, *The Hollywood Writers' War* (New York: Knopf, 1982), 160.

10. Edward Barrett Jr., *The Tenney Committee: Legislative Investigation of Subversive Activities in California* (Ithaca, N.Y.: Cornell University Press, 1951), 4.

11. Barrett, *The Tenney Committee*, 386.

12. Tenney may have had in mind Corwin's play "Untitled," which starred March. March appeared in a number of works produced by Corwin. However, this was the only real war-related radio play that Corwin wrote (as opposed to some of his long radio poems) in which March appeared. Produced as it was before Pearl Harbor, "Untitled," with its "premature" condemnation of fascism, its pro-labor spirit, and its attack on racism, qualified as a ready target for such as Tenney.

13. William N. Robson, *Reminiscences*, p. 29, CUOHROC.

14. Adele Nathan and Blevins Davis, "Beyond the Call of Duty," presented over WOR in cooperation with the National Council of the Young Men's Christian Association, February 14, 1943, CL.

15. Barrett, *The Tenney Committee*, 214.

16. Norman Corwin to Bill Fineshriber, November 11, 1947, as quoted in R. LeRoy Bannerman, *On a Note of Triumph: Norman Corwin and the Golden Years of Radio* (New York: Lyle Stuart, 1986), 198.

17. Robert Hilliard and Michael Keith, *The Broadcast Century and Beyond: A Biography of American Broadcasting* (Boston: Focal Press, 2001), 112.

18. Gilda Block, telephone conversation with author, August 3, 2000.

19. Erik Barnouw, interview by author, Fairhaven, Vt., August 22, 2000.

20. Anton Leader to Morton Wishengrad, July 12, 1948, Wishengrad, 1/58 JTS.

21. Morton Wishengrad to Leader, July 22, 1948, Wishengrad Collection, 1/58 JTS.

22. Norman Rosten to Morton Wishengrad, n.d., Wishengrad Collection, 2/2 JTS.

23. Morton Wishengrad to Norman Rosten, August 14, 1948, Wishengrad Collection, 2/2 JTS.

24. Norman Rosten to Morton Wishengrad, n.d., Wishengrad Collection, 2/2 JTS.

25. Norman Corwin to Robert Malin, Executive Director, American Civil Liberties Union, October 25, 1950, in Norman Corwin, *Norman Corwin's Letters*, ed. A. J. Langguth (New York: Barricade Books, 1994), 130.

26. Joseph E. Persico, *Edward R. Murrow: An American Original* (New York: McGraw-Hill, 1988), 5.

27. Joseph Julian, *This Was Radio: A Personal Memoir* (New York: Viking Press, 1975), 174–175.

28. U.S. Senate Judiciary Committee, *Subversive Infiltration of Radio, Television, and the Entertainment Industry—Hearing before the Senate Internal Security Subcommittee* (82nd Cong., 1st and 2nd sess., 1951–1952), 13–15.

29. Louis Nizer, *The Jury Returns* (Garden City, N.Y., Doubleday, 1966), 234.

30. Oliver Pilat, "Blacklist," *New York Post*, January 29, 1953, vol. 152, no. 62.

31. Navasky, *Naming Names*, 24.

32. Caute, *The Great Fear*, 106.

33. Jeff Kisseloff, "Another Award, Other Memories of McCarthyism," *New York Times,* May 30, 1999, II 27:1.

34. Caute, *The Great Fear*, 521–522.

35. Cogley, *Report on Blacklisting*, 116.

36. This account of Julian's dealings with O'Shea is based on Julian, *This Was Radio*, 179–180.

37. This account of Julian's lawsuit is based on Julian, *This Was Radio*, 182–198.

38. Julian, *This Was Radio*, 180.

39. This account of Robson's experience with the blacklist is based on Robson, *Reminiscences*, 26–28, CUOHROC.

40. The account of Sloane's dealings with O'Shea is based on the author's interview of Sloane on April 15, 1999, at his home in New Canaan, Conn.

41. The account of the effect of the blacklist on Lampell's career is based on Millard Lampell, "I Think I Should Tell You That I Was Blacklisted," *New York Times*, August 21, 1966, IV, 13.

42. Frances Lee Pearson, interviewed by the author, Doraville, Ga., March 19, 1999.

43. Walter Winchell, New York *Mirror*, October 13, 1949, 10:4.

44. Frances Lee to author (E-mail message), November 3, 2000.

45. An undated clipping, "Lee Corrects Winchell," almost certainly from the New York *Mirror*, lies among the various documents in Lee's FBI file.

46. Canada Lee to Ed Sullivan, November 15, 1949, CL.

47. Memorandum from "SAC" (Special Agent in Charge) in New York Division of FBI to FBI Director, October 16, 1952, Rosten FBI file.

48. Report on Robert Crawford Lyon, Jr., July 7, 1950, 8, Lyon FBI file.

49. Memoranda from "SAC" in New York Division of FBI, to FBI Director, October 16 and November 12, 1952, Rosten FBI file.

50. Teletype message, April 15, 1954, Robert Crawford Lyon FBI file.

51. Jane Lyon to author, August 8, 1998.

52. Norman Rosten to Joseph Goldstein, January 12, 1952, Rosten papers, private collection.

53. Jane Lyon to author.

54. Norman Rose, interview by Muriel Meyers, November 2, 1988, NYPL-AJC.

55. Sally Bedell Smith, *In All His Glory: The Life of William S. Paley, The Legendary Tycoon and His Brilliant Circle* (New York: Simon and Schuster, 1990), 301.

56. "Subversive Person in UN Jobs, McCarran Charges, Citing Corwin," *New York Times*, August 9, 1949, 12:3.

57. Bannerman, *On a Note of Triumph*, 212.

58. "Arthur Laurents: Emotional Reality," interview by Patrick McGilligan in *Backstory 2: Interviews with Screenwriters of the 1940s and 1950s* (Berkeley: University of California Press, 1991), 145–146.

59. "Miller Granted European Passport," *New York Times*, July 7, 1956, 15:7.

60. Caute, *The Great Fear*, 529.

61. Ken Roberts, interview by the author, Newark, N.J., October 24, 1998.

62. Rita Morley Harvey, *Those Wonderful, Terrible Years: George Heller and the American Federation of Television and Radio Artists* (Carbondale: Southern Illinois University Press, 1996), 89.

63. Michael C. Burton, *John Henry Faulk* (Austin, Tex.: Eakin Press, 1993), 128.

64. Knight's testimony can be found in U.S. Senate Judiciary Committee, *Subversive Infiltration*, 58–71.

65. U.S. Senate Judiciary Committee, *Subversive Infiltration*, 58–71.

66. Peter Lyon and Alan Lomax, "The First Commando," *The Cavalcade of America*, April 10, 1944.

67. U.S. Senate Judiciary Committee, *Subversive Infiltration*, 98.

68. Caute, *The Great Fear*, 93.

69. Arthur Miller, *Timebends* (New York: Grove Press, 1987), 407.

70. Arnold Rampersad, *The Life of Langston Hughes: Volume II: 1941–1967, I Dream A World* (New York: Oxford University Press, 1988), 215–218.

71. U.S. House Committee Un-American Activities, *Communist Methods of Infiltration (Entertainment-Part 1). Hearing before a Subcommittee of the Committee on Un-American Activities* (83rd Cong., 2nd sess., January 13, 1954), 3851–3877.

72. Navasky, *Naming Names,* 74.

73. Walter White's column in the *Philadelphia Bulletin*, May 16, 1952.

74. Ed Sullivan, "Little Old New York," *Daily News*, May 1952, undated clipping in Canada Lee's FBI file.

75. Abner W. Berry, "Further Thoughts on Canada Lee," "On the Way," *The Daily Worker*, CL.

76. Navasky, *Naming Names*, xix.

77. Anthony Lewis, "Miller Is Cleared of House Contempt," *New York Times*, August 8, 1958, 1:4.

78. U.S. Senate Judiciary Committee, *Subversive Infiltration*, 124.

79. U.S. Senate Judiciary Committee, *Subversive Infiltration*, 181.

80. U.S. House Committee on Un-American Activities, *Communist Infiltration of Hollywood Motion Picture Industry, Hearing* (82nd Cong., 1st sess., 1951, part 1), 189.

81. Deborah Peterson, *Fredric March: Craftsman First, Star Second* (Westport, Conn.: Greenwood Press, 1996), 441.

82. Elia Kazan, *Elia Kazan: A Life* (New York: Knopf, 1988), 441.

83. Nizer, *The Jury Returns*, 427–429.

84. Madeline Gilford, interview by the author, New York City, January 11, 2000.

85. George Berger, telephone conversation with author, April 3, 2000. Berger is an attorney with the Louis Nizer law firm that represented Faulk. He assisted Nizer in the lawsuit against Hartnett.

86. George Berger, telephone conversation, April 3, 2000.

CONCLUSION

> We had a privilege our arriviste successors never enjoyed: complete control over our own words.
>
> —William Robson to Norman Corwin

As the decades passed after the conclusion of the war, radio became a shadow of itself, and its preeminent role in national life was taken up by network television. Initially, television, too, had its own "Golden Age," with several programs that featured quality plays. Even after the demise of those showcase programs, certain other programs, such as *M°A°S°H* and *All In the Family*, continued the tradition that wartime radio began, of focusing on racism and other social problems. Later, however, network television, which, like radio, had started with great promise, decayed into a series of talk shows and reruns. Cable television followed as an alternative to network television. Among its dubious accomplishments, it succeeded, where network television had not been able, in bringing pornography into people's living rooms.

America and the world changed substantially following the end of radio's heyday. America, including Norman Corwin and most of his colleagues, survived the blacklist and McCarthyism. Racially, the

country went through the civil rights movement, but then race relations deteriorated. By the end of the millennium, in addition to the
euphemism "the F word," a new phrase was in common use, this one
among conservative and right-wing politicians: the "L word." Even
liberals avoided calling themselves "liberal." America discovered the
Holocaust in the 1950s. The discovery went into high gear in the following decades with broadcast of a blockbuster *Holocaust*, a nine-and-
a-half-hour, four-part 1978 television series, and later in the 1990s
production of Stephen Spielberg's *Schindler's List*.

And what of the principal players in the story of World War II era
radio drama: the members of that elite wartime fraternity of writers
and directors of radio drama, the actors, and the antagonists on the far
right? First the Red-baiters. After failing to be reelected for Congress
in 1944, Gerald Nye remained in Washington. One of Archibald
MacLeish's, FDR's, and Elmer Davis's nemeses during the war, Nye
eventually became an administrator in the Federal Housing Administration and later a professional staff member of the Senate Committee on Aging.[1]

Claiming health problems, Martin Dies, the plump Texan who first
came to Congress in 1931 and established himself as one of Congress's
most vocal anti-Communists, decided not to run for reelection in
1944. Then eight years later, he won reelection as his district's candidate for both the Democratic and Republican parties. In 1954, President Eisenhower signed into law the Communist Control Act, which
outlawed the Communist Party. The law featured fourteen criteria
that Dies set up to help identify persons involved in Communist activities.[2]

J. Parnell Thomas, another former head of the House Un-American
Affairs Committee (HUAC), served a nine-month prison sentence in
Connecticut for pocketing $8,000 that he obtained by padding his
congressional payroll. Later, in 1954, Thomas, who had served seven
straight terms in Congress, tried to make a political comeback in his
New Jersey election district. But his effort failed by a wide margin.[3]
Thomas's HUAC colleague John Rankin of Mississippi, who saw a
Communist plot behind everyone with whom he disagreed, was
forced from Congress in 1950. The census found that Mississippi had
lost population, and thus the state lost a congressional seat, Rankin's,

it turned out, after district boundaries were redrawn. As a consequence, the South lost one of its loudest segregationists.[4]

Vincent Hartnett left New York and disappeared from public view after John Henry Faulk won a libel case against him. Between 1952 and 1955, he had earned an average annual income of about $20,000. Now, as a teacher in a private school in a New York suburb, he made only a fraction of that amount and was only able to pay off a small part of the judgment from his earnings. Some time later, a representative of Hartnett contacted Louis Nizer's office and negotiated a reduced lump sum, which released Hartnett from the judgment.[5]

In 2000, reached by telephone at his home in Tuckahoe, New York, Hartnett, who once hounded an actor because the back of the man's head appeared to match that of a head in a photo taken at a May Day Parade, told the author, "I don't give interviews. I want my privacy. I insist on my right of privacy."[6] Hartnett in a purely private capacity had delved into the political and personal associations of countless individuals and exposed them to public scrutiny and accusations. He had made his living by frequently bringing baseless accusations against people, from anonymous informants, and then charging his victims a fee to clear their names. But now at the end of his life, he had finally learned what the right of privacy meant.

Subsequently, Hartnett did reply in writing to questions that were submitted to him. Asked whether time had changed his perception of his role in the blacklist era, he replied categorically, "NO." Fifty years after he helped publish *Red Channels*, he was still convinced that the Communist Party had been intent on capturing trade unions in readiness for the day of the final class struggle. Despite voluminous evidence to the contrary, he also continued to maintain that he never sought payment from people to clear their names of allegations that they were helpmates to Communism.

If Vincent Hartnett and J. Parnell Thomas looked the parts that they played in the blacklist, actor Bud Collyer did not. In almost every photograph available, one finds the affable, lanky, brown-haired man with a big and friendly smile on his face. Collyer was a leader of the blacklisting effort within the American Federation of Television and Radio Artists (AFTRA). However, fate managed to keep fuzzy much of the historical record of his role. AFTRA's unwillingness to open its records to outsiders and the disappearance of many of the files of Aware, Inc., one of the key blacklisting organizations, helped Collyer hide his past. In 1996, Rita Morley Harvey published a history of AFTRA. She gave extensive space to remarks in defense of Collyer by Collyer's lawyer son Michael. Michael Collyer presented his father, a fundamentalist Christian, as one of the union's saviors and, despite the record to the contrary, as a tolerant Gentile who moved his family from their hometown "because the country club there adopted a policy restricting Jews."[7]

In 1948, on the eve of the blacklist era, Collyer moved over to television from radio. His son claims that Collyer was pushed from radio because he had become a "hot potato." But when asked to elaborate on his father's career, Michael Collyer declined the author's request for an interview. In any event, Collyer developed a highly successful television career as the host of numerous game shows such as *To Tell the Truth* and *Beat the Clock*.

The careers of Will Geer and Burgess Meredith both prospered in the post-blacklist era. After being shut out of film in the late 1950s, Meredith made a comeback, partly thanks to Otto Preminger, who gave him a role in *Advise and Consent* and several other films. In 1977, Meredith played the role of Joseph Welch in *Tail Gunner Joe,* a television show. Welch was the lawyer who took on Senator Joseph McCarthy in the infamous Army-McCarthy hearings. Meredith considered his playing the role "splendid revenge." In addition to his success as the arch villain Penguin in the television series *Batman*, Meredith became known to a whole new generation and won an Oscar nomination for his role as a boxing trainer in *Rocky* and its several sequels. Toward the end of his life, his distinctive voice was even heard in commercials for Skippy Peanut Butter.

After twelve years on the radio blacklist, in 1963, Geer broke out of it, doing some radio commercials. In 1966, Edgar Hoover wrote a memo to the Secret Service that he still considered Geer dangerous, and, into the early 1970s, the bureau continued to maintain its file on the vegetable-growing actor.[8] But it did so gingerly. "Since the subject is a leading actor appearing in films, Shakespearean plays and television, it is believed that an attempt to interview subject would be an embarrassment for the Bureau," wrote an agent from the bureau's

New Haven office. Only in 1972 did the agency finally cease collecting reports on him. In the last ten years of his life, he also picked up some good roles in seventeen films and various television programs, including the previously mentioned series *The Waltons*.

Fredric March and Orson Welles managed to avoid the blacklist, despite their having views similar to others who fell victim to it. March's career prospered in the postwar period. A gifted and talented actor, by the end of his life in the mid 1970s he had appeared in sixty-nine films.

Welles's postwar career never achieved the greatness of his early work and promise. After the war, he produced filmed versions of two Shakespearean plays, wrote a number of film scripts, and acted in many films. But none of those projects matched the quality of his film masterpiece *Citizen Kane* or his radio spectacular "War of the Worlds." In his last days, Welles was best known for doing voice-overs for radio and television commercials, for Vivitar cameras and particularly for Paul Masson wines. When criticized for "selling out," he replied, "I'd rather do an honest commercial than act in a dishonest film."[9]

The name of Canada Lee faded substantially in the public's memory; his career was short and he died young, at the age of 45 in 1952. But where his name is remembered, it has often been associated with that alleged act of betrayal. A 1973 book about the blacklist by Stefan Kanfer repeats the rumor that to get the persecutors off his back, Lee denounced Paul Robeson as a communist.[10] At least two other publications, another book on the blacklist, this one by Victor Navasky, publisher of *Nation* magazine; and a 1997 issue of *Classic Images*, a magazine that carried an article about Lee, repeated the allegation.[11] However, none of these sources provided any documentation.

Francis Lee Pearson, Lee's widow, vehemently disputes the charge that Lee denounced Robeson. In 2000 she suggested that the FBI was a likely source of the allegation.[12] Her account of FBI agents' efforts to pressure Lee to denounce Robeson before the circulation of the rumors lends credibility to the suggestion. Moreover, Robeson's son, Paul Robeson Jr., told the author that he had never seen or heard any shred of evidence to substantiate the allegation. The heavily blacked out part of Lee's FBI file that the agency released to the author makes no mention of either the alleged denunciation or the two agents' attempt to pressure him to denounce Robeson. One can only speculate about the contents of the pages that the FBI failed to produce.

The lives of the writers and directors of radio's "Golden Age" changed with the blossoming of television in the 1950s. For the most part, they left radio. Ranald MacDougall and Arch Oboler both moved to Hollywood. MacDougall wrote at least forty screenplays before his death in 1973. Oboler dabbled for a while with the short-lived phenomenon of three-dimensional films. Before his death at the end of the 1980s, he sold the rights to his radio plays, which are now marketed on tape for old-time radio fans. Oboler's papers were scattered on the floor of his office in Studio City, California, as a result of a 1994 earthquake. Requests for access over a three-year period to his widow and to his former assistant were unavailing.

Archibald MacLeish, who participated in the 1941 *Free Company* series and served in two government propaganda agencies during the war, became a professor of rhetoric and oratory at Harvard. He continued to speak his mind in the postwar era: against McCarthyism, against American involvement in the Vietnam War in Asia, and against the anti-Communist conception of the Cold War. In the 1980s, in MacLeish's last years, he lived the life of a gentleman farmer in Conway, Massachusetts.

Bill Robson's forced departure from commercial radio was a most difficult thing for him. He had been a creative and highly respected force in radio. For a while he continued writing for radio under pseudonyms. Then, in 1961, Edward R. Murrow hired him to work for him at the United States Information Agency. Despite allegations of disloyalty, Robson easily gained FBI security clearance. In 1970, Erik Barnouw published the second volume of his now classic history of broadcasting. He included in it a discussion of how the blacklist had in varying degrees wrecked or disrupted the lives of Robson and so many others. Subsequently, Robson wrote to Barnouw, telling him that his children had always been vaguely aware that some shadow had been hanging over him. He had never been able to explain what it was all about. "Finally your book came out," wrote Robson, "and I bought several copies and gave one to each of them and said 'This will tell you what Daddy did in the war!'[13]

Frank and Anne Hummert, who lived a secluded life even during the war, eventually retired from radio. In retirement they were even more secluded. When Frank died in 1966, Anne did her best to keep news of his death from the public, and *Variety*, the show business publication, only learned about it a full month later.

After the war, Bill Lewis, Norman Corwin's friend and mentor and once a key official in the Office of Facts and Figures and the Office of War Information, returned as a consultant to CBS and, within a short time, became a vice president of an advertising firm. After his retirement, Lewis was elected chairman of the board of the American Cancer Society and he was influential in promoting anti-cigarette public service commercials and banning cigarette advertising from television.

Millard Lampell, Arnold Perl, and Joseph Liss all did well in the post blacklist era. In 1960, after more than ten years under the black list, Lampell found himself looking at what he called "a wide crack . . . in the wall of the blacklist" when he was offered a film-writing job in London. This led to other work, writing for both the stage (*Hard Travelin'* premiered in Washington, D.C, in 1965) and films. Finally, in 1964, broadcasting opened up to him again, and two years later he won an Emmy Award for an original television drama. In his last years, Lampell taught creative writing at the University of Texas. He died in 1997 from lung cancer, while he was writing his memoirs. Joe Liss made a career for himself in television and publishing, writing more than fifty plays for television's *Studio One* series alone. After the radio blacklist pushed Arnold Perl out, he wrote *The World of Sholem Aleichem*, which had a one-year run as an off-Broadway play. The play featured Jack Gilford and a number of other actors whom the broadcasting industry had blacklisted. Later, Perl was able to resume a career in broadcasting, writing for, among other shows, *The Naked City* and *Eastside/Westside*, a highly successful series.

Norman Rosten and Arthur Miller, who both wrote for the *Cavalcade of America*, developed quite different careers after the war. Although both left radio, Rosten remained in Brooklyn, making a modest living as a poet and sometime writer of fiction and drama. In 1979, he was honored by appointment as poet laureate of Brooklyn. Miller, on the other hand, reached the most dazzling heights of success, writing for both stage and screen. During his short marriage to Marilyn Monroe, to whom the Rostens introduced him, his friendship with Rosten continued. Subsequently, after Miller and Monroe divorced, Rosten and his wife continued their friendship with Monroe and relations with Miller cooled. At the time of this writing, Miller has outlived both Rostens and continues to receive accolades for revivals of some of his older stage plays as well as for his newer ones.

Alan Sloane, who testified as a friendly witness in 1954, regained a writing career in television and took a college teaching job. In later years, despite a debilitating lung condition, he wrote a series of radio plays about senior citizens for Hi Brown. As he told the author, Sloane tried one two occasions to reestablish relations with friends he had betrayed.[14] Once he and his wife attended a poetry reading in Connecticut, not far from his home, by Norman Rosten whose name he had given to the HUAC in 1954. During a coffee break, Sloane approached Rosten. "Allan Sloane!" Rosten yelled out in friendly greeting when he saw him. Sloane felt that he had "stuff in his heart" that he wanted to say to Rosten, but a look in the poet's eyes told him, "Don't bring up the past." They spoke briefly, exchanged some "Let's get togethers," and parted at the end of the evening. Sloane also told the author that he tried to repair a friendship with writer Arnold Perl. At Sloane's invitation, Perl visited him in Connecticut. But Perl found it hard to forget Sloane's earlier betrayal of his friends.

After Norman Corwin left CBS, he worked for a while for the United Nations, where he produced "Document A/777," a plea for an international bill of human rights. In 1951, embittered by radio's commercialism, Corwin wrote "To the writer who wants to do the best work in his power, in defiance of formula, I say: forget radio. At least for the present. Write for a medium that still has diplomatic relations with originality."[15] Corwin appeared to conclude his radio career in the fall of 1955 with another U.N. play, "A Charter in the Saucer," an effort to promote the significance of the U.N. charter that was broadcast on the BBC. Subsequently, he did some film work, which resulted in one case, his script for *Lust for Life*, in an Academy Award nomination. In the following decade he also turned to television.

By 1991, Corwin, now in his eighties, returned to radio, producing "Bill of Rights: Two Hundred" for National Public Radio. Occasionally he received visitors who wished to interview him about his career. National Public Radio broadcast several other new Corwin plays in the late 1990s as well as one on New Year's Day 2000, celebrating the end of the millennium. But Corwin had no illusions that there might be a revival of radio drama. Citing the lack of regular newspaper reviews, he observed that radio drama was mostly a thing of the past. Corwin listened to the latest of his plays from his trophy-filled apartment in Los Angeles.

Among all of Corwin's peers in radio drama from the war era, only Arthur Miller, Allan Sloane, and Arthur Laurents were still alive by the end of the millennium. But the role they all helped play in rallying a nation to the cause of World War II can be remembered. And the penalty they paid for daring to speak their minds lends credence to Thomas Jefferson's warning that "The price of liberty is eternal vigilance."

NOTES

1. Alden Whitman, "Gerald P. Nye Is Dead at 78: Urged Isolationism as Senator," *New York Times*, July 19, 1971, 28:1.

2. "Ex-Rep. Martin Dies, 71, Is Dead; Led Un-American Activities Unit," *New York Times*, November 15, 1972, 1:1.

3. Robert McFadden, "J. Parnell Thomas, Anti-Red Crusader, Is Dead," *New York Times*, November 20, 1970, 44:1.

4. "John Rankin Dies: Ex-Legislator," *New York Times*, November 27, 1960, 86:1.

5. George Berger, telephone conversation with author, April 3, 2000.

6. Vincent Hartnett, telephone conversation with the author, April 11, 2000.

7. Rita Morley Harvey, *Those Wonderful, Terrible Years: George Heller and the American Federation of Television and Radio Artists* (Carbondale: Southern Illinois University Press, 1996), 91.

8. The following citations of Geer's FBI file can be found in Sally Norton, "A Historical Study of Actor Will Geer, His Life and Work in the Context of Twentieth-Century American Social, Political and Theatrical History" (Ph.D. diss., University of Southern California, 1980), 564.

9. Frank Brady, *Citizen Welles: A Biography of Orson Welles* (New York: Scribner, 1989), 558.

10. Stefan Kanfer, *A Journal of the Plague Years* (New York: Atheneum, 1973), 180.

11. Robert Edwards, "Canada Lee: The Othello of the Black List," *Classic Images*, October 1997, C9.

12. Frances Lee Pearson, interview by author, March 19, 1999.

13. Erik Barnouw, interview by author, August 22, 2000.

14. Allan Sloane related the following accounts to the author at Sloane's home in New Canaan, Ct., on May 13, 1999.

15. Norman Corwin, "Radio Writing, U.S.A.," *The Writer* 64 (February 1951): 35.

COLLECTIONS CONSULTED

ACAD   Academy of Motion Picture Arts and Sciences, Margaret Herrick Library, Beverly Hills, California
                  Ranald MacDougall Collection
                  Irving Reis Collection

BU   Boston University, Department of Special Collections, Mugar Memorial Library
                  Norman Corwin Collection
                  William B. Lewis Collection
                  Joseph Liss Collection

BYU   Brigham Young University, Harold B. Lee Library
                  Cecil B. DeMille Collection

CL   Personal Papers of Canada Lee

COL-RB   Columbia University Rare Book and Manuscript Library
                  Erik Barnouw Papers

CSUN   California State University at Northridge
                  Violet Atkins Klein Collection

CUOHROC   Columbia University Oral History Research Office Collection

FBI   FBI file (obtained via request)
IU   Indiana University, Lilly Library
      Orson Welles Collection
JTS   Jewish Theological Seminary, New York, NY
      Morton Wishengrad Collection
LOC   Library of Congress—Manuscript Division
      Writers War Board Collection
      Archibald MacLeish Collection
NA   National Archives, College Park, Maryland
      American Red Cross Central File
      Office of War Information (OWI) Collection
NR   Personal Papers of Norman Rosten
NYPL-AJC   The New York Public Library, Dorot Jewish
      Division
      American Jewish Committee Oral History
      Collection
NYPL-LC   New York Public Library, Lincoln Center Library
      for the Performing Arts
NYPL-S   Manuscripts, Archives and Rare Book Division;
      Schomburg Center for Research in Black Cul-
      ture; The New York Public Library; Astor, Lenox,
      and Tilden Foundations
      Radio Script Collection
PRINCETON   Public Policy Papers, Princeton University
TOL   Thousand Oaks Library, Thousand Oaks, California
      Norman Corwin Collection
WISC   State Historical Society of Wisconsin, Madison
      NBC Collection
      Max Ehrlich Collection
WYO   University of Wyoming, American Heritage Center
      Frank and Doris Hursley Papers
YALE   Yale University, James Weldon Johnson Collec-
      tion, Beinecke Rare Book and Manuscript
      Library
      Stephen Vincent Benét Collection
      Langston Hughes Papers
      Archibald MacLeish Collection

SELECTED BIBLIOGRAPHY

Bacher, William, ed. *The Treasury Star Parade.* New York: Farrar & Rinehart, 1945.

Ballou, Robert. *A History of the Council on Books in Wartime 1942-1946.* New York: Country Life Press, 1946.

Bannerman, R. LeRoy. *On a Note of Triumph: Norman Corwin and the Golden Years of Radio.* New York: Lyle Stuart, 1986.

Barnouw, Erik. *The Golden Web: A History of Broadcasting in the United States. Vol. 2, 1933–1953.* New York: Oxford University Press, 1968.

———. *Radio Drama in Action.* New York: Farrar & Rinehart, 1945.

Barrett, Edward Jr. *The Tenney Committee: Legislative Investigation of Subversive Activities in California.* Ithaca, N.Y.: Cornell University Press, 1951.

Benét, Stephen Vincent. *"We Stand United" and Other Radio Scripts.* New York: Farrar & Rinehart, 1945.

Billips, Connie, and Arthur Pierce. *Lux Presents Hollywood: A Show-by-Show History of the Lux Radio Theatre and the Lux Video Theatre, 1934–1957.* Jefferson, N.C.: McFarland, 1995.

Boyd, James, ed. *The Free Company Presents.* New York: Dodd, Mead, 1941.

Brady, Frank. *Citizen Welles: A Biography of Orson Welles.* New York: Scribner, 1989.

Case, Ann. "A Historical Study of the 'March of Time' Program Including an Analysis of Listener Reaction." Master's thesis, Ohio State University, 1943.

Caute, David. *The Great Fear: The Anti-Communist Purge under Truman and Eisenhower.* New York: Simon & Schuster, 1978.

Ceplair, Larry, and Steven Englund. *The Inquisition in Hollywood: Politics in the Film Community, 1930–1960.* Garden City, N.Y.: Anchor Press/ Doubleday, 1980.

Cogley, John. *Report on Blacklisting: II. Radio-Television.* New York: Fund for the Republic, 1956.

Columbia School of Journalism. *13 for Corwin.* Ft. Lee, N.J.: Barricade Books, 1985

——. *More by Corwin: 16 Radio Dramas.* New York: Henry Holt, 1944.

——. *Norman Corwin's Letters.* Edited by A. J. Langguth. New York: Barricade Books, 1994.

Corwin, Norman. *They Fly Through the Air with the Greatest of Ease.* Weston,Vt.: V. Orton, 1943.

——. *Thirteen by Corwin: Radio Dramas by Norman Corwin.* New York: Henry Holt, 1942.

——. *This Is War: A Collection of Plays about America on the March, by Norman Corwin and Others.* New York: Dodd, Mead, 1942.

——. *Untitled and Other Radio Dramas.* New York: Henry Holt, 1945.

Donaldson, Scott, and R. H. Winnick. *Archibald MacLeish: An American Life.* Boston: Houghton Mifflin, 1992.

Drabeck, Bernard A., and Helen E. Ellis, eds. *Reflections*: *Archibald MacLeish.* Amherst: University of Massachusetts Press, 1986.

Dunning, John. *On the Air: The Encyclopedia of Old Time Radio.* New York: Oxford University Press, 1998.

Fenton, Charles A. *Stephen Vincent Benét, the Life and Times of an American Man of Letters, 1898–1943.* New Haven, Conn.: Yale University Press, 1958.

Fielding, Raymond. *The March of Time, 1935–1951.* New York: Oxford University Press, 1978.

Harvey, Rita Morley. *Those Wonderful, Terrible Years: George Heller and the American Federation of Television and Radio Artists.* Carbondale: Southern Illinois University Press, 1996.

Hilmes, Michelle. *Radio Voices: American Broadcasting, 1922–1952.* Minneapolis: University of Minnesota Press, 1997.

Hollywood Writers Mobilization. *Writers' Congress; the Proceedings of the Conference Held in October 1943 under the Sponsorship of the Hollywood Writers' Mobilization and the University of California.* Berkeley: University of California Press, 1944.

Horten, Gerhard. "Radio Goes to War: The Cultural Politics of Propaganda During World War II." Ph.D. diss., University of California at Berkeley, 1994.

Howell, Thomas. "The Writers War Board: Writers and World War II." Ph.D. diss., Louisiana State University, 1971.

Hursley, Frank, and Doris Hursley. *Atomic Bombs*. Syracuse, N.Y.: Syracuse University Press, 1945

Julian, Joseph. *This Was Radio: A Personal Memoir*. New York: Viking Press, 1975.

Kaplan, Milton. *Radio and Poetry*. New York: Columbia University Press, 1949

Lampell, Millard. *The Long Way Home*. New York: Julian Messner, 1946.

Laurents, Arthur. *Original Story By: A Memoir of Broadway and Hollywood*. New York: Alfred A. Knopf, 2000.

Lawrence, Jerome, ed. *Off Mike: Radio Writing by the Nation's Top Writers*. New York: Essential Books, 1944.

McAleer, John. *Rex Stout: A Biography*. Boston: Little, Brown, 1977.

MacDonald, J. Fred. *Don't Touch That Dial: Radio Programming in American Life, 1920–1960*. Chicago: Nelson Hall, 1979.

Maltin, Leonard. *The Great American Broadcast: A Celebration of Radio's Golden Age*. New York: Dutton, 1997.

Meredith, Burgess. *So Far, So Good: A Memoir*. New York: Little, Brown, 1994.

Millay, Edna St. Vincent. *The Murder of Lidice*. New York: Harper & Bros., 1942.

Miller, Arthur. *Timebends*. New York: Grove Press, 1987.

Museum of Broadcasting. *Orson Welles on the Air: The Radio Years*. New York: Museum of Broadcasting, 1988.

Navasky,Victor. *Naming Names*. New York: Penguin Books, 1981.

Norton, Sally. "A Historical Study of Actor Will Geer, His Life and Work in the Context of Twentieth-Century American Social, Political and Theatrical History." Ph.D. diss., University of Southern California, 1980.

Oboler, Arch. *Free World Theatre: Nineteen New Radio Plays*. New York: Random House, 1944.

———. *Oboler Omnibus*. New York: Dual, Sloan, & Pearce, 1945.

———. *Plays for Americans*. New York: Farrar & Rinehart, 1942.

———. *This Freedom: Thirteen New Radio Plays*. New York: Random House, 1942.

Rampersad, Arnold. *The Life of Langston Hughes: Volume I: 1902–1941, I Too Sing America*. New York: Oxford University Press, 1988.

———. *The Life of Langston Hughes: Volume II: 1941–1967, I Dream a World*. New York: Oxford University Press, 1988.

Savage, Barbara. *Broadcasting Freedom: Radio, War and the Politics of Race, 1938–1948*. Chapel Hill: University of North Carolina Press, 1999.

————. "Broadcasting Freedom: Radio, War and the Roots of Civil Right Liberalism 1938–1948." Ph.D. diss., Yale University, 1995.

U.S. House Committee on Un-American Activities. *Communist Infiltration of Hollywood Motion Picture Industry, Hearing,* 82nd Cong., 1st sess., 1951, part 1.

U.S. House Committee on Un-American Activities. *Communist Methods of Infiltration (Entertainment—Part 1). Hearing before a Subcommittee of the Committee on Un-American Activities,* 83rd Cong., 2nd sess., January 13, 1954.

U.S. Senate Judiciary Committee. *Subversive Infiltration of Radio, Television, and the Entertainment Industry—Hearing before the Senate Internal Security Subcommittee,* 82nd Cong., 1st and 2nd sess., 1951–1952.

Weiser, Norman. *The Writer's Radio Theater.* New York: Harper & Row, 1941.

RADIO SCRIPTS AND TAPES

"This Is Our Enemy" scripts by Bernard Schoenfeld. The series was written and produced under the supervision of the Office of War Information and broadcast over the Mutual Network and WOR late in the spring of 1942. A set of ten of the scripts was distributed to schools and other institutions. Copies of the set are available at Brown University, Special Collections Library.

Many of the radio plays cited here are available on audio tape from commercial vendors. Many of the vendors advertise on the Internet and maintain booths at old time radio conventions such as the annual Friends of Old Time Radio (FOTR) Convention held in October in Newark, New Jersey, or the annual SPERDVAC Convention in Los Angeles, also held in the fall. When applicable, I indicate "OTR tape."

I also consulted tapes in three commercial boxed sets: *Arch Oboler Remembers World War II; Cavalcade of America,* Radio Spirits, Inc. (see www.radiospirits.com); and *Thirteen by Corwin* from LodesTone Audio Theater Catalog (see www.lodestone-media.com).

INDEX

ABOUT THE AUTHOR

Howard Blue is a retired high school history teacher and a genealogist. He has taught in a public school in Moscow and studied at Hebrew University in Jerusalem on a summer Fulbright. His translations of two Russian stories appear in *An Anthology of Russian Literature*, Nicholas Rzhevsky, ed. (M. E. Sharpe, 1996). He lives in Westbury, New York.